Telling Maya Tales

Telling Maya Tales

Tzotzil Identities in Modern Mexico

Gary H. Gossen

Routledge

New York and London

Published in 1999 by
Routledge
29 West 35th Street
New York, NY 10001

Published in Great Britain by
Routledge
11 New Fetter Lane
London EC4P 4EE

Copyright © 1999 by Routledge

Printed in the United States of America on acid-free paper
Text design by Debora Hilu

Detail on cover photo: Portrait of a Chamula storyteller in front of his patio cross.

10 9 8 7 6 5 4 3 2 1

Library of Congress Cataloging-in-Publication Data

Gossen, Gary H.
    Telling Maya tales : Tzotzil identities in modern Mexico / Gary Gossen.
        p.   cm.
    Includes bibliographical references and index.
    ISBN 0-415-91466-3   (HB: acid-free paper).   —ISBN 0-415-91467-1 (PB: acid-free paper)
        1. Tzotzil Indians—Ethnic identity.   2. Tzotzil Indians—Social conditions.   3. Tzotzil Indians—Government relations.   4. Social change—Mexico—Chamula.   5. Chamula (Mexico)—Social conditions.   6. Chamula (Mexico)—Politics and government.   7. Chamula (Mexico)—Ethnic relations.   I. Title.

    F1221.T9G69   1999
    305.897'415—dc 21   98-16529
                                                                          CIP

This book is dedicated to my beloved uncle
Dale David Hamilton —
Kansas iconoclast,
cowboy philosopher,
master storyteller,
all-weather friend.

CONTENTS

Contents

LIST OF FIGURES

PREFACE

TELLING MAYA TALES

>˞˞˞

INDIANS IN MEXICO

No one who has witnessed the massive media coverage of the Maya
Zapatista rebellion that began in Chiapas, Mexico, on January 1, 1994, nor
anyone who has a passing acquaintance with Mexico's remarkable artistic
and social achievements in the twentieth century, can fail to recognize two
great and contradictory themes in that nation's soul. First: Indians, past and
present, have provided enormous symbolic capital, in addition to their bodies and their labor, for the creation and articulation of Mexican national
identity in the twentieth century; it is impossible to imagine modern
Mexico without the biological and cultural legacy of native Mesoamerica.
Second: In spite of their centrality to the Mexican national essence, "real"
Indians have been systematically relegated, in both the colonial and modern
periods, to the demographic, political, social, and economic margins of the
nation. This paradox has, of course, not gone unobserved by the Indian community itself.

The Zapatista rebels demonstrated with poignant clarity that Mexico's
Indians—in this case the Mayas and their Indian neighbors in the Mexican
Southeast—are increasingly aware of their once and future "place" in the
Mexican national idea. They know that they have been central actors in
Mexico's past, and they are demanding a place in its future. Yet where exactly are they today? What will "Indian ethnicity" become in the twenty-first
century? Chiapas serves as a useful setting for posing this question because
it is one of several states in Mexico that have very large (30 percent to 40
percent) and diverse Indian populations. Furthermore, the ongoing Zapatista
movement has placed Chiapas at the epicenter of the politics of ethnicity, as
this subject is currently being debated as a national issue, both among
Mexico's diverse Indian communities and within the nation as a whole.

The essays in this volume present a partial portrait of this ambivalence—
that is, the condition of Indians' being both within and marginal to the

national idea—from the perspective of one Maya *municipio* ("township"), San Juan Chamula, which is located in Highland Chiapas. This Tzotzil (Maya)-speaking community itself has the largest population of any of the predominantly Indian *municipios* in the state. Chamula Tzotzils have also emigrated, during the last century or so, to dozens of new settlements throughout Chiapas, many of which retain the use of the Tzotzil language and other significant cultural features of their *municipio* of origin. Some Chamula Tzotzils, therefore, live in an ethnically homogeneous, culturally circumscribed center (San Juan); others live in various types of noncontiguous settlements that constitute a kind of diaspora. Together, the central community and its emigrant colonies have a population of approximately 150,000 at present, thus making them by far the largest and most influential nonmestizo ethnic group in Chiapas.

I have conducted almost five years of fieldwork (1965, 1967–69, and 1977–79, and 1985) in San Juan Chamula and several of its colonies and have maintained various forms of contact by means of brief visits and correspondence up to the present time. Throughout the past decade, I have been concerned with a set of issues that are familiar themes in social analysis in our time. In particular, I have grappled with the problem of how to place the subjects of my research—that is, Chamula as a local and a diaspora population, and Chamulas as individuals—within that matrix of outside forces that they believe to have some impact, constant or occasional, upon their lives. This multifaceted Other has many expressions, both imagined and tangible. Some of these extralocal forces are as abstract and enormous as the Mexican Nation, the North American Free Trade Agreement (NAFTA) and the so-called neoliberalism of contemporary Mexican political and economic policies; or as mystical and potent as the cosmic and historical forces of their own heliocentric universe. The Other may be as concrete and structurally omnipresent in their daily lives as in the mestizo/Ladino culture that surrounds them and exploits them. The Other may be as concrete and bizarre as a foreign anthropologist living in their midst, or as odd as the occasional long-haired, white-robed Lacandon Maya who comes to San Cristóbal de las Casas to sell bows and arrows to the tourists. The Other may be as intimate and yet indeterminate as the animal soul companion that shares one's destiny as a coessence. The Other also has the face of evil and destruction, as in the myriad spooks and malevolent forces of the universe, some latent, some erratically active, that could end life itself. Finally, the Other lives within the minds of individual actors as the memory of their own prehuman and non-Indian ancestors whose lives and deeds have shaped the contemporary world and continue to do so today.

Simply stated, Chamula social units and individuals are never alone or still, or much less autonomous, any more than we are. Furthermore, neither the diverse settlements that make up the diaspora, nor the individuals who live in them, remain cognitively or politically passive in the ebb and flow of extrasomatic and extralocal forces that influence their lives. Chamulas are constantly engaged, as we are, in assessing both constraints and "windows of opportunity" in their daily lives.

Some of this give and take of coping with daily life has discernible, even predictable patterns; for many Chamula Tzotzils still live in a matrix of sacred cyclical time and related social practices that derive in part from their ancient Maya heritage. However, there are other aspects of modern Chamula experience—such as the recent wave of conversion to Protestantism, political expulsions and reprisals, sometimes chaotic resettlement, voluntary outmigration, partial acculturation, undocumented migration to the United States, experimentation with pan-Indian alliances, and participation in state- and national-level electoral politics—that resist easy interpretation as conventional ethnographic subjects. Stated in a slightly different way, Chamulas live in both an ethnically and linguistically circumscribed universe *and* in modern Mexico *and* in the porous borderland of Greater North America. Neither the existential conditions of their evolving "traditional" world nor, much less, their various experiences with the diaspora, permit a contemporary portrait that is as cohesive and internally consistent as the one I offered in an earlier work, *Chamulas in the World of the Sun: Time and Space in a Maya Oral Tradition* (1974b).

AN ETHNOGRAPHER ENCOUNTERS A CHANGING SUBJECT

Whether it is owing to San Juan Chamula itself, as it has evolved in the complex late-twentieth-century social landscape of modern Mexico, or to my own response to the epistemological doubts and challenges raised by the currents known as the reflexive mood or postmodern turn in social analysis—or perhaps owing to all of the above—I have thought and written about San Juan Chamula in very different ways in the past decade than I was inclined to do earlier in my career. I no longer feel competent to write a traditional monograph or "comprehensive" ethnography, for I believe that the appropriate subject—some culturally, spatially, and morally circumscribed community—of such an enterprise has become increasingly elusive as an easily isolable entity in our time. By this I mean to say that even the most circumscribed ethnic groups in Mexico—such as the one that is the subject of this book—have many expressions of vitality that form a rapidly changing and complex configuration in the late twentieth century. Each expression has a different arena of Others that surround the Maya self and all expressions are, in reality, quite porous in terms of the people, things, and ideas that constitute them. These numerous manifestations of Chamula ethnicity range from the highly defensive, "traditional" municipal center that forcibly maintains a homogeneous community of Indian custom (which is, ironically, underwritten by close cooperation of the local oligarchy with the PRI [Institutional Revolutionary Party] and the Mexican state), to various exile colonies, voluntary agrarian colonies, and loosely organized alliances of displaced Tzotzils with pan-Maya political activists, such as the Zapatistas. This book, therefore, is not a "monograph" in the traditional sense, because it describes more than one space and time in the evolving lives of the Chamula Tzotzils.

I actually tell two tales in this book. First, I offer a multiscenario ethnographic portrait of the Chamula Tzotzils in the late twentieth century. This conservative Maya community now finds itself in the throes of unprecedented change, if not utter fragmentation. Their world mingles chaotically and sometimes violently with the social and political space of modern Mexico, most recently in the context of the Maya Zapatista movement of 1994, on which occasion the ruling oligarchy of San Juan placed the community on guard against this movement. While the forces behind this transformation are familiar Latin American themes—such as conversion to Protestantism, political radicalization, massive out-migration and urbanization—the Chamula "take" on all of this has been original, pragmatic, and multifaceted. Even as they have dispersed to the far corners of Chiapas, they remain the largest and most visible diaspora community in the region. It is, however, no longer (if it ever was) a unified diaspora community. I will tell small pieces of their multivocal tale.

I also tell a second tale: my own. I have observed the transformation of the Chamula Tzotzils over three decades. This period also spans two generations of anthropological thought and related approaches to the ethnographer's craft. Whether it is owing to San Juan Chamula itself as it has evolved in the complex late-twentieth-century social landscape of modern Mexico, or to my own response to recent currents in social analysis, I have thought, written, and taught about the subject in very different ways in the past decade than I was inclined to do earlier in my career. This book, therefore, becomes my own story, just as it is the Tzotzils' story; one that chronicles my own effort to move from "traditional approaches" to experiment with new forms of representation that seem more suited for representing the porous boundaries, contested spaces, and evolving ethnic affirmations that characterize modern Chiapas. The essays that make up this book—some of which have appeared in relatively obscure places, others only in Spanish, and others previously unpublished—were written during the period of 1986 to the present, although the data that are examined span the period of 1965 to the present. These essays reflect my own evolving approach to ethnographic reporting during this period. The reader will find "something old" and "something new." While the essays do not pretend to achieve a holistic or unitary portrait, they do possess a kind of unity that focuses on storytelling in the broadest sense that includes topics from oral narrative to the ritual and political expression of ethnic identity, to the writing of ethnography. In each case, these essays place the local Chamula subject in dialogue with a different set of outside forces that constrain it or condition it—ranging from myself as ethnographic interlocutor and translator to Presbyterian missionaries; from Mexican national ideology to NAFTA and the Zapatista rebels; from the traditional sun deity to individual soul companion/coessences.

Because I am trying to tell several tales that are thematically linked by common contemporary Maya ethnicity, but which nevertheless do not share the same cast of characters, point of view, place or time, the problem of voice—more particularly, of voices—becomes central to this book. I explore a number of alternatives with regard to placing my own authorial voice in relation to that of the Tzotzils—ranging from Gossen the "traditional" ethnographer/translator to Gossen the storyteller/biographer/speculative journalist. In one case (chapter 6), my voice mingles freely with that of my collaborator/coauthor, Richard Leventhal, an archaeologist. In other cases, the voices of Tzotzil narrators join my own voice to tell a multivocal tale.

All of these essays also address the problem of ethnographic truth. The title of this book, *Telling Maya Tales*, refers not only to the Tzotzil storyteller's art and knowledge but also to my own evolving approach to creating ethnographic texts—my own telling of tales—about the Chamula Tzotzil social universe. In other words, telling a tale is also a telling tale, in the sense that getting something said in narrative form invariably reflects both a narrator's conscious agenda and a subtext of conscious or unconscious omissions and distortions. This complex scenario casts all ethnographers as storytellers and also, perhaps, as unwitting prevaricators. But do we have any choice in the matter? Probably not.

In a recent discussion of postmodernism, Madan Sarup (1993) offers a synthesis of Fredric Jameson's position (Jameson 1981) on narrative as an epistemological category:

> he argues that it is hard to think of the world as it would exist outside narrative. Anything we try to substitute for a story is, on closer examination, likely to be another sort of story. Physicists, for example, "tell stories" about subatomic particles. Anything that presents itself as existing outside the boundaries of some story (a structure, a form, a category) can only do so through a kind of fiction. In Jameson's view structures may be abundantly useful as conceptual fictions, but reality comes to us in the form of its stories. Narrative, just by being narrative, always demands interpretation, and so we must always be aware of the distinction between manifest meaning and latent content. Moreover, we should remember that every narrative simultaneously presents and represents a world,

that simultaneously creates or makes up a reality and asserts that it stands independent of the same reality. In other words, narrative seems at once to reveal or illuminate a world and to hide or distort it. (Sarup 1993:178)

None but the most recalcitrant positivists would claim today that the stories we, as anthropologists, tell about the Other are cut from the whole cloth of truth (Rosaldo 1989). Whether the interference that produces the epistemological handicap that limits our capacity "to tell it like it is" be attributed to the languages we speak, to our scientific paradigms, to our own culture (like all cultures) as a form of local knowledge, to postmodern "wisdom," to our personal idiosyncrasies, to the asymmetries of power between us and our subjects, or to the porosity of cultural boundaries in the post-Cold war era, the message is the same: an acknowledgment of humility and constraint and of inevitable distortion in our representations of the Other. We cannot know as much as we once presumed to know. Nor can we represent what we think we know with the degree of certainty that ethnographers used to claim by virtue of "being there" as a fieldworker (Geertz 1988).

Generic treatments of the so-called crisis of representation in the human sciences have become so abundant in the past decade (e.g., Marcus and Fischer 1986; Clifford and Marcus 1986; and Clifford 1988) that the "problem" must surely be well known to, if not acknowledged by, a significant subset of practicing anthropologists. Therefore, I don't think that it serves any purpose to add one more recital of the issues to what is already a large chorus of angst and calls for remaking, rethinking, and reassessing our disciplinary agenda.

I do, however, hope that the present set of essays may provide a useful case study of how the reflexive mood and current postmodern cultural critique have played out in my own thinking and writing about the Chamula Tzotzils over the past decade. Although I hope to have organized this book in such a way that the chapters flow logically into one another, I have nevertheless dated each essay, either by date of original publication or, in cases of previously unpublished material, by date of composition. This dating may serve the reader as a rough index of where the composition lies in what for me has been an exciting period of discovery. Whether this chronology constitutes a guide to "the lies I tell" or to the emplotment strategies (read: theories and paradigms) that seem reasonable in a given era, or to the fast-changing world of my subject of inquiry, is a conundrum whose answer I don't know.

So as to provide a context for the reader to comprehend the perhaps bizarre agenda of this book—a combination of intellectual autobiography and ethnographic portraits of Chamula Tzotzils in modern Mexico—I should like to provide a brief chronology of how I have "come of age"—several times.

HARVARD IN THE 1960S

I came to Harvard in 1964, firmly committed to the idea I would become empowered to understand the wonderfully diverse cultural landscape of Highland Chiapas through the lens of social science. I had glimpsed the remarkable scenario of ethnic diversity in northwestern Guatemala and Chiapas as I returned to the United States by bus from Costa Rica in 1962, where I had spent the year as an exchange student from the University of Kansas. In Costa Rica I took my first anthropology course, and realized that my experience in that benign and lovely country might provide the beginning of a lifelong escape from Kansas. I was "called" to anthropology as my vocation in Costa Rica as a late-adolescent realization that life was, at least then, more interesting abroad than it was "at home." While Costa Rica was a supportive and comfortably pro-American scenario for this discovery, it was, nonetheless, powerful. However, even this illusion dimmed with time. I realized, somewhat sadly, that "white" Costa Rica ("The Switzerland of Central America" as it is celebrated in a popular song) was rather like the United States, in that we and they had created our respective national identities on the ruins of Native American societies that had been destroyed or marginalized in order to make room for ourselves.

My bus trip through Chiapas in 1962, en route home to Kansas, produced the spellbinding realization that there were, indeed, parts of the New World that remained profoundly, pervasively, Indian. Highland Chiapas was no "Switzerland," but rather, a multifaceted living embodiment of an America that was and is. Mexico was different. Wildly exotic costumes, totally incomprehensible languages (not Spanish), unidentifiable foods, and weird smells (wood smoke, incense, and the ineffable essence of tortillas made on wood-fired griddles), fired my romantic imagination. This was where I wanted to be. It was neither Kansas nor Costa Rica.

I learned that Professor Evon Z. Vogt, of Harvard University, had launched in 1957 a long-term project on the subject of continuity and social change in the Indian communities of Highland Chiapas. Eager to be part of this, I found my way to Harvard, beginning graduate study there in 1964. I became one of hundreds of graduate and undergraduate students who eventually—between 1957 and 1990—participated as fieldworkers in Professor Vogt's celebrated Harvard Chiapas Project (Vogt 1994). The intellectual and physical infrastructure of this project proved to be invaluable to me. Training in the Tzotzil language, access to information from dozens of colleagues whose fieldwork preceded and coincided with my own, in addition to the commodious offices and living quarters at the Harvard Ranch in San Cristóbal, provided both an initial orientation and an oasis of security and stimulation to which I could retreat when the physical difficulties and political troubles of living in the Indian communities became acute.

However, despite the relative comforts of working within a well-orga-nized project, the real task—almost five years of fieldwork in San Juan Chamula and its diaspora colonies—did not take shape easily. In particular, the issues of method, theory, mastery of the field language, and the creation of ethnographic texts did not come with the Harvard Chiapas Project nor with the Harvard Ranch. They came from and through me, as I tried to place myself in an "intellectual tradition" and to enable myself to say some-thing about what I observed and experienced. Through what lenses would I analyze thousands of pages of texts and fieldnotes?

As is the case with all of us, my initial approach to this question was condi-tioned by what I perceived to be useful and current models of how to see, how to ask, how to record, and how to report. As I came of age at Harvard and in the field, three approaches came to my attention as plausible ways to proceed.

First, ethnoscience offered what we now know to be the naive notion that any cognitive domain could be elicited from our native consultants and laid out with its internal patterns of native "rationality" if we used the right "ques-tion frames" and stuck faithfully to "native categories of meaning." This was a variant of the old functionalist assumption that any set of exotic beliefs, social classifications, and practices could be revealed by a good anthropologist to have its closet rationality. The task was simply to report this configuration in the chosen domain (e.g., religion, food, firewood, economic practices) and to reveal its inherent order and pattern of articulation with the cultural whole. The observer/ethnographer thus became the translator of the rational order of the Other. He or she labored as the clever Orientalist, in Edward Said's sense of the term—a less-than-innocent, condescending, but nevertheless clever fly on the wall, a facilitator for revealing the truths of the Other, divest-ed of the surface clutter of the culture bearers (Clifford 1998: 259–60).

I took this mandate quite seriously, believing that the large corpus of tra-ditional narratives that I undertook to collect, transcribe, translate, and anno-tate could somehow be made to testify, with my help, to the Chamulas' inner reality. To this end, I paid careful attention to native genre taxonomy, native conventions of oral poetics, and performance rules. I also prepared extensive ethnographic background notes, in consultation with storytellers during translation sessions, that might provide cultural information that was assumed but not overtly stated in dictated texts. The reader will find, in the early chapters of this book, narrative testimony that is cast in this style of ethnographic reporting.

A second analytical approach that captured my imagination was French structuralism. I am now aware that this movement crested and began its rather precipitous decline in the United States even as I was finishing my dissertation in the late 1960s. However, its seductive powers were great: one more tool with which to reveal that beneath the surface chaos of ethnographic data there lay a deep structural template that was not only more or less stable and consistent in a given cultural context but also, if one bought into the full paradigm, a basic feature of mind, of the human spirit. My earlier analyses of Chamula ritual symbolism and ritual behavior relied heavily on a culturally specific application of this approach. It led me to such occasional sophomoric excesses as claiming to offer a "grammar" of Chamula ritual symbolism (Gossen 1971) and claiming to "present the oral tradition . . . as a complete information system" (Gossen 1974b: vii). While I do not disclaim this work, it seems, in hindsight, that I was overly eager to find underlying order and less than fully attentive to the irregularities in the data, inconsistencies from one performance to the next, and to disagreements among my field consultants. An essay that is cast in a modified—perhaps, better said, more circumspect and multivocal—structuralist voice, an analysis of the Chamula Festival of Games, appears as chapter five of this volume. The reader will see that I remain convinced that structural homologies exist that bind together on the ritual stage certain experiential and classificatory truths about diverse aspects of the Chamula social universe.

A third set of approaches that influenced my coming of age as an anthropologist in the 1960s was of course the work of Clifford Geertz and Victor Turner. Geertz's vision of anthropology—not as a science in search of explanation but as a critical strategy for reaching credible interpretations of cultures-as-texts—was already, in *The Interpretation of Cultures* (1963), providing an alternative to the positivistic affirmations of the "great paradigms" and to the Procrustean-bed variant of structuralism. His work has informed and inspired me and given me the confidence to examine my own work critically with an eye to trying to find my own interpretive voice. If texts cannot speak for themselves, and if no overarching paradigm can do the job either, what is left but to place one's own intellectual resources in dialogue with the thought and practices of one's subjects?

In Victor Turner's great Ndembu corpus, I also found respite from the apparent chaos that I sensed, with regard to anthropology's mission, in his distinction between the different levels—exegetical, operational, and positional—at which one could examine symbolic behavior and related social practices. Just as I was impressed by Geertz's bringing together of his empirical concern with the "hard surfaces of social life" and his gift for elegant qualitative analysis, I was taken with Turner's insistence that our own analysis at the positional level must be informed by both native exegesis of practice and our empirical observation of practice.

These approaches that I have just described provided a beginning set of strategies for observation of Tzotzil life and for telling ethnographic tales about it. With them in mind, I went to the field for the first time in the late

1960s. There, Professor Vogt's Harvard Project embraced me—indeed hundreds of us over the next two decades—with his grand challenge to document continuity and change in the Maya communities of Highland Chiapas. In our introduction to the Festschift volume that we edited in honor of Vogt, Victoria Bricker and I have commented on the almost Boasian scope of his vision of Chiapas Project and of his remarkable latitude in permitting, even encouraging, a wide diversity of approaches:

> [We] believe that Vogt is perhaps most similar to Franz Boas [in that his] vision of a basic macro-Maya cultural persistence within Greater Mesoamerica, [led him] to create an ongoing ethnographic archive of culture change in the Chiapas highlands. This phenomenon of continuing cultural integrity that is nevertheless able to adapt to rapidly changing regional political and economic realities is to be understood through what he now calls a "phylogenetic model." ... Franz Boas had a similar agenda in mind as he organized the Jesup North Pacific Expedition, including the Siberian Coast.
>
> In concept and scope, as well as in the large-scale funding and international cooperation necessary for its realization, there are even more similarities between Boas's role as the linchpin in the Jesup Expedition and Vogt's founding and sustaining role in the Harvard Chiapas Project. Along with the similarities in grandeur of conception and the vast production of ethnographic and linguistic archival material must be added the recruitment of "... a diverse staff ..."
>
> It was never a party-line endeavor, neither in theory, style of ethnography, nor mode of reporting. All of us were welcome to bring our own intellectual predispositions and skills to bear on the problems of continuity and change in Tzotzil and Tzeltal communities as these groups have dealt with the forces of accelerating change in the latter half of the twentieth century. We were asked only to work hard, preferably in the native languages, homes, and fields, and to make our field notes available to the general archive of the Harvard Project. (Gossen and Bricker 1989: 3-4)

TOWARD A GLOBAL PERSPECTIVE

The first two decades of my research in Chiapas involved one short field trip (summer of 1965), and two major field trips (1967–69, 1977–79). Throughout this time, I was aware that the field of anthropology, the craft of ethnography, indeed, the shape of social analysis itself, were in the throes of a major reassessment. I realized (as did a number of friends and professional critics of my work) that the community that I once studied and understood as a homogeneous, circumscribed community was, in some respects, porous and multifaceted, and that it was becoming more so by the day. In particular, it became clear to me that I could not pretend to understand continuity and change among the contemporary Chamula Tzotzils without undertaking both a historical and field study of out-migration from the home community, a process that had begun in the nineteenth century. I began visiting and studying Chamula diaspora communities in my 1977-79 field season. After I moved to the University at Albany in 1979, Robert Carmack and I developed a project that would focus on intensive field study of diaspora communities. We began this project in 1983, with the assistance of a number of graduate students from the University at Albany. In the context of this project I made several visits to Chiapas, including one season of field study in the summer of 1985.

Crucial to this phase of my own work on the diaspora was a heightened awareness of the importance of a historical context that would make sense of the diverse processes that caused the out-migration to occur. I was also forced, albeit grudgingly at first, to realize that one could not comprehend modern Chamula without also attempting to reckon with regional processes in Chiapas and also with the Mexican national idea as it has evolved in the postrevolutionary era. These considerations involved political and economic issues well beyond Chamula—not only at the state and national levels but also at the global level.

The pertinence of global issues to the interpretation of local realities in Mexico did not enter easily into my research strategy and aesthetic sensibilities, for I had long thought of anthropology and its focus on the Other as a respite from what I found discordant and ugly in my own culture and in my own life history. However, it became clear as I began serious study of the diaspora in the early 1980s that cultural, economic, and political forces emanating from the United States, Europe, and urban Mexico, had profoundly to do, for example, with the rapid rise of Protestantism as an alternative lifestyle in Chiapas. Furthermore, it has been documented with convincing authority that the pattern of accelerated out-migration from Indian communities—beginning in the nineteenth century and accelerating rapidly in the late twentieth century—had directly to do with economic and political policies made far beyond the boundaries of Chiapas (Collier 1975 and Wasserstrom 1983). That this was incontestably true became obvious to the whole world with the sudden explosion of the Maya Zapatista movement on January 1, 1994, coinciding precisely with the date that the North American Free Trade Agreement went into effect. The lowland jungle of the Mexican Southeast—homeland of the insurrection—has been the destination of thousands of recently displaced individuals and voluntary immigrants, the majority of them being Indians of Maya ethnicity, some of them, Chamula Tzotzils (Collier and Quaratiello 1994).

Most of the essays in the latter half of this book, dating from approximately 1990 (chapters 6 to 10), reflect my attempt to consider Chamula Tzotzil experience against the historical backdrop of the region, the nation, and beyond.

MAYA CULTURAL AGENCY

In the process of raising my own consciousness about the importance of history and global forces in the understanding of the contemporary Tzotzil Mayas, I also came to a new appreciation of the power of local cultural forces as agents of change and adaptation. Tzotzil Mayas are not today, nor have they ever been, passive recipients of outside forces. They have always brought their own cultural constructs to bear on the course that social change would take, even when these outside forces have wielded—since well before the Spanish invasion of the sixteenth century—superior instruments of economic, political, and symbolic power (Hunt 1977 and Bricker 1981).

In attempting to identify durable features of Mesoamerican thought that might figure in the cultural constructs that the Maya have brought to almost a millenium of culture change—first in the shadow of the great empires of pre-Columbian Central Mexico, now as a peripheral region in what Wallerstein has called the World System—I have reexamined Maya religion and ideology from both the pre-Columbian and colonial eras. My brief synthesis of this premodern background appears as a chapter on religion in a recent textbook, *The Legacy of Mesoamerica*, of which I was a coeditor (Gossen 1996). Chapters 6 and 9 of the present book specifically address this deep historical background.

The Chiapas Highlands were marginal to the great seats of political power in the ancient Mesoamerican world system (Carmack 1996), just as Chiapas is today, by most indices of social statistics, peripheral to modern Mexico; it is the poorest, least democratically represented state in the Mexican nation and enjoys the least access to government social services (Ross 1994). It is often observed that Chiapas does not fit the publicly touted national profile of Mexico as an emerging First World nation; rather, Chiapas remains a Third World enclave in a nation that aspires to First World status. Neither the Wars of Independence of 1810–20, nor the Mexican Revolution of 1910–18, effectively changed the white-dominated political institutions and de facto ethnic segregation that were instruments of public policy during the colonial period.

However, in spite of, or perhaps because of, this marginality, Chiapas has been a major catalyst in the genesis of international Indian political activism and pan-Indian cooperation in the Americas in the post-Zapatista era. To cite but one example of this, the Zapatista-sponsored National Indigenous Forum met in January 1996, in San Cristóbal de las Casas, to formulate and promote a new agenda for Indian policy in Mexico. This important meeting was attended by representatives of most of the Indian communities of Mexico, as well as by hundreds of observers from North and South America and Europe. This forum has already produced formal Indian policy changes—though far from full implementation—on the part of the Mexican government (Nash

1997). Some have argued, as I shall in the final essay of this volume (chapter 10), that Maya Zapatistas, who enjoy almost no military strength by conventional measures of firepower, have nevertheless provided major catalysts—the ongoing threat of civil war in Chiapas, an articulate critique of Mexico's neoliberal economic policies, and a steadfast insistence that they, too, are Mexicans—that brought major democratic reforms to the whole of the Mexican political process. We have witnessed this in the results of the municipal, state, and national delegate elections of July 1997; the PRI (Institutional Revolutionary Party), which has dominated Mexico for three-quarters of this century, now must share power with an odd coalition of parties of the right and left, among them the PRD (Democratic Revolutionary Party), that had the strong support of the Maya Zapatistas.

In reflecting on the power of structurally oppressed groups to survive, adapt, and reconstitute—sometimes even to reinvent themselves and their oppressors—through their own agency, I have been influenced during the past decade by a major international project of coordinated research that I helped to organize in 1986 in anticipation of the Columbus quincentenary year of 1992. In collaboration with my colleagues, Manuel Gutiérrez Estévez of Spain, Miguel León-Portilla of Mexico, Manuel Marzal of Peru, and Jorge Klor de Alva, then my colleague at Albany, we launched a project initially entitled "De Palabra y Obra en el Nuevo Mundo" ("Of Word and Deed in the New World," to become "Discourse and Practice in the New World" in the English edition of the seminar proceedings' volumes). This project yielded five international conferences (three in Spain, two in Albany) on the subject of ethnicity, identity construction, and national ideas in the Americas since the Spanish invasion of 1492. (See Gutiérrez Estévez et al. 1992; León-Portilla et al. 1992; Gossen et al. 1993; and Klor de Alva et al. 1995). Held between 1988 and 1992, these week-long seminars eventually involved over seventy-five participants from South America, North America, Europe, and Israel. Included in our number were several representatives of Native American communities in the United States, Canada, and Mexico.

The unifying theme that we sought to highlight throughout the seminar series was to document, from diverse corners of the Americas, sample encounters of Native American and African discourse and practice as these met—almost always in asymmetrical and violent ways—the constructs and practices of the Europeans. Although relatively simple in conception, the goal—to identify alternatives to traditional models of culture change and identity formation in the Americas—proved to be quite elusive. Although almost all presenters agreed that simple models of "hybrid syncretism" did not address the historical and political realities of the European invasion and colonization, neither were they satisfied with static functional interpretations or with conventional Marxist analyses that identified virtually all postcontact New World cultural forms as "colonial creations" that were designed to facilitate exploitation of subject populations. Conspicuously absent also were contemporary or historical ethnographic cases of unfettered cultural continuity from Native American, African, or even European origins.

In essence, the only unanimity that emerged from scholarly examination of dozens of case studies ranging from Canada to southern Chile was the *absence* of any easily generalizable pattern of ethnic formation and expression, even among those communities—such as those of Highland Chiapas—that spoke dialects of the same language and were subject to the same state policies. In all cases, local knowledge, local politics, and local actors seem to have had the last word in determining the form and expression that "belonging to a group" and "acting in history" would assume. Even radical asymmetry of power between parties in situations of cultural contact—such as slavery and indentured servitude—did not strip subalterns of their power to adapt and create cultural forms that expressed compliance and resistance, as well as ethnic affirmation.

Although we did not conceive of this project as an orchestrated testimony to indigenous and subaltern cultural agency, that theme, above all others, emerged as the leitmotif of these five seminars. In a recent commentary on current trends in cultural anthropology, Bruce M. Knauft corroborates our impressions of the importance of this issue:

> Equally important and much less emphasized are the ways in which indigenous people assert meaning, dignity, and resilience or resistance amid these problems. The fact that most people still spend most of their time cultivating their gardens should not be lost sight of. Indigenous practices and indigenous beliefs are far from dead; indeed, they resurface with creative regularity. More than a simple retention to custom, traditions are actively re-created as they are reproduced. The tensions and problems of postcolonialism are legion, but the practical ways in which people find continuities and creative spaces as they engage the possibilities and constraints of change—how they expand and elaborate their received senses of practice and agency—have only recently been opened to understanding and theorization by cultural anthropologists.
>
> Contemporary configurations of practice and agency are thus both understudied and ripe for detailed investigation. This research may be stimulated by theoretical analysis or by programmatic critique but needs in the final instance to be engaged by substantive ethnography of actual social situations. (Knauft 1996:133–34)

REFLEXIVITY

My telling of Maya tales in this book expresses my desire to offer a multi-faceted ethnographic account of the expressive forms and thought of a resilient and self-conscious indigenous community in modern Mexico.

However, this book is also autobiographical, as I have noted above. It tells my own story at midlife. At this point it is appropriate to acknowledge that laying out the doubts, uncertainties, and changes—sometimes even the contradictions and mistakes—in my own thinking about my ethnographic subject, comes with some difficulty. After all, are we not charged, as social scientists, with telling it like it is? If we get it wrong, are we not lying in our representations and lying to our readers? If we don't get it right, then aren't we bad social scientists?

In searching for possible answers to these questions, I am reminded of the baseball umpire story that came to my attention two decades ago in the introductory essay to the *Reader in Symbolic Anthropology* (Dolgin, Kemnitzer, and Schneider 1977: 20). The editors tell the tale of three retired baseball umpires who were enjoying an after-the-game commentary over several beers. They came to reflect on the nature of the game itself, and in due course, perhaps in a mellow haze, each of the three offered an immodest summary of what the game was all about. The youngest of the three spoke first:

"Baseball. It ain't nothin' but balls and strikes and I calls 'em as they are."

Contradicting him, the second said, "Nope. You've got it wrong. Baseball, it ain't nothin' but balls and strikes, and I calls 'em as I see 'em."

The eldest responded, "Nope. You've both got it wrong. Baseball ain't nothin' but balls and strikes, all right, but they ain't nothin' 'til I calls 'em."

The implications of this story for thinking about what we do as social scientists are considerable. Although I am not a baseball fan, I have often reflected on which kind of worldview-of-the-game I would have if I were an umpire instead of an anthropologist. My thoughts on this matter have shifted over the years. Earlier, I would have sided with the first umpire, an earnest empiricist. I now find myself far more sympathetic with the second, for he acknowledges that, while all parties agree that there are ephemeral, "real" events called balls and strikes that are supposed to be subject to rules, each pitch is nevertheless judged and called by the eye, mind, and voice of the observer, the umpire. This scenario, I believe, more or less defines the constraints under which I observe and report as an ethnographer. What about the third umpire? If I were he, I would be a philosopher or a novelist, not an ethnographer.

To come full circle then, if, like the second umpire, I am constrained by my own life and times, but nevertheless wish to tell tales that are not merely fictions, what moves do I make in writing ethnographic accounts that acknowledge both myself and the Other? Many colleagues have addressed this question over the past two decades—obviously enjoying the liberation of what Marcus and Fischer have called an "experimental moment in the human sciences." As Barbara Tedlock and Dennis Tedlock have so elegantly stated the case on numerous occasions, if all ethnographic knowledge derives from dialogue in the broadest sense, then why not place this dialogue in our ethnographic accounts? (See D. Tedlock 1983 and B. Tedlock 1991.) Writing such narrative ethnography typically involves rhetorical strategies for including multiple voices, including that of the ethnographer as a participant rather than as an omniscient fly on the wall. This experimental, multivocal mood has already produced several modern classics, such as Paul Rabinow's *Reflections on Field Work in Morocco* (1977), Dennis Tedlock's *Breath on the Mirror* (1993), Barbara Tedlock's *The Beautiful and the Dangerous* (1992), and Richard Price's *Alabi's World* (1990), recipient of the Staley Prize in 1993. Price's work is of particular interest here, in that he has pioneered rhetorical strategies for writing even historical ethnography in multiple voices.

As I attempt in this book as a whole, and in its several parts, to experiment with different voices, including my own, I realize that the task is not without risk, for it involves the revelation of uncertainties, mistakes, paths not taken, even some downright embarrassing moments. However, I am convinced that these dissonances and glitches contributed to my present understanding of my subject; hence, they become a part of the some of the tales I will tell in this book.

Bruce M. Knauft has recently written of similar feelings of ambivalence about "personalizing one's position" in the writing of ethnography:

> Where do I, personally, stand? For whom do I speak? And why, for most anthropologists are such questions embarrassing? . . . The life one has built—the sum of past choices, constraints, triumphs, and mistakes—confronts one in the present as an externality. There is always tension between living within the confines of this received life and changing or transforming it. This is certainly not a resolvable problem; rather, it is one to be struggled with—a continuing war of position within oneself. Questions of efficacy, personal ability, pragmatic possibility, and paths unexplored are always present. But within this range of ambiguous and sometimes guilty possibilities, it is important not to disempower those eager to confront life's diversities and critique its inequalities, regardless of what racial or sexual or ethnic or class or national position they come from. It is useless to flagellate oneself for not being more of a victim. Paralysis or loss of nerve is not the answer. So, too, inescapable history does not disempower us from productive attempts in the present.
>
> The goal, as I see it, is to appreciate diversity and critique inequality. These goals potentiate rather than preclude the dedication to objectivism as a tool of analysis. Ethnography is subversive because is provides the hard sharpening stone of empiricism through which our concepts are refined, our values engaged, and our unadmitted assumptions brought to light. (Knauft 1996: 276)

LOGIC AND SEQUENCE

The organization of this book has threads of development that seek to tell the several tales that I have promised above. I want to be explicit about this because the plot is fairly complex.

First, with the exception of chapter 1, which is a recent (1993b) reflexive essay about my fieldwork among the Chamulas, the organization moves generally from local (chapters 2 to 5) to regional settings (chapters 6 to 10) in which Chamula and Maya Tzotzil communities are found.

Second, for reasons that I have discussed above, this sequence from local to regional and national foci also represents a rough chronology of the order in which the ethnographic accounts were written. They move from a portfolio of indigenous narrative accounts of the origins of the universe and of the community in chapters 2 through 4, dating from the early 1980s, to a quasi-journalistic essay (chapter 10) on the Maya Zapatistas that was originally published in 1996; the postscript to chapter 10 is actually an editorial that I wrote in January 1998, in an attempt to explain local circumstances surrounding the tragic Christmas massacre of December 22, 1997.

The third logical thread which ties these essays together is historical (as distinct from chronology of composition, discussed above). The first half of the book (chapters 2 to 5) deals with mythical time; that is, local truths that are both time present and time past—timeless—as represented in sacred narrative and ritual drama. The second half of the book (chapters 6 to 10) deals with historical issues, in the Western secular sense, spanning the archaeological record of the Maya Preclassic to NAFTA.

The fourth strain in the plot development of this book is textual. By this I mean to say that the earliest chapters (chapters 2 through 4) depend heavily on the capacity of native texts to speak for themselves; subsequent chapters move progressively to include more voices in the construction of the narrative. This pattern of development expresses my current conviction that neither their discourses nor our discourses speak entirely for themselves. I attempt in chapter 2 to "let the texts speak for themselves," with the help of ethnographic notes, specifically footnotes; in chapter 3, I add more contextual commentary by way of introducing a magnificent long text, retaining the ethnographic notes; in chapter 4, I construct an entire essay around and in response to a powerful native text, retaining all of the above, plus the original Tzotzil text and the narrator's biography. I want to call particular attention to the fact that this section (chapters 2 through 4) includes accounts from five different native storytellers. In this section and throughout the book, I have made liberal use of native drawings as illustrations. I commissioned these drawings from a gifted Chamula artist, Marian López Calixto, who worked independently from me—using only transcribed Tzotzil texts and his imagination to produce his illustrations. I hoped thereby to add a visual medium that might complement, as an aid to interpretation, the content of the narrative text and my ethnographic notes. Continuing the discussion of textual criticism, I embark in chapter five on an extensive discussion of the principal annual Chamula ritual drama of self-representation, the Festival of Games. This essay, originally published in 1986, is a fairly conventional ethnographic description and analysis of this remarkable event. It is amplified here with personal anecdotes (from four occasions of witnessing the festival) and with native texts that are implicit (i.e., known by participants but never articulated) in the text of the ritual.

As I present the second half of this book, native texts tend to disappear as lengthy segments of my own text. What is going on? Why should one abandon the bloodline of ethnographic truth? In fact, natives' and others' narratives share the space.

In chapter 6, I establish a dialogue with a Maya archaeologist, discussing the gendered symbolic space of the Ancient Maya world and of the modern Maya world with regard to religion, specifically the instrumental role of women in the Maya past and present.

Chapter 7, on the nature and history of the Chamula diaspora, is textually saturated with me and other Western scholars in an exercise of historical responsibility. Tzotzils return, however, in the conclusions, for it is argued that women, who control socialization and language use in the home, have fundamentally to do with the cultural continuities that are found in the diaspora communities. Ritual practices are also shown to have a central role in cultural continuity.

Chapter 8, which is an experiment in reconstructing the biography of a major Protestant leader, Miguel Kaxlán, whom I never knew. It depends heavily on a native text composed in Tzotzil by his son, from whom he, the son, was estranged. The entire present text is my own, although based primarily on the testimony of the son as an intermediary. I attempt here to write Miguel Kaxlán's biography against the turbulent backdrop of twentieth-century Chiapas and Mexican history. This implies the incorporation of many points of view, among them the perspectives of the missionaries themselves and those of their allies and adversaries. To this chapter I also add a postscript, a kind of detective story mode of offering an alternative ending to the tale; that Miguel Kaxlán, an antiestablishment radical, was in fact behaving as a traditional Tzotzil hero.

The final two chapters, 9 and 10, deal directly with ancient, colonial, and modern texts in the effort to place some aspects of the contemporary world of Highland Chiapas in historical perspective. In particular, the Zapatista movement, which is considered in both of these chapters, emerged so suddenly and with such an outburst of poetic communiqués and other excellent media coverage, that it made sense for political, aesthetic, and practical reasons to take so-called ephemeral texts seriously as social documents.

A final thread in the development of this book that deserves mention because of its apparent omission and its actual presence, is the point of view of Tzotzil women. Because of the practical limitations of contact that is permitted between unrelated men and women in Tzotzil communities, I have not at any time in my fieldwork spoken freely with or worked at length with Tzotzil women. This has obviously limited my capacity to speak of ethnic identity from the female perspective. However, it will be apparent from early in the book (see chapter 2) that the primordial female presence came first in the order of all things in Chamula cosmology, in the person of Our Holy Mother Moon, who gave birth to Our Lord Sun/Christ. In essence, then, the primordial female power of the cosmos is inextricably linked to all of those discussions of mythical and ritual time that are discussed in the first half of the book. The instrumental role of females in cultural maintenance, cultural renewal, and ethnic continuity—also as victims of exploitation and violence in male machinations for power—is centrally important to the argument of several of the essays (chapters 6 through 8). It is also noted in chapters 9 and 10 that females have, through the Zapatista movement, moved into positions of public leadership; in fact, women's issues are prominent in the Zapatista agenda for social and economic reform. The reader is invited to consider two full-scale ethnographic studies of Tzotzil women's perspectives on their place in contemporary society (Rosenbaum 1993 and Eber 1995). These accounts offer detail and nuances on these issues that I have undoubtedly missed.

ACKNOWLEDGMENTS

This book came into being through dialogue. Not only the ethnographic data but also the impetus to present these essays as book, came to me through conversation.

I am particularly grateful to my colleagues in the Quincentenary Project: Manuel Gutiérrez Estévez, J. Jorge Klor de Alva, Miguel León-Portilla, and Manuel Marzal. My sustained, close contact with them as a group began in 1986 in the context of the planning and editing process related to our multiple seminar series, in addition to the seminars themselves. We spent hundreds of hours together in the Convento de la Coria, in Trujillo, Spain, as guests of the Xavier de Salas Foundation and the Government of the Autonomous Region of Extremadura. In this restored sixteenth-century convent—now the seat of the Salas Foundation, we were constantly aware of the irony of the place. This lovely town was the home of Francisco Pizarro—astute and bloody plunderer of the Inca Empire—and of Francisco de Orellana, discoverer of the Amazon. Vasco Núñez de Balboa, discoverer of the Pacific Ocean, came from another Extremeño town nearby. Indeed, Extremadura proudly touts itself in tourist literature as being the "Cradle of the Conquistadors." (They are revising this, for it did not "play well" during the Quincentenary observance.) To the sobering irony of staging a major project on the processes of postcontact ethnic and national formation in the Americas from this setting was added the counterirony that the taxpayers of Extremadura contributed generously to all stages of this undertaking, including publication of results. As our principal patron, the Extremeño Ministry of Culture—even we, ourselves—came to regard this endeavor as a kind of academic penance in the present for what Bartolomé de las Casas dubbed "the Black legend," referring to the atrocities committed by Spaniards against the Amerindians in the sixteenth century. Indeed, the Spanish title of the project, "De Palabra y Obra en el Nuevo Mundo" is borrowed from the Roman Catholic prayer associated with the sacrament of confession: "My Father, I have sinned against thee in thought, word, and deed. . . ."

Although this backdrop of guilt and atonement may sound maudlin, perhaps even foolish—particularly so in an academic setting—the leitmotif of establishing an understanding and dialogue, via scholarly inquiry, with a few representatives of America's historically oppressed populations, consistently emerged in our discussions and seminars as an ethically and academically responsible strategy for understanding ethnic identities in the Americas. Our central concern came to be the quest for the means of empowering subaltern groups to speak as active agents in witnessing and constructing their own destinies, even as they lived and live today under various circumstances of structural inequality. That we found virtual unanimity among ourselves and among seminar participants on these issues—anthropology as cultural critique and documentation of cultural agency as an active force in social change—may come as no surprise, for one of the mainstreams of cultural anthropology as a whole has focused on these problems in the past few decades. However, the five of us came to this consensus from very different national traditions and intellectual formations—Spanish, Mexican, Peruvian, and North American. I learned much from reflecting on the evolution and expression of our convergence of opinion on this matter. I thank them for reading and critiquing virtually all of the essays in this volume. I also express my deep gratitude to the people of Extremadura, and to Jaime de Salas, secretary of the Salas Foundation, for providing the setting and the means for me to engage in over a decade of sustained international discussion of the subject matter of this book.

The field research and translations that are reported in this book have been generously supported by a fellowship from the John Simon Guggenheim

Foundation (1977–78), and by grants from the National Institutes of Health (1977–79; 1983–85) and the National Endowment for the Humanities (1989–91). I gratefully acknowledge this assistance, knowing that other countries in the world would not have been so generous in support of a project that is, on the surface of it, so far from their "national interest." I hope to have shown in this book that an understanding and appreciation of Mexico, an old and close friend of the United States—now bound to us ever more intimately through NAFTA and through our shared cultural and historical heritage—can never be far from our interests and sensibilities as a nation.

Other significant support for various stages in my research and related conferences and conference presentations has come from the University at Albany, the Institute for Mesoamerican Studies at the University at Albany, the University at Albany Foundation, The Wenner-Gren Foundation for Anthropological Research, and from the Plumsock Foundation. This support is gratefully acknowledged.

I have also obtained valuable help from my colleagues at the University at Albany. I specifically thank Edna Acosta-Belén, Richard Bleu, Louise Burkhart, Robert M. Carmack, James P. Collins, Helen Elam, Liliana Goldin, Gail Landsman, Lee Bickmore, and Richard G. Wilkinson, for reading and commenting on drafts of a number of the essays in this volume. During the same period, I received invaluable feedback and inspiration from a number of graduate students at Albany in the context of seminars in which I presented several of the present essays as working papers. I am particularly grateful to Quetzil Castaneda, Duncan Earle, Antonella Fabri, Estuardo Galdámez, Gwynne Jenkins, Brent Metz, Pedro Pitarch, and Alice Re Cruz, for their assistance and encouragement at various stages of this project. All of them have contributed as much to my education as I hope to have contributed to theirs.

I also express special thanks to Sally and Richard Price and Barbara and Dennis Tedlock, and June Nash, Linda Schele, and Evon Z. Vogt, all of whom have provided me with inspiration through their own highly innovative works and through their encouragement to experiment with my own ethnographic voice.

I also owe a special debt of gratitude to my former colleague Richard Leventhal for many years of friendship and education in Maya archaeology and for his kind permission to allow our coauthored essay to be reprinted here. To my collegue Brenda Rosenbaum goes my deep gratitude, not only for helping to monitor my translations and notes for consistency and accuracy, but also for contributing heroic editorial labors to my larger project of publishing my full corpus of Tzotzil narrative texts.

I express my sincere thanks to former editor Marley Wasserman of Routledge Press for encouraging me to undertake this project, and to the present Publishing Director, Bill Germano, for his patience, encouragement, and understanding in seeing this project to completion.

The last word in gratitute must go to my family. My wife Eleanor, who has been at my side at all stages of this project, provided invaluable bibliographic, technical, and editorial assistance. Without her, this whole project would have languished. I also thank my children—Andrew, Molly, and Nicholas—who read parts of the manuscript with a critical eye for excessive jargon and academese, which they loathe. I hope that they will see the fruit of their demand for clarity.

ORTHOGRAPHICAL NOTE

Aside from a very few colonial sources (Gossen 1985), the modern history of Tzotzil as a written language and literature is very recent, dating from about 1960. Therefore, orthography has not yet been standardized. There are two common modern notions: column 1 is closer to the conventions of the International Phonetic Alphabet; column 2 acquiesces to the realities of available typeface and broader intelligibility to both English and Spanish speakers, and is also closer to the orthography used in older Tzotzil/Spanish—Spanish/Tzotzil manuscripts. Equivalences of consonant notations are generally as follows. Some manuscripts and published texts use a combination of both orthographies, as I shall in this book. All Tzotzil textual extracts in this book have been standardized to use the symbols printed in **boldface** below.

I am using a combination of both notations for these consonants (boldface characters in columns 1 and 2) so as to represent the correct Tzotzil sound value together with simplicity of notation. Other Tzotzil consonants in my orthography are pronounces with their I. P. A. sound values.

(1)		(2)
ʔ (glottal stop) as in	=	7 or ' or **ʔ** as in
ʔ*on* 'avocado'	=	7*on* or '*on* or **ʔ*on***
h as in *hme*ʔ 'my mother'	=	**j** as in **j*me*ʔ**
š (sh) as in š*i* 'he or she said'	=	**x** as in **x*i***
s as in **s*ik*** 'cold'	=	*z* as in *zik*
č (ch) as in č*i*ʔ' 'sweet'	=	**ch** as in **ch*i*ʔ**

č as in *ʔič'* 'chile'	=	***ch'*** as in ***ʔich'***

(glottalization on a consonant is consistently represented by an apostrophe following the consonant)

ȼ as in *ȼeb* 'girl'	=	***tz*** or ***ts*** as in ***tzeb*** or ***tseb***
ȼ as in *ȼ'iʔ* 'dog'	=	***tz'*** or ***ts'*** as in ***tz'iʔ*** or ***ts'iʔ***
k as in ***kom*** 'to remain'	=	*c* as in *com*
k' as in ***k'an*** 'to want'	=	*c'* as in *c'an*
b (glottalized) as in ***nab*** 'lake'	=	*m* as in *nam*

Tzotzil vowels have these sound values:

a [a] as in f*a*ther
e [ɛ] as in b*e*t
i [i] as in b*ee*t
o [o] as in b*o*at
u [u] as in L*u*ke

EDITORIAL NOTE

As I noted earlier in this preface, I have dated each of the essays either with its date of original publication in Spanish or English, or, in cases of unpublished texts, the date of composition. This information, in addition to the setting and circumstances of the composition, is incorporated into brief headnotes for each chapter. In the case of published material, I have deliberately limited my editing to the deletion of redundant material and correction of factual errors. Both the dating and editing decisions are related to the particular goals of this book.

One

THE OTHER IN CHAMULA TZOTZIL COSMOLOGY AND HISTORY: REFLECTIONS OF A KANSAN IN CHIAPAS

This essay represents an epiphany of sorts, an acknowledgment of who I am. It is a coming-of-age story, a middle-aged reflection on my personal and academic formation against the backdrop of Chamula Tzotzils and Chiapas in an era when social change in Mexico and the intellectual transformation of anthropology have moved at an accelerating pace. The acknowledgments at the end of this essay will reveal that this essay began, for me, as an embarrassing fiasco. In a nutshell, I was told by several colleagues whom I respected very much that my presentation at a conference (1990, in Trujillo, Spain) was a very good example of what nobody did anymore.

That judgment may or may not have been accurate, but it hit home. It indicated to me something that I knew but had not acknowledged: that the world was changing, the field of anthropology was changing, and that one should wake up and listen. I did. I scrapped my text and started from scratch. The key point in my reevaluation was that I had previously been approaching the Other in Tzotzil history and cosmology as a structural abstraction without realizing that my culture and I (read: Western civilization) were, among other Others, the Other in our time. Upon reflection, it became clear that the Chamula Tzotzils had been listening to us for many centuries. How could I be so deaf to their stories? How could I be so deaf to my own stories? This essay is a response to these questions.

O wad some pow'r the giftie gie us
To see oursels as others see us!
It wad frae monie a blunder free us
    And foolish notion:
What airs in dress and gait wad lea'e us,
    And ev'n Devotion.[1]

—Robert Burns, "To a Louse: On Seeing one in a Lady's Bonnet at Church."

INTRODUCTION

This passage from Robert Burns, bard of Scotland, came to America and to me via my maternal grandfather, David Hamilton, a Kansas farmer, who was fond of reciting it (neither knowing nor caring about its exact origin; it was just a "Scottish saying") on the occasion of some slip of vanity, foolishness, or insensitivity—qualities he did not view kindly. My earliest memory of hearing this aphorism was one summer day when my mother, aged fortyish, appeared at the milk barn dressed in shorts and a skimpy halter. Long "citified" and happily departed from rural life, she thought nothing of her costume as anything other than appropriate for a hot August day. In the course of events, my grandfather, my mother, and I went into the horse stall to saddle the mare so that I could go out to bring in the cows for milking. While we were saddling the mare ("Mickey"), she apparently found the flesh of my mother's arm irresistible or offensive and took a firm bite. All hell broke loose. My mother yelled and scared the horse. The saddle, not yet properly cinched, slipped to the mare's side, causing her (unusually gentle under normal circumstances) to jump and thrash about, scaring all of us from the stall. The first words uttered by my grandfather were those of the passage cited above. I remember this vividly, for I wondered at that time what on earth this strange recitation had to do with the events at hand. My mother, in both physical pain and rage at her father for his apparent lack of sympathy, departed in a huff, a great black-and-blue welt rising on her arm. Grandad calmed the horse, saddled her up, and off I went for the cows.

In attempting to reconstruct this episode long years later, I believe that my grandfather found appropriate words of scorn for his daughter, my mother, who had opted to give up farm life for college and life in the city. The horse saw her, clad not as a farm woman, but as a stranger, and bit her. My mother did not know why. In other words, she was oblivious to what others, both the horse and her father, thought of her. She did not "see herself as others saw her." Thus, from one perspective at least, she deserved the bite. The lines "O wad some pow'r . . ." told me why many years later.

TO SEE OURSELVES AS OTHERS SEE US

This paper records a set of reflections about myself and other foreigners who, over the centuries, have come as uninvited strangers to the Tzotzil Maya world. Earlier as Nahuatl-speaking merchants and warriors and Spanish soldiers, today as Protestant missionaries, African-American and Guatemalan Indian coworkers on the coffee plantations, and gringo anthropologists—the non-Tzotzil-speaking Other has been a familiar sight to Chamula Tzotzils for centuries. What do they make of us? How do we fit into their social and supernatural landscape? How are we deconstructed, reconstructed, and classified? Are these processes of self-definition in relation to multiple Others ever closed, in the sense of establishing long-lasting classes of who is who? Or are these classes of the Other in relation to the Self ever recast, permeable and subject to reevaluation and negotiation?[2]

These questions are important to me for reasons that are closely related. They matter first of all because I am interested in reflecting on who I am in relation to the Chamula Tzotzil. They have contributed much to my own sense of personal and professional identity since I first went to Chiapas as a graduate student in the summer of 1965. I have not yet seriously examined the asymmetrical conditions of power, resources, and mobility that made my quest for knowledge of the Chamulas possible. These circumstances, particularly the class of being I was perceived to be, undoubtedly conditioned what they revealed of themselves and how they did so. This essay presents the opportunity to reflect on how our appraisal of each other functioned and evolved, and the ways in which it did not and, on several occasions, made all parties unhappy.

I do not conceive of this essay as an *experimental* ethnographic report. I regard what I am trying to do as *narrative ethnography*, following Barbara Tedlock's useful terminology. She discusses this concept at length in a recent article (B. Tedlock 1991), suggesting that the main thrust of the current reflexive mood in ethnographic epistemology focuses on the ideal of coproduction of knowledge. I understand this to mean that interactive Self/Other dialogue not only lies at the center of the production of ethnographic knowledge but also has a place in how we represent this knowledge. As this applies to my present project, it suggests that my quest for entering to some degree into the Chamula Tzotzil world to discover "their identity" has necessarily involved my own identity, autobiography, and experience with my own culture. Upon reflection, it has become clear to me that most of what I purport to "know" about Chamula life and thought has in fact been derived from intersubjective dialogue. However, I have never before explicitly acknowledged and analyzed the nature of what I have brought to the countless conversations I have had with the Tzotzils about "their world." Therefore, in this essay I attempt to provide a reflexive subtext to these conversations.

I also care about the foreign Other in the Tzotzil world because the subject is of relevance to what Renato Rosaldo has called the expanding "borderland" of human affairs in the postcolonial world of the late twentieth century:

> In the present postcolonial world, the notion of authentic culture as an autonomous internally coherent universe no longer seems tenable, except perhaps as a useful "fiction" or revealing distortion. In retrospect, it appears that only a concerted disciplinary effort could maintain the tenuous fiction of a self-contained cultural whole. Rapidly increasing global interdependence has made

it more and more clear that neither "we" nor "they" are as neatly bounded and homogeneous as once seemed to be the case. . . . All of us inhabit an interdependent late-twentieth-century world marked by borrowing and lending across porous national boundaries that are saturated with inequality, power and domination. (Rosaldo 1989: 217)

Finally, the subject of the non-Tzotzil Other fascinates me because Chamula Tzotzils, by virtue of their relatively important demographic presence in Chiapas (100,000 plus, as of 1990), have been in a position to address this issue themselves in both symbolic and substantive ways over the past century or so. San Juan Chamula was the center of violent political and religious movements in 1868-70 and 1910-11 (Gossen 1977 and 1989a). On both occasions, the events involved invocations of Christian and pre-Columbian symbols for the purpose of keeping the community free from different interpretations of these same symbols; that is, the community was divided with regard to whose version of Indian Christianity, and related political control, should prevail. Both movements ended with the dissident elements (those not affiliated with the prevailing view of the traditionalists, allied on these occasions with the Mexican State) purged and expelled. (See chapter 10 for a tragic reprise in 1997.) The issue resurfaced in the 1930s anticlerical movement of the Cárdenas era, during which the small mestizo convent population was expelled. By 1965, when I first visited San Juan Chamula, exclusionary policies had evolved in such a way that there was but one non-Tzotzil household in whole *municipio,* that of the Ladino (mestizo) *secretario* who served as scribe-intermediary for the community in its bureaucratic dealings with the state and federal government. No property in the *municipio* of 364 square kilometers was held by non-Chamulas. In the 1960s and 1970s a group of Chamula Protestant converts launched a new challenge to the ruling civil-religious hierarchy. The movement began quietly enough, but the officials in power soon came to regard the Protestants as a threat to their authority. Between 1967 and 1974, many Protestant homes were burned, and as a consequence, the injured parties became politically active. Finally, the converts were expelled from the community at gunpoint. To this day, they have not been allowed to return. The Chamula Protestant community now numbers several thousand, but all of these converts live and practice their new religion outside the boundaries of the *municipio* (Gossen 1989b).

Even more recently, Chamula civil-religious authorities entered into a dispute with the Chiapas Roman Catholic diocesan authorities over the amount of religious instruction that would be required or parents when their children became candidates for baptism. Although larger issues of diocesan meddling in Chamula popular religious belief and practice were apparently involved, the final result startled both local and national officials. The news even reached the international wire services and resulted in front-page reports in *The Miami Herald* (1987) and the *Los Angeles Times* (Williams

1987). The Chamula Catholic parish simply withdrew itself from the Roman Catholic Church and joined the flock of a self-declared "Orthodox" bishop residing in Tuxtla Gutiérrez, the state capital. This radical change of affiliation was said to be in the best interests of local religious belief and practice.

This brief recital of over a century of efforts by Chamula political and religious officials to control and forcibly edit foreigners' intervention in their affairs is not an attempt to affirm an "authentic" Maya culture that might persist in the late twentieth century. Rather, it introduces a central paradox, both personal and academic, that has haunted me like a shadow in the over twenty years that I have spent visiting and conducting research in the area.

On the one hand, San Juan projects an aggressively separatist and autonomous posture to the outside world through its highly centralized municipal government, and to itself through ritual celebration of its uniqueness as the Sun/Christ's chosen community of the "true people." This image initially appealed to me a great deal; Chamulas, I thought, were truly Other. On the other hand, perhaps because of their relatively large numbers, Chamulas have developed a high profile in Chiapas by actively using most of the well-known strategies for coping with life as poor agriculturists and laborers in modern Mexico: permanent migration to towns and cities; conversion to Protestantism; establishment of privately held, rental, and *ejido*-chartered agrarian colonies; establishment of squatter settlements on private and public land; seasonal employment as day laborers on distant cattle ranches, coffee plantations, and agricultural plots owned by others. A number of Chamulas and other Tzotzils have even gone (legally and illegally) to the United States as migrant agricultural laborers. Most of these economic options present constant opportunities for assuming new cultural, ethnic, and even national identities—the most common of which is to "reclothe oneself" (Sp. *revestirse*) as a Ladino, a bearer of Mexican national culture. Needless to say, this image (and reality) of Chamulas disappointed me initially.

Both "Chamulas" are clearly visible to any observer of Highland Chiapas: a very conservative, separatist community of "Indian" origin, San Juan Chamula survives by continually shedding its dissident elements; yet a diaspora population, variously "Chamula" and "rural and urban Mexican" in identity, has also gained strength in the late twentieth century. This is not merely a large "acculturating" population, though it has such components; rather, it is a diaspora of tens of thousands of people who live in many types of Tzotzil-speaking colonies and maintain a complex network of contacts with San Juan as a focus of their moral, social, and ethnic identity (Gossen 1983, reprinted here as chapter 7). I have elsewhere compared the extended Chamula community to the Jewish diaspora in its capacity to maintain diverse contexts of vitality in contact with other ethnic and national communities (Gossen 1986: 228, reprinted here as chapter 5). How does one make sense of such a complex ethnic puzzle? And how do I, an earnest, uninvited visitor and voyeur, fit into the puzzle?

In considering these questions, I am aware that Chamulas' "Indianness," as with thousands of other Latin American populations, is an historical identity that has been, in part, thrust upon them through the policies of forced segregation and political and economic dependency in the colonial and modern eras (Friedlander 1975; Martínez Peláez 1970; Wasserstrom 1983). Yet it is also the case—whatever the cynical colonial motives and complementary and convergent interests of the local indigenous power elites—that San Juan has chosen to be "Indian" within the greater mestizo world of modern Chiapas and Mexico. The poignancy of this self-appraisal rings true as the main theme of the annual ritual of cosmic renewal known as the Festival of Games, which is celebrated in the pre-Lenten Carnival period of the Christian Passion cycle (Gossen 1986; and chapter 5). This self-affirmation is also unambiguously stated in their preferred description of themselves, not as Chamulas or Indians, but as the "true people" (*batz'i viniketik*), and of their language, not as Tzotzil, but as the "true language" (*batz'i k'op*).[3]

This language of Tzotzil Chamula self-confidence and self-affirmation has never failed to move and fascinate me over the past two decades. Indeed the irony of my pleasure in reporting and rationalizing Chamulas' obsessive xenophobia, and my scorn for much the same attitude on the part of North Americans, Mexicans, and Europeans concerning their own ethnic affirmations in relation to *their* minorities, has been observed by my friends and colleagues, even by my own children. They are right, of course. That is the very subjective paradox that concerns me in this paper: Who is discovering whom? I, the Tzotzils? The Tzotzils, us? I, myself? Or perhaps all of these?

TO BE FROM KANSAS

Those of us who grew up in Kansas and left it learn, sooner or later, that "to be from Kansas" is a Protestant burden to be borne quietly and, if possible, to be overcome. (This dilemma is ironically foreshadowed in the state motto: *ad astra per aspera*, "To the Stars through Difficulty.") Our private memories may be fond, our knowledge of the Sunflower State intimate and subtle. But ultimately, the judgment of our compatriots stalks us and causes us to doubt. Easterners and Westerners typically regard Kansas as an interminable, flat, and boring stretch of the interstate highway system that must be endured on cross-country trips. Amtrak, the national passenger rail service, carefully schedules its long-distance trains to go through Kansas at night. Apparently humorous (I don't think them so) cultural maps of the United States which are available in college bookstores in Cambridge, New York, and Berkeley portray the country as a simple bicoastal phenomenon, with two inflated provinces dominated by Boston, New York, and Long Island (East) and by San Francisco and Los Angeles (West) looming as giant polities joined by a tiny hinterland that condescendingly includes small specks of space representing Denver, Ann Arbor, Chicago, and New Orleans. Kansas does not appear at all.

Kansas has no national parks, no national forests, no major rivers, and no national tourist attractions except perhaps President Eisenhower's boyhood home and library in Abilene and Boot Hill Cemetery in Dodge City, resting place of gunfighters and shrine of the U. S. frontier, cattle, and cowboy culture. To this list of attributes, one could add the state's prosperous agricultural and aerospace economy. ("Where seldom is heard a discouraging word/And the skies are not cloudy all day," recalling the popular classic "Home on the Range.") These virtues appear to be of little interest to anyone but Kansans.

There is, however, an interesting national and international mythology about Kansas that has been called to my attention with frequency, usually in the spirit of humor or mockery. This focuses on two sets of motifs: gangsters and Kansas City (the major city of two twin cities bearing the same name isn't even in Kansas, but in Missouri); and Dorothy, witches, tornadoes, and the Wonderful Wizard of Oz (unambiguously set *in* Kansas). Of these two Kansas myths, the second is by far the more important in that it is vaguely familiar to tens of millions of Americans and foreigners, a popularity that has no doubt been enhanced by the cinema.

For readers who may not be familiar with L. Frank Baum's *The Wizard of Oz* (1956), it is a classic of American children's literature. Like Lewis Carroll's *Alice in Wonderland*, it can be read and appreciated on many levels. Originally published in 1900, it became a successful motion picture in 1939. Starring Judy Garland as Dorothy—now regarded as a classic role for which she was famous all her life—the movie also made imaginative use of the then-brand-new color film technology.

Set in rural Kansas at the turn of the century (the movie version renders this part in black and white), it is the story of an orphaned child named Dorothy who lives with her kindly aunt and uncle and little dog Toto on a small farm. Dorothy is consumed by the sadness of her life and circumstances. One day a cyclone (a type of storm for which Kansas is well known) approaches. Dorothy is unable to make it to the storm cellar because she is trying to rescue Toto, who has taken refuge under a bed.

As the storm strikes, Dorothy is whirled away, as in a dream, to the wonderland of Oz. (At this point, the movie version switches to color.) Dazzled and confused, Dorothy and Toto wander through this other world in the company of new friends, the Cowardly Lion (who lacks courage), the Tin Woodman (who lacks a heart), and the Scarecrow (who has no brain). In the course of the story, in which Dorothy merely wishes to go home, numerous terrifying Others confront them (evil witches and winged monkeys, among others). She and her companions are instructed by a good witch to seek solutions to all of their problems by following the Yellow Brick Road to the

Emerald City of Oz. Here they will find the Great Oz, an all-knowing wizard who will deliver them from their problems if they have the courage to find and confront him. In the end, the all-powerful Oz turns out to be an illusion and a fraud. He is but an old man from Omaha, Nebraska, who long ago, as a young man, had accidentally come to Oz in a runaway helium balloon from a carnival exhibition. Through their ingenuity and courage in confronting him and comprehending him, all of the protagonists gain what they lack; it had been in them all the time. Dorothy returns happily to Kansas and finds reconciliation with her home life with her aunt and uncle; the Lion finds courage; the Tin Woodman, a heart; and the Scarecrow, wisdom.

Thus, although there *are* a few popular images for which Kansas is known by the rest of America, these cannot be regarded as formative or central to public discourse about the United States in the past or present. The images range from dull to destructive, juvenile to conservative and trivial: flat landscapes, tornadoes, Dorothy and Oz, and Dwight D. Eisenhower. The score is *un cero a la izquierda* ("zero to the left"), as they say in Mexico.

My personal score, oddly enough, was highly positive in the beginning. I grew up in Wichita, a dull, prosperous small city but had the luxury of spending summers with my grandparents on their central- and southeastern-Kansas farms that might have served as movie sets for Dorothy's home: small, poor, humbly maintained but utterly beautiful. Both farms, as I remember them from the 1950s, were set in rural communities of great color, integrity, and vitality, and it is from these scenes that I molded my childhood memories.

My paternal grandparents were Low German-speaking Mennonites whose parents, my great-grandparents, immigrated to America in the 1870s from Crimea, then a part of the Russian Empire. They fled Russia, as their forebears had previously fled from Holland, to avoid military conscription and forced assimilation into Dutch and Russian national cultures. Living on one hundred acres of Kansas prairie, my grandparents lived simply, magnificently, seldom doing anything, as I remember them, that did not involve gardening and farming, church, and singing. I was happily involved in all of these activities, and they are, not surprisingly, important to me to this day. On my grandmother's death, in 1954, the farm was rented out; in 1956, the buildings were razed, the orchard bulldozed, and the farm sold as one hundred acres of prime wheat land, which, I suppose, it was and is.

My maternal grandparents were, in a sense, more complex to reckon with in terms of my own identity, for they represented an affective and historical link to the American past that was both old English (my grandmother, whose family, the Hayeses, came from Virginia, claimed a relationship to President Hayes) and new Scotch-Irish stock (my grandfather Hamilton, the H of my own name). Proud but poor, they worked as sharecroppers, until the age of sixty, ever preoccupied with landlords and creditors. Hence my juvenile wonder: Why were the Hamiltons with their "old American links," poorer than the Gossens, second-generation Mennonite immigrants who owned a hundred-acre farm?

Whatever their differences, the Hamiltons shared with the Gossens a rural community life that was like the pastures of heaven. The Hamiltons milked, gardened, threshed, slaughtered pigs, and went to rodeos, cattle auctions, and county fairs. My uncle, who lived with my grandparents, was and is, even in retirement, a cowboy in both style and spirit. Being Presbyterian, they, unlike the Gossens, were not encumbered by rigidity of religious belief and practice. There was somewhat more tolerance for sin and swearing, even though my grandmother ritually denounced these things, particularly when the mention of them occurred in my presence. (I think she secretly enjoyed them, too.) Of particular significance to me, in retrospect, was my grandparents' unusual choice of friends: not WASPS, which *they* were, but the Garraldas (Cruz Garralda, Basque sheepherder from Nevada, married a local woman who had gone there as a schoolteacher; they subsequently returned to Kansas) and the Boulangers (Osage Indian renters who lived on the farm up the road). Thus, my fantasy of early childhood summers was populated with kind and colorful country people, among them Hispanics and Indians, even in backwoods Kansas.

Against these nostalgic cameos of rural life as I knew it in Kansas in the 1950s, I add to my story the fact that my parents opted to abandon these communities to become lower-middle-class immigrants to suburban Wichita. It was here that I actually grew up. And from this dull vantage point, I lamented deeply what my parents had forsaken in order to "better themselves." My home in Wichita, one of hundreds that looked like clones of one another, was in a modest housing development that lay under the flight pattern of Boeing, Cessna, and Beechcraft aircraft companies. The scene was devoid of any of the local pride of place, social intimacy, and color that graced my grandparents' lives. It is of course not possible to verify in my own middle age the truth or fantasy of these memories, for both farmsteads are gone; one has become a wheat field, the other, a cattle pasture. Not only are my grandparents gone but also the places and communities are no more. In 1870, they did not yet exist; by 1970, they, like much of rural America, had vanished.

The qualities of extraordinary impetus for change and social and geographic mobility in American culture have been observed by many, beginning with Alexis de Tocqueville (1946 [1835]) in the early nineteenth century and continuing with Frederick Jackson Turner's great treatise (1962 [1893]) on the significance of the frontier in American history and national identity. This motif of getting away to become something else is a staple in our literature, making regular appearances in each generation. Some more recent examples are Jack Kerouac's *On the Road* (1957) and Robert Pirsig's *Zen and the Art of Motorcycle Maintenance* (1974). However, no one has captured this American obsession more poignantly than D. H. Lawrence. The introductory essay to his *Studies in Classic American Literature*, titled "The Spirit of Place," reads:

All right, then, what did they [the Pilgrim Fathers] come for? For lots of reasons. Perhaps the least of all in search of freedom of any sort: positive freedom, that is.

They came largely to get *away*—that most simple of motives. To get away. Away from what? In the long run, away from everything. That is why most people have come to America, and still do come. To get away from everything they have ever been.

"Henceforth, be masterless."

Which is all very well, but it isn't freedom. Rather, the reverse. A hopeless sort of constraint. It is never freedom till you find something you really *positively want to be*. And people in America have always been shouting about what they are not. Unless, of course, they are millionaires, made or in the making. (Lawrence 1923: 5, italics from the original)

Men are free when they are in a living homeland, not when they are straying and breaking away. Men are free when they are obeying some deep, inward voice of religious belief. Obeying from within. Men are free when they belong to a living, organic, *believing* community, active in fulfilling some unfilled, perhaps unrealized purpose. Not when they are escaping to some wild west. The most unfree souls go west, and shout freedom. Men are freest when they are most unconscious of freedom. The shout is a rattling of chains, always was.

Men are not free when they are doing just what they like. The moment you can do just what you like, there is nothing you care about doing. Men are only free when they are doing what the deepest self likes. (Lawrence 1923: 9–10, italics from the original)

A KANSAN FINDS OZ

D. H. Lawrence was no fan of the United States; yet his opinionated views of U.S. life and culture have helped me to understand and articulate the reasons for my own quest with what to do with American freedom. Lawrence read my parents like a clairvoyant: They fled the structure of circumscribed rural communities in order to get away, period; not *for* something else that they really wanted to do or be. At least, they were never able to communicate this something to me. Deliverance to suburban Wichita yielded little for them other than frustration over what they could not obtain in terms of consumer goods. They lived their lives in domestic strife and alcoholism. They never found "what the deepest self likes." Indeed, the way of life that they abandoned possessed the very qualities (freedom within structure) that Lawrence described as being characteristic of people who have a *homeland*, who gain strength from the spirit of place—those who positively want to be who and where they are.

My career in anthropology has been a quest for such a homeland. If I was destined by birth and culture to flee something in order to be an American, could I not at last break the cycle by turning this flight into a rediscovery of what my deepest self liked: a stable, rural community populated with secure people who liked themselves and wanted to stay that way?

My first encounter with San Juan Chamula did not bode well for achieving this romantic quest. In the summer of 1965, I was introduced to the community by my adviser, Evon Z. Vogt, whose long association with field research in Chiapas greatly facilitated the initial contacts I made there. After the requisite pleasantries and explanations for my presence ("scientific research"), together with bottles of rum and Coca Cola, the municipal authorities granted me permission to stay and Professor Vogt departed. I was promptly placed under what amounted to house arrest. There was no place to house me other than the flea-infested floor of the town hall, as I was a protected stranger without any other credentials for legitimacy. They could not turn me loose, nor could they abandon me.

The Ladino secretario's fat and surly wife brought me tortillas and beans in proper enamel plates the next morning. She had no pleasantries to offer. I was not invited into their home, a one-room adobe structure with a galvanized metal roof; nor, much less, did I get to enjoy breakfast in an Indian home. Never had I spent a more miserable night and morning. I had at last managed to move into San Juan Chamula but had not done so at all. I was a ward of the state, the obligatory charge of the lone Ladino household. Like to like.

There is no way that I can honestly represent my experience with Chamula as a euphoric success story. From the very beginning, my experience with Chamula has been ambivalent. When I was finally allowed to leave the town hall, my next housing arrangement was in the home of a shaman whose son, it turned out, had been employed a few years earlier by the University of Chicago Man-in-Nature Project. In this context, the son had learned to write Tzotzil and also to tolerate, even enjoy, sustained interaction with foreigners. Even though this first opportunity to be in a Tzotzil household had come via previous North American contacts, I was happy at last to have found my way into something "authentic." This living situation failed, however, after only two days, because the shaman's two wives apparently could not agree on which of the two was to receive the twenty-five pesos a day that I was expected to pay for board and room. The problem arose because the house belonged to one of them, the corn supply to the other. The three-way dispute (two wives and husband) continued deep into the night for two nights. Finally, I was asked to leave.

And so it went, from house to house; there was always a reason that it would not work. In one instance, I left because my hosts feared for my safety. The neighbors were saying that I was an *alemán* (German), which did not bode well. Stories were still being told of a German tourist who, a few years earlier, was said to have propositioned some Indian women, whereupon they told their husbands, who promptly killed the German with their machetes. Others said that the German was gesturing for a drink of water and that his innocent intentions were misunderstood. Still others said that the German had not been a German at all, but an earth lord who was inviting the women into a cave in the mountain to make a pact with them. All versions agreed that a white foreigner had been slain. My hosts did not want a similar scandal on their hands, for it would prove complicated since the municipal officials had approved my presence. So I was asked to leave this household. On still another occasion, my status as a guest did not work out because the neighbors were said to be accusing my hosts of making lots of money from what I paid for room and board. These suspicions (apparently expressions of jealousy) turned into accusations of witchcraft against my hosts, and again I was asked to leave.

With time, I found good friends and places to stay in Chamula, although wisdom and consideration for my hosts always dictated frequent short visits rather than long-term residence. In spite of their reputation for hostility to outsiders, they found a place for me and my wife and rationalized our presence as frequent visitors who, though awkward and strange, at least did not fulfill their worst initial fears: that we were Protestant missionaries or Mexican government spies (looking for illegal liquor stills) or "engineers" (Sp. *ingenieros*), seeking ways to change their community without their approval. The anxiety about engineers was caused by alleged problems that had emerged after the Mexican government built a radio transmission tower on Tzontevitz, a sacred mountain in Chamula which houses peoples' animal soul companions and also several earth lords. A severe drought was said to have followed as a consequence of the violation of the earth lord's domain; they have ultimate control over precipitation and were not pleased with the intrusion.

Thus began over two decades of my strange association with the community. While it soon became clear to Chamulas what we were *not*, it was much harder to articulate what we *were* and what we foreigners—with a jeep, obviously prosperous—were doing there. In retrospect, my early insistence that I was a teacher who wanted to learn Tzotzil language and customs so that I could teach them to North American students, must have rung extraordinarily hollow (even though it was, in fact, true), for most of the people with whom I dealt had never gone to school. Those who had gone to school knew perfectly well that the schools did not teach Tzotzil language and customs, but rather Spanish language and Mexican customs. I must have been a liar, they thought, but a relatively harmless one.

The issue of the truth of who I was and what I was doing there eventually became a serious and debilitating question for me as I began to work and talk regularly with a small group of Tzotzil men, most of them neighbors from a single hamlet and within ten years of my own age. I worked with them in the fields and ate and slept in their homes, and they also came to work with me at my home on the outskirts of San Cristóbal, the Mexican trade town and old colonial administrative center of the region.

The topics of interest to me were historical narrative, religion, and cosmology, and in pursuit of this, I was soon happily involved in work (text dictation, transcription, translation, and discussion) and play (joking and drinking) about who was who in the world and what these beings were like. Although I found the encounters and discussions with the Tzotzils to be wildly entertaining at first (for I, in a sense, controlled them), they also increasingly obliged me, as my language skills improved, to talk about myself and my world. Our discussions evolved, at the Tzotzils' insistence, into somewhat more honest dialogue.

As I got to know more people, I was expected to respond, again and again, to the same staple questions. Often asked by the same person, the questions usually followed this sequence: (1) How much did your watch cost? (2) How far is it to your country? (3) What is your country like? and, finally, (4) Do people bite and eat one another there? The first was easy and usually started a conversation about whether my watch was a good buy or whether I had been cheated. The second question, regarding the distance to my country, was also relatively easy to answer once I learned that one speaks not of distance per se, but of days it takes to travel there by bus, truck, or car. I replied that it had taken ten days to drive there from Santa Cruz, California, with all of our belongings, two children, and dog (Rufus, known to Tzotzils as Rupino). The period of ten days by car was usually received with exclamations of wonder when they translated this into days on foot; what is now a two-hour bus ride to Tuxtla Gutiérrez, a frequently used transportation hub, used to take two to four days on foot. Since walking on foot is still the most commonly used means of routine short-distance travel, time of travel on foot is a common measure of distance. Measured in this system, it was clear that we lived far away indeed, more than a hundred days on foot.

This remarkable distance made the remaining two questions in the sequence of logical interest. Being so far away, what was the place like? And what sort of beings lived there? When I explained that California had deserts, seacoasts, and areas of heavy snowfall, the conversations often moved to practical discussions of growing corn, beans, and squash in such a strange place. Beyond agricultural practices, they were always interested in who lived in California. The assumption was always, in the beginning, that people might logically bite and eat one another in a place so far away; and did we in fact do this? No, I would respond, not knowing whether to deny it casually or indignantly. They were willing to accept my denials, but skeptically, since, I learned, they routinely admonish their own children not to run away to Tuxtla or the Ladinos will capture them, cook them, and turn them into tamales. The discussion of the biting-and-eating anomalies took an unusual turn one day when I asked whether anyone in Chamula did this sort of thing. The response, very consistently and amid great laughter, turned out to be "No, but the ancestors did." I later learned that a minor but significant episode in the annual ritual of solar renewal involves ritual consumption of baby-sized (35 cm) bean-and-corndough tamales; they are in fact called *tamali* ʔ*olol* ("tamales made of babies"). The custom of eating their own plump children turned out to be the reason that the Sun/Christ destroyed one of the earlier generations of the Chamulas' own ancestors. It became increasingly clear that outmoded and primitive behavior that they had abandoned long ago might, for them, reasonably survive at a place of such distance as California.

However, as these discussions evolved, they came closer and closer to home. In fact, I soon found myself trying to suppress more and more about myself as I learned more and more what they really—or at least apparently—thought of me. In particular, I learned from jokes (often told about me and at my expense) and stories and anecdotes about the recent past (no longer the ancient past) that familiar parts of my own world, indeed, of my own identity, were consistently rendered in Chamula discourse as evil, amoral, and threatening to them in time present. I *was* Protestant *and* gringo *and* of German and English background; all are classes of beings who come to bad ends or cause serious trouble in historical narratives of the present Fourth Creation. Being white and a speaker of Spanish, I was also logically classed with Mexican non-Indians as a *kaxlán* (from Sp. *castellano*), a class of being about whom there is no end of derision spoken. Their (our) historically dominant economic and political position is well known, even though they (we) are all regarded as descendants of an illicit sexual union of an early (Third Creation) woman and her dog. (See text in chapter 5.) That is why we are thought to smell foul, have bad breath, and engage in unseemly public behavior (particularly between the sexes, as in affectionate rituals of embracing, kissing, and holding hands).

To this rubbish heap of amoral and evil associations, which seemed to fit me like a glove as far as they were concerned, was added the coup de grâce, something I realized one day in silence and was afraid to admit or discuss: I shared a homeland and a national identity with millions of Jews and black people who, in league with the ancient monkeys, were thought explicitly responsible for the death of the Sun/Christ deity, as reported in story after story of the First Creation. (See Figure 1.)[4] Indeed, my very being and "co-beings" seemed to bear moral qualities that were reprehensible to the Chamula Tzotzils—the very people whom I wished to understand and celebrate. My realization of what might be called nonreciprocal affection depressed me and made me ashamed of who I was, for I had, as they say, the best of intentions.

My erstwhile adoptive homeland did not seem to be beckoning me. The stories of murdered Protestants (very true and very recent), slain German tourists (still possible, as my earlier hosts had explained), and serene and white-skinned earth lords living in palatial caves in the earth and bilking poor Indians out of their lives and fortunes, leapt out of my field notes. (See Figure 2. Could the comfortable bearded fellow be a lightly veiled image of me?) It seemed clear that they had my number—I was in all of these texts—and that our friendship was a cruel joke, on both sides. Like Dorothy in *The Wizard of Oz*, I wanted to go home.

Figure 1. A Solar Eclipse
This occasional event recapitulates the slaying of the Sun/Christ deity prior to the first creation. (Drawing by Marián López Calixto, traced from the original drawn in ink and felt pen)
   Translations of the original Tzotzil captions omitted in tracing: 1. "They are killing him there in the sky. They have bound him to a tree and are killing him. He is about dead." 2. "Here is the demon's hammer." 3. "The Demon Pukuj says, 'Ah! The blood is delicious!'" 4. "He shows the gang of demons who are drinking his blood." 5. "The Demon Pukuj says, 'Ah! Ah! Ah! This blood tastes so very, very good! Ah! Ah! Ah!'" 6. "The Demon Pukuj says, 'Eh! Eh! Eh! I crave some of that blood!'"

THE SWEAT BATH AND QUEEN ELIZABETH II

Almost all Chamula households in San Juan and in the extended community have a *pus*, or sweat bathhouse. This is a small, low, earthen structure that is usually set apart from the house proper, although it is sometimes built as an appendage to the exterior wall. It is, however, always included in the social space of the home (*na*), as distinct from cultivated land and pasture (*jamalaltik*) and woods (*teʔtik*). It is like the chicken house, integral to the domestic landscape, but not in the center of it. It is of, but not in the house. The *pus* is

15

sometimes used for routine bathing, but more typically, it is used for ritual and therapeutic purposes, such as postpartum and postmenstrual bathing for women and ritual cleansing of patients in preparation for curing ceremonies. Sweat baths also serve as ceremonial purification for household members who are preparing to assume various types of ritual responsibilities.

Figure 2. A Deal with an Earth Lord and His Wife
A Chamula Attempts to make a deal with the earth lords in their cave home. Note the wings on the female; these express the association of earth lords with angels, which is one of the terms (?*anjeletik*, from Sp. *ángel*) by which they are known in Tzotzil. Also note the snake, which is the familiar of the earth lords. (Drawing by Marián López Calixto)

The *pus* is like a dark, low, rectangular cave that is slightly longer than a human body. The width is adequate for two or perhaps three people to lie down side by side, on wooden planks that make up the floor. Vertical clearance is just adequate for one to sit up. At the far end, opposite the door, is a stone-lined hearth. When the *pus* is readied for use, a small fire is built in the hearth. When it is reduced to coals and the stones are hot, the coals and ash are removed and the bathers strip, gather up branches with aromatic leaves that have been previously collected, and enter the cavelike space, closing the door behind them. They lie flat on their backs, and one person tosses boiling water on the hot hearth stones. The steam and intense heat envelop the *pus* interior, and the bathers beat themselves with the bundles of aromatic leaves until the steam and heat subside, perhaps fifteen to twenty minutes.

At the invitation of a good friend who later became my *compadre* (that is, my wife and I became the godparents of his son), I got to take a sweat bath. The chronicle of this experience is somewhat difficult to relate, for it turned out to be much more than I had bargained for. Indeed, this event, though brief and essentially without conversation, both frightened and confused me. I suppressed the event and never wrote of it my field journal at the time. It is only now, as I write this paper, some fifteen years after the sweat bath episode (1978), that I feel somewhat able to understand what happened.

My friend (I deliberate with his name for I don't want him to be burdened with having to explain this if he does not choose to do so) tossed the hot water on the heated stones, shut the door and instructed me to lie down quickly and to beat myself with the branches. In the intense heat, steam, and darkness, I suddenly felt his hand on my naked crotch. He then found my left hand, which lay next to him, and placed it on his crotch. No words were spoken. So we remained in this intimate contact for perhaps half a minute—I, utterly incredulous and frightened, but not resisting. After that briefest of encounters—which seemed at the time to be an eternity—we both resumed beating ourselves with the branches. Nothing else happened. We emerged after about twenty minutes, dressed, felt refreshed, and had a drink of rum together. Not a word about what had happened was ever spoken between us, much less to our families.

As I reconstruct this many years later, my understanding of it takes shape only by trying to link it to events that followed the sweat bath. Perhaps a week thereafter, I received a letter from a friend in Canada. My soon-to-be *compadre* asked me about the woman whose tiny portrait appeared on the corner of the stamp on the envelope. He knew of Canada and also knew (I'm not sure how he found out) that English was spoken there and that I should be able to explain this odd bit of trivia. I told him that the woman in the picture was Queen Elizabeth II, queen of England. After a halting effort to explain the British Commonwealth of Nations (for my Tzotzil was not adequate to the task), it turned out that my friend was not interested in Queen Elizabeth's symbolic and political functions. He was interested—intensely so—in her body.

Tzotzil oral tradition contains a number of stories of Spanish origin that involve queens as characters, and he was obviously interested in intimate particulars about them, something that the stories don't discuss. The questions were quite direct: Does she eat? Does she have breasts, a vagina? Does she have sex? With whom? Does she urinate and defecate? When I answered yes to all of the above, the conversation became extraordinary. Although he did not call me a liar, he thought my affirmative responses strange. It turned out that queens—strange and apparently powerful beings who live at immense social and physical distance from Chamula—must be like gods and saints and, therefore, though gender-identified, sexless. I asked where the gods and saints came from if not through sexual reproduction. The answer was that they just "are."

17

I then asked what gods and saints ate, and my friend answered confidently, "Incense." If they eat odors and essences, not substances, it followed, he said, that they have no need for organs for elimination of waste and other fluids. Lacking these, sexual reproduction is a nonissue; it is not possible without the equipment. I then asked, since I was acquainted with many Chamula narratives, why the Sun/Christ should want to create a sexed and sexual humanity if he himself was sexless. Would not he want people to be like him, if he created them out of clay in order to exalt him and celebrate him? This turned out to be a stupid question, for, my friend said, it was obvious that people would have to acquire the means of reproducing in order to provide an ongoing line of people to praise him and thank him for their being.

But, I insisted, where did sexuality come from if the Sun/Christ—himself sexless and objecting to sex—did not give it to us? This question was related to an episode in several narratives that reports that the Sun/Christ, who once lived on earth with his children, withdrew to the sky so as to avoid direct contact with them because he objected to their sexual odors.

The answer came back instantly and should have been obvious to me since I knew of such accounts in stories but had not taken the assertion seriously. It was the demon—black and highly sexed—who taught the Sun/Christ's children to reproduce. (See Figure 3.) I subsequently collected many narratives that dwell at length on this subject, and the attribution of sexuality and knowledge of reproduction to the black demon Pukuj's instruction never varies. In fact, the theme of the demon Pukuj's hypersexuality emerges as a key motif in a story that Chamulas love to tell, and claim to be true, of a young man who could not afford the bride-price for a girl he wanted to marry. So he disguised himself as Pukuj, blackening his face with soot, and abducted the girl. He took her to a deserted house and, in effect, raped her. During the heat of this episode, the sweat on the man's face ran and caused the soot to wash away, thus revealing his true identity. The girl is said to have been delighted and agreed to elope with the demon lover, who was in fact the young man she wished to marry. They ran away, and the father of the abducted bride raged. So the story ends.[5]

In this way, I was made to reflect, via Queen Elizabeth II's portrait on a Canadian postage stamp, on certain premises of Tzotzil being and, much later (in fact, now), on the meaning of the sweat bath encounter. Clearly, my world—including Afro-Americans, Jews, Mexican mestizos, queens, and white Europeans—is oddly related to the Tzotzil Indian world, although the complexity of these links is only now becoming apparent to me.

My friend obviously knew I was human. We had previously urinated in the bushes in close proximity. I had two children and a wife, and it could hardly have passed him by that I was sexed and sexual. Yet the complexity of our mutual humanity seemed to be acknowledged in the sweat bath. I will never know whether the discussion of Queen Elizabeth's sexuality and eating habits followed directly from the sweat bath, but I believe that it did. Whatever the meaning of the event, we became close friends and *compadres*. It is primarily to him that I owe my understanding of Chamula as a part of my own world.

I have often wondered about the odd convergence of our life histories; that is, how my *compadre* found both the inclination and the courage to get to know me well. What he revealed of his life made it clear to me that he, too, had come from a defoliated "traditional" world that had not delivered everything he might have wished or expected. Like rural Kansas for me, traditional Chamula proved, for him, to be more difficult to capture than he wished it to be. Both of us found ourselves making pragmatic choices among culturally limited alternatives that were tied to present time. Among these options there emerged the fairly high-risk opportunity of exploring a culturally classified Other at close range. Although neither of us has been profoundly "changed" by our friendship, I feel that both of us have learned something of the fragile, highly malleable cultural construction of the self.

Figure 3. The Demon Pukuj Gives a Sex Lesson

In related narratives about the first people's acquisition of the knowledge of sex, the demon himself demonstrates the sex act with the first woman; she, in turn, instructs her husband. Note that the Moon/Virgin Mary is represented here as blindfolded. She is said to find human sexuality offensive, just as the Sun/Christ is said to find human sexual odors offensive. (Drawing by Marián López Calixto)

I first noted this pattern of flexible self-definition in the evolution of my *compadre's* chosen name for himself. In the twenty-some years I have known him well, he has chosen to be known by three different names. The first was a Tzotzil-rendered Christian name with a Spanish and a Tzotzil patronymic, a system that evolved during the colonial period (Bricker and Collier 1970). He later chose to be known by the Christian name and his father's and mother's Spanish surnames, as is the current Mexican national custom. Even more recently, he has abandoned all parts of both previous surnames and has chosen to be known by the name of a noted Tzotzil labor and political leader who shares a common Christian name in combination with two new Spanish surnames. On all occasions, when these new names surfaced, he simply explained to me, cryptically, that "it is useful and it suits me." I am reminded of the popular song from the California Gold Rush: "What Was Your Name in the States?"

My *compadre*, like many Tzotzils, has also become somewhat marginalized in his own community because of poverty. This has limited his access to certain cultural ideals. During all of the years I have known him, he and his family have lived in his wife's house on his wife's property, since he had not inherited sufficient land from his mother or father to grow even a modest corn supply. He was forced, like many, to part from the ideal norm of patrilocal residence, which led in turn to problems with his wife's family, who, he said, treated him as a poor man who lived on their largesse. But his wife's small plot yielded only two months of the required annual corn supply; so like many Tzotzils I knew, he was obliged to take supplementary employment on the lowland coffee plantations for many months each year. With such modest resources and the long periods of absence while in the lowlands, he was never able to participate in the community's civil-religious cargo system as a ranking official, only as a secondary assistant. The relative failure of his economic coping strategies thus compromised a number of Tzotzil ideals of public and domestic life and led, as he confided to me on many occasions, to a less than happy marriage and to constant problems with his in-laws, neighbors, and children, all of whom accused him of being a poor provider.

I recall a bitter fight related to these matters that erupted in 1978 on the occasion of the Day of the Dead (November 1), a time when the living are expected to set out food and drink for the ancestors to welcome their souls back for their annual visit. This gesture is supposed to please those ancestors who have left property, specifically land, to the living. On the occasion to which I refer, my *compadre* took his ritual responsibility very seriously and sought to enlist his nineteen-year-old son to accompany us on the required ritual visits and distribution of food and liquor offerings. Since these are grueling affairs that last all night and involve a lot of night travel on foot and a great deal of drinking, the son refused to go. He announced that he wanted to get a good night's sleep so as to wake up early and tend his small store. The prospects for trade would be excellent with all of the ritual pilgrims passing by his locale at a fork in the road; he stood to make a handsome profit if he were to open his store at daybreak.

The father was enraged that his son should scorn his ancestors and established custom for the sake of profits. An angry shouting match ensued. The son got the last word: "The ancestors have left you next to nothing and do not expect anything from you. Besides, you cannot afford to buy the stuff. Do not make a fool of yourself." The father and son did not speak to each other for many months thereafter.

The years my *compadre* spent with me as an assistant and close friend may have mitigated some of these tensions and also, no doubt, exacerbated others. However, it is clear to me that his vision of his "traditional" world came no closer to realization in practice than my own. Such, ironically, was the small microcosm of the Tzotzil world into which I fell most intimately and from which I ultimately learned much of what I purport to know of this world.

THE OTHER THAT WAS ALREADY THERE: BLACK, WHITE, AND INDIAN

If the accidents and unexpected encounters of my ethnographic experience revealed an odd reconfiguration of my own world and myself (my cobeings and I were apparently already "there" before the Chamulas even knew me), I was nevertheless puzzled by a central paradox. Why should a people so confident in their own identity as the "true people" live in the very center of a cosmos populated with white-skinned deities and adversaries and black-skinned demons and life forces? Where is the "Indian" in their cosmological, spiritual, and historical landscape? Why is everything that creates, sustains, and threatens the Tzotzil world ultimately attributed to non-Indians? To wit: the creation of life (the white, radiant Moon and Sun deities, identified with the Virgin Mary and Christ); the ongoing overseers and guardians of life (the white-skinned saints); the sexual reproduction of life (the black, bearded, and hairy demon Pukuj) (see Figure 3); the alter egos of individual human lives (animal soul companions who are overseen by white-skinned Saint Jerome); the means of agrarian production (the white Ladino earth lords who control land and water) (see Figure 2); the provision of manufactured goods, books, and calendars (an odd and cynical alliance among the white Sun/Christ, white earth lords; see Figure 4);[6] short-term pacts to gain money and fortune (the black demons and white earth lords; see Figure 5)[7]; even the forces that have destroyed, and may again destroy, life itself (the monkeys, demons, Jews, and even the Sun/Christ himself).

Figure 4. The "Place of the Calendar" (yav kalintario)
(Drawing by Marián López Calixto)
Translations of original Tzotzil captions omitted in tracing: 1. "Here is the courier."(?) [Translation uncertain; *j? ikilex* may mean Englishman, from 'English', or churchman, from Sp. 'iglesia'] 2. "This is the home of the courier and the Demon Pukuj." 3. "This whole area by the Sea of the Setting Sun is the 'Place of the Calendar', and 'Homeland of Hoes, Machetes, and Files.'" 4. " Here is the great expanse of the Sea of the Setting Sun. In no time it will be filling up again [having evaporated from the plunge of the Sun/Christ into it at sunset]." 5. "Here is Our Lord Sun/Christ plunging into the underworld." 6. "This is an axe blade." 7. "This is a file [for sharpening metal blades]." 8. "This is a machete." 9. "This is a hoe blade." 10. "This a calendar book [almanac]." 11. "This is a textbook that we use for learning in school." 12. "This is a calendar that keeps track of the months of the year." 13. "This is a metal coin." 14. "This is a piece of paper money."

Indeed, in over twenty years of working with Chamula folklore and oral history, I have discovered few heroic or supernatural figures who appear as protagonists in historical narratives who are ethnically "Indian." The major heroes and villains of recent (Fourth Creation) Tzotzil oral history are not Indians, but Mexican mestizos (of mixed Indian and European ancestry) and criollos (of European parentage, born in America). For example, both Miguel Hidalgo—of historical fame as the Father of Mexican Independence—and Erasto Urbina—of local fame as a hardware merchant and municipal mayor of San Cristóbal who championed Indian causes in the 1930s, '40s, and '50s—figure prominently and positively in oral historical accounts of the present era. Miguel Hidalgo was a criollo, and Urbina was of mixed Tzotzil and mestizo background (see chapter 4). Certainly, the major villains of recent oral history are also predominantly non-Indian. For example, the revolutionary "heroes" Venustiano Carranza and Alvaro Obregón—both of whom are fondly remembered in Mexican national history—are cast as unspeakable rapists and predators in Chamula accounts. There are also major villains of the recent past who were Chamulas who openly allied themselves with Ladino or foreign patrons. Good examples of this pattern are Jacinto Pérez Pajarito, a Chamula Tzotzil who, between 1909 and 1911, allied himself with a conservative Chiapas bishop, Francisco Orozco y Jiménez, and eventually led a bloody antirevolutionary political movement in San Juan (Moscoso Pastraña 1972), and Miguel Kaxlán, a Chamula Tzotzil who under U.S. Presbyterian tutelage led the Protestant evangelical movement in this community from 1965 to 1982, at which time he was assassinated by his compatriots (Gossen 1989b, reprinted here as chapter 8).

Figure 5. A Blackman/Demon Making a Deal with a Chamula
(Drawing by Marián López Calixto)

The exceptions to this pattern are few and far between. Among those few heroic figures who are ethnically "Indian," perhaps the most remembered in the narrative tradition is an individual named Juan López Nona.[8] Actually he is three men, all brothers bearing the same name. López Nona emerges triumphant in a war with the president of Guatemala. The conflict was precipitated by the Guatemalans' habit of capturing Chamulas for the purpose of taking them back to Guatemala to eat them. The war was fought and won by magical power, and the heroes eventually secured a peace treaty with the Guatemalans. The heroes returned home to live forever in the mountains of Chamula where they could be available if people ever again needed their assistance. To my knowledge, Juan López Nona is silent in the present. Chamulas do not publicly commemorate him or summon his help.

A second set of Chamula heroes slew the "Demon of Bell Cave," who like the Guatemalan enemies of Juan López Nona, killed innocent people for food. After killing the demon, also with the help of magic, they took his severed head to Tuxtla Gutiérrez as proof of their good deed. The governor of Chiapas received them respectfully, commended them for their heroism, and gave them a reward. They, too, are silent in the present.

The third exception to the pattern I have described is an Indian woman and an Indian youth who were involved in the religious movement of 1868-70, known in Mexican history as the War of Santa Rosa, and in Chamula as Cuxcat's War (Gossen 1977). These two individuals are vaguely remembered in historical narratives about this conflict. The woman, named Augustina Gómez Chechev, came into possession of some clay images that she declared had come from the sky. As their sponsor, she announced that she was the Indian "Mother of God." In some accounts, both Tzotzil and Ladino, Gómez Chechev's nephew, a Tzotzil youth of about fifteen years of age, is said to have been crucified on Good Friday of 1869, thus becoming the "Indian Christ," whose cult would deliver the community from the Ladino church authorities. Although both Gómez Chechev and her nephew appear to me to be plausible candidates for heroic stature, neither is remembered in a favorable light. In narrative accounts of this conflict, they emerge as frauds who deserved to be defeated, which they were.

It is striking that none of these protagonists of explicitly Indian ethnicity is remembered seriously. They are utterly ignored in Chamula ritual observance and public memory. Their stories are regarded as unimportant, if true and interesting, accounts of time past. Even the antiheroic figure of La Malinche—the legendary Indian mistress and translator for Cortéz who is ubiquitous in the Mexican imagination as the traitor of and violated embodiment of Indian Mexico—appears in Chamula as a Mexican mestizo whore named Nana María Cocorina (Gossen 1986: 233, 235; also chapter 5). She is antistructural all right, but she has been ethnically altered to become, like the rest of their villains and heroes, non-Indian.

Where does one turn to make sense of this world, which seems extravagantly different and perverse in some ways, and yet is conversant with us, even willing to suppress its own ethnic protagonists in preference to our own? Or are they really "our own"? It is easy, of course, to read Chamula discourse about Self and Other as a symbolic capitulation to cultural "subordination" (Warren 1978). It is also plausible to understand the pattern, as Mary Douglas might suggest, as a logical strategy to find power, both life-affirming and life-denying, through the agency of ambiguous beings and forces (Douglas 1966). However, I do not find either of these approaches, considered alone or together, to be an adequate lens for examining this puzzle. The plot is not that simple.

Unambiguously white-skinned beings are cast as both pro-Indian heroes and villains, just as black-skinned beings are cast as protagonists and antagonists of life. Clearly, a facile reading of the Chamula world as a *colonial creation* must fall short of capturing what is going on, just as assertions regarding an essential, unchanging, fundamentally Maya world, lightly veneered with Western and African symbols, must also miss the mark.[9] The plot is obviously more complex than either of these positions allows.

One solution to this puzzle appears to lie in the power of Maya-derived cyclical time-reckoning to absorb otherness in an ever-evolving historical matrix that consistently yields new end points and renewed identities. In the case of Chamula, this process constantly yields a new set of Chamula communities— a renewed home community and many recently founded immigrant colonies (Gossen 1983, reprinted here as chapter 7).[10] Cyclical time reckoning allows for selective accomodation and comprehension of new actors and new ideas by placing them morally in past time. The dynamism of this logic appears to lie in the capacity of strong cyclical time reckoning to coexist with an equally powerful, progressive, orthogenetic thrust. That is, each destruction and restoration yields a new and better "Indian product." This logic creates a continually evolving present in which "Indianness" is logically foregrounded at the expense of new waves of others who are systematically relegated to a newly reconfigured past. New Others merge with morally equivalent antecedent beings who populated and changed the cosmos over the three historical epochs leading to the present, fourth, epoch. Hence, the possibility that I, a new Other, might, like Queen Elizabeth II and the saints, be sexless.

Unlike D. H. Lawrence's reading of U. S. culture—one in which we are said to be always fleeing from and abandoning past identities ("Henceforth, be masterless")—the Maya appear to absorb and appropriate past adversaries, conflicts, and Others as prior expressions of what they themselves have been in some previous epoch and, most importantly, have superceded.

It is indeed the very historical spectacle of myriad past identities and enemies that they ritually reenact annually in their Festival of Games (see chapter 5). This five-day historical drama—which is, by their own reckoning, the best and greatest of their ritual events—is celebrated in the five-day Carnival period prior to and including Ash Wednesday in the Christian liturgical cycle. However, its content is neither Christian nor Mayan, nor much less a confused mingling of the two traditions. It is more properly understood, as they conceive of it, as a ritual drama of ethnic and spiritual renewal, without which, as they say, "we would die." This spectacular event involves hundreds of actors who play the parts of the very beings, supernatural and historical, who in the past have sought to destroy Chamula.

Chamula is ritually restored in a dramatic gesture of considerable note. The key personnel and their entourages traverse a runway of burning tratch grass (representing the solar orbit) on the fourth day of the festival, which corresponds to the fourth day of primordial creation and to the beginning of the new annual cycle in present time. The fire walk thus marks the end of an immense journey that willfully and mockingly places non-Indian alterity and negation of the Chamula social order in their own past. The bad guys become, as it were, members of their own ancestral lineage. In this manner, Afro-American and European alterity, as well as other forms of behavioral deviance, become necessary conditions for their own evolving identity in present time. It is thus possible for me to comprehend what, for me, are startling facts about Chamula historical reckoning. (See a full discussion of this in chapters 2 and 4.) They repeat again and again in their historical narratives that we—the Europeans, Mexicans, Africans, Jews, and monkeys—are their primitive contemporaries, socially, historically, and morally prior to and inferior to them. Hence Spanish and English become primitive languages, and so forth. It is a vision of the other that echos our own Victorian discourse about "our little brown brothers" in the colonies. Who is inventing whom?

The negative valences of white and black, however, do not provide the whole picture. Chamulas fervently address endless prayers, songs, and florid ritual poetry to their white, sexless Sun/Christ deity: "Great Ladino, Great Patron, Lord of Heaven, Lord of Glory" (respectively *muk'ta kaxlan, muk'ta patron, yajvalel vinajel, yajvalel lorya*). At the same time, they acknowledge that they would not enjoy sex and reproduce without the ancient instruction of the hypersexed black Pukuj. These Tzotzil images echo our own romantic notions of Rousseau's noble savages and the celebration of Afro-American bodies in U. S. athletic and entertainment culture: strength, power, sensuality, rhythm, spontaneity, and so forth. Again, one wonders at moments who learned what from whom?

Where, then is the Indian in Chamula Tzotzil cosmology and discourses. Why are there no significant Indian heroes or gods in the historical narratives of one of the most conservative Indian communities in Mexico? I have attempted to understand this question by searching for myself and my cobeings within their historical matrix in order to glimpse images of ourselves as they see us. I find that all of us—Jews, Afro-Americans, gringos, Mexicans, Europeans, Guatemalans—are consistently historicized in order to foreground and frame and favor an always emergent Indian community in the present. Indianness is thus always present and evolving, at the temporal frontier, as it were. The Other must be captured, evaluated, incorporated, and placed in their own ancestral lineage of experience in order to foreground the Indian Self in the present.

This historical vision contrasts utterly with what I was taught about who

I was as a child in Kansas. I was who I was by virtue of casting off prior identities, not by incorporating them: a Wichita boy, no longer a country boy; an American, no longer an Irishman, a Scot, a Dutchman, or a German; an educated person, no longer a boor (my mother, by the way, often called her own brother, who remained on the farm, "a goddamned illiterate"); a Congregationalist, no longer a Mennonite or a Presbyterian, as my parents were reared. Perhaps this is why North Americans, as a people, so eagerly seek voluntary affiliations; why we seek, for amusement and leisure, the elective and ephemeral homelands of Disneyland (Fantasyland, Frontierland, Tomorrowland, etc.); why we join smoke-free groups; why it has become almost a social necessity and staple of our political rhetoric to identify with athletic teams and sports heroes. We may assume and abandon these affiliations at leisure, and have no commitment to them if it ceases to be convenient. This mind-set is no doubt why I "chose" to be an anthropologist and why I am now, as an adult, a confirmed Anglo-Catholic. My poor Scottish Presbyterian grandfather, whose recitation of Robert Burns began this paper, would roll over in his grave.

RETURN FROM OZ

This essay has been an exercise in reflexivity, an attempt to take seriously the challenge of what has been appropriately called a "crisis of representation" in the human sciences (Marcus and Fischer 1986; Rosaldo 1989). As I understand this challenge, it invites us to seek forms of discourse in social analysis and ethnographic reporting that respond ethically and honestly to the social, political, and epistemological realities of the postcolonial world order. This is a world in which old boundary markers—between scientific discourse and interpretive commentary, us and them, scholars and their subject, the First and Third worlds, objective facts and subjective constructions, practice and discourse, national sovereignties and ethnic identities—are blurring and fading into a vast and complex borderland, to use Rosaldo's terminology (Rosaldo 1989: 196-217). These conditions oblige anthropologists, among others, to seek new ways of identifying subjects of inquiry, framing problems, and doing research. A related issue, bringing us back to the so-called crisis of representation, is how we write about the Other. As Dennis Tedlock has expressed it, the challenge becomes one of trying to write in such as way that "real people sit at both sides of the tape recorder" (D. Tedlock 1983: 3-19).

This paper has been such an attempt. I have tried to show how we and our cobeings are already *in* Tzotzil discourse; they have been actively incorporating and historicizing us for centuries. My encounter with them was no exception. I have also attempted to show how my own life history, field experiences, and culture have conditioned my incorporation of the Tzotzil world into my own identity and discourse. Indeed, the Hispanic and Indian world I encountered in Chiapas was, in an odd way, prefigured in my own biography—my grandparents' Basque and Osage Indian neighbors—before I ever knew Chiapas or the Chamula existed. It was not unlike Dorothy's dream experience in the Land of Oz; the fantastic Other turned out to be a disruption, reconfiguration, and eventual reassessment of familiar images and beings; her deceased parents, her aunt and uncle, and herself—her own world of Kansas. Even the great Oz turned out to be an old man from Omaha.

Like Dorothy in *The Wizard of Oz* and Lévi-Strauss in *Tristes Tropiques* (1976), I found in San Juan Chamula not really an exotic Other, but rather, parts of myself, my cobeings, and my culture reassessed from a different point of view. Both Chamulas and I have participated actively in what amounted to a mutual appraisal, and for me the results are not altogether pleasing or comforting, just as Oz and the slow death of Brazilian native cultures (at the hand of Western culture) were not comforting to Dorothy and to Lévi-Strauss. All three experiences turned out to be stressful, if illuminating, exercises in self-discovery and cultural critique. I found, to my dismay, that Chamulas, unveiled, eagerly consume Coca Cola and Pepsi, and (I am informed, as of January 1992) Japanese video games.[11] These staples of U. S. culture are easily available within shouting distance of the site of the annual ritual of solar renewal. Chamulas, I think, sense no dissonance in this juxtaposition; the problem is mine, not theirs. My illusions are further dashed when I consider that the U. S. Presbyterian missionaries who have converted thousands of Chamulas to Protestantism might have been funded by my own relatives in Kansas. Where are the boundaries?

If Chamulas live in a constructed matrix that actively incorporates us, our objects, and our religions into their world, why and how are they different? Why and how do they choose to stay that way? It obviously has to do with what culture is about, more particularly with how the pieces and ideas in the borderland are put together. The Chamulas' historicized African and European, German and Englishman, Jew and Protestant, Mexican and Guatemalan, may represent real or imagined others who have crossed (or blocked) their path in various ways over the centuries. But they are represented in Chamula narratives and everyday conversation in ways that utterly reconstruct them and merge them to yield themselves, the "true people," in several variants in the present.

I believe that T. S. Eliot best helps to capture what I am trying to say about the Chamulas' historicized Other and emergent Self in cyclical time. Although it may seem odd that an expatriate Anglo-American poet (from Missouri, by the way) who lived much of his life in England, his adopted homeland, might have something to say about Maya history and ethnicity in a rapidly changing world, I think his wisdom is right on target:

Time present and time past
Are both perhaps present in time future,
And time future contained in time past.
If all time is eternally present,
All time is unredeemable.
What might have been is an abstraction
Remaining a perpetual possibility
Only in a world of speculation.
What might have been and what has been
Point to one end, which is always present.
Footfalls echo in the memory
Down the passage we did not take
Towards the door we never opened
Into the rose-garden. My words echo
Thus, in your mind. . . .

(T. S. Eliot, "Burnt Norton," *Four Quartets*, 1963: 175)

POSTSCRIPT

Several colleagues who read drafts of this essay note that is seems odd to give the last word in a study about Tzotzil Other to T. S. Eliot, a voice of high Western modernism who espoused conservative social and political ideas. His worldview, both nostalgic and utopian, does not seem at first glance to clarify, even by way of comparison, anything "Mayan." Eliot's poetic universe sought a still spiritual center amid the unprecedented change and widespread disillusionment, shared by many, with the exhausted political and social arrangements of nineteenth-century Europe. Revolutionary Mexico has expressed a variant of such patterns in the twentieth century, paralleling to some extent the social world against which Eliot wrote and thought: an almost xenophobic nationalism combined with a profound faith in applied science, social engineering, and modernization, even with a component of what Pablo González Casanova has identified as Mexican "internal colonialism" (1970: 71-72). The Chamulas have of course seen, felt, and acted in this Mexican social space while also remaining at the margins of it, seeking, not unlike T. S. Eliot's imagined universe, their own center and their own present. In this manner, then, Tztozil ethnic affirmation and historical reckoning constitute both a creation and critique of the colonial world and its successors in America.

ACKNOWLEDGMENTS

Parts of this paper were first presented under a different title at the conference "The Formation of the Other," held in Trujillo, Spain, in November 1990, under the sponsorship of the government of the Autonomous Region of Extremadura and the Xavier de Salas Foundation. The paper, as presented on that occasion, benefited greatly from critical comments by Manuel Gutiérrez Estévez, J. Jorge Klor de Alva, and Richard and Sally Price. The problems were so numerous that I felt it was necessary to start again, virtually from scratch. A new version of the paper was presented in March 1992, at the eighth Texas Symposium at the University of Texas at Austin, held in conjunction with the annual Maya Meetings, and also at the University of Houston. On these occasions and in subsequent correspondence, I received generous critical commentary and encouragement from many colleagues, among them Linda Schele, Barbara and Dennis Tedlock, Evon Z. Vogt, Victoria R. Bricker, Steven Tyler, Quetzil Castaneda, Antonella Fabri, and William Hanks. At the University at Albany, I received still more constructive criticism and encouragement from John Justeson, James Collins, Helen Elam, Eugene Garber, Liliana Goldin, Gail Landsman, Robert Carmack, Louise Burkhart, Michael Smith, and Thomas Van Alstyne. I also thank Steven Bodio, a freelance writer, for his encouragement to proceed with what, for me, was an altogether new kind of writing. Finally, I express my gratitude to Forrest Robinson, of the University of California at Santa Cruz, for calling my attention to the D. H. Lawrence text that is cited in this paper. This recital of thanks for support in this project is long because my debts are many and my confidence has been, on occasion, slim.

A similar, though not identical, Spanish language version of the present paper appears in Gossen et al. (1993: 37-74), as a part of the edited proceedings of the conference "The Formation of the Other."

Two

TRUE ANCIENT WORDS

I present in this chapter foundational narratives that depict the creation and establish-
ment of order in the universe and in Chamula society. The texts themselves date from
the period of 1965 to 1979, although the translations have been an ongoing enterprise
that has occupied my attention to the present. None of these texts has ever been pub-
lished before. As the introduction will indicate, these narratives are not presented as "the
canon," or even as a representative canon, of Chamula life and thought. Rather, they
are a sample of what I regard as typical expressions of truths whose verity is assumed
by most Chamula Tzotzils. The texts themselves are highlighted here, reflecting my
early and continuing conviction that native discourse speaks clearly, but not necessarily
without interpretive help. The extensive footnotes provide exegesis and clarification
where this seems indicated. I have also used the occasion of this chapter to introduce the
small core of narrators whose stories inform much of the content of this book.

INTRODUCTION

Chamula Tzotzil life and thought—like other Maya cultural expressions, ancient
and modern—moves forward by reassessing the past, in much the same manner
that a weaver moves forward on the frame of a loom, building new fabric by
returning time and again to the pattern of the warp while also adding new material, perhaps also new patterns and new designs. I will argue later that this means
of acting in history does not vanish in times of rapid social change, even with radical departures from "traditionalism," as expressed, for example, in Maya
Protestantism and in the recent Zapatista movement. In this chapter, I turn to
some of the fundamental strands of this warp of memory—the layout of time and
space in the ancient past that produced San Juan Chamula as a moral universe.

I have discussed the general attributes and expressions of traditional
Chamula cosmology in a number of other works. Here, however, I wish to
yield the floor to Tzotzil narrators themselves. The narrative voices that follow
have mattered a great deal to my understanding of the Chamula universe. With
each of the five men whose narratives follow here and in chapters 3 and 4 I
have spent many hundreds of hours, in their homes and fields and in my office

and home. We have also shared countless dirty jokes, drinks, and gossip. Virtually all that I know of Chamula life and thought has come from them directly, or through them indirectly, as they patiently answered countless questions. They also accompanied me here and there, and each became, in his own way, my mentor and teacher. It seems fitting to allow them to speak at length in this chapter. I shall introduce them as each text is presented.

It is relevant to this discussion, and to the larger agenda of this book, to note that all five of these men were neighbors in two small hamlets, Nab ta Petej and Milpoleta, of the one hundred or so that make up the *municipio*. Four of the five were related by lineage and by marriage. Their collective knowledge of their culture was thus truly "local knowledge," and so, therefore, is mine. This means simply that I cannot claim any systematic sampling strategy for my ethnographic reporting because that option was not politically feasible. These men, my close friends, helped me in innumerable ways when other potential sources of information would not and could not work, for reasons that I have discussed above (see chapter 1).

This small group of consultants and friends, however, represents a broad spectrum of the fortunes of men in Chamula Tzotzil society. They are, in the perspective of time present, typical. There are winners and losers. A high achiever, Marián López Calixto, the artist who drew all of the line drawings for this volume, eventually became chief magistrate (*presidente municipal*) of San Juan Chamula and presided successfully over the whole *municipio* in 1988. He is the proud father of nine children and has just constructed a two-storey home with modern materials and amenities in his ancestral hamlet. He is also seeking the means to attend college in the United States. Another of this group now lives as a divorced and politically disgraced exile in the new suburbs of San Cristóbal de las Casas. Two have died of alcoholism and related complications, another, from tuberculosis. This set of life histories, sadly, does not conflict with what we know of the demographic profile of modern Chiapas.

It is also relevant to this discussion to tell the circumstances under which these stories were recorded. None was recorded from an in situ performance. All were written or transcribed from oral recitation in my office at the Harvard Ranch. These texts are neither oral performances nor, fully, the sole product of the written word. They lie somewhere in between. Two of my storytellers learned to write Tzotzil in the International Phonetic Alphabet thanks to the University of Chicago Man-in-Nature Project that preceded my field study in Chiapas. They learned this skill as adults; I was a beneficiary, for they were able to assist me from the very beginning of my fieldwork. I taught two others literacy in Tzotzil. The other was nonliterate. He dictated his stories into the tape recorder and others transcribed the tapes. After their texts were written in Tzotzil, I translated them into Spanish with the author or narrator at my side; this close working relationship is the source of the ethnographic notes that accompany each narrative.

All of this means that the stories recorded in this chapter belong to what might be called a transitional period in Tzotzil literature. The styles remain oral in their composition, and my conversations about the subject matter, as recorded in ethnographic notes, are dialogical in a way that is not unnatural to oral/aural means of transmission. Comment and conversation typically accompany oral performances in Chamula and elsewhere. Dennis Tedlock cultivated this dialogical methodology in his retranslation project of the Popol Vuh (D. Tedlock 1985), which he produced in the company of a contemporary Quiché Maya-speaker. However, the means and the circumstances of recording and transcription in my collection project have created texts that are modern in that they are the literary product of the first generation of literate Tzotzil speakers. The storytellers themselves wrote in a style that is closely linked to the conventions of oral performance, for all had reached adolescence or adulthood as monolingual Tzotzil speakers; they knew none other than the oral style. With the exception of Marian López Calixto, who had received six years of primary schooling in Tzotzil and Spanish, none had been exposed to any form of formal education, with its fairly rigid standards of written exposition. All, of course, were exposed to the peculiar forms of scriptorial assistance requested by anthropologists. (See Gossen 1985 for a full discussion of Tzotzil literature and of the details of various approaches to translation, including the one that is used below.)

The four foundational narratives that follow belong to a genre that is known in Tzotzil as "True Ancient Narrative." This means that they are regarded as true accounts of the first three creations and restorations of the earth and its life-forms. They refer to the formative period of human experience. They are different from the genre called "True Recent Narrative," which includes accounts of the present, "Fourth Creation" of humankind, that is, the period that we would call modern history. The stories in this chapter also contrast with a narrative genre called "Lies," which belongs to a category called "Frivolous Language." These are deliberate fabrications, intended for play and amusement. In contrast, the narratives that follow belong to the formal variant of Tzotzil storytelling; they offer true accounts of time past.

OUR FATHER'S LIFE

Narrated in the Tzotzil Maya language by Mateo Méndez Tzotzek of San Juan Chamula, Chiapas, Mexico, in 1979.

Mateo Méndez Tzotzek, approximately sixty years of age in 1979, reminded me of Santa Claus. He was joyous and forthcoming, never failing to find something pleasant with which to embellish each day, each working session, and every social encounter. A part-time shaman and corn farmer, he was one of the few Chamula men I knew who had never worked as a migrant labor-er. Because of his limited financial resources, he had followed no career in the civil and religious cargo system of public service. He was monolingual in Tzotzil, as close to a "traditional" Tzotzil Chamula as I ever met. He is now deceased. The following text was dictated in Tzotzil and transcribed by other assistants.

I have chosen this text, from many narratives that record these same events in many variants, because it comes closest to representing the funda-mental link that Chamula Tzotzils have forged—through the unknown labors of Dominican missionaries and more than four centuries of local interpreters—between Jesus Christ and their ancient sun deity. The events in the following story begin and end in the center of the universe, San Juan Chamula. To this day you can see (if you pay the appropriate fee) beneath the high altar of the Chamula church, the stone that marks the epicenter of the world, the "navel of the earth" (*smixik banamil*).

Here is an account of Our Father who died on the cross.

Now, Our Holy Mother, the Mother of Heaven, did not understand how she became pregnant.
> **She did not know where or how she had conceived her child.**

Then she looked for a dry stick,
> **One that did not have any leaves.**

Then, without more ado, she presented the stick to Our Father of Nazareth.[1]
> **Our Father of Nazareth was the first one to take the barren branch.**

"Take this dry branch.
> **Let's see if it sprouts buds for you," said Our Mother of Heaven.**

"But why?
> **What is this all about?" asked Our Father of Nazareth.**

"You only have to take the stick to see if it sprouts for you," said Our Mother of Heaven.
> **So Our Father of Nazareth obeyed her.**

He took the barren branch.
> **In fact he took the stick in his hand quite willingly.**

In the end, it did not sprout for him.
> **It did not turn green for him.**

But the truth of matter was that Our Father of Nazareth did not know why he had been asked to take the stick in his hand.

All that mattered was that Our Mother of Heaven saw that the stick did not sprout for him.

She told Our Father of Nazareth to return it to her.
"Give it back to me," she demanded.

"We shall give it to Saint Joseph.
"We'll see if it sprouts blossoms for him.

"It did not sprout for you," she said to Our Father of Nazareth.
Then she gave it to Saint Joseph.

"Take this stick here.
Let's see if it sprouts for you," said Our Mother of Heaven.

"All right, I'll take it," replied Saint Joseph amicably.
So he took it in his hand.

When he took the stick it quickly sent forth living buds.
"Well, now, the stick sprouted for you.

"You are to marry me because I am with child.
But I don't know where I conceived this child.
I don't know how it came to me.

"Suddenly I felt it; it was already there in my womb.
It was moving in my body.

"That is why we are going to get married.
Because we will be able to say that it is your child here in my womb.

"It doesn't really have a father.
That is why you are to be responsible for it.
That is why you are going to be the father of my child,"
said the Mother of Heaven.

"Very well, that's fine. Don't be afraid.
I will marry you," said Our Father Saint Joseph.
Then he did marry Our Mother of Heaven.

Then the son of Our Mother of Heaven was born.
But fortunately, she already had a husband, and he, the newborn, a father.

For this reason, the relatives of the Mother of Heaven never found out that she did not yet have a husband when the child was conceived.
When the child was born, she already had a husband.

For this reason, the relatives of the Mother of Heaven did not know that she did not yet have a husband when the child was conceived.

That was because she married Saint Joseph.

For him, the barren branch sprouted.
> If the stick had not sprouted for him, she would not have married Saint Joseph.

As for Our Father of Nazareth, the stick did not sprout for him.
> That is why they did not get married.

If that stick had never sprouted,
> Humankind would not have happened at all.

Since the stick did sprout,
> It happened that humankind did increase.

Now, when the son of the Mother of Heaven was born, he had a halo.
> The halo of the son of the Mother of Heaven sparkled brightly.

The Jews didn't like it.
> They went to kill the child and his mother.[2]

But the Mother of Heaven realized that she and her child were going to be killed.
> So she fled with her child.

They went off into the cornfield.
> She carried off her son.

There they took refuge in the midst of the cornfield.
> There she nursed her child in the midst of the cornfield.

There, in the midst of the cornfield, some of the Mother of Heaven's milk dribbled down into the earth.
> In this manner Our Holy Mother's breastmilk turned into potatoes.

There in the earth the potatoes grew and multiplied.
> So it is that potatoes are the breastmilk of Our Holy Mother.

Our Holy Mother walked all over the earth with her son.
> As she was carrying her son, her breastmilk kept dribbling out.

That is why there are so many potatoes all over the earth.
> It was because Our Holy Mother walked all over the earth.

Indeed, the Mother of Heaven did not wish to return to where her son had been born.
> She walked all over the earth with her son.
> She carried him bundled there, wrapped in a shawl on her back.

Now, although the Jews looked diligently for the Mother of Heaven,
    They did not find her at all.

They had no idea how to find her,
    For the Mother of Heaven had hidden well with her son.

Then the son of Our Mother of Heaven grew up.
    Neither he nor his mother died.

"Well, Mother, we had better go back to where I was born.
    Let's see if the Jews are still going to kill me.
    Let's see if the Jews still know me.

"Let's go, Mother.
    Let's see if the Jews are still going to kill us.

"Come now, don't be afraid, Mother.
    Let's go.

"If the Jews do kill me, I won't die.
    It doesn't matter if they do kill me.
    I won't die," said the son of the Mother of Heaven.

"All right, then. Let's go.
    But if they kill you, don't blame me.
    If it pleases you, it would really be better for us just to stay here,"
    insisted the Mother of Heaven.

"No, Mother, it would be better if we went to our destiny.
    I think that I am indeed going to die.
    So let us see if I really do die," said the son of the Mother of
    Heaven.

"All right, then. Let's go," said the Mother of Heaven.
    And they went back to the place where the Mother of Heaven's
    son had been born.

Indeed, the Jews didn't like it that the Mother of Heaven's son had a
halo.
    That is why they felt they had to kill him.
    The child's crime was that he had a halo.[3]

But he was no longer a child.
    Now he was a man.
    Now he had grown up.

Then the son of the Mother of Heaven died.
    He was buried.

However, the son of the Mother of Heaven was not a mere person.
    He was Our Holy Father.

This is so because he had a halo,
    Unlike plain people who do not have halos.

Then when they saw that Our Father had died, the Jews went to bury him.
    They buried Our Holy Father right in the ground.

He lay buried there for three days.
    And each day, the Jews went there to see the place where Our Holy Father lay buried.

There Our Holy Father lay buried.
    He had not escaped.

So the Jews now thought that Our Holy Father was really dead.
    There they came every day to see the place where he lay buried.

And every time they came to check up on him, he remained buried there.
    He did not stir.

Then, on the third day, Our Holy Father emerged from the grave.
    He arose into heaven.

Now the Jews saw that Our Holy Father burst forth from the grave.
    They rushed to grab him right away.

But they did not manage to overtake Our Holy Father,
    For he promptly rose up into heaven.

His mother stayed on the earth.
    She was all alone.
    As for Our Holy Father, he ascended into the sky.

Then the Jews saw that there was radiance in the sky.
    "That radiance in the sky is San Salvador!" they exclaimed.[4]

"There he is!
    Let's climb up!
    Let's kill him!" said the Jews to one another.

"But how will we manage to climb up?" wondered some of the Jews.
    "Let's make some steps," said the other Jews.
    With that, they started to make steps, just like a ladder.
    And so the Jews climbed up.

Little by little, little by little,
    The Jews pressed upward toward heaven.

The reason for this was that they didn't want Our Father to live.

That was why they climbed up to kill him in the sky.
But, when the Jews had almost reached the center of heaven,
    The earth lords cried out with a loud voice.
    And all the Jews were cast down.[5]

They died from the beating which the earth lords gave them,
    For the earth lords did not want the Jews to climb up to heaven.

They didn't want them to kill Our Holy Father.
    That is why they beat them up.

So it was that the Jews did not succeed in climbing up to the sky.
    All the Jews fell back to earth from where they were at the center of heaven.

However, not all of the Jews perished.
    Some did not die.

Now, Our Father was there in the sky for three days.
    But on the third day, Our Holy Father came back down to earth.

When Our Holy Father arrived on earth,
    There he found the surviving Jews.

When the Jews saw that Our Father had once again arrived on earth,
    They rushed to kill him.

But Our Father told them:
    "Don't just kill me outright.
    It would be better if you made me a cross.

"There I am going to die on the cross.
    It would be better that way, for I don't want you just to kill me outright," said Our Father.

So the Jews obeyed him.
    They went to make a cross.

Now, when the Jews were busy making the cross,
    Our Father went to the site of their labors.

He went to oversee the making of his own cross,
    To advise them on how big it should be.

And while the Jews kept on working, Our Father stood close by.
    He was watching to see that his cross was well made.

When he saw the wood chips lying there,
    He picked up the wood chips and threw them into the river.

With that, the wood chips turned into fish.

This transformation happened with all of the wood chips.
  It was Our Father who threw the wood chips into the river.[6]

Then, when the cross was finished, the Jews dragged it along hoisted on their shoulders.
  They carried it to the Chamula church.

Then the Jews came into the church.
  They started to raise up the cross.

But they could not raise it at all.
  The cross was too heavy

They found a short stake and drove it into the ground.
  Using this to gain leverage, they pulled on the cross with a rope.

They did it by tying a rope on it there where they had driven in the stake.
  This is how they made the cross to stand upright.
  They anchored it there inside the church.[7]

Then, the stake where they had tied the rope turned into a horse.
  In times long ago, the horse was still a piece of wood, just like this stake.
  And it was this very piece of wood that turned into a horse.

Then, when the cross was standing upright, he commanded:
  "Fine. You are determined to kill me.
  But don't do it now.
  Wait until the Seventh Friday," said Our Holy Father.

First he told them the name of the day on which he would die.
  He told them:
  "First Friday.
  Second Friday.
  Third Friday.
  Fourth Friday.
  Fifth Friday.
  Sixth Friday.
  Seventh Friday—only then are you to kill me," said Our Holy Father.[8]

"All right," said the Jews.
  And the Jews obeyed his orders.

They did not kill Our Father until the Seventh Friday.
  And on the Seventh Friday they killed Our Father.
  He died there on the cross on the Seventh Friday.

So it was that the Jews carried out this murder long ago.
  Once the Jews saw Our Father dead on the cross, they were going to flee.

But, in the end, they did not succeed in fleeing.
They were taken prisoner at once.

The earth lords captured them.
The Jews were not able to get away.

So it was that the earth lords caught the Jews.
They immediately burned them alive in a great fire.

All the Jews died there.
That is why the people of Chamula have the custom of burning Judas every year.[9]
That is because the Jews committed these crimes long ago.

OF OUR HOLY MOTHER MOON IN HEAVEN

Narrated in the Tzotzil Maya language by Manuel López Calixto, of San Juan Chamula, Chiapas, Mexico, 1978.

Manuel López Calixto is the brother of Marián López Calixto, who will be introduced below. Manuel had the gentle manner of Saint Francis. Sweet and unassuming, he took great interest in our children and in our animals. Ever soft-spoken and prone to slow, contemplative, extremely polite interaction, I often thought that he would have made a good monk or poet. I had good evidence of the latter proclivity, as the reader will see below. However, like most Chamulas of his age and modest resources, he had done the routine of migrant labor on the coffee plantations since the age of twelve. He did not imagine that he had the skills of a writer. He came to me looking for work as a gardener, but I found his almost mystical feeling for the natural and social world to be attractive. I taught him to read and write in Tzotzil, and so he came into my circle of close friends and assistants. Manuel's health, always frail, failed in the early 1980s, when he died of tuberculosis.

I include this text in this portfolio of testimonies, for it speaks clearly to the gendered establishment of the cosmos. In a sense, this story picks up where the former left off. What was to become of the Sun/Christ's mother? Here we have an answer.

This is a story of long ago,
An account of long ago about Our Holy Mother of Heaven.

Now, Our Holy Mother was not the first one to ascend into the sky.
That one was Our Lord Sun/Christ.
Our Lord Sun/Christ was the first to ascend into the sky.

So it was with Our Lord Sun/Christ:

Our Lord Sun/Christ in Heaven died.

When her son died, Our Holy Mother in Heaven wept bitterly.
So it was when her son died.

When Our Lord Sun/Christ in Heaven went to the grave,
Our Holy Mother in Heaven wept bitterly for her son.

After that, Our Lord Sun/Christ went to the underworld.
Then, on the third day, Our Lord Sun/Christ in Heaven found his
dwelling place.

When she saw the face of her son, Our Holy Mother in Heaven felt
happy.[10]
So Our Holy Mother in Heaven left at once to take her own place
in the sky.

She went to talk to her son.
So began the conversation between Our Lord Sun/Christ and his
mother.

"You, Mother, you are going to walk at night," said Our Lord
Sun/Christ in Heaven.
"As for me, I am going to walk by day," he said to his mother.

"But we shall walk in the same direction" he said to his mother.
That is the reason why Our Lord Sun/Christ in Heaven and his
mother both move in the same way, according to my late grandmother.[11]

She told me this story a long time ago.
It was of course even longer ago when Our Lord Sun/Christ first
ascended into the sky.

We don't really know how many years ago all of this happened.
My late grandmother said to me: "Don't you see that this took
place long, long ago?

"That is why, when we die, we go to the underworld."
The reason is that Our Lord Sun/Christ passed through the
underworld when he died long ago.[12]

"Then Our Lord Sun/Christ ascended into the sky long ago," continued my late grandmother.
So it happened that Our Lord Sun/Christ ascended into the sky.

So it is that **Our Lord Sun/Christ in Heaven walks together with his mother.**

So it is that **Our Holy Mother shares her secret wisdom with the people.**[13]

ABOUT WHY THE MOON HAS ONLY ONE EYE

Narrated in the Tzotzil Maya language by Marián López Calixto, of San Juan Chamula, Chiapas, Mexico, 1979.

A full and proper introduction to Marián López Calixto would require details of political history that I do not know. He became a political official of the highest status—*presidente municipal* of San Juan Chamula —in the years after our close working relationship. The younger brother of Manuel, introduced above, Marián came to me as an ambitious young man in search of a career as an artist and writer. Although he had received minimal primary education—six years—in San Juan Chamula, he came across to me as a young man on fire with visions of a future as a leader and chronicler of his community. He has effectively achieved both of these goals, and we will undoubtedly hear more from him in the future. Not only has he served with distinction in the highest elective office of San Juan Chamula, but he has also worked as a collaborator in the highly successful Maya Writers' Cooperative (*Sna Jtzi'bahom*) which has labored successfully to produce, in the 1980s and 1990s, dramatic productions, puppet shows, and publications in native languages of Chiapas that have won international recognition (Breslin 1992; Craig and Everton 1993; and Laughlin 1994, 1995). Marián López Calixto is a superstar in the Maya cultural renaissance that is now in progress in Chiapas. His association with me is but a footnote to his many achievements.

I remember him as a wildly colorful young man, with a penchant for highlighting the lurid and humorous in his narratives. He is the artist responsible for all of the line drawings in this book; he is also responsible for tuning me in to the hidden valences of sex, violence, and family intrigue in Tzotzil narrative.

In the text that follows, Marián provides a glimpse of his witty and ironic reading of the traditional wisdom of his community. Here we find that Our Lord Sun/Christ is not only a verbal prodigy but also a mean and scheming younger sibling, and also a rather unambiguous role model for violent male abuse of women, a behavior pattern that persists to this day.

Here is an account of Our Mother Moon in Heaven.
My mother told me this story.

She told it to me at my house.
When the story came up, it was because we had gone outside at night.

And we saw Our Mother Moon in Heaven.
> That is how the story came up.

This is what happened to Our Mother Moon long ago.
> Our Mother Moon in Heaven still lived here on earth.

She wore a skirt.
> She wore clothing just like we do.

Then Our Mother Moon had a son,
> And Our Mother Moon held her son in her arms.

As for Our Mother Moon's child,
> He was given to talking a lot.

As for his mother,
> She listened carefully to what her son said.

As for her child,
> There was no end to his jabbering,
> There was no end to his bossiness.

As for his mother,
> She was overtaken by laughter.

"But why on earth are you carrying on this way?
> You're certainly talking a lot," laughed his mother, amused at the child's strange behavior.

Her son would not pay the slightest attention to what she said.
> And he continued to mutter lots of strange things.

"You, Mother, you and I are going to go to the sky.
> And my brother Marian[14] will stay here on earth," said her son.

"But why are you carrying on like this, Xalik?[15]
> Don't speak such nonsense," said his mother.
> "But what I say is true," said the child.

Then his mother, ignoring Xalik, said to her older son:
> "Let's take a bath, Marián.
> Put some firewood in the sweat bath," said Marián's mother.

"All right," said Marián.
> And the boy put the firewood in the bathhouse hearth.[16]

Then Xalik asked, "Why are you putting that firewood in the bathhouse?"
> So spoke Xalik.

"Because our mother wants to take a bath," replied Marián.
"Oh, all right," said Xalik.

And so his mother said to Marián, "Go to tend the bathhouse."
So spoke Marián's mother.

"All right. I'll go take care of it," replied Marián.
And so he went to take care of the bathhouse.

Then Marián returned to the house to announce this:
"Now it's ready, Mother."

"Shall we go in?" asked Marián.
"Oh, is it ready to go?" she asked.

And in this way Marián's mother continued:
"Where is Xalik?" asked Marián's mother.

"I don't know what's become of him.
He isn't here," said Marián.

Then it happened that Marián's mother called out to Xalik:
"Xalik, where are you?
Come on, let's take a bath."

"But wherever did your brother go?" asked Marián's mother.
"I don't know where he went.
I just saw him here a minute ago," replied Marián.

"Well, let's go ahead and get in, then.
Your brother isn't coming," said Our Mother Moon.
And so they went into the sweat house.

"He'll be along in a little while.
Let him come in later," said Marián.

Then, just after his mother had gone into the bathhouse,
Xalik appeared.

"Mama, I want to come in the bathhouse, too," insisted Xalik.
"Don't come in," said Marián.

"Mama, Marián won't let me come into the bathhouse," complained
Xalik.
"But why didn't you come on time?" asked Xalik's mother.

"But I want to come in, too," insisted Xalik.
"Well, come in, then, but be quick about it.
Take off your clothes," said his mother.

"Fine. Wait for me, then," said Xalik.
    And in no time he had taken his place in the bathhouse.

Then Xalik said, "I am going to toss more hot water on the hearth-stones for you."
    So said Xalik.

"Wait a minute.
    I haven't had a chance to lie down yet," said his mother.

Then it happened that Xalik did this:
    Quickly he threw hot water onto the live coals in the bathhouse hearth.

However, his mother was still sitting up and her eye got burned.
    "Ay! Eee . . . Eee! Now you've gone and scalded my eye.

"Why didn't you wait a minute like I said?" screamed his mother.
    Xalik's mother flew into a terrible rage.

Xalik's mother fled from the bathhouse,
    For her eye was blinded.
    Now she had but one eye!

Once she got out, she yelled:
    "My eye is gone, Marián.
    Come and see!"

"Your younger brother is a shithead, a wicked child!
    My eye is gone!
    Now I am half-blind!
    Why doesn't that child ever learn to behave?" she exclaimed help-lessly to Marián.

"Well, as a matter of fact, I like your face that way.
    Your face looks very pretty now.
    I like it like that," said Xalik, rudely asserting his opinion.

Now, indeed, the sun shone very brightly.
    But as for his mother, she now had but one eye.
    It's because Our Mother Moon's eye was scalded in the sweat bath.

After all of this Our Mother Moon went up into heaven.
    She went there with her son Xalik.

Now when it gets dark, the rays of Our Mother Moon aren't hot.
    The truth is that her son is much hotter.
    His rays are much brighter.

"Well, Mama, I have a plan:
   Let's make the earth and act together to set the order of things,"
   suggested Xalik.

"You're talking nonsense.
   Why are you saying crazy things like that?" asked his mother.

"What I say is just how things will be," said Xalik.
   And so he set off for each side of heaven.[17]
   Xalik went off to travel without end.

Our Father Sun doesn't know how to rest.
   He is always on the go, constantly traveling.

He goes about looking for incense to eat.[18]
   Incense is Our Father Sun's only food.

And that's all there is to this story.

OF HOW OUR LORD SAN JUAN CAME TO CHAMULA

Narrated in the Tzotzil Maya language by Xalik López Castellanos, of San Juan Chamula, in 1978.

Xalik (Salvador) López Castellanos, one of his many pseudonyms, is a man of many identities and many talents. For reasons of his choice and mine, I will not tell much of his life history. What matters most in this introduction is that he has led many lives, most of them sad, in relation to his own community. He has transcended all of these experiences to become a master storyteller and chronicler of his life and times. He came to my attention as an potential assistant for my own research through his association with the University of Chicago Man-in-Nature Project, a context in which he served with distinction. He is thoroughly literate in both Tzotzil and Spanish, and has helped me as a faithful friend for over twenty-five years.

The distinguishing mark of Xalik's narration lies in its historical precision and ethnographic detail. In another life, which he may yet lead, he will be, himself, an ethnographer. So accurate is his attention to detail. I have, needless to say, learned much from him.

The narrative that follows gives an account of the founding of San Juan Chamula. This account (and the one that follows, also about this subject) belongs to the Second Creation in the four-part Chamula Tzotzil register of historical memory. The First Creation established the universe—day and night, the celestial deities, and their gender-linked duties. The Second Creation is more mundane (and more boring). Deities still wander the earth with their wondrous powers, but, somehow, the drama of their lives is diminished. Their lives are thoroughly pedestrian, although empowered with magic. San Juan emerges in the text that follows as a plodding, pragmatic settler. He does not perform truly wondrous deeds as a founder and colonizer; nor does he live in any discernible domestic unit, as his forebears, the Sun and the Moon, certainly did, complete with all of their contretemps. San Juan amounts to little more than a magically empowered bureaucrat, a trait, by the way, that is noted in Chamula ritual observance. His fiesta is dutifully acknowledged in major ritual events on and surrounding his commemorative date of June 24; but this pales in comparison with the truly great event in the annual cycle, "The Festival of Games," which occurs in February, in honor of San Juan's relatives, the Sun and the Moon. (See chapter 5 for an account of this festival).

Here is San Juan's story.

This is a story of Our Lord San Juan of Chamula.[19]

Well, long ago Our Lord San Juan made his home in Chamula.
    But it was no easy task to establish his home.

He first planned to live near a place that is known as Xitalá.
    This is known in Tzotzil as the "Place of our Ceremonial Center in 'Hot Country.'"[20]

But he found that the land was too hot,
    So he did not make his home there.
    His sheep did not thrive there.

The land was not open and level,
    So his sheep had no place to graze.

There were also too many ants.
    His sheep could not thrive.
    The ants bit them.

That is why he did not make his home near Xitalá.
    For he realized that the land was simply too hot.

But he had already worked a great deal.
    He had carried many rocks.
    He had begun to build his house.

But soon he noticed that his sheep refused to eat.
    They suffered from the heat.
    They suffered from the ants.
    His sheep could not stand the heat.

So he began to think about looking for another site for his home.
    He then went to a land called *Hol Ch'umtik*, which is near the hamlet of *Ya?al Ichin*.[21]

Our Father San Juan went to make his home where the land was cooler.
 However, even there, his sheep did not do well and their hearts
 were sad.
 His sheep did not want to live there.

Presently, the younger Lord San Juan spoke up:
 "My sheep refuse to eat.
 Their hearts are truly sad.
 This won't do. They're all dying on me," declared the younger
 Lord San Juan.[22]

"But why are they dying?
 Perhaps you don't give them enough water to drink.
 Perhaps you don't find good pasture for them," speculated the
 elder San Juan.

"What am I to do?
 I take good care of them. I give them plenty of good water to
 drink.
 I find good grass for them," responded the younger San Juan.

"But why are their hearts so sad?
 Why don't they want to eat?
 Why do they do nothing but sleep?

"I had better go look for another site for my house.
 My sheep just don't want to live here," concluded the elder San
 Juan.

"Well, what do you think?" asked the elder San Juan.
 "I really don't know," said the younger San Juan.
 And so it was that they finally decided to look for another place
 to settle.

"But where shall I go?
 Where can there be a good land?

I shall give it a lot of thought," said the elder San Juan.
 With that, he thought very seriously about where he would make
 his home.

"Well, I think we should be off to look around.
 I wonder why I didn't think it over better to start with.
 I didn't look very carefully for a good house-site.

"In those other places I worked for nothing.
 I carried rocks in vain," said the elder San Juan sadly.

They were soon to depart, he and his younger brother and his sheep.
 He now had in mind just where he would build his house.

Soon he arrived at the new site.
It was right there beside a large mountain.

He went to check the site out.
He stood gazing at it from the top of the mountain.

"Good! This is it! Here I will build my house.
This is the place, at last.
I shall go nowhere else."

Whereupon, Our Lord San Juan began to cause the mountain to collapse.
In no time at all, a great landslide happened.
And with that, the lake vanished.

In an instant, as the mountain collapsed, the lake vanished.
And once the lake had disappeared, he began to level the surface
of his house-site with a hoe.

At this time, Our Father San Juan was working all alone.
It occurred to him that it would be good to find workers to help
him with his task.
His younger brother would then be free to tend the sheep.

"You, little brother, you are going to watch the sheep.
Come along and see that they get water.
See that you tend the sheep well.

"As for me, I'm going to get to work.
I'm going to look for beams for our house," said the elder San
Juan.
And with that, he was off to find the house beams.

But first of all, he had to look for stones for the walls of his house.
He went into the forest to gather stones.
He spent the entire day in the woods, looking for stones.

At dusk, Our Father found a place to sleep back at the house-site.
In this place there was a great oak tree.
He slept there under the branches of this great tree.

He spent all of the next day hauling stones with his helpers.
When they got to where the stones were, they heaped them up in
a pile.
They piled them up, right there in the forest.

Then his helpers began to herd the stones along.
They did not carry the stones.
The stones walked along by themselves, just like sheep.[23]
(See Figure 6.)

But there were ever so many stones!
>   And some of them refused to walk along the road.
>   They would flee into the woods.

Whereupon one of the herdsmen would take off after them with his staff.[24]
>   He would go to round them up like a shepherd.

However, some of the stones would not submit to being herded along.
>   They did not want to go to the site of the church.

Some walked obediently along the road.
>   Others refused to cooperate.
>   They went to hide beside the road.[25]
>   So it was with great effort that sufficient stones were forced to go to the future site of San Juan's house.

When the stones finally arrived, the bell rang.
>   This was a large bell which hung there on the large oak tree at the future site of San Juan's house.
>   This bell tolled all by itself when the stones arrived.

But in truth, the herdsmen responsible for all of this were saints;
>   They were not people.[26]

San Juan walked first in line.
>   Behind him came other saints, herding the stones.
>   It was their job to see that the stones did not flee.

Finally, when the stones got there,
>   Our Lord San Juan set to work with his helpers.
>   He began to measure how big he was going to make his house.

When he had finished measuring out the site of his house,
>   He started to dig out a foundation, a place to anchor the stones.

Then, when they had dug out the foundation trench,
>   They began to lower the stones into position.
>   All of this happened when San Juan worked alone with his helpers.

As the project evolved, they could no longer reach far enough to set the stones in place.
>   His assistants threw them up.
>   San Juan himself stood above to catch them.

These were no ordinary stones!
>   One meter to a side.
>   One meter thick.
>   They were very large indeed.

Figure 6. San Juan Herding Magical Stones
(Drawing by Marián López Calixto)

However, for the saints, they were not heavy.
  They threw them up effortlessly.

Likewise for San Juan, the receiver:
  In no time and with little effort he caught the stones.

Now, at the site of San Juan's house, there was a water supply down the slope.
  Indeed, the former lake was still there, although reduced in size.

Our Lord San Juan found that the land was good.
  His sheep would prosper.
  There were no ants.
  There was no intense heat, for it was not hot country.
  The land was very good.
  His children would thrive.
  That is why he built his house there beside the lake.

Now his sheep no longer had sad hearts.
  The sheep of Our Lord San Juan now ate well and prospered.

With these labors, San Juan and his younger brother took up residence in this place,
  Whereas before, they had lived in the wilderness.

They once had a home on Tree Moss Mountain.
But now Tree Moss Mountain would no longer be their abode.[27]

They would now have a permanent home in Chamula.
That is why they call it San Juan Chamula.
Even the Ladinos, all of them from San Cristóbal to Tuxtla
Gutiérrez, know about this.

So it happened long ago.
With great effort, Our Lord San Juan found a site for his home.

A SACRED PLACE

For a casual modern visitor, Mexican or foreign, the town center of San Juan
Chamula in the late 1990s has all of the trappings of an isolated Indian village that has suddenly met the modern world. There are video game parlors,
banks, stores, schools, clinics, electric lights, potable water sources, two-storey
homes, blocks and blocks of paved streets, souvenir shops, etc. Only twenty-
five years ago, this town center had but two gravel-topped access roads, dirt
paths, illumination by oil lamps, and a permanent population of perhaps four
hundred; it is now a modern Mexican town of three thousand.

However, looks are deceiving. This remains an ethnically homogeneous
place with an aggressive and so far successful strategy for staying that way.
Tourists are charged admission fees and are carefully monitored with regard
to photographic privileges and freedom of movement. Mexican mestizos
and tourists abound by the thousands on feast days; they are conspicuously
absent at other times. San Juan Chamula remains today a profoundly Indian
place and apparently intends to stay that way.

How and why is this the case? Although the issue of ethnic continuity
and change is considered in several other chapters of this book, I conclude
this discussion of True Ancient Words by asserting that narrative itself has
fundamentally to do with the creation and re-creation of the Chamula
Tzotzil universe(s) in our time. Countless place names, things, beings, events,
and individual people, have, according to Tzotzil premises, their "secret"
(*smelol*), that is, some formative attribute that is not apparent on the surface.
This hidden attribute almost always implies a story that lies behind the
apparent reality. The opaqueness of reality—a theme, "breath on the mirror,"
which Dennis Tedlock has identified as centrally important to the ancient
Quiché Maya as their lives and times are recorded in the Popol Vuh (see
Tedlock 1993)—has innumerable expressions among the contemporary
Tzotzil Maya. These range from the seldom spoken, yet often dreamed, stories of people's animal soul companions (see chapter 9), to the great mys-
teries of the bodies and deeds of deities, whose presence is revealed to us
only through their radiance, our images of them, and physical evidence of

their good or ill will. For all of this spectrum, from the individual to the cosmos, stories amplify and deepen apparent reality, even as they inevitably distort it and reinvent it. This narrative chain—stories within stories—has its maximum density in the sacred space of the Chamula ceremonial center. Everything started here. From this point of orientation, the center of the universe, the "true people" (*batz'i viniketik*) speaking the "true language," (*batz'i k'op*, as their dialect of Tzotzil is called), trace their deepest genealogical roots and reckon the origins of time and space. This is also the original, if perhaps no longer the central, source of cultural identity in the diaspora communities that are now found all over the state of Chiapas. The latent forces (and hence, the narratives) that have underwritten these many expressions of Tzotzil identity today have multiplied to include many new Others. These new "secrets" (latent, causal forces that lie beneath the apparent reality) now include Protestant missionaries, the Mexican State, NAFTA, the Zapatistas, and numerous expressions of pan-Indian consciousness. However, the narratives that bring these new realities to life and practice are woven on a warp of very old and very local ideas. Tzotzil Ancient Words provide one entree to an understanding of how Chamula Tzotzils think and act in contemporary history.

Three

ON THE HUMAN CONDITION AND THE MORAL ORDER

This chapter highlights a single remarkable text by a virtuoso narrator. The text itself dates from 1969. It was first published in 1993. It concerns the advent of humankind in the cosmos and dwells at length on issues concerning the moral and social order. This chapter continues the reporting strategy used in chapter 2, with somewhat more introductory material and endnotes that are intended to provide an ethnographic context for this entire book. The unusual characteristics of this testimony are discussed in the introduction.

INTRODUCTION

At the periphery of the distribution of folk Catholic traditions of Hispanic Latin America lie tens of thousands of local religious traditions that belong neither to the pre-Columbian nor to the Christian moral universes. These highly localized spiritual expressions—called by Robert Redfield "little traditions" to contrast them with the "great traditions" of the universal or national religions—are best understood as unique belief systems. Each community represents an ever-evolving present that derives from particular pre-Columbian roots and particular experiences with Hispanic-Catholic missionization.

A VOICE FROM THE HINTERLAND

This chapter presents a native Tzotzil Maya text that testifies to popular faith and belief in a community of this type. San Juan Chamula is one of thousands of contemporary peasant communities in Mesoamerica and South America that still speak Native American languages and retain significant elements of pre-Columbian custom and belief. This community and its religion, cosmology, ritual, and oral traditions are described at length elsewhere (Gossen 1971, 1972, 1974a, 1974b, 1974c, 1975, 1976, 1977, 1978, 1979a, 1983,

1985, 1989a; Pozas Arciniega 1959; and Vogt 1973). Also, for comparative purposes, the reader may be interested in several other major studies that consider religious belief, ritual practice, and related art forms in Tzotzil-speaking communities that are adjacent to San Juan Chamula (see Bricker 1973 and 1981; Guiteras-Holmes 1961; Holland 1963; Laughlin 1977 and 1980b; Ochiai 1985; Vogt 1969b and 1976).

The text that is considered here reflects at length on the human condition, spirituality, and the moral order, as they are understood by a sensitive and intelligent Chamula Tzotzil named Xun Méndez Tzotzek. The narrative begins with an account of the creation of the universe from the primordial void. The Sun/Christ deity proceeds to organize the earth and its life forms in the first of four cyclical epochs, or "earths," that the community recognizes. Although it is not mentioned in the present text, this initial moral universe evolves through three subsequent destructions and restorations (a cyclical sequence that is extremely common to the cosmologies of both Mesoamerica and Andean South America) that yield the present era, the Fourth Creation, according to Tzotzil historical reckoning.

The text, written by Mr. Méndez Tzotzek in 1969, testifies to the eternal present that sacred narratives witness. Like the texts in the previous chapter, it belongs to a genre of speech performance known in Tzotzil as "true ancient narrative" (batz'i antivo k'op). Stories of this type provide what is regarded as a true account of the formative experience of humankind in the first three epochs of creation, destruction, and restoration that lead to the present era.

While the narrative that follows belongs to a well-recognized and much-practiced art form, it is nevertheless unusual in several ways. First, it is relatively complex in that it has several episodes rather than a single story line. It also assumes a great deal of cultural knowledge that is not stated in the text itself. For this reason, I have provided extensive ethnographic notes that are the result of conversations about this text with Mr. Méndez Tzotzek. The text is also unusual in that the rhetorical style goes well beyond standard narrative exposition to provide what might be called native exegesis. That is, we are given a sequence of primordial events together with an interpretation of their significance for people's lives today. The content is thus text and homily; text and exegesis of text. The two modes—narrative and interpretation—are in fact implicitly present in all Tzotzil narrative performance, for stories are never told, to my knowledge, for their amusement value alone. They are always told for a purpose—that is, to explain or interpret something. The present text accomplishes this didactic function with unusual clarity and strength. Most other narrative performances have such a "purpose," but I have seldom heard a more artful blend of narrative discourse and teaching in my many years of living and working in Chamula.

Still another dimension that makes this text unusual is that of the circumstances under which it was recorded and transcribed. I served as the audience.

Needless to say, I was far from being a "natural audience," for the information related in the text—as in all narratives, sacred and secular—does not get told in a native setting until particular circumstances make the information relevant to the social context. Otherwise, the information remains latent in the reservoir of collective memory, to be recalled as the need arises. The "need" that was created by my interest must therefore be understood to be nontypical.

At the time I collected and annotated this text, I was in the early stages of ethnographic fieldwork, a time when I was eager to learn all I could find out, in any medium, about Tzotzil Maya mythology and religion. Mr. Méndez Tzotzek was one of several Chamula men with whom I worked intensively in an effort to obtain a broad sample of narratives about the past. Mr. Méndez Tzotzek, about the age of thirty-five in 1969, was never a religious leader. He was what one might call a sensitive "layperson." Not possessing the economic resources to finance a career as a civil or religious official in the community's governing hierarchy, he made a modest living as a day laborer, corn farmer, and part-time shaman. His only remarkable traits were his keen and poetic intelligence and his ability to write Tzotzil. This text represents over two-hundred hours of transcription and subsequent dialogue, as I worked with him translating the Tzotzil to a working draft in Spanish. The supplementary information that appears in the form of numbered endnotes resulted in large part from discussions that occurred during these translation sessions. It should be understood, therefore, that Mr. Méndez Tzotzek's narrative is not presented as a "recitation of the faith," for such a canonic expression of Tzotzil belief and practice does not exist as such. Rather, this testimony can most profitably be read as a personal reflection on the sacred moral order of the Chamula Tzotzil universe, as it is understood by one who lives in its midst.

THE TZOTZIL MAYA

Over six million Maya Indians live today in southern Mexico, Yucatan, Guatemala, and Belize. They are the modern-day descendants of the ancient Maya. Of over thirty Maya languages that were spoken at the time of European contact, about twenty survive today. Tzotzil is one of these survivors, and its number of speakers (approximately two hundred thousand in 1980) is increasing. It is the principal language of nine *municipios* (administrative units below the state that are comparable in some ways to counties in the United States) of the State of Chiapas, the southernmost state of Mexico. Tzotzil is also widely spoken in twelve other *municipios* of Chiapas (see Vogt 1969a; Laughlin 1969).

San Juan is the largest of the Tzotzil-speaking *municipios*. Its population in the home *municipio* and in dozens of immigrant colonies is well over one hundred thousand, most of whom were still, as of 1980, monolingual in Tzotzil. Spanish is spoken as a second language by perhaps 20 percent of the population. Chamulas work as corn farmers, artisans, and day laborers, and most live patrilocally in scattered rural hamlets consisting of fifty to one hundred people. One such hamlet, Nab ta Peteh, is Mr. Méndez Tzotzek's home.

Chamula public religious life focuses on the municipal administrative center, where there is a church that looks superficially like thousands of other village churches in Latin America. It is unusual in that it contains no pews or chairs, and the dirt floor is typically covered with a carpet of aromatic pine needles. An image of the patron saint, San Juan (John the Baptist), dominates the high altar, and some twenty images of saints occupy lateral positions on both sides of the nave. All of the saints are maintained by religious officials called stewards (Tz. *martoma* from Sp. *mayordomo*) and standard bearers (Tz. *alperes* from Sp. *alférez*), who, with their assistants, perform an elaborate round of annual rituals in their honor, focusing primarily on their days of commemoration as dictated by the church calendar. While public ritual life appears to exhibit a full complement of folk Catholic custom, it should be noted that all of the saints and their human sponsors in fact constitute a highly complex, though loosely articulated, cult in honor of the founding deity, "Our Lord in Heaven" (Tz. *jtotik ta vinajel*). Our Lord in Heaven is at the same time the sun deity and Jesus Christ. The Moon, his mother, is associated with the Virgin Mary, and is known as "Our Mother in Heaven" (Tz. *jme?tik ta vinajel*). The saints are vaguely classified as younger siblings of the Sun/Christ deity; hence, they, too, are children of the Our Mother in Heaven.

The public sector that governs corporate community affairs also includes a civil hierarchy of the type that Spanish officials imposed during the colonial period. This group includes an elected chief magistrate (Tz. *peserente* from Sp. *presidente municipal*), and a ranked set of officials who represent the three *barrios* (submunicipal units) of the community. These positions, like those of the religious stewards and standard bearers, are rotating, tenure usually being for one year. Together, these civil and religious hierarchies constitute a variant of local administrative and church authority that is well known throughout Hispanic Latin America in those areas that had significant Amerindian populations at the time of European contact.

While the religious and civil hierarchies of the administrative center are, by our own premises of historical reckoning, the creation of the Spanish colonial authorities (Wasserstrom 1983), the religious practices and beliefs of the small outlying hamlets, where most people live, derive in part from antecedent pre-Columbian forms. Among these are ancestor cults, agricultural deities, earth lords (associated with rain), and animal-soul companions. These latter beings—animal souls— are associated with the health and destiny of each individual and are thus the principal foci of shamanistic practice (and its counterface, witchcraft) at the local level of the domestic unit (Rachun Linn 1989, and chapters 6 and 9 of this book).

Chamulas do not conceive of these sectors—public and domestic—as separate; the whole of Chamula life and being is a body of custom that was created and ordained by the Sun/Christ deity. This moral order is sustained by a cosmology and pantheon of deities that exist under his purview. Thus, although it is easy for the Western observer to note that the public religious sector is predominantly Hispanic-Catholic in its visible expressions, while the domestic sector preserves vital remnants of the belief system of the pre-Columbian Maya, this bifurcated view of Chamula Tzotzil religion bears no resemblance to the sacred moral order in which people believe they live. The text that follows speaks eloquently about this native spirituality and comes closer to expressing its coherent logic and power than scholarly analysis alone could possibly achieve.

The reader will be immediately struck by the apparent similarity between the first chapters of the Book of Genesis and Mr. Méndez Tzotzek's account of the origin of the earth, human beings, sexuality, reproduction, good, and evil. On closer examination, however there emerge some striking differences. First, the creator deity, Our Father Sun/Christ, who is the protagonist of this narrative, was born of Our Holy Mother Moon. This episode—including his birth, death, and resurrection as the sun god—precedes the present narrative and is not explicitly discussed here at all. (See chapter 2.) Thus, the ultimate creative force in the universe is neither the Sun, nor God, nor Christ, but the female Moon, who is understood to be the same as the Virgin Mary. Second, although Our Father Sun/Christ performs major creative acts, as this account testifies, he is but one of a powerful pantheon of life-giving, life-sustaining, and life-limiting forces. These include Our Holy Mother, the demon Pukuj, the earth lords, and the animal-soul companions. Their joint presence in the Tzotzil Maya spiritual universe is clearly apparent in the following account. (See chapter 6.)

OF HOW THE WORLD BEGAN LONG AGO

The verse format of the following translation follows the stylistic conventions of Tzotzil formal style, the foundation of which (as in so many oral traditions of the world) consists of dyadic structure of ideas, sound, and syntax. Details of stylistic patterns of Tzotzil oral tradition, and the details of my translation strategy, are discussed at length in two studies (Gossen 1974b and 1985). Chamula views on the history of language and speech appear in chapter 4 of this book. Here it suffices to say that the dyadic structures (and multiples thereof) that characterize Tzotzil narrative style are marked linguistically; therefore, my decisions regarding how to render the verse structure of narrative texts in translation are for the most part suggested by the original Tzotzil.

Here is an account of how the world began long ago.
How, in ancient times, the world was not at all like it is today.

Long ago, there were only seas.
There were no people.

Well, Our Father began to consider this:
"My children, my offspring, could never thrive here on top of the sea," reflected Our Father.

"It would be better for me to sweep away the sea," said Our Father.
"If I don't, nothing will thrive,

"Neither my children,
Nor my offspring," declared Our Father.

He proceeded to sweep away the sea.
When he had swept away the sea, there remained empty land on all sides of the earth.

There remained nothing but land,
But it was very flat.

There were no mountains,
No people,
No rocks,
No trees,
Only the earth itself, nothing more.

"But where shall I find the seed for my children, my offspring?" wondered Our Father.
"Whatever shall I do?" said Our Father.

He proceeded to dig up some clay.
When he had dug up the clay, he started to mold the clay.

He started to make the head,
He started to give it a face.

He started to give it hands,
He started to put on its feet.

Well, when he had fashioned it,
This clay was in the form of a doll.

Our Father started to make the earth ready.
As he was preparing the land, he watched the doll to see if it moved.

When he saw that it did not move,
　　He went there to the place where the clay doll was lying.

He stood it upright, and watched to see if it could walk.
　　Finally he saw that it remained standing there where he found it.
　　It was not walking at all.

"But whatever am I going to do about this?" wondered Our Father.
　　So he started to think about it.

"I had better take it into my arms," said Our Father.
　　Then, he proceeded to lift the clay doll into his arms.

When he had taken the clay doll into his arms, he started to rub it.
　　He kept on kneading it.

Once he had caressed it, he did it again and again.
　　Then it started to speak.

That which had been clay turned into flesh.
　　Its blood started to form.
　　Its bones started to form.

When he saw that it could speak,
　　He stood it up again to see if it could walk.

He saw that it did not walk.
　　Indeed, he found it standing there in the same place.

He began to remake it.
　　He watched to see if it got up.

Then he saw that it did not get up.
　　He found it in the same place, lying there on the ground.

"But how can I get it to start walking, to start moving?" asked Our Father.
　　"I had better shape it with an axe." said Our Father.

So he began to shape it with an axe.
　　He began to hew its fine details with an axe.
　　And its whole body, which was still made of clay, turned into a person.

Then, when he had sculpted its fine details with an axe,
　　It then began to move,
　　It then started to walk,
　　Its whole skeleton started to take shape.

When all the bones came together,
　　Then it turned into a human being,

61

It was then that which had been clay turned into a man.

Well, Our Father began to consider things.
    "Whatever shall I give him to eat?" asked Our Father.

He was hungry.
    He wanted to eat.

"But whatever shall I give him?
    He's getting sick," declared Our Father.

He thought very hard.
    He began by giving him dirt to eat.
    He patted it on at the side of the man's mouth.

Then he saw that he didn't want to lick the dirt with his tongue.
    There it remained, stuck beside the man's mouth.

"But what shall I give him?
    He's getting sick," said Our Father.

He peeled off the dirt from the side of the man's mouth.
    Then he began to gather grass.

This he patted gently at the edges of the man's mouth.
    But the man did not want to take it with his tongue.

"But what on earth shall I give him to eat?" wondered Our Father.
    He was standing there thinking.

"But whatever can I give him to eat?" asked Our Father.
    He entered into deep thought.

He then started to peel off a little bit of his own body.
    He placed it beside the man's mouth.

When Our Father put his own body next to the man's mouth,
    The man quickly took Our Father's body with his tongue.

When Our Father saw that he quickly took his body with his tongue, he said:
    "Ah! Can it be that it is my body that you crave as food?
    But be assured that you will not eat if you do not work hard.

"Do you know how to prepare a place for my body?" asked Our Father.[1]
    "Do you know how to break the ground?
    Do you know how to cut weeds?

"You will not eat until you learn this, you and your wife and children."
    "Very well. I am willing to work," said the man.

"Well, let's see if you know how to work,
   If you know how to honor my body," said Our Father.

"Very well. I will honor it," replied the man.
   "Good. You are going to go to work.

"I will give you a hoe.
   Let's go out so I can show you how you must prepare a place for
   my body," said Our Father.

"I will show you how to break the ground,
   How to plant my body," said Our Father.

"Take a good look at your hoe.
   I will show you how to use it when you break the ground," said
   Our Father.

With this, he proceeded to show the man how to work,
   How to prepare the place for Our Father's body.

When they came to the place where they would prepare the place for
his body,
   Our Father approached to show him how to prepare the cornfield.

"This is how you do it.
   This is how you proceed.
   This is how you clear the field," said Our Father.
   He showed the man all about the cornfield.

And so, when the man had finally learned about the cornfield, Our
Father spoke:
   "Ah, he really has learned to work," said Our Father approvingly.

And when he saw that the man had learned how to prepare the site for
the milpa,
   He started to show the man about sowing.

"This is how you do it,
   This is how you plant it," said Our Father.

And so, when he had learned about the sowing of the cornfield,
   The seed corn was given to him.

"When you sow it,
   You are to sow it like this," said Our Father.

And so he was given a planting stick for sowing the cornfield.
   "When you sow the milpa,
   You are to open a hole in the ground," said Our Father.

"All right," said the man.
    And so it was that the man started to sow his cornfield.

And when Our Father came later to where the man was sowing his
cornfield, he asked:
    "Is your heart pleased?
    Are you happy?"
    I am quite happy," said the man.

"Do you want a mate?" inquired Our Father.
    "Not really," said the man.

"Well, now, how am I going to get him to look for a wife?' wondered
  Our Father.
    "If he doesn't, there will be no way for them to multiply, my chil-
    dren, my offspring," said Our Father.

"It would be better for me to find a mate for him.
    If I don't do this, he will have nothing to eat,
    No one to make his tortillas," said Our Father.

"We had better look for a wife for you.
    If we don't, you are going to be sad," said Our Father.

"But where shall we find her? Do you have any idea?" asked the man.
    "Perhaps I know where your wife will come from," said Our
    Father.

"But where will she come from? Do you know?" asked the man.
    "Come over to me," said Our Father.

"All right," said the man.
    "She is to come from your rib," said Our Father.

With this, he began to take a rib out of the man.
    When he had taken the rib out of the man,
    He started to stroke it.
    Our Father kept on stroking it.

Then he stroked and stroked it.
    Our Father kept on stroking it.

And, surely, that which had been the man's rib turned into a woman.
    "Good, here is your mate," declared Our Father.

"Here you have the one you will make tortillas for you to eat.
    Here you have the one who will dwell in your house.
    Here you have the one who will make your clothes.
    Here you have the one who will make your food.
    Here you have the one who will sleep with you.
    Here you have the one who will share your food.

Here you have her," said Our Father.
"Very well," said the man.

"As for you, you will go to work," said Our Father.
"You are going to prepare the milpa for sowing.
You are going to bring the firewood for boiling the corn, so that
your wife can cook the food," said Our Father.

"You, then, you are to go to work."
So it was said to the man.

"You, then, you are going to carry water."
So it was said to the woman.

"Very well. I am willing," said the woman.
"Take care of your jug when you carry water," said Our Father.

"Also, if there should be a demon who talks to you when you are out,
Don't take that which he has,
That which he offers you to eat.

"Otherwise, your radiance will be put out.[2]
Otherwise, your husband will not be able to see to do his work,"
explained Our Father.

"So, therefore, pay no attention to what the demon Pukuj says to you,"
said Our Father.
"Very well, then. All right," said the woman and man together.

The man and the woman did not know anything about sex.
"Do you know how to do anything?" inquired Our Father.
"No, we have no knowledge," answered the man and woman
together.[3]

Well, there they were working and trying to accomplish something.
But the man had no knowledge of the woman.

"Well, now. How am I going to get them to multiply?" wondered Our
Father.
For when the man and the woman were sleeping together, they
did not know what to do.

Then the demon came.
The demon Pukuj came to talk to the man and the woman.

The demon Pukuj began by asking:
"You there, don't you and the woman know how to do anything
together?"

"We don't seem to be accomplishing anything," said the man and
woman.

"Come now, that will never do.
    If you don't do anything, you will not multiply," said the demon.

"But what should we do?" asked the man and the woman together.
    "If you want, I will show you what you should do," replied the
    demon.

"Fine. Show us what to do, then," said the man.
    "Okay, I am going to show you," said the demon.

"Lie down, now.
    Let's have a lesson in what to do," said the demon.

The woman was lying down.
    Then, when the woman was lying down, the demon lost no time
    in climbing on top of her.

When the demon was mounted on top of her,
    The man stood there and watched what he did.

Then, when the demon Pukuj had finished sticking in his cock:
    "Did you see what I did?" asked the demon.
    "I did," said the man.

"Now, do just what I did," said the demon
    "Do it just like I showed you," said the demon.

Well, the man started to do it.
    He proceeded to do just what the demon had done.

When the man had finished doing what the demon had done,
    The demon started to ask him questions.

"How was it? Did it feel good when you did it?" inquired the demon.
    "Not bad! It felt great to do it," the man replied.

"Well, you have to keep on doing it like that until you have children.
    Did you learn well what to do with the woman?" asked the
    demon Pukuj.
    "Absolutely," said the man.

Well, when the demon had finished the lesson, he went away.
    And when the man and the woman were alone, Our Father
    arrived.

"What have you been up to?
    Why are you hiding?" demanded Our Father.

The man and woman were indeed hiding.
    They felt ashamed in front of Our Father.

"Why are you ashamed?" asked Our Father.
 "Its's nothing, only that a stranger came by here.
 He came here earlier to leave us a message," said the man and the woman.

"What did the stranger tell you?" inquired Our Father.
 " 'Are you doing anything?' he asked us when he came by," said the man and the woman.

" 'No, there is nothing that we know how to do,' we said to the man."
 So the man and the woman said to Our Father.

"Oh, but that wasn't a man.
 That was none other than the demon Pukuj who came to torment you," said Our Father.

"He said to us: 'If there is nothing you know how to do, you will not multiply.
 I'd best show you what to do,' he told us," said the man and the woman together.
 "He started to show us what to do.

"'Now, you are to do what I do,' the demon said to me," the man said to Our Father.
 "That is why we did just what the demon showed us," said the man.
 He told this to Our Father in the company of the woman.

"Well, if you learned it that way,
 You can go on doing it until you have children." said Our Father.

"But I tell you, it is only proper to continue having sex if you do not seek another woman.
 You may only do this shameful thing with the woman I first gave you," said Our Father.

"But don't have an affair with another woman.
 If you do have an affair with a married woman, then you will pay dearly for it.

"You might be beaten up.
 You might be cut up with a machete.
 You might be stabbed with a knife.
 You might be stabbed with a dagger.
 You might be shot with a rifle.
 You might be shot with a pistol.
 You might be stoned to death.

"You know that it was the demon who taught you.
 So it is that the demon Pukuj wants you to walk with him forever."
 So it was said to the first man by Our Father long ago.

That is why it remains even now that we should not flirt with women who have husbands.
> Whenever we seek women out, there are bound to be killings.

You can see that long ago it was the demon who first taught us to do evil.
> That is why we kill each other when we have affairs with women who have husbands.

"Well, the same goes for you, woman.
> That which the demon did to you felt good.

"You will see what you have gotten yourself in for," said Our Father.
> "You must understand that you will die an awful death if you seek another lover.

"You will see how hard your husband hits you.
> Or, even worse, you will see that your husband will kill you if you do wrong with another man.

"If you do not heed this warning, you should consider the ways you might meet your death.
> Your might be cut up with a machete.
> Or, if not that, you might choked to death by a rope tied around your neck.
> If not that, you might be shot with a shotgun.
> If not that, you might be shot with a pistol.
> If not that, you might be stabbed with a knife.
> If not that, you might be stabbed with a dagger.
> If not that, you might be cut up with a razor.
> That is how you will meet your death.
> Or, if none of the above, you may thrown on the floor.
> These are the ways that you might die.

"Or it may be that you will die a natural death,
> That you will die of an ordinary sickness.

Such will be your reward if you heed this warning.
> For, with it in mind, you will do no evil.

"Or it may be that you will be murdered;
> If so, it will be your own fault."

So it was said by Our Father to the first people long ago,
> At the time when the first people emerged,
> At the time when the earth began in the most ancient times.

And that is why it has stayed that way into the present time:
> That if a woman seeks a lover, her husband will kill her.
> So, also, if a woman looks too eagerly for *compadres*,
> Her *compadres* may be the cause of her death.[4]

You see, it was the demon himself who accompanied the woman for awhile.
> For the other half of the day, Our Father accompanied her.

When Our Father passes his zenith, the demons begin to accompany women.
> You see, long ago, it was the demon Pukuj who showed them how to do evil.[5]

That is why we fight with one another and kill one another.
> This happens when we find out that our women receive compliments from other men.

If our wives talk with other men,
> Or if they seek other lovers, these women will be murdered.

You see, it is because of the demon Pukuj that we lose our tempers;
> That is why it remains to this day that we should not speak to other women,
> That we should not go around with other women.

That is why, if they see us speak to other women,
> Or if they see us going around with other women,
> It bothers them,
> It makes them jealous.

That is why women ought not to receive compliments.
> They ought not to accept company.

You see, it is because of the demon who goes with them;
> That is why one ought not to give them compliments.

You have seen clearly that it was the demon Pukuj who first made love to a woman long ago.
> That is why we ought not to commit sin with just any woman we meet,
> Why we ought not to commit sin in public.

You see, long ago when the demon first showed them about it,
> The man and woman started to be ashamed.

When they committed sin in the company of the demon Pukuj,
> That was when the man learned how to do it.

But the man and woman started to feel shamed when Our Father approached them.
> The man and the woman felt they ought not to come out.

They were both ashamed.
> They were so ashamed that they felt they ought not to go out from the shadows.

Had they done so, they would have felt even greater shame.

"But what shall we do? Do you know?
    Let's cover ourselves as best we can," said the man and the woman to each other.

"But even though we are naked and have sex in private,
    We still can't go around naked in public," said the man.
    So the man and the woman spoke to each other.

"We'd better look for leaves to cover ourselves with," he said to his wife.
    So they started to clothe themselves with leaves.

So it was that they started to cover their genitals with leaves.
    When they had covered their nakedness with leaves,
    It was then that the man and the woman went out to take a walk.

"But my children, my offspring, can't go about like that.
    They're stark naked!" exclaimed Our Holy Mother.
    (See Figure 7.)

Figure 7. First-Creation Utopia
(Drawing by Marián López Calixto)

"This just won't do. Now the weight of work has come to my successor," said Our Mother Moon.[6]
　　"I had best instruct her so she can start to make clothing," said Our Holy Mother.

Then Our Holy Mother started to teach her how to do it.
　　She started the lesson by bringing cotton.

"You had better concentrate on your work.
　　You will be working with cotton. With it, you will clothe yourself and your husband," said Our Holy Mother.[7]

"When you start your work, you begin by fluffing it.
　　You must sort out the seeds from the cotton.

"When you have finished fluffing it,
　　Then you start to card it."

"When you have finished carding it,
　　Then you start to spin it.
　　Then you wind it up."
(See Figure 8.)

"When you have finished winding it up,
　　Then you place it on the warping frame.

"When you have finished placing it on the warping frame,
　　Then you set it with atole.[8]

"When you have finished setting it with atole,
　　Then you stretch it on the sticks of the loom.[9]

"When you have finished stretching it on the sticks of the loom,
　　Then you wait until it dries.

"When it has dried on the loom,
　　Then you start to separate the strands from one another.[10]

"When you have finished separating the strands from one another,
　　Then you start to weave.

"When you have finished weaving the piece of cloth,
　　Then you have to shrink it and felt it.

"When you have finished shrinking and felting it,
　　Then you stretch it out to dry.

"When it is dry,
　　Then you start to make clothing with it.

Figure 8. The First People Receive Instruction in Domestic Tasks
(Drawing by Marián López Calixto)

"That is the task which you will carry with you.
　　You have no other duties.[11]

"You must do this every day.
　　It will be your work every day until you have clothed my children.

"Well, so be it. Take care of your tools.
　　You are to work with them.

"Take care of your spinning bobbin,
　　Take care of your loom,
　　Take care of your warping frame.
　　You are to work with them."

So said Our Holy Mother when she explained her tasks to the first woman long ago.
　　That was when the earth was created in the most distant antiquity.

72　That is what Our Holy Mother told her.
　　That is why it has remained like that until today,

That we have clothing.
That is why we no longer walk about naked.
That is why we feel shame when we have no clothes on.
That is why women keep on learning this kind of work even today.

You see, Our Holy Mother taught it that way,
  Back when the first people came forth,
  Back when people first began to fill the earth in the most distant
  antiquity.

At the time when people first began to multiply,
  Jaguars started to be born,
  Coyotes started to be born.

Animals started to be born.
  All the animals there are on the earth started to be born.

The jaguar was the first. Next came the coyote,
  Then came the lion and the bear.

The jaguar was first to come out.
  You see, that is how he came the be the animal-soul companion
  of half of the people.
  The other half had the coyotes as their animal-soul companions.
  This was because the large animals came first.[12]

You see, the people were occupied in increasing their numbers.
  So it was when the first people emerged.

Later it came to be that jaguars accompanied some of them;
  Coyotes accompanied some;
  Weasels accompanied others.

But those whom the jaguars accompany,
  These are richest.

Those whom the coyotes accompany,
  These are not so rich.

Those whom the weasels accompany,
  These people are poorer.

Those whom the foxes accompany,
  These are the poorest,
  Rather like those of the weasel.

As for the human counterparts of both the fox and the weasel,
  These unlucky ones do not live very long.

There was once a person whose baby chicks had been eaten by some
animal.

The owner of the chicks saw this.
He shot the culprit, a weasel, with a shotgun.

After the weasel died,
    It was only a matter of three days until the owner of the chicks
    died also.
    He had shot his own animal soul, and so died quickly himself.

So also with the fox.
    He who has the fox as a soul companion does not live very long.

This one, the fox, likes to eat chickens.
    When the owner of the chickens sees that the fox is catching his
    baby chickens,
    The fox quickly meets his end at the point of a shotgun.

Then, when the fox dies of shotgun wounds,
    He who has this fox as a soul companion lives for only three days.

The person who has the fox as soul companion may be a man or a
woman.
    So it is, whoever we are, we die just as our soul companions do.

You see, long ago it was Our Father who thought about all of this.
    Our Father long ago gave us dreams about our animal-soul com-
    panions.

That is why it remains the same even today,
    That not all of us have jaguars as animal souls.[13]

There are several kinds of animals that Our Father has given to us as
soul companions.
    For this reason it is often unclear which soul companion Our
    Father has given to us,
    Whether it is a jaguar,
    Whether it is a coyote,
    Whether it is a fox,
    Whether it is a weasel.

These, then, are the kinds of soul companions that Our Father provides.
    That is our heritage, even into our time.
    You see, long ago it was this that occurred to Our Father,
    At the time when he started to make the earth ready for us.

You see, long ago there were no mountains, no forests,
    Only flat land.

There were no rocks,
    Only the earth itself.

On the third day, trees started to grow.
    This was when the seas dried up long ago.[14]

Trees started to grow;
    Grass took root.

This was on the third day of creation.
    It was then that the forest started to be.

The animals went to live there.
    So it happened that the animals have their homes there in the forest.

But the fact was that there had been only land.
    It was just flat land.

The seas had not fully dried up.
    The forests could not grow well.
    The surface of the earth was soft and unstable.

"But how am I going to harden the earth?" wondered Our Father.
    "If I don't do it, my children won't survive," said Our Father.

"It would be better for me to anchor the earth with rock supports."
said Our Father.
    "I shall pull things down.
    Let's see what some landslides will produce," declared Our
    Father.

With this, he caused the earth to quake and tremble.
    So he provoked great landslides.
    And so the earth's surface itself quickly collapsed.

As the earth continued to cave in upon itself,
    Suddenly, stones and caves emerged,
    Suddenly, mountains were born,
    Suddenly, rivers were born.

Springs came forth,
    Sinkholes came forth, places where rivers sink into the earth.
    Small cracks for the door to the house of the demon Pukuj began
    to appear.[15]

Then, as the rocks and caves kept forming,
    Caverns for the homes of the earth lords started to form.[16]

When the rocks and caves had been created,
    They acted as supports for the earth so that the earth would not
    collapse.

That is why there are rocks embedded in the earth itself,
    And also why there are huge caves lacing the earth.

It happened that Our Father thought that there ought to be rocks and caves.
> And the earth has remained that way to this day.

Long ago, the earth was still unstable,
> There were no rocks;
> There were no great caves;
> There were still no mountains.

Then, when the mountains were formed,
> The large animals went to live there.
> Those who would be our animal-soul companions went to live there in the mountains.

So the great caverns came to be the homes of the earth lords.
> So, also, the great caves.

That is why the mountains were created,
> Why the great caverns were created.

All of this is what Our Father decided to do when he started to prepare the First World long ago.
> Back when the earth was created by Our Father, long ago.

So this story ends.

Four

~

LANGUAGE AND INDIANS' PLACE IN CHIAPAS

This essay presents a comprehensive analysis of a single text concerning the origin and political and moral issues surrounding language. Composed by the same gifted narrator whose testimony appears in chapter 3, and dating from the same time period of collection, transcription, and translation, this text and the accompanying commentary have never been published before. This testimony is remarkable in that the narrator lays out not only a native theory of language and ethnicity but also a theory of history. As such, this chapter provides background on the logic of cyclical time reckoning and the politics of ethnicity that underlie many of the other discussions in this book.

Because this chapter concerns language per se, I have chosen to include here the full original Tzotzil text so that readers have the opportunity to observe how I have tried to capture the conventions of Tzotzil narrative style in English translation. The presentation style and my commentary (composed in 1995) reflect my current conviction that complex texts may benefit from somewhat more exegesis than that provided by extensive ethnographic notes alone.

The present essay has as its centerpiece a Tzotzil Maya narrative account of the origins of the linguistic and political inequality between Indians and Ladinos (bearers of Spanish-speaking Mexican national culture). Xun Méndez Tzotzek, a bilingual man from San Juan Chamula, Chiapas, Mexico, wrote this testimony in 1969. My initial translation to Spanish, together with ethnographic notes, was prepared in close consultation with him. I consider this text to be an important document because it records the views of a sensitive Indian observer on the close ties between language, ethnicity, and asymmetrical political power in the Highlands of Chiapas, Mexico. This text provides us with the opportunity to examine, from the Indian point of view, a volatile current topic that is certain to become a hot issue in the state, indeed in the whole nation, in the near future.

I use the word "volatile" advisedly, for the directorate of the Zapatista insurrection movement of 1994—whose constituency is largely Maya Indian peasants—has made numerous demands of the Mexican federal state, none of which has been resolved as of this writing. These demands are not only for political and economic reforms but also for cultural autonomy. This specifically implies development of public educational policy and pedagogical materials that treat Indian languages, culture, and history not as afflictions to be overcome, but rather, as respected features of Mexico's de facto ethnic pluralism.

Mexico has postponed dealing with this challenge for four and a half centuries, and the piecemeal solutions that have been proposed have invariably derived from the wisdom and political interests of the conqueror/tutor/missionary state rather than from the Indian communities themselves. This is not to say that the politics of language and literacy have been absent from the public forum; only that Indian communities have typically been the recipients of these policies, not consultants in their formulation and implementation.

THE COLONIAL LEGACY

Beginning with the creation of New Spain from the ruins of Mesoamerica's pre-Columbian civilizations in the sixteenth century and continuing even as this is written in January 1995, Mexican mestizo and criollo (white European) authorities have been concerned with finding ways to assert to themselves and to persuade the outside world that they preside over a Western polity; this in spite of the fact that native speakers of Indian languages constituted, until approximately 1800, a numerical majority. Even today, twelve milion (about 11 percent) of Mexico's ninety million people speak one of more than fifty distinct Native American languages as their first language. Native American biological, cultural, and linguistic forms have mingled with European and African bodies, ideas and languages to create a modern Mexico that is truly the quintessential mestizo ("mixed") nation of the Americas. Everything from the lexicon of Mexican Spanish (which has hundreds of loan words from Indian languages, particularly Nahuatl), to the food in market stalls, to the faces on the street, expresses the pervasiveness of the mestizo roots of this nation.

While it is impossible to imagine modern Mexico without its Indian past and present, public policy has always treated Indians and Indian languages as problems to be overcome. Early in the contact period, the priests faced the challenge of evangelizing the Indian community and found that they could not do so without learning native languages. If the sixteenth century produced a pragmatic political and religious interest in using native languages as a means of facilitating conversion and subsequent tutelage in Christian doctrine, this interest diminished in the seventeenth and eighteenth centuries. Deposed native political leaders became the local agents of Crown policy. Typically descending from the elite families in the old social order of the Indian communities, these men were taught Spanish and brought into the colonial power structure as intermediaries— political *caciques* ("local bosses"), *sacristanes* ("sacristans"), and *maestros de capilla* ("choir masters")—who gained exemptions from taxation and forced labor by "facilitating" the delivery of labor and tribute from their Indian compatriots to Crown authorities. These local Indian leaders were also expected to encourage their subalterns to follow daily and annual religious observances in compliance with dictates of priests who often visited the villages only a few times a year to perform baptisms, weddings, and memorial masses for the deceased.

This colonial system was, by design, conceived as a caste system (to be Indian literally carried with it, according to ecclesiastical and civil codes, the legal "duty" to bear the burden of *casta*). This policy effectively segregated Indian communities in the countryside from the Spanish criollo and mestizo populations of the town and cities. These two "republics" had separate and unequal tax and legal codes as well as different expectations for religious observance and participation in the sacraments. Until well into the nineteenth century, schooling for other than the local elite leaders was out of the question. When schooling was available, it was, with few exceptions, delivered in Spanish and conceived entirely within the curricular framework approved by the church. With a number of notable exceptions (particularly those documents numbering in the many hundreds dating from the sixteenth century), works written in and about Indian languages were not widely available in Mexico; with the exception of a few scholars and clerics, native languages held little interest for the rank and file of the colonial establishment. Although thousands of religious, legal, and census documents written in Mesoamerican Indian languages, dating from the colonial period, survive today, it is nevertheless true that educated mestizos and criollos held Indian languages and verbal art forms to be inferior human expressions, to be used only as a matter of administrative and evangelical necessity.

To a great extent these colonial social, ethnic, and linguistic attitudes survive remarkably intact in our time. If anything, public policy and local practice in the nineteenth century exacerbated the social and economic asymmetries of Indians in relation to the state. The nineteenth century, with the exception of the period of liberal reforms in the 1850s and 1860s, saw almost no progress in the education of Indians, even in Spanish. The pattern of local rule, discussed above, continued, and with it, the pattern of local elite bilingualism which served the purposes of the state. Social and economic circumstances of the Indian communities deteriorated to conditions that were decidedly worse than those that prevailed during the colonial period. After independence from Spain, the criollo and mestizo elites who had controlled public life under Crown authority were free to exploit Indian land, labor, and production without any encumbrances in the form of church and state responsibility for Indian welfare under what had been called the duties of the Crown as the head of a "missionary state." Indians by the hundreds of thousands were obliged during the nineteenth century to become debt slaves of criollo- and meztizo-owned ranches, plantations, and mining operations. This caused a marked depopulation of demographically isolated Indian communities, for the men in particular often had to spend many months a year working as day laborers far from their home villages. Just as often whole families were forced to migrate to the ranches and plantations where they worked under a system that was, in effect, debt peonage.

Against the backdrop of this massive political and economic exploitation, which reached its peak during the long dictatorial regime of President Porfirio Díaz (1871–1910), Indian languages and literatures and Indian education found themselves where the Indians themselves were—at the very bottom of the heap of national priorities. The state found it convenient to ignore the demographically isolated (and linguistically conservative) Indian communities as long as the flow of cheap labor continued. Most Indian villages had no schools at all, nor much less other social services. These thousands of isolated Indian populations became what Aguirre Beltrán has called *regiones de refugio*, suggesting that they were forced—demographically, culturally, economically, and socially—to the very margins of national life (Aguirre Beltrán 1967).

THE MEXICAN REVOLUTION AND INDIGENISMO

It is well known that the epic Mexican Revolution (1910–17) attempted to address many of the social ills that I have just described. The theme of *pan y libertad* ("bread and liberty" or, more generally, economic, social, and political justice) underlay not only the revolution itself but also the creation of modern Mexico. This is neither the time nor the place to discuss this theme at length. However, it is relevant to the present discussion to observe the irony that has most recently been noted by the Maya Zapatistas themselves; that although the revolution was fought in the name of Mexico's poor and oppressed, both mestizos and Indians, many of the structural inequalities that created economic and social misery for millions of the urban and rural poor in pre-revolutionary Mexico remain in place today. Some observers, ranging from academic historians to Subcomandante Marcos of Maya Zapatista fame, contend that the revolution never even happened in Chiapas. Indeed, with all of Mexico's golden age of agrarian reform in the Cárdenas era (1930s), its incredible artistic and literary florescence throughout the post-revolutionary period, and its post–World War II economic prosperity, crowned most recently by the boom years of the 1980s and the passage of the North American Free Trade Agreement (NAFTA) in 1993, it remains the case that the poorest state in Mexico is Chiapas, and it is the rural poor, including hundreds of thousands of Maya-speaking Indians, who are at the bottom of the heap. Mr. Méndez Tzotzek, whose account follows below, speaks to us from this social and economic space.

It would be mean-spirited, indeed historically irresponsible, not to recognize that Mexico has implemented literally hundreds of policies and programs in the post-revolutionary period that have focused on the improvement of the economic and social circumstances of the nation's rural and urban poor. Indian communities themselves have been targeted for special attention in this regard. Indeed, a whole body of policy legislation and related health, educational, and economic programs—known as *indigenismo*—has evolved since the 1920s with the specific goal of bringing the thousands of Indian communities into the cultural and economic space of modern Mexico. Many *indigenista* programs have been enormously successful. For example, the *municipio* of San Juan Chamula, the source of the text below, did not have a single public school or clinic in 1910. It now has dozens of one- and two-room rural grammar schools, plus an upper school and a clinic in the town center.

However, as I noted at the beginning of this essay, Spanish language, Mexican ethnicity, and social place are still so indelibly linked within national culture that virtually all programs aimed at social and economic "progress" for Indians follow the state-initiated pattern of colonial and nineteenth-century public policy thinking. Indianness and Indian languages are viewed by public policy makers as problems to be overcome (and sometimes as "background noise" to be ignored), not as integral parts of the nation's historical and present identity. In particular, throughout the twentieth century, Indian education has been conceived and delivered with an eye to remedial intervention. The initial goal is always *castellanización*, that is, to teach literacy in Spanish together with the standard curriculum of Mexican schools so as to liberate Indians from the social and economic disadvantages that are thought (by Mexicans) to be linked to their Indianness. Invariably, Indian language syllabaries and reading materials are abandoned once a child is able to understand, read, and learn in Spanish. Briefly stated, the state retains today many of the same tutorial functions that the church exercised in the colonial period. There is but one route to social and economic adaptation, and the structurally dominant Spanish-speaking state defines this. Indians can take it or leave it. The subtext has not changed much since the sixteenth century: Indianness is a social, linguistic, and spiritual condition that should be corrected. (See Lomnitz-Adler 1992: 261–281 and Modiano 1973.)

CHIAPAS IN MEXICO

Along with Oaxaca and Yucatán, Chiapas is among the states of Mexico that have the largest and most conservative Indian populations. Perhaps half of the *municipios* in Chiapas are made up of 50 to one 100 percent monolingual or bilingual speakers of native languages, most of them of the Maya family of languages. Among the most important of these languages are Tzotzil, Tzeltal, and Tojolobal. Until the mid-nineteenth century, most of the Indian population of Chiapas lived in the demographically isolated communities that I have described above. In large part by colonial design, Indian *municipios* evolved as unique cultural isolates; each one had its characteristic dialect of an Indian language, colorful traditional clothing, a particular variant of a civil-religious hierarchy of ritual officials, and a particular cycle of public ritual observances in honor of the saints. This pattern survives today in many of the *municipios* of the Central Highlands. This vibrant ethnic mosaic also, ironically, attracts the national and international tourist trade. Indian traditionalism is thus not only a source of cheap labor and produce; it is also a marketable commodity from which the Ladino community reaps considerable economic benefit.

However, beginning in the nineteenth century, for reasons that have been discussed above, thousands of Indians emigrated from these closed communities to several sparsely populated regions of the state in search of employment on cattle ranches, coffee plantations, and other commercial agriculture operations. (See chapter 7.) These areas of recent immigration lie to the northeast and east of the Highlands (the valley of Simojovel and the Lacandon jungle), and to the southwest (the Grijalva River Valley and the Pacific coastal strip and foothills). This out-migration pattern has continued unabated in the twentieth century, and the reasons for it have been not only the desperate quest for land and economic opportunity but also political and religious exile from people's communities of origin. The most recent wave of this exodus has been the result of missionary activity. Protestant evangelical activity began in the 1950s and lay Catholic mission activity (post–Vatican II) began in the 1960s. Even more recently, in the 1970s and 1980s, the more radical Roman Catholic Liberation Theology movement has been active in these areas of recent immigration. Initially, at least, all of this missionary activity proceeded with the blessing of the Mexican state, for, it was argued (and still is), mission activity shares many of the tutorial goals of state *indigenista* policy. Missionaries, like Mexican state officials, believe that planned change—e.g., literacy programs, access to modern health care, improved farming techniques—will benefit Indian communities in ways that their traditional lifestyles and customs cannot accomplish. All of these various mission initiatives tend to hold a highly negative opinion of what they regard as the spiritual and political tyranny of traditional Indian lifestyles and community organization. Although the nuances differ from one mission group to the next, the critical theme is similar. They agree that economic and social "progress" are incompatible with traditional Indian customs. Thus, the missionary critique of traditional Indian customs has often gone hand in hand with support for modernization and closer interaction with the Mexican state and its social and economic institutions. This has generally been the Protestant and Catholic Action message. Sometimes (as with Liberation Theology), the focus of the critique is the blatant collusion of traditional Indian *caciques* with the Mexican state, a pattern of cooperation that enriches the *caciques* at the expense of their own Indian subalterns. Sometimes (as with the Protestants), the reasons offered for conversion center on the paganism and evil of Indian religious practices; they also note that taxes levied for the celebration of village festivals drain limited financial resources that would be better invested in improved nutrition and health care for one's own family. They are also adamant about the evils of alcohol, its excessive cost, and its relation to domestic violence. Thus, there is the promise of economic progress and personal "betterment" if one abandons core elements of Indian traditional life.

These missionary groups also agree generally on the importance of education and literacy. Protestants have been successful in encouraging literacy in both Spanish and Indian languages (and in providing Bible translations and other religious tracts to read). They all agree, also, on the de facto importance of Spanish as the lingua franca of the nation.

All of these forces for social change have had a particularly strong impact on the areas of recent immigration, beyond the Central Highlands. As for the highland Indian communities themselves, many have reacted violently to these challenges to their local autonomy and related political authority. Many of these traditional *municipios*, most notably San Juan Chamula, have reacted by purging Protestant converts from their communities at gunpoint, stripping them of their land and property and quite literally sending them into exile. This has led to decades of conflict and litigation, and also to the massive out-migration of Protestant converts to new communities in both urban and rural regions of the state.

In summary, Chiapas today is a region of great social unrest, demographic displacement, and political flux. The 1994 Zapatista movement expresses the desperate circumstances that thousands of Chiapas Indians perceive to be their lot. By virtually all measures of social statistics, Chiapas is a Third-World enclave in a nation that aspires to First-World status. The gap between the rich and the poor is enormous, and this pattern is exacerbated by the ethnic and linguistic diversity of state. Any solution to the social and economic problems will undoubtedly have to come to grips with politics of language, literacy, and ethnicity, for the Zapatistas have made it clear that they are *both* Mexicans *and* native peoples with rights to their own ethnic and linguistic heritage. Social and economic progress cannot come, as state officials might wish, at the cost of Indian identity.

LANGUAGE AND ETHNIC IDENTITY

The number of speakers of Indian languages in Chiapas is growing with each new census. As noted above, massive change has come to the region, but outright acculturation (or Ladinoization) to Mexican national culture is apparently not the strategy of choice for many hundreds of thousands of speakers of Indian languages who live in the state. While bilingualism is undoubtedly on the rise (particularly so in the areas of new immigration, where there *is* no common language other than Spanish), it is also the case that Indians value their linguistic heritage, for tradition has taught them that their very being as humans, and their identity as individuals and members of social groups, reside in their language. Indeed, language is the most fundamental marker of Indian identity. It typically continues as the defining attribute of Indianness even when people abandon their traditional dress and traditional customs. This pattern of linguistic conservatism characterizes hundreds of Maya Protestant congregations in the state; their songs, religious services, community, and home activities are conducted in Maya languages. All Maya-speaking people in Chiapas refer to their particular dialect of their language as "the true or real language." It is ironic to note, in contrast, that Ladinos in Chiapas do not typically even recognize Indian languages as languages; they call them *dialectos* ("dialects"). Indians are well aware of the condescension implied in this designation, for it constitutes but one more gesture of Ladino contempt for Indians and Indian identity. The barriers of *casta* are obviously still in place. Because an understanding of a problem from the point of view of all parties involved often precedes the formulation of possible solutions, it makes sense to take seriously just what Indians think about the history and nature of language and its related verbal art forms.

Language is not, for the Indian community, an easily negotiable or expendable part of their collective and individual being. Chamula Tzotzil sacred narratives pay a great deal of attention to the key role of language (*k'op*) in the evolution of the human condition over the four cyclical creations and restorations that make up the history of the earth and its life forms. Mayas (indeed, most Mesoamerican Indian communities) link language and dialogue to the dawn of consciousness in their creation narratives. In time present, as in time past, language, with its wide range of rhetorical, poetic, and musical embellishments, has served as a sacred symbol which allows humans to share qualities with, and communicate with, gods. In effect, beautifully executed speech and song are the only substances that the human body can produce that are accessible to and worthy before divine beings. Ritual speech, prayer, song, and sacred narrative performance share with other sacramental substances—such as liquor, incense, tobacco, fireworks, aromatic leaves, and flowers—the quality of metaphorical heat. They all produce "felt" intensity of message (i.e., heat) that is essence, not substance. All of these sacraments share the quality of transcending substance through heat, smell, sound, smoke, and feeling (as in drunkenness), which are media which Our Lord Sun/Christ and other deities both understand and consume; it is, quite literally, their only "food." In the case of language, it is said to be the "heat of the heart" of the performer (which invariably expresses itself in the intensified messages of couplets and other forms of stylistic redundancy) that makes it reasonable to classify ritual language, song, prayer, and sacred narrative as sacraments. (See Gossen 1976.)

Thus, language matters a great deal to the Tzotzils. Its mastery qualified protohumans for true humanity in the time of the ancestors. In its embellished forms, it serves as food for the sustenance of deities. In the individual life cycle, minimal mastery of its complex art forms constitutes basic competence as an adult. Political and religious officials and shamans must master it with even greater aplomb in order to be credible as community leaders. It therefore makes sense to Tzotzils to cultivate language and to take it seriously.

XUN MÉNDEZ TZOTZEK'S NARRATIVE

The following text refers to events in the Third Creation. This is what might be called the "heroic period," in Chamula historical reckoning. Prior to this period (in the First and Second Creations), the creator sun god (Our Lord Sun/Christ in Heaven) had created humankind a number of times from clay or mud, sometimes sticks. Although different narrators disagree on particulars of what happened to these earlier experiments with humankind in the First and Second Creations, all agree that learning to eat corn and learning to speak, sing, pray, and dance were diagnostic of the dawn of human consciousness. It is also remembered in the oral tradition that the failure of early beings to learn these things caused Our Lord Sun/Christ great frustration in his creative labors, so much so that he destroyed his trial beings because they could not do these things adequately.

It is also true of all the narratives that abuse of the gift of food (for example, the use of their own babies as meat filling for corn tamales) and speech (as in the narrative that follows below) caused Our Lord Sun/Christ to take radical action in changing the course of human history. In the case of the baby tamales, Our Lord Sun/Christ caught them in the act of pitching their live babies into a kettle of boiling water and immediately changed them into monkeys, condemning them to live forever without maize, to subsist on fruits and seeds of the forest. (See chapter 5.) In the case of the abuse of language, as documented below, people sought, through the construction of a great cement stairway (a labor that was facilitated by having Spanish as a common language), to be too close to Our Lord Sun/Christ, even presuming to reach his domain on the third and highest layer of the heavens. In this narrative, which is of course reminiscent of the biblical Tower of Babel story, Our Lord Sun/Christ could not abide the presumption to power and knowledge that derived from people's having a universal language. (Might this historical memory lie behind the so-called linguistic conservatism of the Chiapas Maya? Might it also lie behind their reluctance to commit themselves, once again, to a common language, Spanish, that caused such difficulty for their ancestors in the past?)

The text that follows belongs to a speech genre known in Tzotzil as True

Ancient Narrative (*batz'i antivo k'op*). This is a type of sacred narrative that is regarded as a true account of premodern times; that is, it reports events that are attributed to the First, Second, and Third Creations in their cyclical reckoning of human history. The "truth status" of events reported in this story is comparable to that of the historical present (the Fourth Creation), which is reported in accounts known as True Recent Narrative (*batz'i ?ach' k'op*). Thus, the text that follows has the truth and reality status of events which happened yesterday. Tzotzils carefully discriminate in their native taxonomy of speech genres between invented stories (*jut k'op*, "lies" and *?ixtol k'op*, "jokes") and true stories. The following is thus, by Tzotzil reckoning, a true story.

Although I intend to discuss the text at some length after it is presented, three final introductory comments are appropriate. The first has to do with the style of the translation. It is rendered in verse couplets and multiples thereof. This translation style and its rationale are described at length elsewhere (Gossen 1985). Here it suffices to say that Tzotzil oral performance is keyed to dyadic structures of speech. This is explicitly manifest in the hundreds of fixed formal couplets that are used in the composition of ritual language, prayer, and song. The semantic couplet is also, perhaps by extension, the stylistic "center of gravity" that is used in the composition and performance of important historical narratives. This dyadic style, which is noted by the numbered verses in the following text, is characterized by semantic redundancy, which is marked linguistically in spoken Tzotzil by verbal "punctuation marks," known as enclitics. The couplet style, therefore, is central to how Tzotzils tell stories. What is missing, of course, is that at each pause (that is at the end of each verse) we, the listeners, would be invited to participate in the storytelling with exclamations like "Is that so?", "No way," "Really?", "Can it be so?", "I don't believe it!", or "Far out!" The reader must imagine these embellishments as s/he reads the following text.

The reader may also be interested in knowing something about the narrator. When I first heard Mr. Méndez Tzotzek's recitation of this narrative in 1969, I lost no time in realizing that it was important, both to him—for it revealed in poignant detail parts of how he viewed his life and circumstances as a landless, poor Tzotzil—and to me—for it provided a local history of language and of the close ties of language to the politics of ethnic subordination of Indians to the dominant Ladino, Spanish-speaking social order. Xun Méndez Tzotzek was in an excellent position to comment on these parts of his community's historical memory, for life had not treated him well. Like so many Chamula Tzotzils, he was born into a densely populated, land-poor rural hamlet where he had no hope of ever making it as a subsistence farmer, although this was the ideal. Therefore, until the time he was thirty-five years old—in 1969, when this narrative was written by him—he had spent most of his adult life as a migrant day-laborer on the coffee plantations and large-scale corn-farming operations of the Pacific lowlands. Although he was able to support his family minimally with this income, he never accumulated sufficient savings to allow him to assume a position in the civil-religious hierarchy of the town center. This disappointment notwithstanding, he nevertheless sought local prestige and modest income through the practice of traditional curing. His career as a shaman failed when he became an alcoholic and could not manage to get through the long prayer recitations that were involved in curing rituals. He had enjoyed a brief interlude of economic success in the late 1950s and early 1960s, when he worked as a paid assistant for U. S. anthropologists. It was in this context that he learned to write Tzotzil. However, alcoholism also compromised this employment, and he resumed his usual pattern of migrant labor to the coffee plantations, which he had begun as a young man.

Méndez Tzotzek worked with me as an assistant for many months in 1968 and 1969, and during this time I came to respect him a great deal for his keen and poetic intelligence. He was particularly patient and adept at explaining during our translation sessions what was obvious to him but not explicitly stated in his written texts. These discussions are the source of most of the ethnographic notes that appear at the end of this essay.

The narrator, therefore, is typical of most Tzotzil males of his generation in his inability to cope economically at home and in his inevitable decision to enter the migrant labor market. In this context, like virtually all of his compatriots who were obliged to do the same thing, he experienced first-hand the exploitation and humiliation of being an unskilled Indian day laborer in Ladino-controlled economic and institutional settings. The bitterness of these memories, together with his carefully considered rationalization and understanding of his experiences with the Ladino world, are clearly evident in what follows.

A third proviso is offered as I present this text. It reads like a Tzotzil rendering of Genesis 11: 1-9, which tells the story of the Tower of Babel. Is it a Maya account at all? It is, and it isn't, as I shall discuss below. However, there can be little doubt that the Dominican missionaries must have told their version of this story to the Tzotzils and told it well. Babel was the Hebrew rendering of Babylon, and it is well known that this city represented everything that was reprehensible to the Israelites. The Tower of Babel represented the ultimate pretense to temporal and secular power on the part of the Babylonians. They had to be foiled. And God did this, according to the Bible, with his mandate for the confusion of tongues. However, the Tzotzil rendering of this story casts the Spaniards and their language, quite unambiguously, as the Babylonians of the New World. What hath God wrought? Listen to this story.

THE GREAT CEMENT STAIRWAY TO HEAVEN

1. Here is an account of long ago about Ladinos,
   Of where they came from.

2. Long ago there were only Ladinos and Our Father.
   It happened that Our Father Sun/Christ first gave
   souls to the Ladinos.
   It happened shortly after he had first molded them
   from clay.

3. When he had formed the first person,[1]
   Only then did he begin to make the second person.

1. ʔoy jun loʔil yuʔun kaxlanetik to voʔne,
   bu talik.

2. veno, ti voʔne lae ʔaʔ li jkaxlanetik ti jtotike.
   jaʔ la baʔyel la jyak'be xch'ulel li jkaxlanetik ti jtotike.
   jaʔ la baʔyel las spat ti ʔach'el.

3. k'alal la ti la spat ti baʔyel vinike,
   jaʔ to la lik spat ti jun tz'akal vinike.

4. After Our Father Sun had formed them from clay,
   The clay came out looking just like little dolls.
   It was then that he began to give to the clay
   images their souls.

5. This happened at the time when we were being
   placed on the earth.
   It was then that Our Lord Sun/Christ molded the
   clay.
   The first of these images to whom he gave a soul
   was the first whom he had made.

6. He began by rubbing and rubbing the molded
   image, over and over.
   In this manner, he proceeded to place a soul in the
   first person.[2]

4. k'alal la ti lah spat ʔach'el ti jtotike,
   k'alal la ti lah xlok' ta chak k'uchaʔal santo ti ʔach'ele,
   jaʔto la lik yak'be xch'ulel ti ʔach'el.

5. k'alal la ti meltzajtik ta banomil,

ti ʔach'el spatoj ti jtotike.
jaʔla baʔyel laj yak'be xch'ulel ti bu baʔyel la spate.
6. *lik la sjuch' ta ʔox juch'tael,*
    ti k'alal la lik yak'be ti xch'ulel ti baʔyel vinike.

ᗑ ᗏ

7. When he had placed a soul in the first person,
    It was then that he began to place a soul in the
    second person, the second one he had formed
    from clay.
    Just as this image was the second one in Our
    Father Sun's order of creation, so it was the second
    to receive a soul.

8. When Our Father Sun had finished giving these beings
    their souls,
    That which had formerly been only clay began to
    change into people.
    These were the ones whom Our Father Sun had
    first wrought from clay.

ᗑ ᗏ

7. *k'alal la ti laj yak'be xch'ulel ti jun baʔyel vinike,*
    jaʔto la lik yak'be xch'ulel ti ju tz'akal vinike, ti tz'akal spat
    ti ʔach'ele.
    haʔla tz'akal laj yak'be xch'ulel ti tz'akal vinike.

8. *k'alal la ti laj yak'be sch'ulel ti jtotike,*
    lik la pasuk ta viniketik ti ʔach'el toʔox.
    lik spat ti jtotike.

ᗑ ᗏ

9. When the two images began to become human,
    They walked alike.
    They worked alike.
    They talked alike.

10. Indeed, both people spoke only Spanish.
    Long ago, Spanish was still the only language.
    Tzotzil, the true language, did not yet exist.[3]

ᗑ ᗏ

9. *k'alal la lik pasuk ta kirsano ti chaʔ voʔ viniketike,*
    koʔol la ta xanavik,
    koʔol la xʔabtejik,
    koʔol ta xk'opojik.

10. *ta puru kastiya ti chaʔ voʔ viniketik*
    ti voʔne lae jmoj toʔox la ti k'op ta puru kastiyae.
    muʔyuk toʔox la ti batz'i k'ope.

11. The people began to multiply.
    As they multiplied, they talked alike, in just one language, Spanish.

12. Since they had but one common language, the people talked among themselves and got ideas.
    "Perhaps we should go to find Our Father Sun up above?" they wondered.

13. "But how shall we climb up?
    Any ideas?" they asked.

11. lik la boluk ti kirsanoe.
    k'alal la bol ti kirsanoe, jmoj la ta xk'opojik, ta puru kastiya.

12. k'alal la ti jmoh ta xk'opojike, lik la snop sk'opik.
    "mi xak'anike ba jtatik la jtotik ta ʔak'ole," xiik la.

13. "pero k'usi xkutik chijmuy.
    xanaʔ ʔun," xiik la.

14. "Come, it would be best to make a stairway.
    We can climb up and find Our Father Sun and talk to him," said the people.

15. "But how shall we build a stairway?" they asked.
    "It would be best to build a great stairway of cement," said the people.
    So they began to build the cement stairway.

14. "jaʔ lek laʔ jpastik tek'obal.
    yoʔ chijmuy ʔo jtatik ta k'oponel ti jtotike," xiik la ti kirsa-noetike.

15. "pero k'usi xkutik xanaʔ xkak'tik ti tek'obale," xiik la.
    "jaʔ lek jpastik muyel tek'obal siminto pilal," xiik la ti kirsa-noetike.
    lik la spasik ti tek'obal simintoe.

16. As they began to make the great cement stairway,
    Some prepared the mortar,
    Some gathered the stones,
    Some put the stones in place, layer by layer.

17. The great cement stairway was still not finished when
they ran out of stones.
"Bring more stones!
Bring more mortar!

　　　🖙　🖙

16. *k'alal la ti ʔocik ta spasel ti tek'okal pilal simintoe,*
　　　yan la ta sjuy meskla,
　　　yan la ta saʔ talel ton,
　　　yan la ta slatz muyel ti tone.

17. *xkechel toʔox la ta meltzanel muyel ti tek'obal pilal simintoe, k'alal*
la ta xlaj ti tone.
　　　"tzako me tal ton.
　　　tzako me tal meskla.

　　　🖙　🖙

18. The stones are all gone!
Bring some more!

19. The mortar is all gone!
Make some more!" they said.

20. "Come build it up!
The mortar is all gone!
Come build it up!" they said to each other with
full understanding,
For the language that they spoke was the same.[4]

　　　🖙　🖙

18. *"laj me ton.*
　　　saʔo xa me tal.

19. *"laj me meskla.*
　　　juyo xa me talel," xiik la.

20. *"ʔak'o xa me muyel talel.*
　　　lah xa me meskla.
　　　ʔak'o xa me muyel talel," xiik la,
　　　jmoj la ti sk'opik ta xk'opohike.

　　　🖙　🖙

21. The stairway they were building quickly grew upward.
Different people came every day to help build the
great cement stairway.

22. They all spoke the same language.
They understood the same tongue.

23. "Well, it simply won't do for them to speak the same

language."
So said Our Father Sun when he started to think about it.

✎   ✎

21. ti tek'obal la ta spasike jlikel la muy yuʔunik.
yantik xa la xmuy yuʔunik jujun k'ak'al ta pasel ti tek'obal pilal simintoe.

22. jaʔ la ti jmoj ti sk'opike.
jmoj la xaʔik ti k'ope.

23. "veno, pero leʔ ʔune mu xtun ma li jmoj sk'opik ʔune."
xa la lik snop ti jtotike.

✎   ✎

24. "Just look! They've almost reached me!" exclaimed Our Father Sun.
"No, it won't do for them to talk alike."
So said Our Father Sun when he started to think about it.

25. "It would be better for me to change their languages.
"We'll see if they understand one another when they talk now.
"We'll see if they understand one another when talking among themselves about what they are doing," said Our Father Sun.

✎   ✎

24. "k'elavil ʔun, sk'an xa xistaik ʔun," xi la ti jtotike.
"moʔohe, mu xtun li jmoj ta xk'opojike."
xi la lik snop ti jtotike.

25. "jaʔ lek ta jelbe ma sk'opike.
ta jk'eltik mi xaʔik ta sk'opon sbaik tana un.
ta jk'eltik mi xaʔik k'alal k'usi ta xʔalbe sbaike k'usi ta spasike," xi la ti jtotike.

✎   ✎

26. When Our Father Sun changed the languages, the people were right in the middle of their work,
Right when they were in the midst of building the great cement stairway.

27. When their language changed, they could no longer understand what they were saying to one another.
As they worked, they no longer understood what their companions were asking for.

✎   ✎

26. *k'alal la shel ta k'op ti jtotite, syakelik la ta abtel,*
      ti k'alal la ti syakelik ta spasik ti tek'obal pilal simintoe.

27. *k'alal la hel ti k'ope, mu xa la xaʔik k'usi la ta xʔalbe la sbaik.*
      ti k'alal la ta xʔabtejike, mu xa la xaʔik ti k'usi ta sk'anbe
      sbaik.

ᐟᑏᐣ ᐸᑎᐟ

28. Just as they were in the midst of building the great
      stairway, they abandoned it, half-finished.
      This happened because they no longer understood
      what they were saying to each other.
      This happened because Our Father worked great
      changes in language itself.

29. It happened that he started to oblige us to speak
      nothing but Tzotzil, the true language,
      Those of us who are Indians.

30. It is for that reason that we only speak Tzotzil, the
      true language,
      Those of us who are Indians.

ᐟᑏᐣ ᐸᑎᐟ

28. *ti k'alal la ta smeltzanik ti pilal tek'obale, te la kechi yuʔunik*
      smeltzanel.
      jaʔ la ti mu xa la xaʔik ti k'usi la ta xʔalbe sbaike.
      jaʔ la ti lah sjel ʔep k'op ti jtotike.

29. *jaʔ la ti lik yak' puru batz'i k'op chijk'opojtik,*
      ti k'uyepaltik ʔinyotike.

30. *jaʔ yuʔun la ti ta puru batzi'i k'op chijk'opohotik,*
      ti k'uyepal ʔinyotik lae.

ᐟᑏᐣ ᐸᑎᐟ

31. You see, it happened their souls entered their bodies
      second in the order of creation,
      The bodies of those ancient ones, our forefathers.[5]

32. Those of us who were the children of the second
      person were separated from the others.
      We were left with the name of "Indians."

ᐟᑏᐣ ᐸᑎᐟ

31. *xavil la jaʔ la tz'akal ʔoch xch'ulel,*
      baʔyel totik kuʔuntik la ti voʔnee.

32. *ja? yu?un la kich'tik ch'akel ti k'u la yepal snich'nab ti tz'akal vinike.*
    ha? la kom ta ?inyo sbi.
          ⤜ ⤛

33. It was different with the first person.
    It was this one who was the first to receive a soul.
    It was this one who was left with the name of Ladino.[6]
    It was this one who received the first language.

34. Everyone still spoke just Spanish in ancient times.
    That is why it happened that Ladinos are also called "Spaniards."
          ⤜ ⤛

33. *yan la ti ba?yel.*
    ?och xch'ulel ti ba?yel vinike.
    ja? la kom ta kaxlan.
    ja? la yich' komel ti ba?yel k'op.

34. *ti puru kastiya to?ox la ti xk'opojik ti vo?nee.*
    ja? yu?un la ti ja? la kom ta j?espanyol sbi li kaxlanetike.
          ⤜ ⤛

35. They speak only Castilian.
    That is why we are obliged to learn Spanish.[7]

36. You see, it was the first language that Our Father Sun assigned to the ancestors long ago.
    It is for this reason that there is but one common language, Spanish.
    All are thus obliged to learn Spanish.

37. You see, the Ladinos speak only Spanish
    That was because Our Father Sun first gave souls to the Ladinos.
          ⤜ ⤛

35. *ja? ti ja?ta xk'opohik ta puru kastiya.*
    ja? yu?un la ti ja? la ta persa ta jchantik li kastiyae.

36. *xavil la ti vo?ne ja? la ba?yel k'op la jyak' komel ti jtotik vo?nee.*
    ja? yu?un ja? no?ox la jun k'op, kastiya.
    ta persa ta x?ich' chanel li kastiyae.

37. *xavil la li jkaxlanetike ja? la puru kastiya ta xk'opojik.*
    ja? ti ja? ba?yel la jyak'be xch'ulel ti jkaxlan ti jtotike.
          ⤜ ⤛

38. When Our Father Sun changed the languages, people began to split up.
    They scattered;
    Some went to the lowlands,
    Others, like ourselves, scattered here and there in the highlands.
39. Those who went off together were those who had the same language.
    The different groups were divided according to those who had the same language.
    >━ ━<

38. k'alal la ti jel ti k'ope, lik la xch'ak sbaik ti kirsanoetike.
     tanijik la;
     yan la ʔolon,
     yan la ʔak'ol la jbatikuk.

39. jaʔ la jmoj la xch'ak sbaik ti bu koʔol ti sk'opike.
     slekoj la xch'ak sbaik ti bu koʔol ti sk'opike.
     >━ ━<

40. So it is true that different groups do not understand each other's languages.
    That is why we remain separate, very separate, those of us who still speak Tzotzil, the true language, today.

41. In all lands there are those of us who speak our native languages,
    All over the earth.

42. It is different with the Ladinos; they all speak but one language.
    They speak Spanish.
    >━ ━<

40. jaʔ la ti mu la xaʔibe sba sk'opike.
     jaʔ yuʔun la tana ti slekoj ti batz'i k'optik komem hasta ʔora.

41. ta jujun lum ti ʔoy jbatz'i k'optik,
     ta skotol banomile.

42. k'ajomal jkaxlanetik jun noʔox k'op.
     ta xk'opojik ta kastiya.
     >━ ━<

43. As for those who are Indians, they speak only their native languages.
    This is true of all native peoples.

44. So then, when the people split up long ago,
   The different groups of people went separately to
   find land to build their houses.
   So it was that the Ladinos went separately to look
   for land where they could settle.

>᠁ ᠁<

43. k'u yepal puru ʔindijena ta puru batz'i k'op to sk'opojik.
   skotol ʔindijena.

44. veno, k'alal la ti la sch'ak sbaik ti kirsonoetik to voʔne lae,
   bat la saʔ yosilik bu la xuʔ spas naik to hchop la ti kirsanoe.
   jech la ti jkaslanetike slekoj la bat sa yosilik bu xuʔ snakik.

>᠁ ᠁<

45. So it was that they found their homelands.
   There they began to build their houses.
   There they multiplied.

46. When they had multiplied, it seems to me that the
   Ladinos began to reflect upon who they were and
   what they should do.
   Indeed, the correct name of those whom we call
   "Ladinos" ought to be "Spaniards."

47. Now, then, soon thereafter, the Spaniards began to
   harass the native people.
   They began to oblige them to do forced labor.

>᠁ ᠁<

45. veno, sta la ti yosilike.
   te la lik spas naik.
   te la bolik.

46. k'alal la ti bolike, lik la snopik ti jkaxlanetik, xkaltike.
   pero li sbi la ta kastiya jʔespanyol la sbi.

47. veno, ti jʔespanyole lik la yutilan ti kirsano ʔindijenae.
   lik la tzakik ta ʔabtel.

>᠁ ᠁<

48. When the Indians worked, they were not given rest
   periods when they grew tired.
   Although they were thirsty, they did not permit
   them to drink water.

49. Only when their work time was over could they rest
   from their labor.

And if they chanced to fall asleep during their assigned work time, they were sure to receive a sound beating.
This was their fate if the Indian workers should fall asleep.

>rr⌒ ⌒rr<

48. k'alal la ti ta xʔabtej ti ʔinyoe, mu la xʔak'bat xkux k'alal xlube.
ʔak'o la chak' yuch' yaʔi ʔoʔ mu la xʔak' yuch? ti ʔoʔe.

49. jaʔ to la mi sta ti ʔorae, jaʔ to la ta xkux ta ʔabtel.
pero k'alal ta ti ta xʔabteje, mi vayi la jlikeluk
ta ʔabtel lek la jun majel ta xʔich'.
k'alal mi vayi la ta ʔabtel ti ʔinyo vinike.

>rr⌒ ⌒rr<

50. **This was what happened to them in the daily round of their labor.**
The Spaniards watched over them and tormented them a lot while they were working.

51. **Their hateful ways carried over into the manner in which they feigned to "baptize" people.**
They didn't really baptize them in the churches.
There *were* no churches.

52. **Instead, what really happened was that they did nothing more than brand them, just like horses.**
That was how the Spaniards of long ago humiliated and mistreated the Indians. (See Figure 9.)

>rr⌒ ⌒rr<

50. jech la jujun k'ak'al la spasbat.
ti ʔilbaj ta xʔutilan la tajmek ti k'alal la ta xʔabteje.

51. jech la xtok k'alal la ta xʔich'ik ʔoʔe.
muʔyuk la bu ta xʔich'ik ʔoʔ ta ch'ulna.
ch'abal la ch'ulna.

52. k'ajomal la ta xʔak'bat smarkail chak k'uchaʔal kaʔ.
ʔilbaj toʔox la yutilan ti ʔindijenaetik ti ʔespanyoletik ti voʔne lae.

>rr⌒ ⌒rr<

53. **Soon, Our Father Sun felt that there had been enough of this.**
He didn't want us to be abused and hurt by whippings,
Nor to be humiliated by threats and scorn from the Spaniards.

Figure 9. Spaniard Soldier Branding an Indian
(Drawing by Marián López Calixto)

54. When Our Father Sun felt that there had been enough
    of this, the warfare began:
    The Spaniards began to make war with the
    Indians.
    It was they who made war.
    Indeed, it was a war that lasted for perhaps four
    years.
    It was they, the Spaniards, who made war.

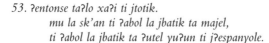

53. ʔentonse taʔlo xaʔi ti jtotik.
    mu la sk'an ti ʔabol la jbatik ta majel,
    ti ʔabol la jbatik ta ʔutel yuʔun ti jʔespanyole.

54. k'alal la ti taʔlo xaʔi ti jtotike, lik la ti letoe.
    lik la spasik leto xchiʔuk ʔinyo ti jʔespanyole.
    jaʔ la spasik ti leto.
    laj la spasik chanvikuk ʔavil ti puru leto lae.
    jaʔ la spasik ti letoe.

55. It was hard to solve these problems.
    The one who managed to do so was one who suf-
    fered through the fighting and triumphed.

〜〜 〜〜

55. *vokol la meltzaj ti k'ope.*
     ja? la meltzaj yu?un ti kuch yu?un pas leto.

〜〜 〜〜

56. It was Miguel Hidalgo who prevailed and caused peace to come.[8]

He stopped the old custom of branding us as though we were horses.

He began to show them how to baptize us in the church.

He began to show us how to pray to Our Father Sun.

He began to tell us what we should say in prayers.

He began to show us how to work.

He began to show us how to read and write.

He began to show us everything.

〜〜 〜〜

56. *ti mikel ?idadkoe, ja? la la skomtzan ta lek ti k'ope.*
     ja? la ta xch?ay ti ta to?ox la xkich' jmarkailtik.
     ja? lik yak' ?iluk ta xkich'tik ?o? ta ch'ulna
     lik la yak' ?iluk ta jk'opontik jtotik.
     lik la yal k'uxi ta jpastik resal.
     lik la yak' ?iluk k'uxi chij?abtej.
     lik la yak' ?iluk chanvun.
     lik la yak' ?iluk skotol.

〜〜 〜〜

57. It was Miguel Hidalgo who accomplished these good works:

It was he who settled the conflict a long time ago.

It was he who left the problems well solved.

It was he who hunted and chased the Spaniards back to their own ancestral homeland where they really belonged.

It was he who forced them to return to Spain, as their country is called.

〜〜 〜〜

57. *k'usitikuk ?abtelel ti mikel ?idadkoe.*
     ja? la smeltz'an ti k'op vo?ne lae.
     ja? la la skomtzan ta lek ti k'ope.
     ja? la snutzik sutel to j?espanyoletike ti bu la sta ti yosilik ti j?espanyol ti vo?ne lae.
     ja? la ti sutik batel ti ta ?aspanya, sbi ti lume.

〜〜 〜〜

58. **That is why they celebrate his fiesta every year on the 16th of September.**

    That is when Don Miguel Hidalgo was shot to death.

    You see, he left the earth in good condition long ago.

    >ᴛᴛ͛ ͣᴛᴋ

58. *jaʔ yuʔun la ti ta xlok' sk'inal ta jujun ʔaʔvil, ta vaklajuneb semiembre.*
    ti k'usi la ti cham ta tuk' ti don mikel ʔidadko lae.
    xavil jaʔ la la skomtzan ta lek ti banomil ti voʔne lae.

A MORAL EXEGESIS OF ETHNIC AND LINGUISTIC SUBORDINATION

The reader will undoubtedly have noted themes in this text that link it to the Biblical text of the Tower of Babel, discussed above. The narrator also reveals to the listener/reader that he is a keen observer of his own life and times with regard to the asymmetries of Indian and Ladino economic power and social prestige. He is also clearly conversant with Mexico's own mytho/historical accounts of its own history. All of these constitute clearly identifiable and easily understandable strands of historical memory that enter into the composition of the narrative.

There are other themes, however, that do not lie so close to the surface and are not so easy to comprehend. In particular, although it is never stated here (for it belongs to other accounts of Chamula history), a fundamentally Maya vision of cyclical time and moral evolution informs this entire narrative. I refer to the startling placement of Ladinos and Indians, Spanish and Tzotzil, in precisely the opposite chronological order from that which we assume to be common knowledge. Don't all of us, Indians and Westerners, know perfectly well that thousands of years of Indian civilization preceded the Spanish invasion and conquest of what is now Mexico? And that no one in the New World had heard of Spanish until it was violently foisted upon Amerindians as a colonial language? Doesn't this muddling of chronology come across as a naive conflation of stories from "our own tradition" that Tzotzils don't quite get right? I answer "yes" and "no," to all of the above, for all knowledge, including our own, is situated in particular historical contexts and social constructs. The Tzotzil Maya world was and is different from our own in terms of the rhythm of historical process. Ours has a dominant linear, progressive theme, with occasional cyclical moments that startle us. For example, the press is currently reminding us of Nazi and Allied parallels to what is currently happening and not happening in Bosnia. The Maya world, in contrast, is keyed to a basically cyclical vision of historical process, with a secondary progressive, linear theme; the structure of current events inevitably recapitulates the pattern of the past to provide the opportunity to correct past mistakes.

Cyclical time reckoning thus allows for, even invites, human progress *if* it is understood that old structural grids regulate, condition, and limit this progress. These structural grids also demand a due placement of new historical "others"—such as the Spaniards—in a moral slot that suits them. The text above performs this historical surgery quite effectively. Spaniards are banished to the very distant past, a chronological place that renders them morally inferior to, and prior to, Indians in the order of creation.

Maya-derived four-part cyclical time does not posit a mere repetition of former time periods. There is, rather, an orthogenetic thrust, a kind of "moral progress," that underwrites the unfolding of historical experience. In this sense, present-day Chamula Tzotzils believe themselves to be at the cutting edge, the frontier, as it were, of moral progress. This is why they unabashedly classify themselves as the "true people" and their language as the "true language." At one point in their history, as recorded in this text, they shared important aspects (notably the Spanish language and associated human arrogance) with Ladinos. Ladino culture, therefore, figures as a part of their own ancestral lineage, more particularly, a primitive phase of it. They shared, in times past, the moral weaknesses of their present adversaries. They have "progressed"; Ladinos have not. Ladinos (and, indeed all white Europeans) figure not exactly as ethnic others, but as depraved, primitive versions of themselves. (See chapter 1.)

The theme of relegating morally inferior beings to their own ancestral past rings as a powerful leitmotif to virtually all of Chamula cosmological and historical reckoning, including the ritual representation of these ideas. For example, the crime of infanticide, discussed earlier in this essay, was not the sin of ethnic others, but of their own ancestors, and this crime is dutifully represented ritually in the preparation, exchange, and consumption of "baby tamales" in their annual ritual of solar renewal, known as the "Festival of Games." This ritual reproduces a great historical drama of the four creations of human experience, and virtually all of the barbarous behavior and immoral beings, real and imagined, who have crossed their paths over the ages figure as motifs in this festival. These events and beings include the Spanish conquest, Spanish soldiers, Mexican soldiers, Guatemalan soldiers, transvestite camp followers, monkeys, demons, Ladinos, and European tourists. All of these motifs are placed in their own journey through the trials of moral progress and they, themselves, play these parts and reenact these events which are, for them, morally reprehensible. They triumph over all of this immoral landscape of the past in the climax of this ritual, which consists of purging these immoral aspects of their lineage in a ritual race through a path of burning thatch grass on the fourth day of the festival. This path of fire represents the solar orbit, and in it, and through it, the Chamula actors purge the negative aspects of their past and emerge purified, exonerated, and transformed from the depravity of their own past. They ritually create a new present in which they are the victors and their adversaries (who also reside within their own genealogy and consciousness as a people), vanquished. (See chapter 5.)

Language figures prominently in the symbolic content of the ritual I have just described. The monkey characters and other immoral beings speak Spanish, in a manner that can only be described as farcical mockery. Indeed, the charter document that is recited during numerous episodes of the Festival of Games is called the "Spanish Letter." Recited in Spanish by a ritual personage known as the *pixcal* (from Sp. *fiscal*, "public prosecutor" or "district attorney"), this is a call to war, and calls upon the Chamulas themselves to engage, as Spanish soldiers, in the military destruction of their own community. It is precisely this theme of foreign military invasion of Chamula that makes up the nonstop ritual activity of the three and a half days that precede the firewalk. Involved here are not only Spanish soldiers and the theme of the Conquest but also Guatemalan and Mexican soldiers, specifically named, who were leaders in wars of the nineteenth century. All of these adversaries spoke Spanish and their human and moral qualities were dubious at best. For example, the common Norway rat—predator, scavenger, and bad citizen par excellence—is known in modern Tzotzil as *karansa*, named after Venustiano Carranza, revolutionary hero and president of Mexico.

It can thus be seen that the attribution of Spanish language and Ladino ethnicity to the first-made of Our Lord Sun/Christ's creation is an elaborate and quite elegant joke; Ladinos were destined to be primitives and must therefore work harder, even than Indians, to overcome this affliction.

While the immorality of Spanish-speakers and Ladino culture is unambiguously and scathingly reported in both the Festival of Games and in the text above, it is also true that the text speaks charitably of the "good Ladino," Miguel Hidalgo, who is in fact recognized by all Mexicans as the "founding father" of the whole nation. At this point, Méndez Tzotzek seems to buy into Mexican public mythology about its own past in acknowledging that Spaniards (*gachupines*) were in fact evil and that they did in fact exploit Indians mercilessly. Furthermore, one of their own (i.e., Hidalgo) realized that this was so and acted forcibly to correct it.

Thus, Ladinos are not, as an ethnic category, relegated to unredeemable evil. They clearly have, in their own genealogy, leaders who are capable of acting on behalf of all Mexicans, Ladinos and Indians. It is surely this same logic that accounts for the presence of white gods and saints, including Our Lord Sun/Christ himself, as redeeming, compassionate, creative beings in Chamula historical reckoning. Indeed, in deepest antiquity, the creative force of life itself is attributed to deities with shining, white, radiant faces. The problem is that most Ladinos have "forgotten" this opportunity for goodness and redemption in their own lineage, preferring instead to remain mired in their own primitive past, fossilized somewhere between the very dawn of creation and the present. It is undoubtedly this same logic that makes the mestizo revolutionary hero, Emiliano Zapata, and Subcomandante Marcos, also a white Spanish-speaking Mexican, plausible as symbolic and real paladins of the Maya Zapatistas' cry for social justice in our time.

In conclusion, therefore, Chamula Tzotzils, perhaps also all Indian people in Chiapas, recognize that their own language and ethnicity share important historical experiences with Ladinos. Ladinos, thus, have the opportunity not only to become moral beings but also to recognize that they, the Ladinos, share a past with Indians. Neither should be expected to give up the identities embodied in their languages, for as the text tells us, this diversity was part of the creator's plan. Perhaps there is an opening for dialogue here. The final passage in Méndez Tzotzek's text offers a moving appeal for redemption and reconciliation in the centuries-old Mexican chronicle of ethnic, class, and linguistic conflict. The conciliator is not a parochial Indian hero or god; he is Miguel Hidalgo, mestizo parish priest and national hero, one of the central figures in Mexico's own story of itself. Méndez Tzotzek, and through him, Hidalgo, seem to be reminding Mexicans that their diverse languages and cultures belong to all Mexicans as the heritage of their great nation.

Five

THE CHAMULA FESTIVAL OF GAMES:

NATIVE MACROANALYSIS AND SOCIAL COMMENTARY IN A MAYA CARNIVAL

The main corpus of this essay was published in 1986. The 1986 text is reproduced here in its entirety, with minor editorial changes that omit redundant ethnographic background material. There are three addenda in the present version, all of which amplify the ethnographic account in ways that would not have seemed relevant to me a decade ago.

The first of these addenda is a reflexive and anecdotal prologue that provides a glimpse of the fluidity of the Carnival's mood. Far from being a fixed text, Carnival rolls with the punches; my account of the English people and the Monkeys is but one of such unscripted moments, without which Carnival would not be Carnival.

The second addendum consists of textual sidebars that provide Tzotzil narrative accounts of cultural memory that all participants vaguely "know," but which do not get articulated in the verbal or dramaturgical text of the event. These sidebars are, as it were, culturally significant footnotes. The narrators, who are identified in each sidebar text, have been introduced above (chapters 2 and 3).

The third addendum is graphic. Included are several line drawings by Marián López Calixto. These drawings, whose strategic place in my research agenda is discussed in the Preface to this volume, were produced by Mr. López Calixto as a kind of independent critical commentary on events and characters in narrative texts. Since the Festival of Games, as a ritual chronicle of ethnic memory, refers constantly to who was/is who in their social universe, it seems appropriate to reproduce these verbal images of actors whose being informs the script of the ritual.

PROLOGUE: MONKEYS AND ENGLISHMEN

It was 5:30 on a foggy morning in 1978. Driving my Jeep, I had just begun to descend into the small eroded basin in which the Ceremonial Center of San Juan Chamula, a Tzotzil Maya community of Highland Chiapas, is located. It was mid-February, Carnival time, and the community was in the midst of its great annual super-bash, the "Festival of Games" (*k'in tajimoltik*). This event is the feast of feasts in San Juan Chamula, the event which attracts the greatest attendance of any in the ritual-heavy annual cycle. It attracts the eager participation of many thousands of Chiapas Highland Maya as well as foreign tourists and Mexicans. It is among the great traditional rituals of the Americas.

As I drove my Jeep down the steep road that leads to the Ceremonial Center, I noticed a scene straight out of a Fellini movie. A foreign tour group, obviously well-informed about when to be where to take in the Maya traditional festivities, was parked in a sheep meadow just off the road that led down to the Ceremonial Center. The bucolic scene of grazing sheep and cornfields was swathed in the swirling fog of early morning. The vehicle that sat parked in this landscape was also a Jeep that had attached to it an aluminum trailer with a rear door. The door was open and a confident but soft-spoken group of eight people sat in folding lawn chairs placed in a semicircle around the open door. They were drinking tea from white ceramic cups, waiting for the action to start in the Ceremonial Center some two hundred yards further on down the road. The group consisted of four middle-aged couples, all dressed in sensible wool plaid jackets and worn trousers. They were obviously experienced tourists; the otherworldly setting did not daunt their sense of self-possession. Their sense of calm and entitlement was remarkable as they sipped their tea in the half-light of early morning.

I pulled over to the side of the road, overwhelmed by curiosity at this incongruous spectacle. A shameless voyeur, I had to know who they were. How could they be so composed? Didn't they know that Chamulas were known to be tough and mean to outsiders? Didn't they know that this was the fourth day of Carnival, the day of the ritual destruction and reconstitution of the universe?

I introduced myself in Spanish and received curious stares, since I had the appearance of an eccentric tourist myself and ought to have spoken English to start with. "Good morning," was the response. "We don't speak Spanish," declared a portly sixty-year-old woman. The accent was British. The scene might have become a pleasant intertourist exchange of banalities, complete with tea for me, had the Chamulas not appropriated their own domain.

The Fellini movie scene developed further. The trailer, parked illicitly in someone's sheep pasture, was suddenly besieged. Straight out of the swirling fog, now rising with the heat of the day, came a rush of bodies and a chorus of aggressive and angry whoops and hollers. Eight Chamulas approached the scene, clad in costumes that startled the Western souls of the English tourists. The intruders were dressed in conical black animal-fur hats, dark sun-glasses, black cotton frock coats, white shirts visible beneath them, and knee-length black breeches, lined with red piping. Dried, hollow cow horns were suspended from their snake skin belts. Brandished in one hand were dried bull-penis whips; in the other, gourd rattles which they shook furiously while announcing their precipitous arrival with war whoops.

Most astonishing to the English tourists, the aggressive Chamulas did not at first speak in any language at all. The message was delivered in whoops, hollers, chattering noises, screams, and angry gestures, including clenched fists and threatening slashes with their whips. Although I knew that the Chamula visitors were none other than the famous monkey characters of Chamula Carnival fame, their appearance come off like a true show-stopper. Not only did the

English tourists not expect them at that time and place, but they were utterly terrified. Furthermore, the monkey characters were trying to make a point, quite vehemently so, for the yelling and whooping would not stop.

The composure of the English was utterly dissolved. They could not leave, for they were surrounded. They couldn't communicate, for the Chamulas were behaving like savages. Several teacups fell off into the grass amid the flurry of packing up the chairs and the table in the hope of a quick departure. However, the Chamulas would not permit this. It was a moment of utter panic. Finally, I stopped being amazed and delighted long enough to realize that I might be of some use in moving the crisis off dead center.

Switching from whoops to Tzotzil, one of the Chamula monkeys told me, when they recognized me as a familiar face, to translate the following messages to the tourists:

> Message 1: They would have to take their car and trailer out of the pasture.
> Message 2: They would have to purchase a tourist permit at the city hall.
> Message 3: They would have to keep their photographic equipment absolutely away from obstructive locations during the big events to come.

I dutifully translated and was not, myself, alarmed by the bizarre incident, for such encounters abound in my field notes and I thought I "understood" what was going on. The monkeys were simply doing their job. However, the English people were nonplussed. They spoke no further word to me or to the Chamula monkeys, but finished packing up their folding chairs and propane stove and prepared to depart. On the part of the monkeys, there were no hard feelings. Amid raucous laughter, they lifted their siege to let the English people leave, even giving them a helpful push when the tires began to spin on the frost-covered grass. I regretted not being able to listen to the content of the English group's conversation as they roared off, unharmed but terrified.

The irony of the episode just narrated delighted me because I thought, after having had four opportunities (in 1968, 1969, 1977, and 1978) to witness and participate in the extraordinary festival that the English people missed, that I understood what was happening, even in this spontaneous sideshow that no one had rehearsed. In fact, the English people were quite unwittingly characters in the ritual proceedings. In truth, they would have been welcome and even made the party merrier if they had stayed and followed the modest rules that the monkeys had announced, for they, like the monkeys themselves, were the invited conquerors. They might even have been invited to the great banquets of midday, at which the host ritual personages, the Passions, would ritually celebrate the destruction of Chamula society by giving away free food to all comers. The invaders, the "others," would ritually triumph. It was the day for the monkeys, the Lacandones, the Guatemalans, the English, the Spaniards, the Mexicans, the whores, and the transvestites to triumph.

The point is that the role that the poor English people started to play but could not bring themselves to complete, is scripted by the logic of the festival, which is a massive historical drama of the destruction and reconstitution, by fire and the renewed Sun/Christ, of Chamula society. If they had just stayed to play their parts as foreigners, the party would have been merrier.

INTRODUCTION

It has become commonplace in critiques of Mesoamerican Indian studies from inside Mexico (Bonfil 1970; Stavenhagen 1970; Warman 1980); and from Europe (Favre 1971), Japan (Ochiai 1985), and North America (Wasserstrom 1983; Friedlander 1975) to observe that the vast bulk of ethnographic work in the area, primarily done by North Americans, has ignored economic and political systems as well as the histories of these systems. This work, the critiques run, has emphasized functional analysis of so-called closed corporate communities (Wolf 1957), while ignoring the historical, regional, and world milieu in which Mesoamerican Indian communities have actually evolved in the modern (post-1800) era. These studies have also been criticized for emphasizing the so-called "epiphenomena" of religion, expressive behavior, and worldview of Indian populations of the area, while ignoring the situation of dependence, economic servitude, and class exploitation from which Indians suffer (Wasserstrom 1983; Friedlander 1975).

THE COMMUNITY AND ITS CARNIVAL

The purpose of this paper is to offer a case study of native macroanalysis and social commentary which will show that at least one minority Indian population of Mexico is acutely aware of its "real" economic and political circumstances. I will focus on this real world as I believe it is perceived by San Juan Chamula, a Tzotzil-speaking Maya community in the central highlands of Chiapas (see general ethnography in Gossen 1974b; Pozas 1959; Linn 1977). In particular, I will describe and analyze a major festival in the ritual cycle, showing specifically how this annual event appraises the Chamula moral community both internally and externally, with reference to the world beyond its boundaries. The language of this social commentary is ritual action and related expressive forms. These forms are but some of the cultural codes that carry this information, yet they speak with unusual clarity. Victor Turner has demonstrated with his Ndembu data (1967), and more recently with cross-cultural data (Turner and Turner 1982), that ritual action has the characteristic of representing explicitly in the ritual microcosm of time and space that in which in daily life is nebulous, implicit, and diffuse in the social fabric. In other words, ritual action renders accessible and visible those truths that are basic but not customarily articulated in everyday life because they are bigger than life.

My topic is an annual Chamula festival known in Tzotzil as k'in tajimoltik ("Festival of Games"). Although the festival is cognate with Christian Carnival time, in that it is always celebrated during the five days preceding and including Ash Wednesday, the Festival of Games is at the same time a major winter solstice festival, replete with symbolic inversions of many normative themes in Chamula life, ancient and modern, pre-Christian and Christian, sacred and secular. It is primarily, by Chamula exegesis, a cult to the Sun/Christ deity,[1] a celebration of the cosmos and its beginning in antiquity. The festival also carries a complex set of themes relating to Indian ethnicity and ethnic conflict, which derive from events of the colonial and modern Mexican periods of Chiapas history (Bricker 1973: 85-89; 1981: 133-35; Rachun Linn 1982). Finally, the Festival of Games addresses a whole range of normative themes in everyday Chamula life, from sex roles to political integration, the agricultural cycle and worldview. Thus, the festival celebrates virtually all aspects of Chamula everyday custom, internal ethnic identity, and historical reckoning, while also acknowledging, without charity, the wider world of the Mexican nation, the state government of Chiapas, even Guatemala, Spain, and foreign tourists.

Because the festival considers these themes so poignantly and so self-consciously, even angrily, it is not an exaggeration to attribute to the event a powerful political statement about who the Chamulas are. They state in countless ways, banal and sublime, that they are not about to be engulfed by Mexican national culture. They reenact once a year just how untenable and immoral cultural assimilation—better said, capitulation—would prove to be. I wish to show that Chamulas are not innocent victims of "false consciousness," but rather astute observers of their own place in the ethnic and class configuration of the modern world.

Chamulas are by far the largest and most influential of the Maya Indian groups of Chiapas. Perhaps because of this, mestizo Mexicans of the state of Chiapas typically use "Chamulita" as a generic, somewhat condescending term for all Indians of the highlands. Chamulas have also played an important role in the history of Chiapas, being at the epicenter of two modern Indian political movements in the Chiapas highlands, those of 1868-70 and 1910-11 (Gossen 1974b, 1977; Bricker 1981). Their importance today is acknowledged by modern Mexican presidents, governors, and minor bureaucrats, for when they choose to make a token appearance before a representative Indian community in the state they typically go to San Juan Chamula. The most recent of these events was in January 1984, when then-President de la Madrid arrived by helicopter to address thousands of Chamulas who had arrived on foot, truck, and bus from their outlying hamlets to see the ʔajvalil ("lord" or "top official") from Mexico City. Apparently, he only appeared briefly and did not speak. The Chamulas were satisfied.

If San Juan Chamula is acknowledged by many to be both the real and symbolic center of Indian cultural presence in the Chiapas highlands, this situation has been a conscious creation of Chamulas themselves. It is one of only a handful of Indian communities in the Chiapas highlands that does not permit non-Indian Mexicans or foreigners to own land or even to spend the night in their boundaries without specific permission of municipal authorities. During the 1930s, with the blessing of the anticlerical regime of Mexican President Lázaro Cárdenas, local authorities drove out a convent population of thirty nuns. In 1974, they expelled a parish priest who had been allowed to live in the church complex in the Ceremonial Center. Between 1974 and 1977, authorities banished at gunpoint all of the Protestant convert population of three thousand, contending, correctly it seems, that this was a serious challenge to community autonomy and separate ethnic identity.

The community is infamous among other Indian groups and Mexicans alike for being ruthless to foreigners and Mexicans who wander in its boundaries without permission. True stories of murdered Germans and arrested Swiss tour groups are very much alive in both the Indian and local Mexican gossip networks. Furthermore, the municipal authorities are fiercely centralist in their political stance, forbidding any church or other civic structure to be built in outlying hamlets, for this is viewed as a threat to central political and religious authority.

On the demographic front, Chamula is terribly overpopulated, density being over one hundred persons per square kilometer. Thus, Chamulas go by the many thousands into the work force of coffee plantations and lowland cornfields to earn money to buy what they cannot produce at home. In fact, Chamulas supply the labor that produces a significant percentage of Mexico's entire coffee crop—not a trivial item in Mexico's international trade. In response to the population pressure, thousands of Chamulas have permanently emigrated in dispersed colonies all over the state of Chiapas. These new Chamula colonies tend, rather strikingly, not to become assimilated into modern Mexico and their inhabitants return frequently for festivals in the home *municipio*.

Chamula is a paradox. It is both the most widely dispersed, yet the most hermetically sealed of the Chiapas Indian communities. To a great extent Chamulas depend on mestizo-controlled state and national economies for jobs and for trade, yet they hold mestizo Mexico in considerable contempt, and Mexicans, like other foreigners, are not welcome in Chamula except as day visitors. Chamulas remind one of the Jews in their capacity to retain a powerful moral community in spite of their geographic dispersal and their long history of strained coexistence with other ethnic groups. How do all of these highly visible defense mechanisms work? What do they mean? Why are they important?

THE FESTIVAL OF GAMES IN TIME AND SPACE

Chamulas describe the Festival of Games affectionately as the best (*mas lek*) of all the events in their annual ritual cycle. It is the best attended of more than twenty major public ritual events that occur annually in the Ceremonial Center, bringing hundreds of men home from the coffee plantations and thousands of families on foot and by truck to see the "Lost Days" of "Crazy February." These terms refer to the crucial temporal framework of the festival. "Crazy February" is a translation of *loko febrero* (Tzotzil rendering of Spanish). The term Crazy February refers to the well-known carnival season immediately preceding Lent in the Christian calendar. However, like so much of the thematic content of the event, there is both a Christian and a traditional Maya referent for most symbols. The festival also coincides with the Tzotzil Maya month of *ch'ay k'in*. This month name means in Tzotzil "lost festival," "lost days," "lost heat" and is related to a Yucatec Maya word for "lord" or "priest," *ah k'inh* (León Portilla 1968). This unusual month fell around the time of the winter solstice in the ancient Maya solar calendar and was the five-day odd month in this system, known as the *ha?ab* (eighteen months of twenty days, plus a five-day special month=365 days). This calendar still persists in Chamula and remains in use as an agricultural almanac (Gossen 1974a, 1975). However, the five-day month of *ch'ay k'in* is adjusted by officials to coincide with the traditional pre-Lenten Christian carnival of four days (Saturday through Shrove Tuesday), plus Ash Wednesday. Whatever its Christian and ancient Maya history, the festival now falls in a time of agricultural dormancy—the cold, dry season—a betwixt and between time when no one is either planting, tending, or harvesting corn.

The anomalous time in the annual cycle complements other peculiar traits of the festival. It is five days in duration; all other festivals in the annual cycle are three days long. It is also the most expensive festival in terms of ritual sponsors' expenses, and comprises the major annual effort of the highest-ranking religious officials. However, it is also peculiar in that it takes place entirely outside the church and involves no cults to the saints. It is a time of barbarism, of demons, precultural monkeys, armed warfare with Mexicans, Guatemalans, and Spaniards, a time of abandon and suspension of rules and ordinary behavior.

A native key to all of these anomalous themes is the name of the event itself, *k'in tajimoltik*, the "Festival of Games." It is a time of intense ritual play and games, a reenactment of the awful childhood of humankind, before the establishment of day and night, a time when there were no rules—cosmic, supernatural, or human; a time before the sun had risen into the sky to differentiate day from night and to give the first heat that destroyed the sun's mythical adversaries.

There is a well-known Chamula mythical referent that provides the details of the death of the Sun/Christ deity at the hand of the forces of evil: the precultural monkeys, demons, and Jews. Briefly paraphrased, the story is as follows:

> The Sun/Christ is born to the Moon/Virgin Mary as her second son. He is slain and nailed to a tree, but comes back to life. On this, the first day of the primeval myth era, he goes to the edge of the earth, marked by the western horizon, known in Tzotzil as the place of "waning heat." On the second day he descends into the southwestern quadrant of the universe, which is the Underworld. On the third day he moves past the nadir of the universe, still in the Underworld, and into the southeastern quadrant of the universe. On the fourth day, he rises from the eastern horizon, emerging from the Underworld into the northeastern quadrant of the universe. This marks the great cosmogonic moment, the first rising of the Sun/Christ into the new universe. Upon reaching the zenith of the sky at the end of the fourth day of creation, the Sun/Christ gives to the universe for the first time sufficient heat and light to kill his adversaries. On the fifth day order is established in the universe as the Sun/Christ moves into the northwestern quadrant, descending to the western horizon to mark the end of humanity's first "real" day. With this, the categories of time, space, and cosmic order are established in the beginning of the First Creation. This creation is subsequently destroyed and restored three more times by the Sun/Christ as punishment for human ineptitude. The last of these is the present, Fourth Creation.[2]

For the present discussion, it is relevant to emphasize that it is precisely the five primeval days of the First Creation, as discussed above, that are recapitulated ritually in the five-day Festival of Games: four days of chaos and anticipation, culminating in a Firewalk over burning thatch, symbolizing the first ascent of the Sun/Christ to the zenith, at noon of the fourth day; the fifth day is the first day of Lent, known in Tzotzil as "Fish-eating Wednesday" (*melculix ti? choy*).

Figures 10 and 11 summarize the information above and also indicate the extraordinary complexity of the place of the Festival of Games in Chamula spatial, temporal, social, religious, and agricultural symbolism. Note that its time of occurrence, in the southeastern quadrant of the Chamula time-space cosmological scheme, has all of the following symbolic associations:

1. Childhood in the life cycle; naiveté, play; these are symbolized in the Festival of Games by the themes of abandon and precultural references to monkeys (*maxetik*), who are important ritual personages in the festival. Unnamed children are known in Tzotzil as "monkeys."

2. Darkness and night, specifically the period between midnight and dawn.

3. Rising aspect of the Sun/Christ, yet still in darkness; anticipation of light, yet still in predawn phase of the day.

4. Short days, long nights, with steadily increasing relative length of day in the annual solar cycle.

5. Dry season in Chiapas highlands.

6. Time of frost and cold.

7. Period of agricultural dormancy.

8. Third primeval day of Sun/Christ's mythological trip through the Underworld after his death, immediately preceding his emergence on the eastern horizon at the beginning of the fourth primeval day.

9. Southeasterly orientation in the overall cosmic scheme.

10. Dark of the moon.

11. Beginning of male-dominant time in the day and year.

12. Left hand location of Sun/Christ deity as he faces the cosmos to begin his daily arc across the sky.

13. Periphery (edge) of the universe, in close association with antisocial forces and beings.

These themes—precultural chaos, childhood, play, and close association with evil, antisocial elements—together with the temporal backdrop of the five-day

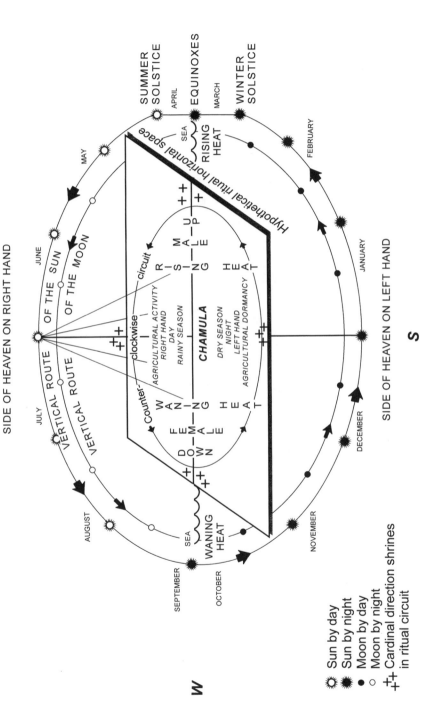

Figure 10. *Temporal and Spatial Categories in Chamula Cosmology*
(Chart drawn by Ellen Cesarski)

N

E

W

S

SIDE OF HEAVEN ON RIGHT HAND

SIDE OF HEAVEN ON LEFT HAND

SUMMER SOLSTICE

EQUINOXES

WINTER SOLSTICE

APRIL

MARCH

FEBRUARY

JANUARY

DECEMBER

NOVEMBER

OCTOBER

SEPTEMBER

AUGUST

JULY

JUNE

MAY

OF THE SUN

OF THE MOON

VERTICAL ROUTE

VERTICAL ROUTE

SEA

SEA

RISING HEAT

WANING HEAT

Hypothetical ritual horizontal space

Counter-clockwise   clockwise   circuit

CHAMULA

AGRICULTURAL ACTIVITY
RIGHT HAND
DAY
RAINY SEASON

DRY SEASON
NIGHT
LEFT HAND
AGRICULTURAL DORMANCY

RAM-SANUNG MALUPE HEAT

DEFENMAG WANUNG HEAT

○ Sun by day
✹ Sun by night
● Moon by day
○ Moon by night
+ Cardinal direction shrines
+ in ritual circuit

month of *ch'ay k'in*—"lost heat" or "lost festival"—are orchestrated into the great ritual drama of the Festival of Games. With this background, I will now proceed to discuss particulars of the event.

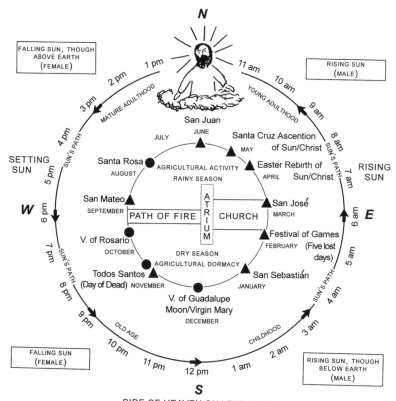

DAY, LIGHT, SUN ABOVE EARTH
SIDE OF HEAVEN ON RIGHT HAND

SIDE OF HEAVEN ON LEFT HAND

DARK, NIGHT, SUN IN THE UNDERWORLD

▲ Male deity fiesta
● Female deity fiesta

Figure 11. *Symbolic Associations in the Festival Cycle*
(Chart drawn by Ellen Cesarski)

PERSONNEL

To the best of my reckoning, based on four field seasons' observance and participation in this festival, the grand total of individuals with official roles to play in the festival each year comes to the astonishing figure of 2,066. While this figure is surely but an approximation (it varies from year to year), it is an index of the monumental scale and organizational complexity of the event in this community of one hundred thousand. Some general characteristics of the organization of festival personnel will enable the reader to assimilate the personnel list that follows later in this section.

In the first place, the festival requires the participation of two hereditary positions that are passed from father to son. These are the positions of Lord of the Drum, *hbajbin*, of which there is one for each of the three *barrios*; and Master of Ceremonies or Crier, *pixkal*, from the Spanish *fiscal*, meaning "fiscal official" and "prosecuting attorney for the state" as well as the court's "crier" or "chief spokesman." There is but one Crier for the whole community, and he is also the sacristan of the Chamula church. These hereditary positions are few, but central to the festival performance.

There are, in addition to the very few hereditary positions, a large number of rotating positions. These are costly public-service jobs, and they are requested many years in advance; waiting lists are kept in the town hall in a locked safe. All of these positions exist in triplicate, for each of Chamula's three political divisions or *barrios*—San Juan, San Pedro, and San Sebastián. Furthermore, each of the rotating positions must be occupied twice, in two consecutive years, first as an incoming official, then as an outgoing official. So, in effect, tenure for rotating positions is two years.

Finally, there is a veritable army of supporting personnel required for each of the official positions, both permanent and rotating, for all have complex service responsibilities involving preparation and distribution of ritual meals and elaborate exchanges of ritual goods. Each must establish a temporary household in the Ceremonial Center that is capable of maintaining his entire entourage for the duration of his ritual tasks, which last for almost two months in each of two years.

The Passions

The principal sponsors and leading ritual figures of the Festival of Games are the *paxyonetik*, or "Passions," named for the Christian Passion, which is one of the historical overlays represented in this pre-Lenten festival.

There are six Passions—one incoming, one outgoing, for each of Chamula's three *barrios*. They are striking figures to behold. Outgoing Passions wear a costume that looks rather like a loose, two-piece suit of red pyjamas with knee-length legs. The headgear consists of a long piece of white cotton that is wound as a great turban, with the loose ties hanging in the back. The color symbolism is important. Red is the symbol of the rising sun and the east, and white is the symbol of north and the sun at zenith, in most ancient and contemporary Maya communities. It is useful to consider the Passions as symbols of the festival itself, for they embody two opposing aspects of good and evil, like many of the dual-aspect deities of Mesoamerican antiquity. The Passions are the custodians of, sponsors of, and actors in the cult to the head of Sun/Christ, who is the principal deity honored at the festival. The head of the Sun/Christ is represented by four metal flagpole tips, each of which bears the name of a saint and is at the same time an aspect of the Sun/Christ's totality. Each of three sets (one for each *barrio*) of flagpole tips is kept in a sacred wooden chest, which is brought out during the festival and, during the rest of the year, is maintained in the outgoing Passion's home in an elaborate chamberlike shrine made of hanging bromeliads. The Passion renews the flowers every twenty days, with prayer, incense, and rum liquor, according to the schedule dictated by the months of the ancient solar calendar. At festival time, the flagpole tips are attached to poles (the skeleton of the Sun/Christ) and banners (the body of the Sun/Christ), and clusters of multicolored ribbons (symbolizing his radiance) are attached to the poles to create four flags with ribbon clusters below the tip. These flags represent the four positions of the Sun/Christ in his vertical orbit-rising, zenith, setting, and nadir. Other interpretations state that the four flags are aspects of the Sun/Christ's divinity; accordingly, they bear four saints' names that express this quadripartite whole. Together, these four flags, carried in a counterclockwise circuit, represent the totality of the Sun/Christ. The Passion, as the sponsor of this cult, is the "bearer" or "carrier" of the Sun/Christ's burden on earth, according to the language of his oath of office. At the Festival of Games the Passion becomes "as the Sun/Christ," and is addressed as "Lord of Heaven, Lord of the Sky." He also wears a ribbon necklace, which restates the ribbon motif of the flags. His ribbon-encircled head is like the head of the Sun/Christ and people who address him ritually bow to touch or kiss his necklace before speaking.

With all of this positive "valence," each Passion is also the quintessence of evil. The evil aspect is easily discernible in an alternate set of titles used to address and speak of the six Passions, comprising three teams of two, incoming and outgoing. These terms are ranked, as Chamula society itself is ranked, from senior to junior. Each year the three *barrios* rotate the titles. The most senior, in this context the most evil, is the Soldier Passion, who is associated with Spanish, Mexican, and Guatemalan armies that have invaded Chamula over the centuries. The second-ranking Passion is also known as the "Lacandon Chief." This title refers to a conservative lowland Maya group, the Lacandones, whose remnant members (a few hundred) still live in the jungle to the east of Chamula. Chamulas fear and dislike the Lacandones, whom they regard as savage and primitive. (See figure 12 and following.)

THE LACANDON PEOPLE
(*Narrated by Marián López Calixto*)

This is an account of the Lacandon people of Chiapas.
    People say they are very bad.
One cannot tell if a person is a man or a woman;
    They have the same hair styles,
    They have the same clothes,
    They have the same tunics,
    One doesn't know if it's a man or a woman.
For this reason, this is what people say:
    There in the land of the Lacandones, they bite,
    For those people are no more than beasts of the forest.

What's more, for dogs, they keep lions,
>   For cats, they keep jaguars.
>   That's what people say.
Indeed, they have no dogs,
>   Not even cats,
>   Nothing of the sort.
>   The Lacandones raise nothing but wild animals.
What's more, if their lions and jaguars are not fed, they bite.
>   Their dogs are very mean.
And they don't even keep chickens,
>   For they have no place to hatch their chicks.
>   This is because these people themselves live in the depths of the jungle.
They have no way to kill even wild animals efficiently.
>   They possess only bows.
>   For guns, they possess only arrows.
>   That is what these people are like.
When they want to marry,
>   They feel around in each other's crotches to find out if they are men or women.
When people wish to find mates,
>   They ask each other if they are men or women . . .
"Are you a woman or a man? I've no idea," the Lacandones say to one another.
>   And even if they are women, they have beards.
>   That is why one can't tell if a person is a woman or a man.
This is what the Chamulas say about them:
>   They say they are like wild animals, for they aren't sure whether these people are good or evil.
They say they have great long mouths,
>   And that their ears are very big.
When it is time for baptizing their children, they do it with a big stick.
>   And they don't even have *compadres*.
>   They just stand there alone when their children are baptized.
>   There isn't even a church to use for baptisms.
What's more, if it turns out that they don't like their children very much, they don't even nurse them.
>   And when they die, they don't even bury them.
They toss their children away to rot in the streams.
>   When they have decayed, the buzzards come.
They treat their children like any old dog.
>   They toss their children away.
As for their penises, these people have great long ones.
>   The Lacandones have got penises just like an old jackass's.
As for the vaginas of the women, the same story:
>   They are stretched long and wide.

Figure 12. Portrait of a Maya Lacandon Man/Woman
(Drawing by Marián López Calixto)

Thus the second Passion is a symbol of Indian adversaries, of which the Chamulas had many before the Conquest, among them the Toltecs and Aztecs of central Mexico. The second-raking Passion is also known as the *ska?benal paxyon*. This is best translated as "Linking Passion," suggesting a function of "linking" the Soldier Passion to the third-ranking Spanish Lady Passion (see Bricker 1973: 98 for a discussion of the etymology). The third-ranking Passion has a female title, that of *Sinyora* (from Spanish *señora*, "lady"), or *xinulan antz* ("stinking woman"). The Spanish Lady Passion represents the Mexican mestizo cultural presence and also the cult of Malinche, Cortez's Indian mistress and interpreter, who is much celebrated throughout Mexico as a traitor to her own people, the native Mexicans. Among the Spanish Lady Passion's entourage is a female impersonator (actually a man found guilty of sexual infractions in the Chamula court), who wears a dirty white, antique Mexican wedding dress. He behaves as a clown, flirting and cavorting as a whore in the Passion's entourage. He even, at one point in the ritual, simulates sexual contact with the sacred drums. He is at liberty to make suggestive remarks to ritual personnel. With all of this negative burden, the Spanish Lady Passion in his positive aspect is also addressed as the "Holy Mother of Heaven," referring to the Moon/Virgin Mary deity.

Thus the three titles of the Passions simultaneously represent the ultimate moral forces in the universe—the Sun/Christ with his mother the Moon/Virgin Mary—and various adversaries of the moral order—invading armies of non-

Chamulas, foreigners, and other Indians, even the enemy within, immoral sexual behavior. (See Figure 13.)

The Flowers

Each of the six Passions (incoming and outgoing for each *barrio*) has associated with him a second-ranking personage called *nichim* or "Flower." The Flower, like the Passion, contributes heavily to the annual maintenance of the cult of the Sun/Christ. However, whereas the Passion is in charge of the head of the Sun/Christ (the flagpole tips and ribbons), the Flower is in charge of the body (the banners) and the skeleton (the poles). The four banners (flowered cotton cloth on various colored backgrounds) are kept carefully folded in a wooden chest, receiving a regular twenty-day flower renewal ritual. The chests are kept within bromeliad-decked chambers, which look much like those of the Passions' shrines for the flagpole tips. The flagpoles are kept wrapped in white cotton, lying horizontally behind the chest that contains the banners.

In an explicit sense the Flowers and Passions are a team, being responsible for different parts of the Sun/Christ's body. During the Festival of Games, the Flower must ritually present the chest containing the Sun/Christ's body and the bundles containing his skeleton to the Passion, who then ritually assembles the four aspects of the Sun/Christ's whole body, adding the four metal tips and ribbons to the four poles and banners.

Figure 13. A Mexican Soldier Rapes a Chamula Woman
(Drawing by Marián López Calixto)

While the Flower has his positive aspect as custodian of part of the Sun/Christ cult, he, like the Passion, has his negative aspect. He is "Captain" in the respective army of his Passion. He also, therefore, shares one of the three representations of evil (Soldier, Lacandon chief, or Spanish Lady) that is associated with his commander. He is simultaneously helpmate and representative of the Sun/Christ and his enemy. The positive aspect is present in his ribbon necklace, which, like the Passion's necklace, represents the Sun/Christ's radiance. The negative aspect is expressed in his full cooperation with the Passion's ritual warfare activity.

The Commissaries

Each of the six Passions also has associated with him a second-ranking officer, the *comisaryo*, from Spanish *comisario* or "Commisary." This officer is the messenger, runner, and deputy of the Passion. He has as his principal ritual task the carrying of the sacred chest which bears the symbols of the head of the Sun/Christ for the Passion. His negative aspect is expressed in his military mode as inquisitor and policeman in charge of managing the subjects, presumably the Chamulas themselves, who have been ritually defeated by the Passions' armies (see Bricker 1973: 90 for further discussion of the etymology of *comisario*).

The Ordinaries

Each of the six Passions also has associated with him a third-ranking officer, the *ortinaryo*, from Spanish *ordinario* or "Ordinary." This officer is the messenger, runner, and deputy of the Flower. He has as his principal ritual task the carrying of the sacred chest which contains the banners and the bundles that contain the poles of the Sun/Christ.

In his negative, counter mode the Ordinary is the assistant, servant, and deputy of the Flower or "Captain." Thus, he also functions as a police official in charge of conquered subjects, assisting the Commissary in this military duty (see Bricker 1973: 90 for further discussion of the etymology of *ordinario*).

Monkeys

No one who has ever attended Carnival in Chamula can fail to come away impressed and possibly terrified by the hundreds of men and boys who roam the festival and follow the action dressed as nineteenth-century French soldiers, complete with red and black frock coats, with tails, short trousers, and conical monkey-skin hats, perhaps taken from European bear-skin models. Bricker (1973: 91-93) has demonstrated that the origins of this bizarre costume are fairly recent, probably dating from Maximilian's time, the well-known period of the "French Intervention" (from 1861 to 1867) in Mexican history. Whatever their origin, they are called *maxetik*, or "Monkeys," and according to the common exegesis, represent the evil monkeys of primeval antiquity, who, with the demons and the Jews, killed the Sun/Christ. They state this antisocial theme in other ways. They wear belts of snakeskin, symbolizing the capricious earth lord of their pantheon. According to the Chamula explanation, this being, who lives in caves and controls rain and monetary wealth, is associated with Mexican mestizos. The Monkeys carry dried bull-penis whips, of the type used by traditional mestizo cowboys, and wear dark sunglasses, also associated with the modern Mexican cultural sphere. They also carry horn vessels filled with rum and powdered chile, which they drink freely.

The Monkeys, their faces blackened with charcoal, represent the evil aspect of the cosmos, the bad shadows, the foreign, the primitive, and the hostile. (See following.)

THE DESTRUCTION OF THE FIRST PEOPLE
(*Narrated by Salvador López Sethol*)

Monkeys were still people long ago.
  The people became monkeys because they were evil.
And what were the deeds of these people long ago?
  They used to eat their own children long ago.
What size were their children when they ate them?
  They were already nearly grown up when they ate them.
  For it is said that they were at the age of seeking wives when they killed them to eat.
How did they slay their children to eat them?
  The monkey people clubbed their children to death with sticks.
  That is how they did it when monkeys were still people long ago.
Were all the people changed into monkeys long ago?
  Not all of them.
  Some of them simply died.
What happened to the companions of the monkey people who died?
  To these survivors Our Lord Sun/Christ in Heaven gave a punishment.
What punishment did Our Lord Sun/Christ in Heaven give them?
  He gave them a great flood as a punishment.
How great was the deluge that Our Lord Sun/Christ sent down?
  The waters had reached halfway to Heaven when the companion of the monkey people died.
For how many days were the flood waters gathered when the companions of the monkey people died?
  The flood waters lasted for three days.
Where were the monkey people who did not die when their companions died?
  They escaped in box-boats when they realized that the flood waters were coming. . . .
As the flood waters receded,
  Down came the monkey people floating there in their box-boats. . . .
Remember that they were still not monkeys.

They were still people when our Lord Sun/Christ came down.
"What are you doing here?" asked our Lord Sun/Christ.
  "Nothing," they replied.
  "We're just lighting a fire," said the monkey people.
They had spoken but three or four words,
  When at once they were given monkey tails and monkey fur.
Once they had monkey tails and monkey fur,
  They were banished to the woods forever,
These monkeys were never given corn to eat again.
  "I shall never again let you have corn," said Our Lorn Sun/Christ.
"From now on you can f ind your own food there in the woods," said
  Our Lord Sun/Christ.
  "All right, then," said the monkeys.
When Our Lord Sun/Christ went back up to the sky,
  The monkeys began searching in the woods for their food.
These monkeys had been people long ago.
  They were changed into monkeys because they had done evil.
(See Figure 14.)

Figure 14. A Person is Transformed into a Monkey
(Drawing by Marián López Calixto)

The monkeys even speak a mocking Spanish mixed with animal noises instead of Tzotzil, as a part of their verbal routine. They are clowns and tricksters, constantly milling about, joking and threatening, with explicit obscenity. Thus, like other ritual personnel at the festival, they have a dual aspect. They represent not only the forces of evil and the primitive human condition but also the policemen of the festival, keepers of the public order. They serve as the guards of ritual personnel and also as their conscience; they are charged with watching ritual officials constantly to ensure that they keep the rules of sexual abstinence. There are Attached Monkeys and Free Monkeys. The Attached Monkeys, in groups of four, are a formal part of each official's entourage. Thus, for each of the six full personnel groups (consisting of Passion, Flower, Commissary, and Ordinary), there are sixteen Monkeys, making a total of 96 Attached Monkeys. Any man can dress as a Monkey, even the chief civil official, the *presidente municipal*. They roam about laughing, joking, singing, and engaging in all manner of threat and obscenity in the presence of anyone. As Monkeys, they are not bound by normal everyday rules of human conduct, yet they are charged with keeping public order. They are precultural beings policing an enactment of precultural chaos. It is a contradiction that in the context of the festival makes perverse sense. Finally, the Monkeys' color symbolism, predominately black, is associated with the west, the direction of "waning heat," and with death and negation, precisely the cosmic opposite of red and "rising heat," which are dominant symbolic associations of the Passions.

Game Constable

Each Passion appoints a *mayol tajimol* or "Game Constable," whose job it is to supervise ritual dancing around the sacred drums at the ritual feasts.

Chilonero

The *chilonero* or "Belt Man" assists the Game Constable in attaching a jaguar-skin belt to each dancer at the ritual feasts. It is also his duty to ring the bells that are attached to the neck of the jaguar skin as each dancer performs.

The Crier

The post of *pixkal* or public "Crier" is hereditary, as discussed above, and is also the same individual as the church sacristan. There is one for the whole community and he serves as a kind of master of ceremonies for the whole festival. His main duty is the reading of the "Spanish Letter" on dozens of occasions throughout the sequence of the festival. The text of this letter is given in full below.

The Lord of the Drum

The "Lord of the Drum" (*jbajbin*) is, like the Crier, a hereditary position that is passed from father to son. The drum in question is a highly sacred object, and

123

it has a regular ritual maintenance cult similar to that of the objects that represent the Sun/Christ. The three drums (one for each *barrio*) are actually double ceramic drums, each part of which is covered with a porous animal membrane. They are approximately 20 cm high and 12 cm in diameter. When they are to be used, the ceramic jars are filled with water at different levels, which creates a two-tone effect upon being played with the hand. The drums are associated with a well-known mythical account of an earth lord's daughter who marries a human. (See following.)

About the Earth Lord's Daughter
(*Narrated by Manuel López Calixto*)

The following extract is from a longer narrative of the Second Creation. Prior to the events that follow, the male protagonist, "an ancient one" (not yet a modern Tzotzil Maya) wins as his bride the fair daughter of an earth lord as a reward for rescuing him from a trap where he had been caught (in his alternative form as a snake). They begin their strange marriage on a bad foot, caused in large part by the human husband's lack of understanding of his wife's miraculous powers:

When she made tortillas, she made plenty.
    She had but a little bit of dough, but she made it stretch a long way.
In this way, the woman made her corn increase so that it produced many tortillas.
    Even though she had but a little bit of corn, she made this corn increase in volume a great deal.
    She also made the beans increase.
    Thus, even though the household had but a little bit of food, she made this food increase.
Whenever she went out to get sweet corn, she would bring back plenty.
    When she went out to harvest sweet corn, she would return with lots and lots.
She really did not harvest many ears of corn.
    She would actually pick but two ears of sweet corn.
    But when she returned, she had a large carrying net full of sweet corn.
And so it was with the beans:
    When she went to pick beans she picked only two pods.
    But these few beans became many.
For her seeming wastefulness, the man scolded his wife.
    "Ah, but I gathered a very little bit," said the poor woman, trying to defend herself.
So it was that this ungrateful and mean man, her husband, became furious.
    It was because of this that he hit her.
    His wife's only fault had been her success in causing the corn to increase.

In a fit of peek, he landed a blow against his wife's nose.
  This caused blood to flow profusely from her nose.
One of the nets of sweet corn was close by.
  From it she grabbed an ear of corn.
She wiped her bloody nose on this ear of corn.
  That is why red corn is known as "the blood of the earth lord's nose."
After the woman had suffered this awful beating,
  Her father came at once to take her away.
  It was the woman's father himself.
Now, at that time the sky had been completely clear.
  Then suddenly the clouds gathered!
  Then suddenly the thunderstorm broke!
When it had just started to rain a bit,
  A great bolt of lightning struck close to the man's house.
  How the thunder crashed!
At the very moment when the thunder sounded, the man's wife
  disappeared.
  Right then, the earth lord came to rescue his daughter and take her
  away.
No sooner had his daughter suffered the beating
  Than the earth lord quickly came to carry his daughter away . . .
As for this woman,
  She, too, was an earth god.
  However, the woman's situation was not simple:
  She had borne human children.
She left her children here on earth.
  The children were forced to fend for themselves.
When her children began to cry,
  She lost no time in returning to take care of the little ones.
"Why are you crying?" she asked her children.
  "Because we're very hungry," replied the children.
"Don't cry. I'll bring pots of food for you," said their mother.
  Then their mother went to bring the pots of food for her children.
Presently their mother returned.
  She gave the food pots to her children.
"I have some things for you here.
  Here is a tortilla gourd bowl for you.
  Here is a bean pot for you.
  Here is a corn-cooking pot for you."
  So she spoke to her children.
"When you run out of tortillas,
  You must turn your tortilla gourd upside down.
When you run out of beans,
  You must turn your bean pot upside down," said their mother. . . .
When they ran out of tortillas,
  They were to lose no time in turning the tortilla gourd upside down.
When they had turned them upside down,

> They were to beat on their food pots like a drum.
> When they had finished drumming on them,
>   They were to place the food pot upright.
> They were to do this until they saw that their bean pot was full;
>   And that their tortilla gourd was full.
> Then they would have tortillas.
>   Then they would have beans in their pot.
>   And in this way her children had food to eat . . .
>
> The story continues by relating how the jealous father demands to know the secret of their magical food supply. They are forced to reveal their secret; whereupon he smashes their wondrous pots. In anger and pity, the mother returns to take away her children forever. The father is bereft and sad, and lives out his life in solitude.

It is this narrative that forms the background for understanding the central role of the drums in the Festival of Games, for the Passions are expected on several occasions to feed the multitudes. The drum is associated with a plenteous food supply, as in the myth cited above. In a sense the drum facilitates this, for it is played before, during, and after the ritual feast that the Passions must provide for the multitudes. This feast is called *kompiral* (from Spanish *convidar*, "to invite"). The Passion feels great social pressure to provide such an abundance of beef and cabbage soup, bean tamales, white bread, rum, and sweetened coffee that all present may partake. Thus, the playing of the drum as a ritual focus for the dances at the feasts matches closely the orphans' rubbing of the magic pot in antiquity to produce an unending food supply in the absence of their mother. Indeed, the two pots are jokingly referred to as "breasts." The Lord of the Drum therefore links the cult of the Sun/Christ to the female principle, and to the cult of the earth lord, which in turn is explicitly associated with the Mexican mestizo cultural sphere in Chamula narrative tradition. In a sense, joint economic dependency of the Indian world upon itself and upon goods from the Mexican economy is acknowledged in the drum cult. One of the foods "produced" by the drum at the feast is, notably, wheat bread rolls, "Mexican bread," (*kaxlan vaj*), which is radically unlike the everyday corn-based Indian diet.

Nana María Cocorina

I have noted above that one of the *barrios* each year has Passions who are known as the Spanish Lady Passions. This reference has already been discussed in relation to the Malinche cult, which is known throughout Mexico. The individual who dons a tattered Mexican wedding dress, to play the role of *xinulan antz* ("stinking woman") and act as the Passion's consort, Nana María Cocorina, is often a male criminal who has been accused of sexual wrong-doing of some sort by the Chamula traditional court. Thus, the Malinche figure at one and the same time symbolizes the integrity of the Chamula moral code and the emptiness of other Indian, Spanish, and Mexican moral codes. (See following.)

The Origin of Ladinos
(Narrated by Mateo Méndez Tzotzek)

Long ago, the Ladinos had a dog for their father, and this is how it happened.
> It happened when a stinking Ladino woman[3] came along with her dog.

Now, long ago there were still open grasslands[4] all over the earth.
> There were still no houses; times were different.

It was at this time and place that the dog started to fuck his mistress.
> Indeed, the stinking woman encouraged him and helped him.

Then and there, the dog fucked her.
> The Ladino woman was there waiting for him on her hands and knees.

Well, they did it lots and lots of times.
> And sure enough, he got the Ladino woman pregnant.

Now, the stinking Ladino woman had her baby.
> Her child was born.
> And he turned out to be the ancestor of modern-day Ladinos.

Well, as soon as the Ladino woman's child was born,
> She and her dog set up housekeeping.
> Slowly but surely the Ladinos began to multiply.

That is why Ladinos have no shame.
> They flirt and speak with each other on the road.
> They hug and put their arms around each other in public.
> They even kiss each other in public.
> This is all because they had a dog for a father long ago.

Nana María Cocorina is specifically noted in the text of the "Spanish Letter," which is given below.

Musicians

All twenty-four major ritual officials (Passions, Flowers, Commissaries, and Ordinaries) at the Festival of Games have as an integral part of their respective entourages a group of musicians. The musicians for each official constitute a ranked group of six. First in rank are the harpists (positions one, two, and three); second in rank are the guitarists (postitions four, five, and six). They play and sing at all stationary segments of the prefestival and postfestival activities and for endless hours during the five-day festival itself. Their role is of critical importance, for the words of their songs, in traditional couplets, offer a running narrative of what is happening at every stage. They also serve as informal prompters and advisers to the ritual officials themselves.

Miscellaneous Servants

In addition to all the above, each major ritual official has a large number of servants who help him to fulfill his vast network of obligations. A typical list follows. This was the Outgoing Passion's supporting staff in 1979:

- 1 Ritual Advisor (who must be a past occupant of his patron's position). He is actually a teacher and prompter who guides the current occupant in his duties.

- 1 Embracer (whose duty is to move dancers through the drum dance and "lift" them ritually out of the dance.

- 1 Incense-bearer (whose duty is to maintain and carry incense burners).

- 4 Flower-bearers (whose duty is to gather and decorate shrines in the Passion's home and in the Ceremonial Center). These typically have a total of about twenty assistants.

- 1 Chief Cook (who manages preparation of ritual foods). Working under him are about thirty women.

- 1 Chief of Gruel (who manages ritual preparation and cooking of great ceramic jars of sweetened corn gruel).

- 1 Chief of Drinks (who manages provision of rum liquor in bulk containers and measurers it into liter bottles for ritual distribution).

- 1 Personal Servant (who helps the official with dressing, holds pieces of ritual paraphernalia, and retrieves dropped items).

- 4 Fireworks Bosses (who are in charge of hand cannon detonation and the firing of skyrockets).

- 6 Porters (who carry food, gifts, and drinks from one locale to another).

- 2 Sweepers (who are in charge of ritual sweeping and maintenance of public spaces).

- 2 Butchers (who are in charge of ritual slaughter and dressing of a bull, which provides meat for the feasts).

- 1 Meat-tender (who is in charge of keeping flies away from meat that is hung for many days to age before cooking).

- 50+ Wood-gatherers (who must cut, carry, and stack firewood for the massive cooking operation needed for feeding the staff and for preparation of ritual foods).

- 30+ Bull-pullers (who are usually young men and boys charged with bringing the bull for slaughter; this involves holding ropes tied to the bull as he is escorted amid great fanfare into the Ceremonial Center on the Tuesday before the festival begins).

It should be noted that all titled roles are male roles in this patrifocal society. However, all wives of major officials are held in great honor and are known by the female honorific *me?* ("mother" or "female"), as in *sme? paxyon* ("Madam Passion"). Wives of major officials do not do manual labor at the festival and are waited upon by male servants of the ritual official. They also stay in sexually segregated groups, as do male officials and servants, for the duration of the five-day festival, during which complete sexual abstinence is required of all who have ritual responsibilities, great or small. To break this prohibition causes rain, which of course wreaks havoc on a massive, five-day outdoor spectacle of this nature. In 1979 it rained. The Outgoing Passion ended up in jail for allegedly having sex with his wife during the prescribed prefestival period of abstinence. Other accounts (which became "official") alleged that the rain had come because the Passion got drunk during the execution of his public duties.

SEQUENCE

The magnitude of the Festival of Games, its primacy in the annual cycle, and its clear role as the feast of feasts in the hearts and minds of Chamulas, demand some gesture on my part that captures its special qualities. Let me simply remind the reader that, for nearly all of the months of January and February, virtually all of the social energy of the community is directed toward this event. For weeks on end, thousands of families discuss it around the fires in the evening. It is the impetus that brings hundreds of men home from months of labor on the coffee plantations. It regulates the plans of truck owners in the far-flung Chamula colonies all over the state, as they contemplate how to increase passsenger runs to meet the demand for space. The Chamula universe coalesces around this event because it re-creates the Chamula universe in a manner so vivid and so all-encompassing it is simply not to be missed. One has only to contemplate the sight of ten thousand people assembled in a barren mountain basin of about three square kilometers for four days without sleep or housing to realize that something extraordinary is going on. In this section I shall give a chronology of the main events, using the calendar of 1978. It will, of course, vary each year with the situation of Lent and Easter in the Christian calendar.

It is helpful to visualize the whole event as a ritual destruction and reconstruction of Chamula society. The festival begins, physically and symbolically, in the distant hamlets as a three-part plot to destroy Chamula society. The aggressors are, of course, the three *barrios*, led by the Passions. The Passions, the earthly custodians of the cult to the Sun/Christ, will, in their negative valence—as soldiers,

129

foreigners, and amoral beings—consort with monkeys and whores to destroy the Sun/Christ's universe.

Ritual perparation for the festival begins on January 1, when all civil officials take their oath of office in the Chamula Ceremonial Center. This sounds ordinary enough, but it must be remembered that the Passions are actually neither civil nor religious officials. They are not part of the civil hierarchy, which involves all traditional civil officials (*presidente, jueces, alcaldes síndicos, alcaldes, gobernadores, regidores,* and *mayores*) or, properly, of the religious hierarchy, which involves the *mayordomos* and *alféreces* who sponsor cults to the saints. The Passions and Flowers and their entourages are betwixt and between, for the cult they sponsor is both above the civil/religious system and outside of it. Indeed, it deals with the supreme power of the cosmos, the Sun/Christ deity, which is logically and temporally prior to civil, religious, and cosmic order. This is symbolized by the anomalous social space where the oaths of office for the Festival of Games personnel take place. This happens in the southwestern corner of the walled atrium of the church. The location is neither *in* the church (where religious officers are installed) or in the Town Hall (*Ayuntamiento,* where civil officers are installed), but in the southwestern, most negative, quadrant of the atrium external to the church (see Figures 10, 11, and 16). The oath-taking is thus subject to neither civil nor religious authority. The time of oath-taking is also bizarre in that it is on the day of civil cargo oath-taking (January 1), but not in the *Ayuntamiento* where other officials are installed, as decribed above. Yet neither are they like religious officials (*mayordomos* and *alféreces*) who assume their duty in the church and at the temporal slot in the annual cycle as defined by the Christian calendar, according to the saints' feast days. In a word, Passions and Festival of Games personnel are outside the "system" and will be outside the system until the Chamula moral and social universe is reconstituted on the fourth day of the festival when all personnel are ritually purged by the Firewalk. But that puts us ahead of the story. Let us backtrack.

Before January 1.

All festival personnel must enlist their servant corps and entourages with ritual gifts of rum. Housing in the Ceremonial Center must be rented and costumes borrowed or made.

January 1.

All major festival personnel receive the oath of office at around noon from the Crier at the southwestern quadrant wall of the church atrium. This is *outside* the church, away from the navel of the universe, which is located under the central altar, *inside* the church. Names are read from sign-up lists established years prior to this date.

January 21.

This is the day of the Feast of San Sebastián in the Chamula ritual cycle. On this occasion, which is a major festival in its own right, all Festival of Games personnel appear in full costume at around noon to enter a formal petition to the *presidente municipal*, requesting permission to stage the festival. All personnel, surrounded by their entourages of Monkeys and other servants, get on their knees, again at the southwestern corner of the walled atrium compound of the church, and beg the *presidente* for permission. This is granted and the Crier announces the dates (taken from the annual Catholic calendar/almanac, which is published in Mexico as *El calendario del más antiguo Galván*). The Crier then stands on a pedestal and reads to the massed armies the charter myth of the Festival, which is called, in Spanish (it does not have a Tzotzil name) the *Carta Española* or "Spanish Letter." This is the first of many occasions on which the exhortation is ritually read during the Festival of Games. The Crier reads the script in brutal, almost mocking, Spanish. It is an incitation to war, destruction, and immorality. Here is a translation from the 1979 script.

Chamulas!
Crazy February!
Today is the twenty-fourth of February.[5]

The first soldier came to Mexico [City];
He came to Guatemala;
He came to Tuxtla [Gutiérrez];
He came to Chiapa [de Corzo];
He came to San Cristóbal [de las Casas];
He came with flags;
He came with drums;
He came with trumpets.
Viva! Viva!

Fellow citizens!
The second cavalier came to Mexico [City].
He came to Tuxtla [Gutiérrez];
He came to Chiapa [de Corzo];
He came to San Cristóbal [de las Casas].
He came with flags;
He came with drums;
He came with trumpets.
Viva! Viva!

The last cavalier came to Mexico [City].
He came to Guatamala;
He came to Tuxtla [Gutiérrez];
He came to Chiapa [de Corzo];
He came to San Cristóbal [de las Casas].
He came with fireworks;
He came with cannons;
He came with fifes;
He came with bugles;

He came with flags;

He came with trumpets.

Mariano Ortega and Juan Gutiérrez came with their young lady, Nana María Cocorina.

They went together into the woods to make love.

They returned eating toffee, eating candied squash, eating blood sausage.

Viva Mariano Ortega!

Note that this oration is a kind of mock celebration of war. All personnel join in the three raucous choruses of "Viva!" as they raise fists and agree to celebrate the destruction of their world. Not only is it delivered in Spanish, the precivilized tongue that all people spoke before the Sun/Christ brought order to the universe, but it also gives a kind of litany of the provenience of historic threats from the periphery—Mexico, Tuxtla Gutiérrez, Chiapa de Corzo, San Cristóbal de las Casas, and Guatemala (see chapter 4 on Spanish as a "primitive" language). All of these places are associated with the foreign, Spanish-speaking world, and all, over the centuries, have been the origin of armed incursions into Chamula territory. The symbols mentioned—cannons, drums, trumpets, explosives—are the accoutrements of war. The two names mentioned—Juan Gutiérrez and Mariano Ortega—are actual military and political figures who figured prominently in the nineteenth-century history of Chiapas.

Mariano Ortega (historically Juan Ortega) was a political reactionary who supported the empire that was established by Maximilian in Mexico during the French Intervention of 1861-67. On May 7, 1863, Ortega invaded and occupied the department of San Cristóbal, which at that time included Chamula. The occupation lasted until January 24, 1864. He then became a roving marauder for the centralist cause. Ortega, therefore, came to be identified as a military adversary of Chamula autonomy, which was expressed in the so-called Chamula Caste War of 1867-70, also known as the War of Santa Rosa. During this period, Chamula was aligned with Juárez's federal troops who fought to defeat Mexican centralists and French imperialists. The federal troops lost, and in the process Chamula's revitalization movement, which had been tolerated by Juárez's government, was destroyed. Ortega is also identified with the boundary dispute between Mexico and Guatemala of the same period, for many of his troops were recruited from Central America, and because he used Guatemala as a base for his attacks on the towns of Chiapas (Bricker 1973: 87).

Juan Gutiérrez was a supporter of federalism and local autonomy for the state of Chiapas during the first half of the nineteenth century. He became governor of Chiapas in 1830 and during subsequent years led federalist troops in raids throughout Chiapas. He engineered an attack on the conservative stronghold of San Cristóbal de las Casas. This event indirectly involved Chamula (Bricker 1973: 87-88).

In spite of the direct links with the written record of Chiapas history, it is actually "generic" war and foreign intervention that are the referents of the "Spanish Letter" text. It is a telescopic commentary on all foreign intervention, reaching back even to the Conquest and perhaps even to the pre-Columbian period. The latter is suggested by the link of the second cavalier with the

Lacandon Chief. The association with the Conquest is suggested by Nana María Cocorina, who is clearly linked to the image of Malinche. Furthermore, the place names noted, particularly Mexico City and Chiapa de Corzo, are significant. Mexico City was, of course, the site of Cortéz's major Conquest vistory in 1521 in Tenochtitlan. Chiapa de Corzo was the site of the first decisive military victory of the Spaniards over the Indians of Chiapas in 1524.

It is significant that the "Spanish Letter" is first read and that Festival of Games preparations begin in earnest on San Sebastián's feast day. This saint, who is also important in other Indian communities of the Chiapas highlands, is known in Chamula tradition as a traveling merchant who was shot and killed (with arrows) by other Indians. Local icons of him throughout Highland Chiapas suggest this, but of course the Christian legend of the martyr reports that he died pierced through by spears, at the hand of Roman soldiers. In particular, the Roman emperor Diocletian is held responsible for St. Sebastían's death.

January 28, Wood-gathering Sunday.

In the afternoon of this day, all major personnel meet at their homes with their ritual entourages. A ritual meal is held, after which the officials go to several sites in the outlying hamlets to make a ritual appeal to those who are attracted by the fireworks. The speech given by the official is as follows:

> Please, for the sake of his firewood,
>> For the sake of his fire,
> Of the Lord of Heaven,
>> Of the Lord of Glory,
> He who pays for our guilt,
>> He who buys us out of difficulties,
> He who gave us our souls,
>> He who gave us our spirit,
> It is his firewood
>> It is the fire of Our Father Sun.
> Please, I beg you,
>> Eight days from now,
> We shall await you in the forest;
>> You shall hear where to find us in the forest;
> There the horn will be blasting;
>> There they will be firing skyrockets;
>> At three o'clock in the morning.
> Please, I beg you.
> (Gossen 1974b: 178–79)

This speech is delivered amid war whoops from the Monkeys, skyrockets, hand cannon explosions, trumpet blasts, and general bedlam. Recruits receive ritual gifts in exchange for a promise to appear on a designated day, early in the morning to cut, split, carry, and stack the vast amount of firewood needed for the festival in the Ceremonial Center.

February 4 (*or any convenient day; it is specified in the recruiting speech*),
Wood-gathering Expedition.

It is significant that this, like so many events of the Festival of Games, begins at night. All people who have agreed to help appear at about 2:00 A.M. at the official's home in the Ceremonial Center. A modest meal is served and then the party heads for the woods. The Monkeys and their ritual officials lead the procession, which even in 1979 was still done by the light of pitch-pine torches. I call attention to the nocturnal theme because precultural chaos, darkness, and cold are major motifs of the symbolic ambience of the festival. This, of course, relates to the days of the festival themselves; they fall in the dark of the moon because Easter is so situated in the Christian calendar (first Sunday after the first full moon after the spring equinox). This invariably places the four days preceeding Ash Wednesday in the dark of the moon and the earliest phases of the new moon.

Another important motif of the festival is first stated at this event. This is the theme of primitive, collective food preparation out-of-doors. Beginning with this event, all ritual meals of the festival are prepared in crude shelters made of poles and branches outside of the ritual official's home. The interior hearth fire is extinguished (as in Chamula funeral rituals). Although this has obvious practical value (for vast amounts of food must be prepared), this also recapitulates the themes of negation of heat and light, which are central to the destruction theme of the first phases of the Festival of Games. Ordinary domestic and public life are specifically suspended; this involves not only mass cooking out-of-doors but also the total segregation of males and females in all activities, including seating and eating. Rules of sexual abstinence have already been in effect since the oath-taking on January 1.

After the wood-gathering expedition, which lasts approximately ten hours, the group returns for a feast at the ritual official's home in the Ceremonial Center. The theme of this meal is primitive food and primitive behavior. The menu is beef tripe soup, beans, and tortillas. The tripe soup is significant because it is greasy, which is specifically repugnant to Chamula food aesthetics. It is resonant with the primitive theme, however, in that greasy food is associated with Mexicans (Indians believe that Mexican bodies small of lard) and the ancient people. There is a well-known narrative of the First Creation that states that the early people made tamales of their own children when they were two or three years old, presumably still plump with baby fat. Although the ancients enjoyed eating their own children, particularly savoring their fat, the Sun/Christ destroyed them for this crime. Related to this theme is the admonition that Chamulas give to their children about going too far from home; for example, "Don't go to Tuxtla or the Mexicans will kill you and render lard from you." This theme is repeated later in the Festival of Games itself, when, on the Friday before the festival starts, the Passions' wives exchange a ritual giant bean tamale, which is called the "baby tamale." They are, in effect, ritually indulging in the crimes of the ancients. (See following.)

INFANTICIDE
(*Narrated by Xun Méndez Tzotzek*)

Well, long ago the people of the First Creation didn't live very long.
  The reason was that they insisted on eating their children.
They did not increase at all,
  Because they persisted in eating their children.
When their children were born, they let them grow six months.
  At six months old they killed them.
They killed their children in pots of boiling water.
  While the pot was boiling, a woman faced her child.
She danced with her child.
  She hugged her child—for the last time.
  Her baby was soon to be her meal.
When she finished dancing,
  She cast the child into the pot,
  Where the baby boiled to death.
When she threw it in the pot,
  The baby was still crying.
When she pulled it from the pot,
  The baby was quite dead.
When she saw the child was dead,
  She diced it with a knife.
Once her babe was chopped to pieces,
  She stuffed the meat into tamales.
  She wrapped the flesh in corn dough.
The people enjoyed the baby-filled tamales.
  They also enjoyed the baby broth.
This is what everyone did.
  Thus, they did not multiply at all.

As the story unfolds, Our Father Sun/Christ discovers them in the act of preparing baby tamales and sends all of the First Creation people to death in a poetic rain of boiling water. (See Figure 15.)

Figure 15. The Preparation of "Baby Tamales" in Ancient Times
(Drawing by Marián López Calixto)

On the occasion at hand, the Wood-gatherers feast, the Monkeys perform a ritual chant with the accompaniment of a rattle, in which they celebrate the greasy qualities of the meal they are about to receive.

Here is the text of the chant, including the original text and translation:

Chanted: *asite veʔlil*
Greasy food,
   asite komer
Greasy food,
   asite ʔitaj
Greasy cabbage,
   asite napux
Greasy turnip greens.

Sung: *La la ti la lai*
   La la ti la lai

Chanted: *asite chenek'*
Greasy beans,

asite prijol
Greasy beans,
asite ve?lil
Greasy food,
asite komer
Greasy food.

Sung: *La la ti la lai*
        La la ti la lai
        (Gossen 1974b:180)

Note the presence of Spanish words: *asite* (Sp. *aceite*, "oil"), meaning "greasy"; *komer* (Sp. *comer*, "to eat"), meaning food; *napux* (Sp. *nabo*, "turnip"), meaning "turnip greens"; and *prijol* (Sp. *frijol*, "bean"), meaning "beans" in Tzotzil.

It is highly significant that the Monkeys celebrate and praise the virtues of greasy food, Mexican food, *in Spanish*. This is appropriate for the Monkeys, like Mexicans, are by Chamula classification their primitive contemporaries and, therefore, naturally fond of grease. The Monkeys perform with mockery and laughter and offer the audience drinks of rum from their cow-horn flasks. The Passions watch this with benign approval, for it is all part of the plot, ever-thickening, to thrust Chamula into the dark ages of primitivism during the Festival of Games. The feast follows and the entourage disperses.

February 4–16.

This period mobilizes all of the ritual personnel to their final preparations for the onslaught of the great events to follow. This time comprises the two weeks prior to the beginning of the festival. There are three major sets of events that occur during this period.

1. All Passions and Flowers must present formal ritual petitions to the Lords of the Drum to appear with their drums at appropriate times during the festival. This early morning event takes place at the home of the Lord of the Drum and involves both the Incoming and Outgoing Passions and Flowers, together with their retinue of Monkeys and personal servants. The Passions give gifts of *pox* (rum *aguardiente*) and present their petitions. After this is a ritual of acceptance. There is a brief drum dance performance, followed by a routine meal of tortillas, cabbage soup, beans, and coffee. The crowd disperses.

2. The second major task that the three Outgoing Passions must attend to during this period is to arrange for the bull that will be ritually sacrificed to provide meat for the ritual meals of the festival. These arrangements require that the bull be brought to a holding site, which is within a half-day's walk of the Ceremonial Center. This arrangement is necessary so as to allow all three sacrificial bulls (one for each *barrio*) to be brought in ritual procession from the hinterlands to arrive by twilight on the Monday preceding festival week. This assures that the sacrifice can proceed with proper triple symmetry at dawn on Tuesday.

3. A third major task of this period is the dispatching of the Flower-gatherers for each of the twenty-four major ritual positions. This involves crews of four to twelve men who go by foot, truck, or bus to tropical and subtropical areas to bring necessary plants and flowers for the adornment of altars, porticos, and shrines in the prescribed manner. In addition to bringing the special bromeliads from the lowlands, the Flower-gatherers must bring sufficient nets of pine needles to cover the floors of their patrons' homes with the required carpet of green. These exeditions often take several days and are marked by ritual meals of departure and return.

February 17.

This is the Saturday one week preceding the launching of the Festival of Games. On this occasion, all members of the entourage of the twenty-four officials meet at the respective homes of the officials in the distant hamlets to accompany their patrons to their ceremonial homes. This is "moving day." Each of the major officials moves his household in great fanfare, amid fireworks and dancing by the Monkey assistants, to his temporary rented home in the Ceremonial Center. These moving parties are major events, for they involve transportation of sleeping mats, cooking utensils, ceremonial clothing, and large supplies of rum liquor that will be used in upcoming events. At all roadside shrines the large parties pause to rest amid exchanges of liquor and fireworks. Upon arrival at the ceremonial homes in the center, the officials expect to find their Flower-bearers hard at work putting finishing touches on bromeliad-decked house shrines and pine-needle carpeting on the floors. The official's parties arrive around noon and immediately set to work establishing the temporary households that will serve for the duration of the festival. A ritual meal is served and the Monkeys dance. Drinks are offered and fireworks detonated.

February 18, Name-recording Sunday.

Early in the morning, the officials are ritually dressed by their servants after blessing ceremonies and prayers. At around noon, all twenty-four officials, eight from each of the *barrios*, go with their entourages to the southwestern wall of the atrium of the church in the Ceremonial Center. The Crier reads the "Spanish Letter" to the enthusiastic *"Vivas!"* of participants. This is, in effect, an incitement to arms. The Crier then checks each official on his list of committed participants, which has been established on the previous New Year's Day. After receiving orders from the Crier to appear at the required times during the next two weeks of arduous activity, each party retreats to its headquarters and consumes a ritual meal.

February 19, Bull-pulling Monday.

At three in the morning, the three Outgoing Passions arise and offer ritual drinks to the sixty or so men who have assembled the night before in anticipation of the great day of bringing the sacrificial bull to the Ceremonial Center. This is a raucous affair and the party departs in the early morning darkness, amid fireworks and laughter, for the site is in a distant hamlet, where the bull is being held for the sacrifice. The Monkeys and Passions in full costume lead the party by lantern and pitchpine torchlight to the hinterlands. These trips are affairs of great abandon and much drinking, the goal being to fortify the bull-pullers for the great task that lies ahead.

At the destination, which is usually reached by midmorning, the Passion addresses the keeper of the bull with elaborate ritual formulas, thanking him for his services and offering ritual drinks of gratitude. There is then a dance of the Monkeys, more fireworks, more drinking, and a ritual meal. The bull is then lassoed and placed in traces consisting of two 13-meter ropes that lead from either side of the lasso that secures the neck. Lines of men and boys grab the lines amid great hoopla, and the party departs for the Ceremonial Center. During the return trip, there is ritual use of *moi*, which is powdered native tobacco mixed with lime. This is used by all participants as snuff and is said to fortify the bull-pullers. It is also rubbed on the neck and shoulders of the bull to give him strength for his final journey. Prayers are also said for the bull as he is annointed with the tobacco. An older woman is appointed as the tender of the bull. She is designated *jalal me?tik* ("Holy Mother Moon") and deals with the bull as though he were her son. The primeval myth is being reenacted: the Moon/Virgin Mary is tending her son, the soon-to-be sacrificed Sun/Christ.

The five-to-six hour return trip with the bull is wild. The bull tries to get away and the lines of men and boys must restrain him. Much of the trip is spent running and the pace is broken only by rest stops at roadside shrines, at which time there are more ritual offerings of tobacco snuff, liquor, and fireworks, for strength. The party arrives at the Ceremonial Center in late afternoon, and the bull is tied to a tree or post in an outlying area, to be held for the early morning sacrifice on Tuesday. A small group of men and boys feed and watch over the bull all through the night. The others receive a ritual meal and drinks and retire.

February 20, Bull-killing Tuesday.

Several hours before dawn on Tuesday, the Outgoing Passion rises and goes with his Monkey servants and bull-pullers to the holding area where the sacrificial bull waits. Drinks are exchanged and thanks given by the Passion, who also prays over the bull, stating pointedly that the bull is not only the Sun/Christ, but all of us, our *k'exol*, our "substitute." Fireworks punctuate the arrival and departure of this group. The bull is led, in the earliest glimmer of morning light, to a snubbing post in an open area near the Passion's home. The ritual butcher takes over and prepares the bull for sacrifice. A lasso is placed on one hoof, and the neck lasso remains in place. This enables the group to throw the bull on its side. Front hooves are bound together, the back hooves likewise, and then the front tie is linked to the back tie. The bull-pullers hold the body while the butcher pulls the neck rope taut to the snubbing post in such a way that the head is thrust upward and the neck and breast are thrust upward and exposed. Just before the sun appears over the eastern rim of the Ceremonial Center basin, the Passion prays and offers drinks to all participants, again praising the bull for acting in their stead. At this point, mint leaves are stuffed into the bull's anus and nostrils so as to retard spoilage of the meat. As the sun appears, sky-rockets are launched and hand cannons fired in all three sacrificial sites. At this signal, each of the butchers, in his respective site, thrusts his knife into the jugular vein of the bull's exposed throat. The bawling and agony are long and terrible. As the blood rushes out, it is caught in buckets and taken away to be dumped in a cooking pot in the outdoor kitchen.

At this point all adult women who are not menstruating are invited to file by and kiss the bull's breast between the front legs. This ritual act has the goal of retarding spoilage and of emphasizing the "life-for-life" sacrificial theme. After the kissing ritual is concluded, the butcher proceeds to split the carcass with an axe and remove the entrails. The entrails are removed in buckets and taken for washing. The testicles are given to the young boys to play catch with, and the penis is removed for drying, after which it will be used as a whip by future Monkeys. The carcass is then skinned and quartered and hung by ropes, two portions on either side of the front door of the Passion's home. The bull's head is mounted precisely above the front door of the Passion's house. A guard is posted to fan the flies away from the meat until it is to be used the following Saturday.

The rest of the morning is spent in a ritual of thanksgiving, sponsored by the Passion and his Monkey servants. There is ritual drinking and relaxation as members of the Passion's entourage watch the events while the cooks prepare the blood soup that will be eaten as a noon meal. As with all events at the festival, men and women remain in explicit spatial isolation from one another.

The noon meal is served ritually in gourd bowls. It consists of blood soup, which is made of the bull's blood, water, *epasote*, and chile. It is accompanied by sweetened coffee and bean tamales wrapped in calla lily leaves. After all have partaken—men first, women second—the group disperses for rest. The afternoon is spent preparing the main dish for the evening meal, which consists of soup made from the heart, liver, pancreas, and lungs of the bull. It is seasoned with chile, salt, and *epasote*. The two hundred or so members of the Passion's entourage reassemble for the evening ritual meal, which consists of entrail soup, beans, tortillas, and sweetened coffee.

February 21, Shopping Wednesday.

The Passion's entourage departs at sunup for the Ladino commercial center of San Cristóbal de las Casas. They may go on foot or in trucks. Either way, this trip has considerable symbolic significance as a collective ritual shopping expedition. It is marked by much drinking and exchange of ritual language. It is also useful to note that all of the goods to be purchased are explicitly Ladino, non-Indian goods. In particular, the group will purchase thousands of Mexican sweet buns, made of wheat flour, in addition to coffee and sugar. They must also purchase many bags of citrus fruit from the lowlands, which will enter into ritual exchange requirements of the festival. Other items on the shopping list are ceramic bowls and enamel (or ceramic) cups, which each Passion must have by the hundreds in order to feed the multitudes at the ritual banquets. Finally, they will purchase hundreds of handmade skyrockets and bags of gunpowder for the hand cannons.

Another purpose of this shopping trip is to bring hundreds of kilos of corn for custom grinding into flour for use in the vast amounts of sweet gruel that will be prepared on Friday of this week. The advantage of this arrangement is that the large-volume machinery of the San Cristóbal tortilla factories can achieve in a few hours what would require hundreds of hours of grinding time by the traditional *mano* and *metate* method.

By early afternoon the shopping expedition returns home with dozens of burlap bags of purchases, including food and processed corn. It is abundantly clear from these events that Chamula depends substantially and symbolically on the Mexican Ladino trade sphere in order to stage its festival.

February 22. Sweeping Thursday.

All twenty-four major ritual personnel are required on Thursday to send cleaning crews to sweep rubbish and remove stones from all major thoroughfares and paths in the Ceremonial Center. Their Monkey servants are sent as marshals to supervise these activities. They conduct the affair as a "forced labor" event and ritually threaten their "slaves" if they do not work well. These ritual cleaning expeditions prepare not only heavily traveled routes but also obscure routes to the sacred mountain shrines and water holes. Combustible rubbish is purposefully and explicitly burned, perhaps anticipating the firewalk to follow on the fourth day of the festival. In addition, these sweepers must remove rocks and rubbish from the shrines and water holes and be sure that proper decorations of ritual plants and pine-needle carpets are in place. All of these massive ritual cleaning events are sponsored by the ritual officials and must be launched and concluded by rituals of thanks and acknowledgment, involving meals, dancing, fireworks, and drinks.

February 23. Gruel-cooking Friday.

This is the day of massive food preparation. The spectacle of Chamula Center on this last day before the festival is like an idyllic scene from the archaic world. Literally thousands of people are at work preparing durable food items that will last for the five-day ritual blowout, which begins on the following day. Each major and minor official has his entire entourage assembled for this final day of preparation. All realize that they will not be allowed to sleep or even rest for the next five days. The tone is one of intense excitement, domestic activity, and anticipation.

The major food items prepared are tens of thousands of bean tamales. They are prepared like large jelly rolls. The corn dough is spread with mashed, cooked beans, then rolled and cut. The individual pieces are then wrapped in calla lily leaves and steamed for many hours. In addition, hundreds of gallons of sweet gruel must be slowly cooked in great clay pots.

Although all ritual officials prepare the main festival food items, the principal foci of this activity are the Passions' houses, for they must feed not only their entourages but also thousands of casual visitors over the next four days.

141

The two food items that require the most preparation time also have ritual significance of a high order. These are the gruel and bean tamales. The gruel is required as a "snack" food to be offered as a gesture of hospitality to any guest. The gruel also symbolizes the radiance of the Sun/Christ deity and the life force itself, for it is made of corn, which is said originally to have been given to humankind by the Sun/Christ, who created it from the flesh of his own inner thigh. The word *ʔul*, which means gruel, is also the colloquial word for semen, and indeed the two substances look remarkably alike. Thus, there is a direct link between the Passion's role as symbolic bearer of the Sun/Christ's responsibilities on earth, and his role as ritual maker, provider, and distributor of gruel, for the deity is the supreme creator of all life, including humankind itself. Therefore, much is made of the ritual preparation of gruel. This event involves eight hours of penance, in which the Outgoing Passion isolates himself with his Monkey servants and the Chief of Gruel. He is required to stir the gruel in a vast clay pot in an enclosed room over a very hot fire. It is made inside so that drafts will not break the pot. During all of this ritual stirring, he prays over the pot and sings the gruel-making song, which observes the symbolic link of the gruel to the Sun/Christ's radiance:

> **Now it is surely descending as rain,**
> **Your blessed radiance.**
> **Now it is surely descending as rain,**
> **Your blessed shadow, Great Patron . . .**
> **Now it is surely descending as rain,**
> **Your blessed ritual meal,**
> **Now it is surely descending as rain,**
> **Your blessed heart, Great Patron . . .**
> (Gossen 1974b: 228)

The Passion works in seclusion, sweating in the intense heat and smoke in the company of only his Monkey servants and gruel maker. He is ritually preparing the life force for guests, who are, in effect, all of us. He is also paying the price of life—toil—for all of us.

The complexity of the Passion's multivocal symbolic role is apparent shortly after he emerges from the gruel-making ritual. At this time, he and his wife go in ritual procession to present a "baby tamale" and freshly made gruel to the Incoming Passion of the same *barrio*. While the gruel is the symbol of the life force, the baby tamale (actually a life-sized, baby-sized bean tamale wrapped in calla lily leaves) is a symbol of mythological sins of the ancestors, who had the custom of eating their own children as toddlers. Specifically, they made tamales of them and consumed them greedily. For this crime, people were destroyed by the Sun/Christ deity at the end of the First Creation. It is of utmost importance to an understanding of the events of the Festival of Games to realize that these symbolic gifts of life and death—gruel and baby tamales—are in fact the very contradictions celebrated by the whole festival: the forces past and present, internal and external, which give life and destroy life.

The stage is now set for the great ritual dismemberment of society. After half a night's sleep, all parties are up to witness the invasion of the Passions and their armies.

February 24, Saturday, First Day of the Festival of Games.

The first of the "Lost Days" begins shortly after midnight. Following collective ritual cleansing baths, all Passions and their entourages of Flowers, Commissaries, and Ordinaries convene for prayers for strength in the races, battles, and dancing to come. At about 1:00 A.M. the Lord of the Drum and his assistants arrive at the home of the Incoming Passion and the Dance of the Warriors begins. It is first performed here; then the entire entourage runs to the home of the Outgoing Passion and then returns to the Incoming Passion's home. The duration of this three-episode dancing and ritual running is about twelve hours, culminating at around noon on Saturday with the first of the great banquets (*kompiral*). This banquet is served by each Incoming Passion to all comers and consists of dried beef broth with chile and cabbage, coffee, sweet rolls, gruel, bean tamales, and tortillas. Throughout the day, personnel from each of the other *barrios* pay ritual visits during which prescribed gifts of fruit, tamales, and liquor are presented to the host. On all of these occasions visitors from other *barrios* are invited to participate in the Dance of the Warriors. The focal activity of the entire day is the Dance of the Warriors, which takes place around the sacred kettledrums on a dance ground located in front of each Passion's patio shrine. Figure 16 shows the layout of this activity.

As the Passion, his entourage, and the musicians watch from a bench located in front of the shrine, hundreds of men from the community are captured, in rank order, and "recruited" to the Passion's army. They are forced to become followers and are "initiated" through the dance. It is worth noting that in the course of the four days during which this dance is performed almost incessantly, virtually every man who has ever in his lifetime performed a civil or religious job, great or small, is reincorporated into the corporate community through this medium.

Victoria Bricker has provided a vivid description and interpretation of the dance:

> The Messenger fetches all the civil and religious officials, one by one in rank order, to take part in this dance. He has two assistants called the Bell Ringer (*jtij chilon*) and the Lifter, or Embracer (*jpetvanej*). When the Messenger walks up to an official, the Bell Ringer accompanies him, carrying the jaguar pelt, which he slips over the chosen official's head. The Messenger walks in front of the jaguar impersonator carrying his ribboned staff; the Bell Ringer walks behind him, shaking the pelt so that the bells ring. The designated official carries one of the Passion's flags, capped by the "Head of God." The Drummer sits on a little chair, his drums resting on a bed of pine needles. The Embracer stands outside the circle waiting for the moment when he will lift the man wearing the jaguar skin. After the jaguar impersonator has circled the drums several times, the Embracer lifts and walks him three steps into the center of the circle, then three steps away from the drums, while he waves his flag in the four cardinal directions, and finally carries him over to the cross, where he sets him on his feet. Immediately, the Bell Ringer snatches the jaguar pelt from his head, the Messenger seizes the flag,

and both run off to recruit someone else, the next-highest-ranking male present, to take part in the dance. The lifting episode is described as being "raised beside the kettledrum" (*muyel ta bin*).

The jaguar skin represents God's jaguar, who defended him when the demons (Jews) tried to kill him. Formerly, jaguars wore bells around their necks so that they could signal each other's presence in the forest. That is why there are bells attached to the jaguar skin. Whenever a man puts on the jaguar skin, he is impersonating the jaguar who tried to defend Christ. Therefore, no man can refuse to participate in the dance, for to do so implies refusing to protect God from evil. The jaguar impersonator carries the flag with the "Head of God" on top and protects it from the Monkeys (demons), who follow behind him. When the dance ends, both God and his jaguar are lifted toward heaven, symbolizing the resurrection of Christ. (Bricker 1973: 110-12)

To Bricker's interpretation of this focal event must be added the heavy multivocal symbolism carried by the monkeys, jaguars, and soldiers. They are simultaneously associated with the Passion in his destructive mode—as a foreign soldier—and with the Passion in his affirmative mode—as the Sun/Christ deity. Thus, each "recruit" who is marched through the Dance of the Warriors is embarked on two missions. He joins the Passion's search-and-destroy strategy for destroying the Chamula social order. He also commits himself to the Passion's alternate agenda, which is to place the Sun/Christ once again in the heavens, with the help of his jaguar soul companion or coessence. (See chapter 9.) This affirmative mode will prevail, at last, on the following Tuesday in the Firewalk.[6]

At odd intervals throughout the Dance of the Warriors—almost as a "fight song" in praise of the jaguar, the presumed coessence of the politically powerful participants—the Passion's musicians play and sing what might be called the theme song of the Festival of Games. It is called *bolomchon* ("the Jaguar Animal"). Here is the text:

> **Jaguar Animal in heaven,**
>> **Jaguar Animal on earth.**
> **Patron of heaven,**
>> **Patron of earth.**
> **Your legs are lame, Jaguar Animal,**
>> **Your legs are long, Jaguar Animal,**
> **Your whiskers are spiny, Jaguar Animal**
>> **Your whiskers are long, Jaguar Animal.**
> **Get up, Father,**
>> **Get up, Mother.**
> **Stand up, Father,**
>> **Stand up, Mother.**
> **Rise up, Father,**
>> **Rise up, Mother.**
>
>> (Gossen 1974b: 221-22)

Performance of this cryptic song of praise for the power of the jaguar is inter-spersed in the sequence of more standard narrative songs that focus explicitly on the cult of the Sun/Christ—"The Lord of Heaven, The Lord of Glory." The con-stant juxtaposition of the two motifs—Sun/Christ and jaguar—suggests they are indeed aspects of the same unitary concept, embodied in the Passions.

The banquet—consisting of free food for thousands, served by the Passion's entourage—occurs from about noon to 3:00 P.M., after which each official and his entourage return to his home via the central plaza, which must be circled three times, running with war whoops. After brief rests, each Passion's entire complement of officials and their parties reassemble at his home, to begin an afternoon cycle of reciprocal visits between the *barrios*. Dancing and ritual drinking of gruel and rum occur during these visits, producing what is actual-ly a series of triple stagings of the Dance of the Warriors. Finally, late at night after a modest evening meal, each official (literally) runs home with his entourage. They rest for an hour or so, exchanging drinks, but not sleeping, only to reassemble at midnight for a new onslaught.

February 25, Sunday, Second Day of the Festival of Games.

This, the second of the "Lost Days," is like a replay of the first day except that fatigue and excitement make the events somewhat zanier and wilder than the first day. The focus of the Dance of the Warriors this time is the home of the Outgoing Passion of each *barrio*. He gives a feast that is similar to that of the Incoming Passion. However, as Outgoing Passion he has somewhat greater prestige ("ritual heat") and is expected to provide the banquet for even more people. Since attendance is greater, there are even more individuals to move through the Dance of the Warriors. Hence, events are considerably longer. Fatigue also increases, tempers flare, drunkenness increases, and maintenance of public order becomes even more challenging as over ten thousand people converge in the small mountain basin. There is a huge influx of vendors from all over the highlands, for Sunday is the reg-ular market day. This brings not only a larger crowd but also a more diverse crowd, including tourists. It is as though Chamula is indeed being invaded by cultural "others," in a sense fulfilling the war proclamation of the "Spanish Letter," which behaves as a kind of charter document of the festival. Little do the outside vendors and tourists know that they actually have a ritual role to play.

This escalating invasion mode is expressed by the prominence of the Spanish Lady character in the ritual proceedings on Sunday. The reader will recall that the third Passion is also known as the Spanish Lady, "Señora Passion" or "Consort Passion." It is he who keeps Nana María Cocorina (the female impersonator char-acter) as his mistress. She accompanies him everywhere, wearing her tattered white wedding dress, flirting with the Monkeys and other officials even as she is cuddling up to the Passion himself. As if in sacrilege, she also carries at all times a sacred incense burner. She embodies not only the Malinche symbol (of Indian betrayal of Indian Mexico), but also the promiscuity and other forms of immoral sexual behavior that are attributed to Mexican mestizos and to foreigners.

Bricker describes Nana María Cocorina's visit (in 1973) to the Soldier Passion's compound, in the company of her Consort Passion. Like all members of the visiting delegation, she is "captured" and incorporated into the Dance of the Warriors. Bricker writes:

> Nana María Cocorina takes part in the Dance of the Warriors, but the Embracer does not lift her at the end of the dance. Nor does she carry one of the flags with the "Head of God" on top; instead she continues to carry her censer. After she has circled the kettledrums three times, she approaches the drums, stops in front of them, and waves her censer over them three times with a circular motion. Then she turns around and dips her buttocks over the drums three times, suggesting the thrusting movements of sexual intercourse. The expression ?ak'be ve?el means both "to feed" and "to have sexual relations with." Chamula men refer to the genital organs of a woman euphemistically as the "meal" (sve?el) of her sexual partner. Thus Nana María Cocorina "feeds" the drums both spiritually and sexually.
>
> The spectators laugh and comment on the actions of Nana María Cocorina: "Oh, but the lady is doing an obscene thing—he is putting her skirt into the head of the drum!" They call out to the Messenger: "Don't pull the tit of our younger sister [Nana María Cocorina]. Her breast is full of milk because she is pregnant. And don't poke her stomach, because she is already several months pregnant!"
>
> The Messenger replies: "Never mind if her breast bursts. Someone can drink her milk. But her child is already very big. Who knows if it won't soon be born."
>
> Nana María Cocorina laughs: "Well, never mind if my child is born. We'll look for another (head of) cabbage which can be stuck in; ha, ha, ha."
>
> Nana María Cocorina is pregnant because she made love with Mariano Ortega and Juan Gutiérrez in the woods, as announced by the master of ceremonies the week before:
>
> Mariano Ortega and Juan Gutiérrez came with their young lady, Nana María Cocorina.
> They go together into the woods to make love.
> They return eating toffee, eating candied squash, eating blood sausage.
>
> When she finishes participating in the Dance of the Warriors, Nana María Cocorina goes over to the bench in front of the cross to join the Passions, Commissaries, and Ordinaries seated there. As she approaches the bench, the Passions laugh and one of them calls out to her, "Come here, lady, for I feel very cold. Come sit here!" He wants her to sit beside him and warm him with the wool clothing customarily worn by women. (Bricker 1973: 117–18)

Thus, with the escalating invasion, and the increasing complicity of the three Passions in the effort to destroy Chamula, the moral order appears to be collapsing as well.

The layout of the second day's activities otherwise follows that of the first day, except that the banquet is better, being based on the fresh beef of the sacrificial bull. The first course is gruel, the second beef stew, the third sugar water and sweet rolls.

February 26, Monday, Third Day of the Festival of Games.

Monday is also known as *lunex ʔuch voʔ* ("Water-drinking Monday). It is so called because there are no banquets this day; the only ritual item formally given to all is rum. The Dance of the Warriors proceeds as on Saturday and Sunday, and the Passions' servants are busy preparing the food for the massive banquet that will be served on the following day.

February 27, Tuesday, Fourth Day of the Festival of Games.

The events reach fever pitch and climax on Tuesday. It begins with a spectacular torch and lamplight procession to Mount Calvary at around midnight Monday (early Tuesday morning). The three *barrios* have their respective Mount Calvaries, all of which figure prominently in the sacred geography of the community (see Figure 16). The Mount Calvary cross shrine is the most important of the many cross shrines visited by the ritual entourage during the festival. The shrine on Mount Calvary probably represents, ostensibly, a station of the cross in Christian symbolism. Bricker suggests that the ritual ascent of Mount Calvary early Tuesday morning may represent Christ's procession from Pilate's house to Calvary Hill (1973: 124). Whatever its Christian significance, it also represents explicitly the defeat of the Chamulas at the hand of the generic invaders, for all people, in order to be admitted to the mountaintop shrine, must present tribute payment (*patan*) in the form of broken potsherds, pieces of dry horse manure, or ritual bouquets of iris leaves that have been given the previoius day as tokens ("tickets") at the banquets. These offerings are placed at the foot of the shrine to which the flag poles representing the Sun/Christ's body will be tied.

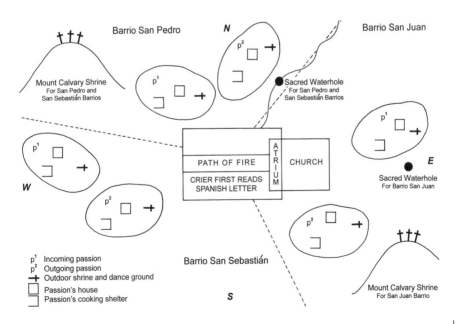

Figure 16. Chamula Ceremonial Center during Carnival
(Map drawn by Ellen Cesarski)

The Dance of the Warriors proceeds all night. Shortly before dawn, at a signal from skyrockets and hand cannons, the three masses of people representing the three *barrios* descend from the mountains raucously, running and shouting, for the final assault on Chamula. The masses converge on the walled atrium of the Church to witness the symbolic nailing of boards across the main entrance to the Chamula church. After this event and a final, triumphant reading of the "Spanish Letter," the three mobs move to the sacred water holes of their respective *barrios* (see Figure 16). After ritual offering of potsherds to the water holes (again called *patan*, "tribute"), the Passion presides over still another long episode of the Dance of the Warriors, but this time the site is in close proximity to the sacred water hole. This location seems to symbolize the final "taking" of the Chamula hinterland from its rightful owners. It symbolizes the conquest achieved. Chamula has been lost, center and periphery, to the invaders and foreigners.

At around noon the feast begins, with all present receiving an elaborate free meal consisting of beef, cabbage, and chile broth (each guest receiving three tiny pieces of beef), bread, tamales, sweetened coffee, and rum. While the feast is being distributed, the Passions' Monkeys recruit some teenagers and Free Monkeys to form two teams of about fifty individuals to participate in a mock battle of Mexico and Guatemala, or between the Carrancistas and Pinedistas.[7] The two armies group on two facing hillsides and, at the signal of a trumpet, charge each other. They reach the low point between the two hills, throwing hard pellets of horse manure as ammunition. There are three engagements. In the first Guatemala wins, in the second Mexico wins, and the third is a draw. At the end of the war, the soldiers rush to the spring for a drink of water. All of this proceeds with great cheering and laughter from the assembled onlookers. It is not lost on the crowd that the mock battle carries kernels of truth; they have never, in their view, benefited from Mexico's heroic military exploits.

As this is occurring, a team of assistants previously appointed by the Passions and supervised by the Passions' Monkeys, gathers a large amount of old roof thatch from an abandoned house and carries it to the Ceremonial Center. Here it is spread at a depth of about 20 cm to form a path about 6 meters wide that stretches clear across the central plaza, from the church atrium (east) to the cross shrine at the opposite side of the plaza (west). This path, called *sbe jtotik*, the "Path of God," is about 80 meters long and represents, when ignited, the path of the Sun/Christ across the sky (see Figures 11 and 16).

At a signal from the cannoneers (a massive surge of skyrockets and hand cannon detonations), the six Passions' entourages run to the plaza. They run around it, counterclockwise, three times, and then assemble at the eastern end of the path of thatch. In the meantime, the Monkeys have their hands full with the police effort involved in keeping the crowds off the "Path of God." It is regarded as sacred space and unauthorized people who step on it are driven back with whips.

At about 2:30 P.M. the thatch is ignited, and while the flames are still high, the key officials from the three barrios run back and forth—east to west, then west to east—three times over the flames and coals. This event never fails to achieve a stunning dramatic effect. The crowd is mesmerized, and it is easy to understand why. It is, after all, the dramatization of the cosmogonic moment, the first ascent of the Sun/Christ into the heavens, purging evil and vanquishing the evil forces of the cosmos. With the event, the ambiguity of the Passions ceases. They are on the Sun/Christ's side. Have they not traversed the very "Path of God"? Have they not sacrificed half of an average life's income and great personal hardship for the privilege of leading Chamula to its own destruction at the hands of foreigners—Spaniards, Mexicans, Guatemalans—and to its redemption and salvation in the hands of the Sun/Christ?

With the fireworks over, the tension and stress of the four previous days dissolves into a kind of secular carnival. The church is reopened, the market resumes, and live bulls are baited and chased in the plaza. It is as though life and order have at last returned. The slow, agonizing death of the sacrificial bulls at dawn just one week ago becomes but a memory, as very live and self-sufficient young bulls harass a delighted multitude.

February 28, Wednesday, Fifth Day of the Festival of Games.

Wednesday is known as "Fish-eating Wednesday" (*melkulix ti? choy*). It is obviously linked thematically with Ash Wednesday in the Christian annual cycle. The major themes of the day in Chamula are anticlimax and rest. Tuesday night has brought the first night's sleep in four days, for no one is allowed to sleep from Saturday to Tuesday afternoon.

Early on Wednesday morning all of the ritual officials gather in the Chamula church, which has been ritually reopened since the conclusion of the Firewalk. There are long prayers of penance in which the Passions seek forgiveness for their failings during the previous four days. At noon, the Passions give their final banquet. Formerly this consisted of dried fish and potato broth, but the menu now consists of beef broth, tamales, and tortillas, which are left over from the previous day's feasting. The older tradition is kept alive in Barrio San Juan by placing three dried fish on the banquet table.

In the afternoon the Passions and their entourages engage in reciprocal visits to their counterparts in the other *barrios*. These events are not well attended by the public, but are necessary for protocol. In particular, all participants are ritually thanked for their help during the previous two months.

Finally, in the evening, there are rituals of dismembering the body of the Sun/Christ. This consists of properly removing the flagpole tips (the head) from the poles (the skeleton). The banners (the body) are also removed from the poles. All of these objects are censed and wrapped in white cotton before being placed in their respective storage boxes. The boxes are then placed in the bromeliad-laden shrines in the officials homes, where they will be censed and blessed at twenty-day intervals throughout the year by their caretakers. This activity, by the way, seems to be a clear case of continuity of calendrical ritual from the pre-Columbian period. The reader will recall (see above) that the annual solar calendar of eighteen months of twenty days is still used in the community (Gossen 1974a).

The final event on Wednesday is the preparation for sale of the ribbons (the radiance) from the top of the flagpoles. These ribbons are regarded as a "spent" component of the Sun/Christ's body and must therefore be renewed every year. The used ribbons are sold by the Passions and Flowers on Thursday as amulets, which when attached to collars around the necks of sheep are believed to have great power in protecting them from disease and parasites.

On Thursday, the only festival-related event is the sale of these ribbons to people who drop by the Passion's house for this purpose. Otherwise, the community quietly regains its wits and cleans up the chaos left by the celebration of the "Lost Days."

CONCLUSION

Why does San Juan Chamula invest such time, such social energy, and, relatively speaking, such vast sums of money and resources in staging an event whose script is set and whose outcome is fixed? Why does it matter so much? No single answer suffices, but the most compelling answer to this question comes from the Chamulas themselves. They respond quite simply: "It is the custom. If we don't do it and do it properly, we will die." What, exactly, are they getting at?

I believe that they are appraising, in a complex idiom, who they are as a successful, if besieged, minority in modern Mexico. Victor Turner, in one of his many brilliant forays into the meaning of ritual actions, said that ritual expresses "quintessential custom . . . the refined extract . . . of many long-standing customary ways of behaving, thinking, and feeling" (Turner 1968: 23). Elaborating the idea in another way, he said that ritual is "the periodic restatement of the terms in which men of a particular culture must interact if there is to be any kind of coherent social life . . . it creates, or re-creates, the categories through which men perceive reality—the axioms underlying the structure of society and the laws of the natural and moral orders" (Turner 1968: 6-7).

The Festival of Games achieves such a self-appraisal by ritually destroying and reconstructing the moral community. Chamula stages and wins a moral, military, and ethnic battle that is not unlike its everyday battle with disruptive forces from within and with intrusive ethnic forces from without. The slow motion of ritual action at the beginning of the festival is focused on peripheral social space, the forests and lowland cattle ranches, both of which are associated with evil beings and with the Mexican mestizo world. The disruptive forces invade the Ceremonial Center itself as preparations for the festival proceed. At an accelerating pace, the familiar daily scenes—the hearth, sleep, work, leisure, sex—fall by the wayside, as Chamula returns to its primeval mode, its own childhood. The fires go out inside homes and life "goes primitive." There is no work, sleep, or sex, only running and the feverish activity of warfare and destruction. The ritual victory of the negative valence of human experience is achieved as the triumphant armies descend from the mountaintop shrines on Tuesday morning to vanquish all of Chamula, from periphery to center, with the ritual boarding up of the church door. Finally, the Sun/Christ triumphant prevails, the jaguar and the Sun/Christ defeat the soldiers and Monkeys, as the whole ritual entourage purges its negative mode by running the "Path of God," (the Firewalk), as though they themselves were the Sun/Christ embarked upon his first ascent into the heavens. Thus, Chamula reconstitutes itself through the Festival of Games, taking the whole community on an immense journey through space and time. Along the way, they re-create on the ritual stage what Chamulas have experienced as a people within the greater social universe of Mexico and the world at large. Ultimately, they "feel" why it is crucial to keep the center of the moral universe, San Juan Chamula itself, free from foreign intervention and moral corruption.

The following tabular representation (Figure 17) sketches the great breadth of social commentary that is to be found, implicitly and explicitly stated, in the language of ritual action in the Festival of Games. While this does not pretend to be an analysis–for the festival is itself a self-analysis–the table does attempt to synthesize and translate the magnitude of what is being said.

For each of the domains labeled in the left margin, the Festival of Games provides three vistas. The first vista (the left column in Figure 17) is a glimpse of life primeval, from whence they came. This knowledge is carried in the oral tradition; hence, it is implicit knowledge that does not necessarily get stated at the festival itself. It is taken for granted. I have attempted, in the description above, to provide this background information. The festival itself provides only shorthand reminders of what are in fact complex narrative referents. For example, one must know that Spanish was the lingua franca of the primitive world, and that it survives among the Chamulas' primitive contemporaries, the Mexican mestizos, in order to appreciate the mocking, derisive use of Spanish in many of the ritual episodes.

The second vista (the middle column in Figure 17) is the chaos of the coming of order, which is the principal theme of the first four of the five "Lost Days." These themes are actually life primeval, with consciousness of good and evil in combat. It appears that evil—life without rules—will prevail. It is precisely these four days, following the Sun/Christ's death and his subsequent descent into the Underworld, which are depicted in the first four days of the festival.

The third vista (the right column in Figure 17) begins with the re-creation of order in the Firewalk. This is the cosmogonic moment that yields the modern world and re-creates the contemporary social order. It is time present.

The Festival of Games relives the dialectic of the story of creation, of the past and present conflict between rule-governed and non-rule-governed forces. It is a folk commentary in the mode of macroanalysis, a reenactment and appraisal of centuries of ethnic conflict that Chamulas have seen and survived as a people. It shows clearly that they are aware of where they have stood in these centuries of conflict as tribute-paying victims, not beneficiaries, of the larger world's interventions in their affairs. The festival sheds some light not only on why Chamula has assumed a defensive posture toward the world at large but also on how they have coped with the threat of intervention. They do so by keeping a fanatically centralized political and religious organization that systematically purges unwanted foreign presence and militantly discourages intra-community factionalism. This well-known political style of Chamula is expressed in the obligatory ritual reincorporation of past and present officials into the central moral community through the Dance of the Warriors. As though this gesture were not sufficient, undesirable behavior and devious motives are finally purged through the Firewalk.

The Festival of Games is also an economic commentary. It clearly acknowledges economic dependence on the larger Mexican community, but also states that Chamula wants Mexico's goods and services on its own terms, in the service of the Sun/Christ in Chamula, not in the service of becoming Mexican. The festival is also a poignant commentary on the traditional agricultural cycle, an appeal to the Sun/Christ for another warm growing season, and to the earth lords at the water hole to supply rain, in order to make the sacred food-producing drums and the Passions' banquet an everyday possibility, not just symbolic tokens. Even the burning grass of the Firewalk and the horse manure of the mock battle are actually key elements in Chamula traditional agriculture. Each spring, corn stubble, dry grass, and weeds are burned in the fields. The resulting ash, together with any available sheep or horse manure, is dug into the impoverished soils of Chamula to encourage another annual crop of corn.

The festival is also a commentary on human psychology that is not unlike Freud's notion of ambivalence in human consciousness. Just as the Passions are at once the representatives of the Sun/Christ and of ethnic forces who would destroy Chamula, so each Chamula is an amalgam of ethnic patriot and potential Mexican mestizo, an amalgam of good citizen and sheep thief. The ambivalence in the Passion—with his coteries of evil monkey servants on the one hand and his holy coffer containing the symbols of the head of the Sun/Christ on the other—is perhaps in all Chamulas, and may be in all of us.

I conclude by returning to the beginning. Chamula's self-portrait, as revealed in the Festival of Games, can hardly be dismissed as a naive folk spectacle of an isolated community that is unaware of the external and internal forces that impinge on its fate. It is in fact an eloquent dialogue with these very forces. Chamulas emerge from this self-appraisal as a highly self-conscious, historically conscious, and class-conscious people. Perhaps this provides some insight into the extraordinary success that San Juan Chamula has achieved as the dominant Indian community in the state of Chiapas.

Figure 17. What is Happening at Carnival?

SUBJECT Before First Creation, Life Primeval	Sun/ Christ Born and Slain	Four Days of Festival of Games Life Primeval in Combat with Moral Order	Fire- Walk, Sun/ Christ Alive	Fifth day of Festival of Games, Time Present, Moral Order Restored
Space				
Ouside cosmos Distant space Periphery		Chamulas forests Outside of houses Perimeter of Ceremonial Center (mountain tops and water holes) Fields deserted		Normal focus of houses and fields, Daily round
Outside moral universe Wasteland		Themes of woods, water holes and cultural periphery		Return of Ceremonial Center to center of moral universe Central religious and political authority is restored
No churches No saints		Church is locked Saints are not for- mally honored		Church is reopened Saints regularly vis- ited and honored by ritual officials
No houses Evil beings, monkeys, demons, etc. live in forest		Houses destroyed for old thatch to kindle Firewalk		Proper houses, with thatch, tile and metal roofs
Raw foods consumed		Household hearths extinguished Cooking takes place in rustic outdoor shelters made of brush		Household hearths rekindled Cooking in houses
Evil beings every- where, for spatial categories are not delimited		Theme of Southwest (evil, left, south) quadrant of public space for censing flags, reading of Spanish Letter		Emphasis on East in all ritual and everyday motion Northeast (good, right, north) is most positive Association with rising Sun/Christ

SUBJECT I	II	III
Ethnicity		
Non-Chamula Animal behavior Animal foods	Lowland Mexican trade goods consumed: tropical fruits, wheat bread, coffee, sugar, beef, fireworks	Highland Chamula Ethnically pure Everyday highland food: maize, beans, cabbage, squash, tortillas
Ancestors are said to eat their own offspring Monkeys Precultural beings hostile to birth of Sun/Christ	Ritual officials dress and behave as foreign soldiers and monkeys Life-size "baby tamales" ritually exchanged and consumed	Restoration of moral behavior
No language "Primitive Spanish"	Ritual use of Spanish as foreign tongue	Use of Tzotzil (*batz'i k'op* "the true language") in both everyday and ritual context
Time		
Before temporal cycles No night No day	Dark of the moon *ch'ay k'in* ("lost day," "lost time," "lost festival," "lost heat"), five-day odd month in ancient Maya solar calendar, is the five-day period of Festival of Games No light or heat	Normal months in 18 x 20 + 5 calendar Normal seasons, festival and days
No days or festivals	five-day festival	three-day festivals
No sun in the sky Monkeys, demons, and Jews prevail (-)	Sun/Christ pursued and killed by evil beings, death lasting until the fourth day	Sun/Christ sets all time in motion and maintains temporal cycles with help of ritual officials (+)
	Ritual officials are both sun (+) and monkeys and soldiers (-)	

Subject	I	II	III
	Time of warfare, pursuit, aggression	Passion makes war on Chamula with help of monkey servants and foreigners	Peace Only legal defensive measures to keep Chamula pure
		Monkeys demand tribute: food, broken pots, horse manure, and stones	Only legal taxes from Chamulas to Chamula
	Aggression	Theme of constant running and pursuit	No aggression except for legitimate defensive action, for no one is afraid
	Gestation and birth of Sun/Christ in womb of Moon/Virgin Mary	Ritual officials become children, soldiers and monkeys, intent on destroying moral order promised by Sun/Christ	Chamula is "adult" Play only for children Children classified as "monkeys" until named
	Demons and Jews pursue and kill him	Emphasis of Festival of Games on irresponsible, immoral, childish behavior	Mainstream of adult morality and social responsibility
Economics	Goods unexploited, for consciousness of them does not exist	Passion gives free banquet of "foreign" food to thousands Theme of magical reproduction of food via sacred drums Theme of tribute	Food and goods available through labor, money, and service to Mexican economy Only legitimate taxes
		Theme of begging handouts	Families should provide subsistence needs

SUBJECT	I	II	III
Animals			
	Wild animals, particularly monkeys and snakes	Ritual officials become monkeys and snakes and jaguars	Ritual officials kill monkeys, control snakes, and accept powerful soul guidance of jaguars
		Bull sacrificed	Bulls return to life (post-Firewalk bull-baiting) Ribbons (rays) of the Sun/Christ protect sheep and provide woolen clothing
Politics			
	No ritual officials No order No control Chaos	All ritual officials, past and present, in and out of Chamula, reincorporated as equals in Dance of the Warriors (*communitas*)	One set of ranked civilians and religious officials, with strict deference relationship and hierarchy
		All bear both monkey (-), jaguar (+), snake (-) association, along with soldier identity (-) Ruling *presidente municipal* wears monkey costume All officials subject to immoral conduct	All officials are charged with bearing Sun/Christ's burden of moral conduct in defense of the community
		Three barrios separate entities as invading armies	Three barrios unified by common community responsibilities

SUBJECT	I	II	III
Social Organization and Family	Primitive promis-cuity among animals	Monkeys make obscene jokes, propositions to anyone Theme of Nana María Cocorina (Malinche figure) played by sexual offender Rules of sexual abstinence for ritual officials, combined with great verbal license	Strict rules of male/female respect and avoid-ance, except by cultural norms, marriage, bride-price payment, ritual kinship, etc.
		Negation of pro-creation Consumption of "baby tamales" Immoral sexual con-duct of foreigners Mockery of bride-price gifts (citrus fruit) in presenting them on behalf of Nana María Cocorina, the sol-dier's mistress Segregation of rit-ual officials from	Proper procreation
Language	No language Animal noises	Theme of precultur-al noise (rattles) of monkeys Theme of the ritual mockery of Spanish, the lan-guage of the ancient people Spanish Letter (in Spanish) as a dec-laration of war	Return to *batz'i k'op* "the true lan-guage" (Tzotzil)

Subject I	II	III
Agriculture		
Not known	Magical and foreign provisions of food	Firewalk brings heat, sun, light for growing season, ash for fertilizer
	Theme of "lost heat" and "lost days" of festival	
	Drought	
	Frost	Promise of warming weather
	Agricultural dormancy	Proximity of rainy season (May)
	Horse manure is played with as ammunition for war	Horse manure as key fertilizer ("swords into ploughshares")
	Water holes as receptacles for tribute	Water holes as givers of life
Food only from wild plants	Food comes by supernatural good will, as a gift, and by begging	Food is grown by expert agricultural knowledge and purchased by labor
	Free banquet provided by Passions	Food is earned

Six

〜〜〜

THE TOPOGRAPHY OF ANCIENT MAYA RELIGIOUS PLURALISM: A DIALOGUE WITH THE PRESENT

My coauthor Richard Leventhal, a Maya archaeologist, and I published this essay in 1993. It was originally presented as a contribution to the area of religion and ritual at an invited Dumbarton Oaks conference in Washington, D.C. held in 1991 on the subject of Maya culture in the eighth century A.D., a period known as the Late Classic. We sought to bring the archaeological data and glyphic inscriptions dating from that period together with modern ethnography of the Maya-speaking people of Mexico and Guatemala in an effort to use contemporary religious beliefs and practices as sources of inference for the interpretation of religious precepts and ritual practices from more than a thousand years ago.

This experiment in the use of ethnographic analogy must be regarded as informed speculation, for it is of course impossible to "prove" what was in people's hearts and minds in a distant era. Furthermore, most of what we do know empirically about this ancient world consists of material remains and glyphic texts that took their shape and content under the aegis of the states that ruled at that time; therefore, this evidence might logically be expected to reflect the interests of the elite who ruled the public sector of these theocratic states. This ancient world, as reflected in inscriptions and iconography, had a patrifocal bias. What was going on in the homes and fields of the nonelite population?

Our interest in modern ethnography, therefore, derived from the knowledge, provided by the modern Tzotzil Maya, that although public ritual for the most part focuses on male participation and a male authority structure, numerous domestic rituals—such as those associated with life crises, shamanism, ancestor cults, and agricultural propitiation—and public moments of social movements of the postcontact era—have involved the central participation of women.

We thought this exercise in ethnographic analogy would add substantively to debates in archaeology, historical ethnography, and modern ethnographic interpretation. This essay is twice multivocal. First, we attempt to mount a dialogue that moves across time. Second, we attempt to move between the gender-valenced categories of public (male) and private (female) sacred space to present a hypothetical, holistic topography of religious pluralism in both the ancient and modern Maya world.

This essay also sets forth a model of a typically Maya historical process (with initial female phases and subsequent male phases) that, we believe, characterizes both ancient and modern Maya societies as they have acted in history. This model is further applied in the arguments of subsequent chapters, particularly chapters 7, 8, and 10.

INTRODUCTION

Now, as we approach the quincentenary of the encounter between the New and Old Worlds, much is known of the religious beliefs and practices of the ancient Maya. Beginning with the great synthetic works of J. E. S. Thompson (1966, 1970), based largely on a careful, if fanciful, reading of the archaeological and ethnohistoric record; and continuing in our time with the incorporation of massive testimony from hieroglyphic texts, rendered by the ancient Maya's own hands (Schele and Miller 1986; Marcus 1976); and the sensitive new translations and interpretations of well-known texts (notably D. Tedlock's Popul Vuh [1985] and Edmonson [1982]), our dialogue with the Maya past is changing significantly. It has shifted from a once-prevailing interpretive framework based upon a European analogy (i.e., Maya religion was similar to Greek polytheism), to a more cautious approach that is based upon axiological premises of the Maya themselves.

However, the interpretive tradition in our time continues to regard Maya state religion as homogeneous, omnipresent, and universally embraced by one and all, from princes to peasants, from merchants to farmers, and by inhabitants of all the cities throughout the Maya lowlands (Hammond 1982; Thompson 1966, 1970). We seek in this paper to present an alternative view, one that directly addresses the evidence for religious pluralism, perhaps even competing cult affiliation, among the ancient Maya.

The dialogue we try to generate within this paper between an ethnologist and an archaeologist is not based upon a belief in the direct historical approach (e.g., Vogt 1964, 1994), although the reader may well infer such an association. We are aware of and accept that change has been dramatic from the eighth century A.D. to the present, but feel that this dialogue will help us identify structural principles that will allow us to make comparisons and to use the present to examine the past and the past to understand the present. By "structural principles," we mean to suggest relational patterns of beliefs, discourse, and practice within whole symbolic systems; a metaphysics of who's who in the social and supernatural universe. The content of these cultural systems may vary radically from past to present; structural patterns may indeed be fairly conservative.

It is essential at this point to clarify a point of terminology that occurs frequently in our discussion. As both ancient and modern Maya societies are state-level societies, consisting of city centers and outlying political and economic dependencies, we are dealing in both cases with two distinct types of moral communities; what Robert Redfield (1941, 1960) called Great Traditions, consisting of official state-level ideology and religious practice, and Little Traditions, consisting of local variants of the state-level ideology and alternative local ideologies and religious practices. We shall attempt to adhere to Redfield's terminology so as to avoid ambiguity and misunderstanding inherent in such distinctions as center/periphery or core/periphery. It is well understood, following Redfield's well-known concept of the folk-urban continuum, that the gradient between the ideal types, while permeable, nevertheless tends to express—in the Little Tradition at the folk extreme of the continuum—a collection of cultural traits which are local, circumscribed, and typically conservative; these traits may antedate the advent of the current prevailing Great Tradition that is associated with the urban centers.[1] We would like to emphasize that, as with Redfield, we are aware of the great variation found along this folk-urban continuum. However, we feel that the identification of the two ends of this continuum, the Little and Great Traditions, provides us with a starting point for our analysis.

Specifically, we utilize modern Maya ethnography as a stimulus for discussing the points of articulation between Classic Maya state religion and the ideologies of the Little Tradition. While the inferential leap is large and potentially cluttered with more than a thousand years of cultural baggage, there is evidence from elsewhere in Mesoamerica that this is not a fruitless strategy. Flannery and Marcus have used such a structure of inference for interrelating the ideational principles of ancient Oaxaca (Flannery and Marcus 1976). The Maya area also has a few powerful case studies (Hunt 1977; Bricker 1981; Farriss 1984) that show that the intellectual, ideological, and religious spheres of Maya life have, because of their quiet embeddedness in language and esoteric knowledge, proved to be resilient and functional in the colonial and modern eras.

The general issue of identifying points of continuity and change in the New World as it has evolved since contact with the Old World has been argued into a kind of fruitless impasse by the polarization of positions between those arguing for continuity and those arguing for a fundamental transformation of the Indian world into a peasant periphery of the "world system." Within the Maya region of Mexico and Central America, there can be little doubt that both positions have been overstated. Any reasonable discourse on the subject must take as a first premise that both continuity and change are operative today, just as they always have been in the past. It is clear that public economic, religious, and political affairs—even the social organization of Indian communities themselves—have been altered at the convenience of colonial and national interests for more than four centuries (Kendall, Hawkins, and Bossen 1983; Chambers and Young 1979; Wasserstrom 1983). It is also indisputable that such groups as the Mam (Watanabe 1983), Quiché (B. Tedlock 1982), and Tzotzil (Gossen 1974a; Morris 1987; Bricker 1989) preserve in their living Maya languages, beliefs, and related expressive forms clear continuities from earlier periods. The task in establishing a meaningful dialogue between past and present, therefore, becomes primarily one of identifying areas of discourse in the modern Maya world where one is most likely to find beliefs and practices that have proved to be either "unthreatening" to the dominant Hispanic Christian world or relatively "invisible" to its authority structure. Such a cluster of relative immunity from forced intervention and change is to be found in the Little Tradition of the Maya area in the realm of domestic social life and economic production and in the art forms, belief systems, and cosmology surrounding the domestic unit. The most important anchor point of this conservatism of Maya Little Tradition is language itself; more than six million people in contemporary Mexico, Guatemala, and Belize live in Maya-speaking households. It is therefore to the private sphere of modern Maya domestic life, particularly to the local knowledge that is carried in Maya languages, that we turn for the clues to continuity that guide our dialogue between the past and present.

We began considering the issues presented in this paper using a more or less formal model based upon the city, bearer of the Great Tradition, and contrasting outlying communities, bearers of the Little Tradition. As the paper evolved, this model began to weaken as we discovered the power and ambiguity of women in ancient and modern societies. In fact, the categories of the model became permeable rather than rigid. It is precisely this permeability and flux, rather than rigidity, that guides us in our central concern, which is the whole configuration of religious belief and practice in ancient Maya society.

Within the limited space of this paper, we have set for ourselves a large task in the examination of ancient Maya religion. We realize that we will not be able to cover all possible subjects and their implications. Rather, we envision this paper as an opportunity to present numerous ideas, their implications, and some of the archaeological and ethnographic material to support these ideas. We will not present these ideas in the form of testable hypotheses with a series of test implications. Rather, below are a series of models that we hope will stimulate others to examine these questions in both the archaeological and ethnographic record.

CYCLICAL AND LINEAR TIME IN THE PEASANT PERIPHERY AND CENTER

Cyclical time as an intellectual and theological artifact of ancient Mesoamerica was first expressed in the Calendar Round in the Preclassic period (Aveni 1989). The fifty-two-year cycle, based on intermeshing cycles of the 260-day and 365-day calendars, preceded the Classic Maya Long Count by about six hundred years (Aveni 1989), and has, in its modern permutations, survived the Maya Long Count by more than one millennium (Gossen 1974a, 1989a).

Because the old solar calendar still survives, largely in the domestic, private sector of contemporary Maya communities, the function and logic of sacred cyclical time may be understood in a full ethnographic context. It is significant that the modern Tzotzil solar calendar carries with it a dependent set of corollary cycles, such that the structure of the solar year is homologous with the structure of the day; the human life cycle; the agricultural year; and the four-part cycle of creations, or restorations, of the cosmos. Modern Tzotzil cosmology not only preserves a variant of the philosophy of sacred cyclical time but also incorporates without dissonance the Gregorian calendar, a linear system with a single anchor point in the past. Therefore, it is possible to examine how a conservative cyclical system of Maya time-reckoning interacts and intermeshes with a more recently introduced linear system.

How can such a case suggest insights into the Maya past? Modern Tzotzil public ritual and administrative life are regulated by the linear Gregorian calendar that was forcibly introduced, as a new "long count," with Dominican missionization in the sixteenth century. The dates of the saints' days and liturgical cycle, particularly those dates of the variable part of the cycle (Ash Wednesday to Pentecost), are published each year as an inexpensive religious and agricultural almanac called *El calendario del más antiguo Galván*.[2] This linear calendar enjoys a high profile of importance among the religious and political leaders; indeed, it is an indispensable document. Its written form, as with the Maya Long Count inscriptions, contributes to its symbolic power through its association with central administrative authority. In addition to serving as a basis for the public festival calendar and providing the administrative and fiscal schedules of the civil authorities, the Western linear calendar's cumulative and sequential years provide the register of future ritual obligations. Waiting lists for individuals who will assume religious offices (involving sponsorship of saints' cults) are kept in this system. For some offices, these waiting lists, kept under lock and key in the town hall, run well into the twenty-first century. Thus, both present and future orchestration of Chamula public life—a current local expression of Mexico's Great Tradition—is focused on the administrative center and depends upon the linear calendar.

Nevertheless, the Western linear calendar is conceived by Tzotzils to be no more than a cumulative reckoning system within the "Fourth Creation," the present epoch in the four-part cycle of creations of restorations recognized in Chamula cosmology. Thus, to summarize, the linear Gregorian calendar, a recent introduction, functions as a subset within a larger Maya system of cyclical time. This four-part cycle subsumes the linear system not only logically but also historically, for the major cycles of creation and destruction were undoubtedly in place before the Conquest.

At this point, it should be noted that it is primarily male political and religious authorities who need and use the linear calendar to manage the affairs of Chamula public life; indeed, most Chamula women, the large majority of whom have never been to school, do not even use or understand years in the Christian era. The linear calendar, therefore, functions as a symbolic and practical tool of the male-dominated administrative center. In contrast, the cyclical concepts within which the linear calendar is logically embedded are diffused in nearly everyone's collective knowledge (male and female, humble and powerful) and may be said, therefore, to be omnipresent in the sense of both social and physical space.

Just as knowledge of the larger cyclical framework of the linear calendar is diffused in all of the community, so the modern descendant of the old Maya solar calendar (Calendar Round) also survives as an important time-reckoning tool that is widely known and comfortably coexists with the Gregorian calendar. Known in Tzotzil as the *?otol k'akal* ("counter of days"), the old solar calendar of eighteen months of twenty days plus a five-day nineteenth month is used for two principal purposes, neither of which involves central statecraft in the Great Tradition. Typically kept in the form of a wooden tablet with charcoal tally marks, the old Maya solar calendar still functions as an agricultural almanac that identifies propitious days for engaging in traditional economic activities ranging from roof-beam-cutting to the planting of maize (Gossen 1974a). It also serves as the schedule for "flower-changing rituals," which must be staged every twenty days by ritual officials who sponsor saints' cults. Unlike the public spectacles of the saints' days, these rituals occur in the privacy of officials' homes and are not open to the general public. Furthermore, unlike the case of the Gregorian calendar, knowledge and use of the old solar calendar is as common among women as among men. In fact, the version of this calendar which has been analyzed came from the home of an elderly woman who is a shaman (Gossen 1974a).

It should be noted for comparative purposes that not only in the Maya area, but throughout the Americas and elsewhere, asymmetrical gender relations have figured prominently in the dynamics of states and the articulation of their patrifocal Great Traditions with their more egalitarian Little Traditions. The Tzotzil-Tzeltal region provides a number of well-documented cases of female instrumentality, esoteric knowledge, and political activity, most of it linked to the nonpublic spheres of life, extensive knowledge of oral narrative and oral history (Laughlin 1977; Karasik 1988), and key roles in subversive religious cult activity (Bricker 1981). In Guatemala, the Mam (Watanabe 1983) and Quiché (B. Tedlock 1982) are well-documented cases of females (and males) as repositories of traditional knowledge regarding cosmology and divination. Elsewhere, in the Andes, females were, apparently by community consensus, actually designated as "keepers" of tradition, even as males were forced during the colonial period to become religious and political agents of the new Indian puppet-state. This arrangement apparently received the unwitting endorsement of the colonial establishment, since women were regarded as irrelevant to its vision of local rule (Silverblatt 1987). Perhaps something comparable was going on in the Maya area.

We believe, therefore, that gender relations, as articulated with time-reckoning, narrative, and cosmology, provide a useful and hitherto unexplored angle from which to consider conceptual parallels between ancient and contemporary Maya religion.

THE NATURE OF TIME AND HISTORY AMONG THE ANCIENT MAYA

At this point, we would like to summarize several introductory points: (1) ancient and modern Maya cosmologies are strongly linked by a central logical structure based on cycles; (2) both ancient and modern cosmologies emphasize cyclical time as the more dominant and conservative time-reckoning system, and cyclical time is primarily associated with the Little Tradition of both ancient and modern Maya communities; and (3) linear time is the more ephemeral and pragmatic time-reckoning system and is associated with the creation and maintenance of political authority in the Great Tradition. We argue that both ancient and modern political and religious systems and authority in the cities, derived from and recorded in linear time, are in fact subject to the structural rules of the cyclical perception of time and history that preceded these authority systems and ultimately outlived them.

It has long been understood and discussed that the ancient Maya conception of time and history was cyclical in nature (Thompson 1966). A simplistic statement of this principle is that what has occurred in the past is also occurring in the present, and will occur in the future. There is an entire series of cyclical calendars through which the ancient Maya marked time. These include the 260-day Sacred Round (*tzolkin*), the 365-day Solar or Vague year (*haab*), a combination of the *tzolkin* and *haab* that forms the fifty-two-year cycle called the Calendar Round, as well as the nine-day Lord of the Night cycle, which cycles every 467 years with the Calendar Round. Other cycles existed, but these were the primary ones used by the ancient Maya. This cyclical nature of time appears to relate specifically to the ritual activity of the Maya.

In contrast to the Calendar Round and the cyclical nature of time is a more linear view of time as presented in the Long Count. We believe that there is evidence that the ancient Maya viewed this calendrical system as being both linear and cyclical in nature. The Long Count is a time-counting system based upon the 360-day "year" or *tun*. It is cyclical in that it focuses upon a cycle of thirteen *baktuns* or 5,200 *tuns*. The Maya used this to mark the beginning and the end of the previous and present-day worlds. The creation of the present world for the Maya occurred on 11 August 3113 B.C. and the destruction will come in the year A.D. 2012. Although it is cyclical, the length of the cycle is so long—5,200 *tuns* (360-day periods)—that the history of the Maya and the present day fall into the same creation of the world, and it therefore presents a more linear view of time than that of the Calendar Round and its components.

There is also evidence that the Maya perceived the Long Count as a linear count of time. The basic components of the Long Count are the *kin* (a single day), the *uinal* (a period of twenty days), the *tun* (a period of 360 days), the *katun* (period of twenty *tuns*), and the *baktun* (a period of twenty *katuns* or four hundred *tuns*). However, we have evidence from several monuments that the Maya continued to expand this basically vigesimal system beyond the baktun to include the *pictun* (a period of twenty baktuns), the *calabtun* (a period of *20 pictuns*), and the *kinchiltun* (a period of twenty *calabtuns*). For example, Tikal Stela 10 bears a date of 1.11.19.9.3.11.2.?, which presents a time or time period well beyond the reach of the basic Long Count cycle of thirteen *baktuns* (Jones and Satterthwaite 1982).

However, Coggins argues that, within the midst of what appears to be a predominantly linear calendrical system, the development of the importance of the *katun* ending or *katun* completion marks the imposition of a cyclical structure (a twenty-year cycle) upon the linear Long Count (Coggins 1979, 1980). Coggins argues that the identification or celebration of the *katun* ending first appears at Uaxactun at 8.16.0.0.0 and then at Tikal at 8.18.0.0.0, and marks the arrival of Teotihuacanos at Uaxactun and Tikal (Coggins 1980).

Therefore, within the basic calendrical systems of the ancient Maya, we find a combination of the two concepts of time or types of experiences defined by Leach as: (1) a notion of repetition, and (2) a notion of nonrepetition (Leach 1971). Leach argues that within "primitive societies" the notion of repetition predominates due, he argues, to the psychological repugnance to death. Leach continues and states that death and birth are therefore equated, creating a repetitive view of time.

However, within the ancient Maya, we see the continued use and importance of both a nonrepetitive or linear system and a repetitive or cyclical system. How can we begin to understand the correlation of these calendars that represent both a linear and cyclical view of time? Schele and Miller (1986) discuss the calendars as "an overlapping set of cycles, each different in duration and reference." Again, according to Schele and Miller, the primary reason for the use of such a complex set of cycles was, as with other people, to record "the history of human events." However, this does not explain the utilization and interrelationship of the linear and cyclical calendars. Although the Maya did not utilize the Calendar Round as the final cycle of renewal and rebirth as did other groups in Mesoamerica, such as the Aztecs (Schele and Miller 1986), it was a primary method of identifying time and history. The two parts of the Calendar Round have a certain amount of antiquity which cannot be ascribed to the Long Count, which is fairly recent and dates to the seventh *baktun*.

We argue in this paper that the development and utilization of the Long Count in Mesoamerica, and its widespread utilization throughout the Maya lowlands, is due to the development of a lineage-based kingship within the Gulf Coast, Pacific Coast, and the Maya lowland area. This lineage-based kingship, in order to legitimate not only the living king but also his successor, needed a linear calendar of time.

The earliest and most secure Long Count dates in Mesoamerica are found on Stela 2 at Chiapa de Corzo ([7.16.]3.2.13 [6 Ben 16 Xul]); Stela C at Tres Zapotes 7.16.6.16.18 6 Etznab [1 Uo]); and monuments from El Baul, Abaj Takalik, and La Mojarra (Winfield Capitaine 1988). The earliest monuments with a Long Count fall within the beginning of the first century A.D. and relate to developments during the Late Preclassic in Mesoamerica. The societies located within the Gulf Coast, Chiapas and Guatemalan Highlands, and the Pacific Coast have all been characterized as being complex and stratified in their political and social organization. Most often, these societies, such as the Olmec or the Izapa people, have been slotted within the chiefdom level of sociopolitical complexity (Flannery 1982; Sharer and Grove 1989). However, anthropologists have realized that the term chiefdom is rife with possible meanings and cultural interpretations (Drennan and Uribe 1987).

We argue that chiefdom-level society, a developmental phase between egalitarian society and complex state-level organization, can be equated with two forms of control of leadership. Flannery (1972) has argued that within a chiefdom-level society, the institution of chief exists separately from an individual who holds that office. There is no direct succession to the office of chief. We would argue that as some chiefdom-level societies become more complex, a lineage-based succession or descent system develops and it is at this point that the Long Count, or a more linear view of time than had existed previously, is utilized to legitimize this different political system. The appearance of the Long Count at Chiapa de Corzo, at Tres Zapotes, and at La Mojarra, all indicate to us the existence of a lineage-based chiefdom society at these sites and within these areas. We will not argue that full state-level complexity is the next step within these geographic and cultural regions. Rather, it is the lowlands (the Maya area) and some parts of the highlands (the Valleys of Mexico and Oaxaca) that develop into the more complex state-level organizations.

We are not arguing for the preeminence of the Long Count and a linear view of time and history in any of these Mesoamerican societies. Rather, we feel that there is an important integration of linear and cyclical time that provides for a different type of chiefdom-level organization, and possibly even state-level organization within the Maya lowlands. Cyclical structure still provided the basic underpinnings of the society, but this linear construction allowed for a different type of legitimization of power and rulership.

We can identify this same type of integration of cyclical and linear views of time and history within the modern Maya of Chiapas. Gossen has demonstrated that several aspiring historical actors in Chamula central political life—each of whom has proposed radical political and religious transformation of the central authority structure of the community—have in fact been both raised to power and destroyed by logical exigencies that literally existed before they were born. In this sense, the careers of Maya leaders, past and present, are also both constrained and assisted by cyclical time. Structurally and culturally speaking, individual Maya may be said to live before they are born, so powerful is the capacity of the past to structure the present (Gossen 1977, 1988).

One such case is the Chamula revitalization movement of 1867-70, known as the War of Santa Rosa. In this violent religious and political separatist movement, Chamula protagonists behaved not so much as new actors in history, but rather as reenactors of the mythological past as they understood it. It is recorded that among the actors was a Tzotzil woman, Augustina Gómez Chechev, who declared, upon receiving sacred images from the sky, that she was the new "Mother of God" (referring to the Moon/Virgin Mary deity), and was commanded by the Sun/Christ deity to form an new Indian religious cult, separate from the Ladino (Mexican-Hispanic) religion (Fig. 18). The climax and ultimate downfall of this cult came with the crucifixion of an Indian youth, Gómez Chechev's relative, who was, through his death and expected rebirth, to become the new Indian Sun/Christ. This bizarre event caused outrage among Ladino church and government officials, and the ensuing separatist movement was destroyed by Ladino troops in 1869-70, but only after its protagonists rose and fell as new representations of old mythological players on the Maya Tzotzil stage (see also Gossen 1977; Bricker 1981: 119-25).

Another case involves a very recent Tzotzil culture hero named Miguel Kaxlán, who founded the Chamula Protestant movement in 1965. He was eventually assassinated by traditionalist adversaries in 1981, but only after living a long life that bore striking structural similarities to the life history of the founding creator deity, the Sun/Christ. Thus, even in moments of radical culture change that do not look favorably on Maya traditionalism, the Maya produce actors who are not really modern pragmatists and rationalists, but rather haunting semblances of their mythological forebears (Gossen 1988, reprinted here as chapter 8).

Figure 18. Augustina Gómez Chechev and Her Cult Followers
(Drawing by Marián López Calixto)

In pursuing the dialogue between the Maya present and the past, this model suggests to us that the Classic Maya dynasties were morally underwritten and legitimated by the Long Count as a divine "historical" genealogy. These dynasties and the use of the Long Count were subject to cosmological exigency to reflect the past as dictated by the more dominant structures of a cyclical view of time and history. There is ample evidence for the importance of the ritual cycle within the structure of the genealogical history of the ancient Maya rulers. Long Count dates on stelae and other monuments within the lowlands are constantly found in association with calendar round dates and other cyclical dates. Although the linear perception of the Long Count is an integral part of the elite/kingship of the Great Tradition, it is intimately tied to the cyclical construct of the Little Tradition.[3]

In the present-day surge of hieroglyphic translations and presentations of the ancient Maya past as presented by the documents and other forms of material culture, it is important to recall an article by Dennis Puleston in 1979. Within this article, Puleston argues that the thirteen-*katun* historical cycle (256-year Short Count) was not only a primary factor in the development of historical events during the Postclassic and Colonial periods but also structured history during the Classic period. "It is clear that the Maya conception of historical repetition did not entail an exact repetition of past events but rather a conformance of history to certain underlying, predictable patterns as revealed in the katun prophesies" (Puleston 1979: 63). This concept of the death and rebirth of cycles and of time can be seen with Puleston's argument for the thirteen-*katun* cycle, the thirteen-*baktun* cycle, or Long Count as it relates to the destruction and creation of the world, and numerous other cycles including the individual *katun* cycle emphasized by Coggins (1979). This cyclical perception of time and history will therefore have an impact both upon the way events unfold and also, importantly, upon the way these events are perceived and constructed in a written form. This argument goes beyond Puleston's and necessitates new approaches to our "writing of Maya history."

Carlson (1980) raises the issue of what he calls "tampering with history" in terms of the genealogical structure and ritual time of the ancient Maya. We believe, however, that it is not an issue of "tampering with history," for the concept of what is history remains uncertain. We argue that Maya kingship "history" was constructed. What we would like to emphasize is a point presented above of "people who live before they are born." One can argue, as Schele and Miller (1986) or Lounsbury (1980) have, that the historical dates are set in time as records of actual events and that the ritual cycle was utilized to justify or legitimize the actions or activities on these dates. However, we would like to turn this around and argue that the Calendar Round and other cycles structured history and provided the framework within which the Long Count could ideally record the construction of history. Mythical ancestor gods, mythical ancestors, and important ancestors such as a lineage founder may have provided the life-cycle structure—perhaps even specific date—for more recent rulers. This is not "tampering with history." Rather, the ancient Maya worldview is structured upon and exists within a long tradition of the cyclical view of time and history. A more recently imposed linear calendar, utilized for kingship, is embedded within this cyclical system.

MODELS

We have thus far spoken of a highly structured and conservative template of underlying logic of the Maya cosmos that is based upon cyclical time. We have asserted that such a paradigm may account for striking patterns of similarity that exist between the structure of religious authority systems in the Classic Maya and those of the contemporary Tzotzil and other Maya groups. In this section we will sketch the derivation, outlines, and corollaries of the model.

DERIVATION

Practice and empirical social life simultaneously derive from and reify belief. To turn it about, as Clifford Geertz has so felicitously phrased it, sacred symbols are models of and for social reality (Geertz 1963: 123). In the context of this discussion that means the structure of everyday Tzotzil domestic life is the wellspring of the social reality of the cosmos. Religion articulates the essential qualities of both spheres. The paradigm we propose, therefore, derives from mythology—the past, and contemporary social life—the present, for each simultaneously sustains, reaffirms, and continually re-creates the other. The model proposed is thus necessarily paradigmatic (pure structure, that is, timeless) and syntagmatic (structure realized in time and history).

TZOTZIL DOMESTIC LIFE—A MINIPORTRAIT

Tzotzils who are not public officials live in patrilineal compounds scattered in hamlets among the cornfields and sheep pastures. Women traditionally move from their patrilineal compounds of birth to those of their husbands after extensive bride-price transactions and initial matrilocal residence are concluded. Women maintain the household and attached kitchen gardens and small livestock. For many months each year, women run these households in the absence of their husbands, who move about in a more distant orbit of economic activities and public service that takes them frequently to the Chamula center and to the commercial and political centers of mestizo Mexico. Thus, the peasant periphery and Little Tradition of the Tzotzil world is permanently and primarily occupied by women.

It should be noted that the Tzotzil language itself suggests this association in the term of reference *yahval jna* ("The owner of my house") that a man uses for his wife. This term is used even when (as is the typical case) the house is located on land owned by his own patrilineage. It is also the case that the traditional custom of bride service requires that a newly wedded couple live matrilocally at the wife's home compound for several years before moving to the husband's compound. The labor provided by the husband for the maintenance of the wife's home household is considered part of bride price. Tzotzil men, therefore, live in close association with female-dominated domestic arrangements both as young children and as newly wedded husbands. Both childhood and adult life for men are initiated in a surrounding environment with a female locus. Even death, in particular the preparation of the corpse for burial, is exclusively in the hands of women.

Although males dominate most aspects of modern Maya public life most of the time, and are the customary articulators of the community with Mexico's Great Tradition, it is nevertheless the case that women have occasionally risen to public power as founders and prophets of a new or revitalized Great Tradition. Notable cases that are discussed elsewhere in this paper are María de la Candelaria, founder of the Tzeltal Revolt of 1712, and Augustina Gómez Chechev, founder of the 1868-69 Chamula movement (note that even Ladino history associates this movement with Santa Rosa [Bricker 1981: 125]). On these occasions and others (the 1911 Pajarito movement and the more recent Protestant evangelical movement), women have risen to prominence in public affairs as leaders and symbols of proposed "new" Great Traditions, based on native priesthoods. Their moments in power have been brief, and in all cases they have been preceded and succeeded by male public leaders.

However, to reiterate the point, females and the Little Tradition with which they are associated are foci not only of beginnings and endings but also chief actors in the transitional and critical moments in the life cycle and historical process. Although the female principle is not typically or even consistently high in the public profile, it is nevertheless the permanent force on which this patrifocal community depends for initiation, revitalization, and final marking of cycles. Femaleness is ambiguous and anomalous in Maya society; it is therefore powerful not only in the maintenance of the status quo in the Little Tradition but also powerful in the public arena when the Great Tradition experiences critical moments of transition, revitalization, and renewal.

Roots in Myth

The pattern of domestic division of labor is reproduced in the interaction of the solar (Sun/Christ) and lunar (Moon/Virgin Mary) deities in the primordial creation myth of the cosmos. It should be noted that Tzotzil mythology assigns primordial sexual identity in the cosmos to the female, who then brings male sexuality into existence only to have it (that is, him) usurp her own primordial power. The following is a paraphrase and synthesis of many narrative versions of the origin myth from Gossen's transcribed corpus of narratives:

> Before the First Creation, the world was a single surface of mud and slime and it existed in total darkness. This world was populated by precultural and asexual monkeys, demons and (thanks to the Dominicans) Jews. Our Mother Moon (Virgin Mary) was alone in this primordial chaos. She becomes pregnant and was aware that the being in her womb was full of heat. The demons were also aware of the potential force in her womb and they pursued her so as to kill her child upon birth. Shortly after he (the future Sun/Christ) was born, the demons and their allies killed him, but he came back to life and fled west to the edge of the earth platform and went into the underworld, pursued by the demons. He spent two days there. On the third day, he began to rise from the eastern horizon as the nascent sun. When he reached the zenith of the heavens, his heat and light destroyed his enemies. With these events, the world experienced its first day and, simultaneously, the cosmos received its configuration and spatial limits, for these were traced by the Sun/Christ's orbit by day (heavens) and by night (the underworld).

A Tzotzil Cosmological Paradigm

Figure 19 is a schematic synthesis of the spatial and temporal categories that are implicit and explicit in the cosmos, according to Tzotzil premises, as revealed in narrative and interviews. Note the homologies that prevail among the daily and annual solar cycles and the cycles of annual agricultural activity and the life cycle. Also note the shifting gender valences of the quadrants of the day and the annual cycle, which are created by the combined values of light/darkness (male/female), on the one hand; and ascending sun/descending sun (midnight to noon/noon to midnight) on the other. Chamula belief asserts that female power becomes dominant each day and each year in the descending phase of the sun. (See chapter 3, page 67, and endnote 5 for the mythological source of this important point.)

Figure 20 represents the stages of the cosmogonic narrative of the First Creation, which also constitute the logical sequence of major narrative accounts of the three subsequent creations (or restorations). Since the sequence of narrative logic (A1 to A2) is homologous with the pattern of daily life, it becomes a kind of timeless template that generates the possibilities for historical action in the present and future. It is suggested that this pattern (A1 to A2) forms a deep structural backdrop for decision-making (with cognitive accounting) whenever any part of it is expressed historically with new content, new actors, or new challenges. In this manner, mythology provides the pattern for historical action in the present. It is both paradigmatic and syntagmatic.

A Grammar of Narrative and Social Change

The model presented in Figures 19 and 20 has been applied to the interpretation of Tzotzil ethnohistorical texts (Gossen 1977), contemporary biography (Gossen 1988), and ritual drama (Gossen 1986). In each case, human circumstances begin with an initial phase of social uncertainty or ambiguity (see A1 and B1 of Fig. 20). This ambiguity is taken away or clarified by means of female mystical force or creative power (see C1 of Fig. 20). In the case of the cosmogonic myth, the Holy Mother Moon has this role as the primordial creative power in the universe, for she is (or is to be) the mother of the Sun/Christ. No sooner is the primordial female power made manifest as a source of new being and creation than a male personage (see D in Fig. 20) appears and attempts to take away or capture the power of the female, be it her reproductive capacity or her mystical power as the "mother of god" or oracle for new cults. Once the woman or her power has been subdued and put away under male patronage (see C2 in Fig. 20), male protagonists enter into conflict with other males in order to dominate the flow of events in short- or long-term public history. It is at this point (B2 in Fig.

20) in the paradigm of cyclical history that male-dominated periods of linear history are typically expressed. Some of these male actors win (A2a) and some lose (A2b), the same in local affairs as in the public political and religious forum. This paradigmatic drama begins as a local conflict between the sexes and inevitably becomes a public conflict between male adversaries for political, economic, and religious power. The paradigmatic drama is realized on a small scale in the history of ephemeral but violent revitalization movements or in long-term historical trends. In all cases, the pattern is paradigmatic in that it is simultaneously the pattern of the day, year, and human life cycle, the logic of the cosmos, and historical change.

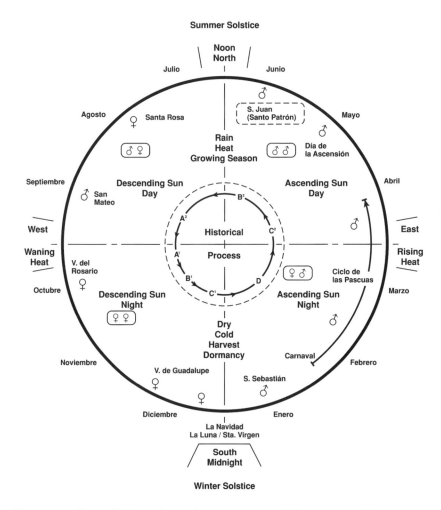

Figure 19. Tzotzil Cosmological Categories and the Historical Process

Figure 20. Toward a Tzotzil Maya Theory of History

A¹ Initial State – Malaise
Nothingness; steady state; coexistence of potential adversaries; pessimism; primeval muck

B¹ Chaos
Awareness of plight; threat of war, natural disaster; rising expectations; national political vacuum; local corruption, incompetence; poverty

C¹ Apparition of Female Divinity
Moon/Virgin Mary; Indian 'Mother of God'; martyrs; oracles; virgins; foreign female impostors

D Male Broker/usurper with new words:
sex, cult, knowledge, magic, power; words in female's name or own name; wrests mystical power from female; often foreign or nonhuman (animal or supernatural)

C² Male Ascendancy
Male organization forms and takes over, forming aggressive posture

B² Militarism
Male cult organization assumes total control, forcibly recruiting followers; slaying enemies; not tolerating 'otherness'

A²ᵃ New Steady State (Victor)
Purged patrifocal element reasserts its power over society (conservatism) or New patrifocal order takes over society (change)

A²ᵇ Vanquished – Final State
Defeat, Death, Exile, Political Fission; Transformation of Protagonists into animals or antiheroes who even in 'death' create threat to New Steady State (A2a), and may be impetus to new Initial State (A1)

THE GENDER VALENCES OF TIME AND SPACE

The early and concluding phases of narrative and historical sequences involve instrumental female power. The Tzotzil narrative tradition is full of such cases, as is the Western written record of postcontact Tzeltal and Tzotzil history. For example, the Tzeltal Revolt was precipitated by the declaration of María de la Candelaria that she had been designated by the Virgin as spokesperson for a new cult. This led to an effort to establish a separate Indian Church, apart from the Spanish Church and from the authority of the Spanish political officials (Bricker 1981: 59–66). Again, in 1868, Augustina Gómez Chechev precipitated the Tzotzil separatist movement described above. In 1910, a Chamula Tzotzil woman came to power as the "Holy Mother" of a violent religious and political movement known as the Pajarito Rebellion, which was (in league with conservative Catholic clergy) concerned with purification of Chamula religion against the godless revolutionaries who were soon to produce the Mexican Revolution (Moscoso Pastraña 1972). Even more recently, the post-1965 Chamula Protestant movement is said to have found its initial success in conversion through sympathy inspired by two sisters. These little Chamula girls became heroines for the cause of Protestant conversion after they survived severe burns inflicted by the ruling oligarchy of Chamula, who ordered the girls' home burned as punishment for their faith (see chapter 8).

In all of the cases just cited, these Maya religious movements began outside the local administrative centers, within the Little Tradition, in periods of rising expectations for local autonomy or local reform that were associated with periods of political malaise or transition in the national society. In 1712, the greater backdrop was the shift from Hapsburg to Bourbon administration of Spanish Crown policy toward the church in relation to local communities in America. In 1867–70, the Juárez anticlerical and federalist reforms were in full swing in the Mexican national government, giving considerable latitude for expression of local ethnic autonomy. In 1910, the anticlerical forces of the early years of the Mexican Revolution were being felt at the local level, thus diminishing Mexican central church authority over local Indian religion. In the 1960s, the national oil boom had shifted policy priorities to encourage industrial transformation at the cost of continued agrarian reform in peasant communities. Protestantism promised prosperity (that the government was accused of no longer delivering through land reform) to marginal peasants through radical change in their own lifestyles.

In all the cases just cited, the initial female impetus, which was fundamental in launching the movement, was captured by a male leader who sought to shift the movement from secondary to primary importance. In all cases, the females faded from view as males brought the movements into violent confrontation with other male-led interest groups.

The point of this discussion is to suggest that the ideology of cyclical time appears to have given to all of these movements a remarkably similar pattern of genesis and development, in spite of their diverse origins and different contexts. Given that all of the movements were of Tzotzil and Tzeltal Maya origin, and that these communities are fundamentally patrifocal in the structure of their political and religious affair, the female role in founding these new political and religious movements is striking. We believe that this instrumental female role can be understood as an expression of the initial phase of a timeless template of historical process that existed before the events themselves. We further suggest that this is a fundamentally Maya template, based on cyclical solar time. Perhaps it is a very old one.

It is important to note at this point that the pattern of gender associations just proposed appears to bear a strong resemblance to well-worn interpretive themes that associate females with hearth, home, and "nature," and males with the public arena and "culture." Is not the primacy of the female principle everywhere dominant in the semiotics, psychology, and biology of the human experience? Is femaleness not universally associated with the domestic sphere, local customs, continuity, conservatism, and with the early phases of ontogenetic development of the individuals? Although the apparent answer is "yes" (Ortner 1974), we argue in this paper that a broader view emphasizes the importance and power of women not only during the initial phases of development but also during transitional and terminal phases. It is also during these periods of change where female symbolic dominance is clearly identified in both the ancient and modern Maya domestic sphere (Little Tradition) and, most importantly, within the historical process of the public sphere (the Great Tradition).

For comparative purposes, it is important to note that we are not observing something bizarre or anomalous in the adaptive behavior of the Maya, but rather, a typical response of underclass individuals to their opportunities for political empowerment in stratified, patrifocal, or state-level societies. Instrumental female involvement in political movements that eventually involve the public sector is well-documented cross-culturally, and there is, we believe, good reason to incorporate the politics of gender into our consideration of the ancient Maya theocratic states. Irene Silverblatt (1988: 451–52 [footnotes omitted]) has eloquently summarized this challenge as follows:

> Studies in European and American history remind us that the state is not a monolithic event or institution that merely fulfills functional requirements of power and economy. Western histories, along with the variability of earlier states, have illustrated the complex nature of the relationship between any particular state and the gender relations within. They have also shown that as states contributed to the definition of womanhood, so did women contribute to the definition of states.
>
> Women conspicuously and collectively participated in the political movements protesting the traumatic changes in social relations and circumstances wrought by the expansion of capitalism. From the religious uprisings during

the British civil wars, to food riots in France, to religious challenges in Italy, to tax riots in Holland, women noticeably—to eyewitness observers and often belatedly to scholars—clamored against the threatened diminishment of their lives. Women's protests throughout the world assumed varying shapes and were centered on diverse issues. The nature of state power, the organization of work, the character of class divisions and transformations (each including their gender aspects), cultural expectations regarding legitimate standards of living, practice, and gender activities—all tied to specific state-making, colonial, and economic histories—contoured the possibilities of women's alliances and political engagements.

No uniform history of women in the state can account for the complex, often contradictory, histories of how women have engaged their particular political worlds. Some women's movements have been "enlightened" and progressive, while others—like the robust one that was integral to Nazi rule—have not. Justice to progressive feminism requires honest assessment of its limits, as well as of women who passionately embrace fundamentalism, the veil, and the "right to life." Feigning innocence of power, ambiguity, and contradiction ultimately demeans women's struggles, as it denies their potential.

FEMALES IN THE ANCIENT MAYA WORLD

Women played important roles within the ancient Maya political and ritual world. Little research has focused on the role of women within the Little Tradition of ancient Maya society. This is an area of research that is lacking in our understanding of the ancient Maya past. However, we can turn to the elite sphere or the Great Tradition and study the role of women within a historical context.

In examining historical figures, there are two areas of discussion we would like to pursue within this paper. The first will be the role of women as powerful figures within the ancient Maya political structure and as rulers. The second is the relationship between women and blood sacrificial rites.

We have emphasized above that within modern Maya communities, women play a multiplicity of roles: first, they are the focus of the conservative folk cult or Little Tradition and can be associated with ancient cyclical concepts of time and history; and, second, they are transitional and initiate change or serve as harbingers for new crises in the system, particularly within the Great Tradition. The power of women within modern and (as will be shown below) ancient communities is the contradictory structure they provide—both conservative and dynamic in their form.

This ambiguous and contradictory nature of women is evident within the hieroglyphic texts and iconographic representations of the elite and rulers of Maya centers. On the one hand, women provide a conservative structure that allows for the maintenance of the ruling lineage. Relationship glyphs or parentage statements, often found on monuments, document the apparent ties of the present ruler to his/her parents (Schele 1982). Another system-maintaining mechanism for women is the utilization of marriage alliances between centers to create connections for political power and growth (Molloy and Rathje 1974; Marcus 1976).

The Popul Vuh is a good place to start in the identification of the role of women within Postclassic/Colonial Maya and possibly within Classic period society (D. Tedlock 1985). Two women figure prominently within the story and provide us with good examples of both the conservative and transitional nature of women in Maya society. The point of intersection between Xmucane, the grandmother of the Hero Twins, and Blood Woman, their mother, clearly identifies the roles of women as we have discussed above. Blood Woman marks the point of transition between many aspects of the world. As the daughter of one of the Xibalban or Underworld Lords, she marks the transition point between the underworld and the Earth. In addition, within the story of the Popul Vuh the world seems to be in disorder, for the Xibalban Lords have defeated One Hunahpu and Seven Hunahpu; but the story is not finished for Blood Woman is pregnant with the Hero Twins. We would argue that with the birth of the Hero Twins, Blood Woman restores order to the world.

In contrast to her daughter-in-law, Xmucane demonstrates the conservative side of women. She realizes that Blood Woman is her daughter-in-law and pregnant by seeing the mark of the carrying net in the dirt of the corn field. Dennis Tedlock (1985: 40) makes an insightful comment when he states:

> To understand how Xmucane is able to interpret the sign of the net we must remember that she knows how to read the auguries of the Mayan calendar, and that one of the twenty day names that go into the making of that calendar is "Net." . . . The event that is due to come next in the story is the rebirth of Venus as the morning star, which should fall, as she already knows, on a day called Net. When she sees the imprint of the net in the field, she takes it as a sign that this event is coming near, and that the faces of the sons born to Blood Woman will be reincarnations of the face of One Hunahpu.

Xmucane as a "daykeeper" maintains and understands the past, while Blood Woman signifies change and transition.

At the same time, within the contradictory fashion of women within Maya and other societies, women who have become rulers have caused a dramatic transition within the genealogical structure of the kingship. Women are identified as rulers or powerful elite at numerous sites including Palenque, Naranjo, Copan, and Caracol, to name just a few (Schele and Miller 1986; Chase and Chase 1987).

The Palenque genealogy with its women rulers is one of the best documented in the Maya area and will be discussed here. According to Schele's reconstruction of the Palenque genealogical chart for the ruling lineage at Palenque (Schele 1991), two women come to power within a short span of time. Lady Kanal-Ikal accedes to the throne of 9.7.10.3.8 and dies a little more than twenty years later. She is followed by a male ruler, Ac Kan, who lasts fewer than eight years on the throne. The second woman, Lady Zac-Kuk, then comes to the throne for a short period and apparently steps aside when Pacal reaches the age of twelve and takes on the mantle of power. In terms of relationships, Lady Kanal-Ikal is the grandmother and Lady Zac-Kuk is the mother of Pacal. Schele and Freidel (1990) identify some anomalies with the accession of these women on the monuments of Palenque. First, Pacal portrayed both women twice on his sarcophagus. No other ruler is presented as such and there is no apparent explanation of this anomaly. Second, the identification of Lady Kanal-Ikal's accession to the throne follows the standard pattern according to Schele and Freidel (1990). However, Lady Zac-Kuk is not identified specifically by name but rather by a concept that refers to her as the "mother of the gods" (note the similarity in the role played by Augustina Gómez Chechev, discussed above). Schele and Freidel argue that these two anomalies are Pacal's way of justifying his position on the throne—by emphasizing the importance of his grandmother with two representations and by arguing that his mother is a god. Pacal, himself, becomes a god.

This elaborate manner of justification by Pacal is needed because these two women, with their identifiable positions of rulership, cause a transition or change within the lineage structure at Palenque (Schele and Freidel 1990). In a patrilineal system, when women come to the throne, the accession of their offspring causes a shift or jog within the patrilineage. The offspring of each of these women are tied to their mother's husband's lineage, not to their mother's father's lineage; therefore a shift in descent occurs. It might almost be called a moment of transition or even crisis, caused and perhaps resolved, by these women as rulers. However, as our model agues, once this period of transition or crisis, precipitated by women and even resolved by women, comes to an end, the new structure of the Great Traditions is returned to men. Again, power at Palenque is created within the hands of the male ruler Pacal.

It is interesting to note that these women at Palenque experience periods of reign very close to each other in time. This may mark a general period of transition and change within the Palenque community. At the same time, note that this conspicuous clustering of women rulers falls at the end of the "hiatus," another period of change and transition that affects most of the entire lowland Maya area. It might also be possible to speculate that Lady Zac-Kuk and Lady Kanal-Ikal are mythical rulers who were created to justify the genealogical shift to a new or different lineage structure. Such a creation may explain what appears to be an overly energetic justification of presentation of these women as rulers.

We would like to present one more example of an identified female ruler in the Maya lowlands who marks what appears to be a point of transition at a site. The ruler is Lady 6 of Naranjo. Lady 6 as been identified by numerous scholars including Berlin (1968), Marcus (1976), and Closs (1985).

Closs has divided the inscriptions and "history" of Naranjo into three periods: the early period of 9.8.0.0.0 to 9.10.10.0.0; the middle period of 9.13.10.0.0 to 9.14.15.0.0; and the late period of 9.17.10.0.0 to 9.19.10.0.0 (1985: 65). Although he acknowledges a hiatus in the inscriptions, Closs indicates that there is continuity in the dynastic structure between the middle and late periods at Naranjo. The reign of Lady 6's apparent son, Smoking Squirrel, and of Lady 6 herself marks the end of the middle period at Naranjo—a clear transition point in the history of this site. Naranjo's power as a major center is waning at this time and does not reemerge until about 8.17.10.0.0 or the beginning of the late period.

Whether or not Lady 6 of Naranjo or Ladies Zac-Kuk and Kanal-Ikal of Palenque are real is not the question. The point must be made that at major transition points in the life cycle of an ancient Maya city, women, either real or mythological, were often identified as powerful figures who may have caused this period of transition or even helped resolve the apparent lack of order within the world structure.

Images of women are often associated with the bloodletting ritual. At sites such as Yaxchilan, Bonampak, Piedras Negras, Naranjo, and Nim Li Punit, females are either performing a bloodletting ritual themselves or in conjunction with another person, usually a male, or are associated with the males who are performing this ritual (Schele and Miller 1986). We do not want, within this paper, to get into a discussion of whether such rituals were actually performed. There are iconographic representations of bloodletting rituals; whether real or not is unimportant. The questions remains: Why are women associated with the bloodletting ritual? We would argue that bloodletting, within Maya culture, is an act which takes place at a transitional period (Schele and Miller 1986), and therefore, women who are transitional actors within the Maya world view are part of this ritual. Bloodletting is transitional on several levels. First, the act was performed or was stated to have been performed at periods of transition within the life of a lord/ruler and within the life of a city. These transitional periods included accession, birth, death, warfare, or even period endings, and are associated with the political world. At the same time, these bloodletting rituals, which mark transition points, are utilized to maintain the status quo and legitimize the lineage. Again, we see the ambiguous nature of women within Maya society, both as sustaining symbols and instigators of change.

A bloodletting ritual is also a transitional period from a spiritual perspective. This ritual, which is analogous to shamanic acts, marks the actual transition of a person from a physical body into a spirit, an animal spirit, in order to communicate with the gods. It is a transition from this world to another. Therefore, as a primary transition point or force in religious ritual, women play an integral role in ancient Maya society.

THE TOPOGRAPHY OF RELIGIOUS PLURALISM

We have asserted that deified cyclical time is the older, latent moral order on which ancient Maya society and its theocratic authority system rested. We have also asserted that linear time was not pansystemic (i.e., subscribed to by all inhabitants of a city's surrounding settlement). Rather, the cults of the Great Tradition based on linear time were relatively short-lived and potentially fragile systems that required periodic genealogical adjustments as dynasties that ruled with the authority and legitimacy of these systems rose and fell. The more fundamental rhythm of cyclical time constituted the logical underpinning of linear time.

We also contend that the dynasties of kings, similar to Catholic cults and the Mexican civil government in Chamula, were male-focused expressions of the Great Tradition that coexisted with numerous cults of the Little Tradition. The dynasties that ruled through the authority of linear time were tuned to "faster turnovers" and were more malleable, in terms of content, than those of the periphery. The cults of the periphery, on the other hand, were and are today, more conservative and stable than those of the center in that they are concerned with the rhythm and maintenance of domestic social life and domestic economy. The cults of the periphery are tuned explicitly to deified cyclical time and articulate easily–if often in token fashion–with the cults of the center. Why? Because the periphery is logically prior to the center in origin and has consistently, in both the pre-Columbian world and the modern world, outlasted it.

MODERN RELIGIOUS PLURALISM

We should now like to sketch the panorama of particular religious cults and supernatural transactions that coexist in the contemporary Tzotzil world of Chamula, in the hope that the logic of their location and function in social space (though not their content) will provide a possible source of inference about the configuration of ancient Maya religion.

The vast majority of all Chamula Tzotzil live in scattered hamlets that lie outside of the administrative center that is the focus of all public civil and religious activity—the local expression of Mexico's Great Tradition. Although all people occasionally visit the central church (there are no outlying chapels) periodically for private petitions to particular saints, virtually all life-crisis and curing rituals of a personal or family nature take place in the homes, hamlets, woods, and fields that lie outside of the administrative center. Christian baptism—in effect, a naming ceremony—is the only exception to the pattern in that it requires the presence of a Catholic priest who performs the ritual in the Chamula church. All other ritual markings of the life cycle—birth, first baby-tooth loss, first menses, bride-petitioning, selection of *compadres*, house-entering ceremonies (i.e., marriage), burials, and annual offerings to ancestors (male and female, who return to visit the living on November 1)—take place in the outlying hamlets. These domestic rituals contrast with public rituals in that they may involve active participation of both male and female lineage elders.

Similarly, male and female shamans, who number in the many hundreds, have equal stature and perform their services of health maintenance in the homes of their clients. The supernaturals invoked in life-crisis rituals are male and female saints, the sun (male) and moon (female) deities, and the all-important animal-soul companions of patients. An animal-soul companion, of a particular species and of the same gender as the human counterpart, is assigned to each individual at conception. These special animals, known as *chanuletik*, share a tongue-soul (*ch'ulel*) with their human counterparts, and their two aspects, junior and senior, live in a mountain corral (junior home) and in the third layer of the sky dome (senior home) (see chapter 9 and Rachun Linn, 1989). The destiny of each animal soul—health, injury and sickness, wealth and poverty, life and death—is shared with its human counterpart and is the object of supernatural intervention on the part of the shamans.

Just as life-crisis rituals, other domestic rituals, and shamanistic practice are located almost entirely in the periphery and involve a strikingly egalitarian participation of male and female practitioners and supernatural beings, so witchcraft is practiced and ritually exorcized on what might be called a gender-blind basis in the periphery, often in the woods and caves. Witches and their victims may be male or female, just as shamans who deal with remedial measures against witchcraft may be male or female. Likewise, there is a widely practiced, though clandestine, tradition of divination that focuses on oracles known as *kaxaetik* ("talking boxes"). These boxes or coffers have owners or spokespersons—male or female—who will consult the oracles for a fee if a client has a particular problem or desire for information that cannot be dealt with through regular shamanistic practice.

In addition to the cults just discussed that focus on personal welfare, there is also present in the Little Tradition a complex body of beliefs focusing on the earth lords (*yajval banamil*). The earth lords live in caves and underground passages and are ultimately responsible, in their manifestations as clouds, lightening, and thunder (*anjeletik*, "angels"), for rain and the water supply. The earth lords live in families (usually mother, father, and children) in caves and are typically represented as wealthy, white-skinned Ladinos. In addition to their association with water, they are believed to control material wealth in the form of metallic money. Thus, they are the subject of many and frequent transactions between humans and their realm. They are the recipients of a major annual ritual offering that is performed at all local water holes and springs as a petition for rain; this occurs annually on the festival of Santa Cruz (May 1-3). Furthermore, the earth lords are the subject of many narrative accounts of promises of human loyalty and service to them in the exchange for monetary wealth. Significant in these transactions is the role of the daughter of the earth lords as a contact person. This woman typically offers herself as an attractive sexual companion or as a snake in distress. With these guiles, she lures human males into caves and into often catastrophic transactions of labor bondage or marriage in exchange for unlimited money and food supplies. Thus, it is clear that the earth lord complex is heavily linked symbolically with economic aspects of both the Little Tradition of the periphery (i.e., earth, rain, and agricultural productivity) and the Great Tradition of Mexican society (i.e., labor-bondage and money). The earth lord complex is "invisible" or absent from public religious practice, but visible in its realm (the periphery) as an important cult focus that is associated with instrumental female power.

In addition to all of the above, there are numerous minor spooks and supernatural beings, of both sexes and of an asexual nature, who inhabit the periphery and with whom individuals must, on occasion, deal. Among them are male demons (*pukujetik*: winged, hairy, black creatures who inhabit underground tunnels and caves), the female wind deity (*me?ik'*), and the female "charcoal-cruncher" (*xk'ux ?ak'al*). All of these creatures cause human misfortune and are, in various ways, ritually placated or tricked so as to protect humans from their malevolent activities.

In summary, Chamula supernatural belief and practice form a multifaceted complex of competing and overlapping cults. The continuum stretches from the highly visible public cults of the center that are, for the most part, dominated by male practitioners, to the nonpublic, even clandestine, cults of the periphery, that are essentially egalitarian with regard to gender of supernaturals and cult practitioners. Many, in fact, are solely female or involve females as the instrumental actors.

The great presence of female supernatural power in the periphery enters and subsumes the central male cults in the great festivals of the period spanning the fall equinox to the winter solstice (the Virgin of Rosario in October and the Virgin of Guadalupe and the Moon/Virgin Mary in December). Temporary female primacy in the center reaches a climax in the Christmas ritual, which is culminated by an all-female procession at midnight on Christmas Eve. Women also enter central political activity when the central male cults are "in trouble" or in transition; it is here that women become the new "mothers of god" and may potentially precipitate experiments with new or revitalized cults in the center, as exemplified by the "rebellions" or the lineage adjustments of the Classic period discussed above. This "intrusive female" role is also ritualized annually in the prominent role of Malinche—actually a male ritual official dressed as a Ladino woman—in the year-renewal ritual of Carnival, which occurs in February (see chapter 5).

Conversely, periods of crisis in the Tzotzil centers routinely send central male authorities to the "female" domain of the mountains and caves, where both male and female ancestors and earth lords are asked for help. A recent case involved petitions for relief from a major drought in the 1970s. An even more recent crisis (1994) sent male ritual officials to cave shrines to petition the earth lords for deliverance from the Zapatistas (Peres Tzu 1996).

Thus, the periphery maintains many cults and supernatural complexes that coexist with those of the center. These peripheral cults are more individualistic and egalitarian, with both female and male practitioners and deities. These cults do not compete openly with the cults of the center, for they have different rhythms, functions, and agendas. They do not really depend on the central cults, although they passively acknowledge them. Rather, in the last analysis, the center depends, both cognitively and spiritually, on the periphery for survival and renewal.

PLURALISM IN THE ANCIENT MAYA WORLD

In developing this section on the ancient Maya world, we wish to emphasize that we do not propose that the Little Tradition of the ancient Maya bears specific resemblance to that of the modern Tzotzil described above. We do, however, propose that the ancient Maya Little Tradition is certain to have existed in some form. A responsible reading of the ancient Maya world must proceed with an appreciation that there was undoubtedly a complex realm of individual and domestic supernatural practice that did not find its way into the formal inscriptions and iconography of the centers. We propose that its content will reveal a cosmos in which state religion was but one of many voices of supernatural vigilance over human affairs.

We can easily begin, as Leventhal and others have argued (Leventhal 1983; Proskouriakoff 1962), that Maya religion on all levels is based upon ancestor worship. Within the centers, ancestor worship is highly complex and structured for it is, de facto, the state religion. Outside of the center, within the periphery, ancestor worship is also evident but it is a more localized version, clearly different in each family's case. Within the Little Tradition of the periphery, there is an integration with state religion of the Great Tradition, which provides a canopy under which the individualized ancestor worship can function.

The existence of a complex Little Tradition which exists alongside the state religion of the centers has been argued many times in the past.

Probably the strongest proponent of such a model was Stephen de Borhegyi, who identified the existence of what he termed the "folk cult" or "folk tradition" that was omnipresent in the ancient Maya cultures of the highlands and lowlands (Borhegyi 1956). Borhegyi perceived this folk cult as a stable manifestation that survives, relatively unchanged, within the lower strata of society, among the farmers and the peasants. During periods of highly complex, centralized state-level religious and political organization, the folk cult, according to Borhegyi, continues to exist but disappears in terms of its material manifestations. The material culture is controlled by the state religion. During periods when the centralized state religion does not exist, the material remains are dominated once again by the folk cult, similar in form to their previous existence.

We agree with Borhegyi's picture of a complex series of distinct "subcultures" that existed within ancient Maya religious organization. However, we feel that the physical manifestations or remains of these cults did not disappear completely during periods of centralization such as the eighth century A.D. The great number of incense burners, household altars, handmade and moldmade figurines, and family shrines found in direct association with residential structures at numerous ancient Maya sites including Copan (Leventhal 1979) argues for the existence of localized cults.

These Little Tradition cults are integrated within the centralized state religion within the settlement and outlying hinterland surrounding the Maya cities. For even within these outlying plaza groups, we find evidence of the centralized state religion of each city in the form of shrines, oratories, altars, and caches. These are found at such sites at Seibal (Tourtellot 1988), Copan (Leventhal 1979; Willey et al. 1994), and at Tikal (Haviland 1963) to name a few.

The picture of the ancient Maya religion continues to become complex and clouded when one turns to the center and identifies the existence of not only ancestor worship but also the worship of a series of deities tied to the natural world (Schele and Miller 1986). These deities have become formalized with specific features and markings to identify them, and they are used as a setting for the ancestor gods. Good examples include the Celestial Monster, the Cauac Monster, the Jaguar God or the Sun God, and, most importantly, the Maize God. The existence of these formalized "natural" gods within the centers of the ancient world emphasizes the difference between the ancient and modern Maya worlds. This is a contrast between the internal, autochthonous development of ancient Maya complexity and those forms that resulted from imposed conquest situations.

Within the ancient world, the city centers were, at an earlier time, a part of the periphery. They were single family household groups that grew and gradually became the focal points of cities for numerous reasons not to be examined here. The center, therefore, is the periphery transformed, writ large, and formalized. Ancestor worship becomes structured and the animal souls, spooks, and natural deities of the periphery become formalized into a state religion.

CONCLUSION

To merge beginnings and endings will, we trust, be acceptable in this setting. As we conclude, it should be noted that we have not once defined the phrase, "the topography of religious pluralism," which appears in our title. What, at last, do we mean? To read it literally, topography is a representation of what is where in a physical landscape. To extend this, we have attempted to sketch what is where in the supernatural and metaphysical landscape of Maya thought.

Modern and ancient Maya religious organizations are complex systems which both define and organize the surrounding world in the past and present. We have attempted to present what we argue is a deep structural template that allows us to examine the past and the present in relation to one another. The template provides us with a model that emphasizes the conservative periphery and the more fluid center. It is the conservative periphery that allows us to examine the ancient and modern worlds. And, because the fluid centers and Great Traditions of the ancient world are indeed a formalized periphery deriving from the Little Tradition, we are able to gain insights into the entire spectrum of the ancient Maya world at the eighth century A.D.

Seven

INDIANS INSIDE AND OUTSIDE OF THE MEXICAN NATIONAL IDEA: A CASE STUDY OF THE MODERN DIASPORA OF SAN JUAN CHAMULA

Composed in 1983 and published in Spanish language editions in 1983 and in 1992, this essay appears here for the first time in English. It records for the most part historical data pertaining to the Chamula diaspora, dating from at least the mid-nineteenth century. Internal migration ranks with (and sometimes is in tandem with) conversion to Protestantism among the most important sources of culture change relevant to Chamula and other Maya communities as they move into the twenty-first century.

The intent of this essay, however, is not merely to provide a historical account of the diverse types of communities that make up the Chamula diaspora but also to make sense of the tendency of many Chamula colonies—some of them in existence for more than a century—to retain their language, ethnicity, and various forms of typically Chamula cultural expressions. Indeed, the numbers of people who claim Tzotzil as their native language is increasing with each census.

I advance here the argument that the typical Chamula domestic unit of the diaspora population, like that of the home municipio, is primarily "owned by" and permanently occupied by monolingual Tzotzil-speaking women, who, in the frequent absence of their partially bilingual husbands for reasons of outside employment and other forms of interaction with "new neighbors," tend to socialize their children as ethnic Indians, the primary identity marker of which is the use of Tzotzil as a first language.

This essay, therefore, relates directly to previous and subsequent discussions of the instrumental importance of women in the renewal, reproduction, and creation of new Chamula Tzotzil cultural forms. I argue that the primacy of women as relatively low-profile cultural conservators, adaptors, and creators in Chamula Indian communities is not unrelated to the role of Mexico's Janus-faced Malinche/Guadalupe complex as the simultaneous traitor/genitrix dynamic in the construction and sustenance of Mexican national culture.

INTRODUCTION

I recently learned an idiom of Mexican Spanish usage that was new to me. *Se le sube el (lo) indio a uno* ("to lose one's cool" idiomatically translated into American English) is apparently used with some frequency as a mode of commentary on a wide variety of situations in the flow of Mexican life. A typical context that might elicit the phrase from an observer results when another person suddenly loses control and abandons customary, conforming behavior, as in sudden anger, unexpected stubbornness, drunken excess, or an outburst of violent or emotional behavior. This example serves as a useful entree into the subject matter of this paper, which is about adaptive strategies that Mesoamerican Indians have used historically as a means of surviving in and coping with the postcontact social context of Mexico. Indeed, the idiom reminds us that whatever their historical fate, Indians will survive in perpetuity for *el indio* lies in the consciousness of all Mexicans. It is always ready to reemerge in its many guises.

The issue of "where is the *indio* in Mexico?" is far from trivial, for Mexico is, by any reckoning, the quintessential *mestizo* (mixed European and Indian) nation of the Americas, such that even if one is a recent Lebanese immigrant, one soon realizes that to be Mexican is to acquire, feign, or, minimally, to acknowledge an Indian spiritual heritage. Then one is free to deny and hide it, only to manifest it in moments of stress . . . *cuando se le suba*. The history of Mexican life and letters is full of anomalies that underline its unique love-hate relationship with its Indian heritage. It is well-known that most of Mexico's national symbols and national heroes, as well as her artistic and intellectual achievements, acknowledge and celebrate forthrightly the nation's complex Indian heritage.

I shall cite only a few of the most obvious cases. The Virgin of Guadalupe endowed Mexico, from the sixteenth century forward, with an indelible Indian spirit. Morelos and Hidalgo were among the few heroes of the Latin American Independence movement who sought autonomy from Spain without the criollo ideology that accompanied the movements elsewhere in Hispanic America. Indeed, the issues voiced in the *Grito de Dolores* (traditionally attributed to Hidalgo):

> Fuera el mal gobierno/Down with bad government!
> Mueran los gachupines/Death to the Spaniards!
> Viva la Virgen de Guadalupe . . . /Long live the Virgin of Guadalupe! . . .

were harbingers of the Mexican social upheaval and cultural fluorescence of the twentieth century. The great Benito Juárez, Mexico's superhero of the nineteenth century, was of Zapotec Indian origin. Finally, Mexico's great epic revolution and its vast legacy of arts, letters, and social legislation in our time, are all colored with the nation's past and present Indian heritage.

As the idiom *subirle el indio* says, the *indio* is latent in the Mexican spirit;

it has always been there and will never go away. Yet, just as surely as *el indio* is in all of mestizo Mexico—if not genetically, then spiritually—there remain many, many millions of contemporary Indians who as yet do not move and think within the great cultural traditions (in Robert Redfield's sense of "great tradition," i.e., national culture or civilization, as contrasted with "little local traditions") of modern Mexico. The Mexican great tradition, however ambivalently, is compelled to include *los indios* in its national ideology and political agenda, but it also excludes them because the abstraction *indios* is actually spoken in common Mexican usage as the condescending and diminutive term *inditos*, referring to many millions of contemporary, mostly rural, people who do not share the national heritage of which they are, ironically, an integral part.

Some parts of Mexico—notably its regions of heavy Indian population, such as Oaxaca, Yucatán, and Chiapas—retain to this day a de facto social order based on *casta*, one in which most Indians are obliged to find some way of coping either as relatively isolated ethnic *indios* or as menial, marginalized participants in the rural and urban labor force. In these areas, where the dual culture is a way of life, the Ladino/mestizo sector—which bears the language and customs of the national culture—behaves as a separate social order from the indios. It depends on the goods and services of the Indian sector, but does not include indios in its everyday and institutional life. Indians have exercised a number of options for coping with this asymmetrical institutional life. These options range from conscious assimilation (*Ladinoization*) to militant separatism, along with many patterns of pragmatic coexistence with the Ladino/mestizo sector.

What does this matrix of subjugation and subordination look like from the perspective of those who live outside the Ladino/mestizo sector and seek admission to their "own house"? Do they even want to go into their "own home"? Or does their own home lie permanently elsewhere, outside the fabric of Mexican society? The answers to these questions are neither simple nor consistent from community to community or from individual to individual. Indians, indeed all Mexicans and people everywhere, have their own pragmatic agendas for coping and finding a way through their lives and times. I believe, therefore, that large-scale generalizations about social change and acculturation in Mexico and Latin America are likely to be either trivial or wrong.

In this chapter I hope to provide a small-scale comparative study that will illustrate, on the regional level, the complexity of the process of Indian adaptation to Mexican national life in the late twentieth century. My subject is the diaspora of the Chamula Tzotzil Indians in the state of Chiapas, Mexico.

This chapter will tell the extraordinary tale of a thriving and vital Indian community that both coexists and competes with the Mexican state, a community that is both dispersed demographically in at least 130 immigrant colonies and also, paradoxically, a community that willingly avails itself of educational, economic, and political opportunities provided by the Mexican state, but whose numbers of monolingual speakers of Tzotzil increase significantly with each census. Sometimes known as the "Jews of Chiapas," the Chamulas have successfully adapted to many different social and environmental niches of the state.

In what follows, I shall provide ethnographic and historical background for the Chamula diaspora and then offer a classification of the types of colonies that make up the extended community. By "extended community" I mean the parent community of San Juan Chamula and its 130 colonies. I shall then discuss the social and ideational strategies that bind the extended community, with all of its genuine diversity, into what might be called a "federated" moral and ethnic community that seems to have remarkable power to persist even as the modernization process swirls about Mexico and Central America.

THE BIG PICTURE: THE TZOTZIL AND TZELTAL PEOPLES IN CHIAPAS

Since approximately 300 A.D. the Tzotzil-Tzeltal-speaking family of Maya Indians have lived as corn farmers in the oak-and-pine forested highlands of what is now Chiapas, the southernmost state of Mexico. Although continuously transformed and influenced by great waves of political, ideological, and economic powers greater than they—spanning the period of the Olmecs (600 B.C.–200 A.D.) to that of the Nahuatl-speaking Aztecs (1300–1521 A.D.), then the Spanish colonial enterprise, and now the great forces of twentieth-century Mexican national culture—the Tzotzil-Tzeltal Indians of the area have persisted as a significant human presence in Mesoamerica. They are heirs in some ways to the Ancient Maya. They are part of what is today the largest contiguous complex of historically related Native Americans left in all of North and Central America. In all, the contemporary Maya people of Mexico number some 2.5 to 3 million, and are concentrated in the states of Chiapas, Yucatán, Tabasco, and Quintana Roo; and in Guatemala, Belize, and Honduras, some 4 million.

The Tzotzil and Tzeltal peoples of Chiapas make up but a fraction of this Maya complex, yet they constitute the majority population of some twenty *municipios,* or townships, in the central part of the state of Chiapas. They live for the most part as subsistence corn farmers, artisans, traders, and day-laborers in Mexican-owned commercial agricultural operations. They are therefore highly visible as ethnic "others" is the social and economic character of central Chiapas. Most significantly, their language, customs, dress, and general outlook on the world distinguish them from Ladinos, bearers of the mainstream Spanish-speaking national culture of the area.

Whether one regards the Tzotzil-Tzeltal peoples as a disadvantaged rural proletariat, created by the capitalistic "world system" (Stavenhagen 1970; Wasserstrom 1977; Wallerstein 1974) or as cultural entities which are ideologically separate from the Western world (Vogt 1964), or by their own definition as the Sun/Christ deity's chosen people on earth (Gossen 1974b), one is forced to recognize some fundamental facts about them. First, they constitute a significant minority population in the region. Second, they are critically important as laborers and producers in the region's agricultural economy. Third, different Tzotzil-Tzeltal communities have responded in strikingly different ways to the social and economic forces of our time which have thrust these groups into a face-off encounter with variants of Western culture. Some of these communities will disappear as distinct cultural entities within a generation. Others will persist, perhaps indefinitely. Finally, by any form of reckoning, qualitative or quantitative, Tzotzil-speaking Chamulas are likely candidates for persistence. This is their story.

From the early 1940s to the present, the Tzotzil-speaking area of Highland Chiapas has been the focus of several major ethnographic and linguistic research projects and many independent investigations. The cumulative modern ethnographic, linguistic, and ethnohistoric record of the Tzotzil peoples is remarkable in scope, quantity, and detail. (See Vogt 1978 and 1994b for the extensive Harvard Chiapas Project bibliography; McQuown 1959 for the Chicago Man-in-Nature Project bibliography; Aguirre-Beltrán 1978 for Mexican and foreign research in the area; Gossen 1985 and Laughlin 1975 and 1977 for language, literature, oral tradition, and linguistics; Wasserstrom 1977 and Calnek 1962 for documentary sources, archaeology, and ethnohistory.) With all of this—many hundreds of titles, published and unpublished— the record is strikingly unbalanced. Almost all major monographs and articles have considered Tzotzil communities in their home municipalities; no major monograph has dealt with out-migration in general or with specific Tzotzil emigrant colonies. A small corpus of Mexican research has recently been done (Münch et al. 1980; Olivera and Salazar 1977; Pérez Castro 1980 and 1981; Salazar 1977, 1981a, 1981b, n.d.). However, this work is only partially published and deals with one municipality (Simojovel) of the many in which Tzotzils have colonized. This hiatus in the emigrant literature of Chiapas is significant in light of the fact that so many Tzotzils now live outside of their home municipalities. It should be noted that the Chamula out-migration, while among the more striking cases, is far from unique. It characterizes other Tzotzil and Tzeltal peoples as well. It is in fact a demographic and political problem of considerable magnitude in the state as a whole, for vast areas which are officially destined for petroleum and timber exploitation and cattle-grazing lands are also occupied by thousands of Tzotzil and Tzeltal squatters and other thousands of "legal" Indian colonists. The conflict of interests is a fundamental one of large- versus very small-scale exploitation of public lands. This study of the Chamula diaspora will not only fill a large ethnographic gap in what is otherwise a well-studied region of Mesoamerica, but will also open new vistas regarding a significant demographic and human problem in what is one of Mexico's richest and fastest-growing regions.

Within this region the home *municipio* of San Juan Chamula is among the communities which are fairly well-documented. Pozas (1959 and 1962), Gossen (1974b), Rachun Linn (1977), and Wasserstrom (1977) are all full-scale studies. Pozas emphasizes economic and political organization; Gossen, general ethnography, worldview, cosmology, and oral tradition; Rachun Linn, civil and religious organization; Wasserstrom, documentary history and ethnohistory of Chamulas and other highland Indian communities. The home *municipio* of San Juan Chamula also figures prominently in several regional and comparative studies of Indians within the broader framework of the state of Chiapas and the Mexican nation. Most important among these are Favre (1971), Köhler (1975), Wasserstrom (1977), Cámara-Barbachano (1964), and Collier (1975).

While the ethnographic record is strong, this body of research has been fairly criticized by those who note that the Tzotzil have participated for centuries in regional social, political, and economic entities which are greater than the small, insular *municipio* which has typically been the unit of ethnographic description and analysis in the area. Several historians and sociologists, as well as anthropologists (Wasserstrom 1977, 1980; Favre 1971; Köhler 1975; Stavenhagen 1976) have observed that Indian communities have never lived in economic and political vacuums, that they have at least since the colonial period coped as poor peasants in a wider political and social orbit over which they had no effective control. Thus, in this view, native municipal boundaries as ethnic boundaries are seen as creations of colonial authorities for their own convenience and perpetuated by anthropologists who persist in viewing them as closed corporate communities. While this is a fair criticism of Tzotzil studies in particular and Mesoamerican studies in general (Chambers and Young 1979), it is also clear that many native communities are now explicitly conscious of their separate ethnicity and wish to preserve it while at the same time availing themselves of the advantages to be obtained through well-informed dealing with the state and federal governments. Indeed, it seems clear that some of the Chamula and other Indian colonists have found it easier to exploit economic opportunities as corporate Indian entities rather than as Indian individuals or as acculturated Indians (Earle 1979; Siverts 1969).

There are scattered studies in Chiapas, greater Mesoamerica, and elsewhere which indicate that my reading of the Chamula situation is neither improbable nor unique. In the Tzotzil-Tzeltal area, Siverts (1969) has offered strong evidence to this effect from the community of Oxchuc, observing that Indian ethnicity offers compelling advantages even when individuals have the opportunity through education and other means to make the jump to mestizo ethnic status. Spicer had documented similar patterns of Yaqui ethnic tenacity as they have moved from their homeland into mestizo communities in northern Mexico, and even into southern Arizona (Spicer 1961a, 1961b, 1969, 1972). Casagrande observes a similar phenomenon in Ecuador (1964), as Falla (1978) and Carter (1969) do in Guatemala.

It is the common wisdom of the political left and right of academic social science and applied social science that marginal peoples must inevitably be brought into some form of participation in the respective national cultures under which they live. This is the explicit thrust of Mexican national Indian policy as embodied in its philosophy of *indigenismo*: to "facilitate" full participation in national culture for all Mexicans. Acculturation theory generally views this process as inevitable (Foster 1962; Adams 1970). Regional and world-system theorists (Wallerstein 1974) claim that it has already happened; that local cultural diversity is illusory. On a somewhat different tack, a common view of cultural syncretism is that each encounter between a dominant and minority population yields a new synthesis which is unique, but generally favors the dominant contributor (Adams 1967; Madsen 1967). The Chamula diaspora has much to contribute to consideration of these issues, in that Chamulas seem to have sorted out over the centuries of ethnic encounters with dominant powers (Toltec, Aztec, Spanish, Mexican, and Western) a bipartite adjustment in which cultural forms associated with conduct of public life (e.g., contact languages, government, adjudication of disputes, economic pursuits, public religious observance) yield quickly to new demands and new masters. Yet those cultural forms linked with the domestic, private sphere of life (e.g., division of labor in household production, management of the supernatural world, ethics, basic assumptions of worldview, time, and space) remain largely intact. (See chapter 6.)

If I am able to identify the processes which sustain an ethnic moral community which is nevertheless dispersed and noncontiguous, following a line of research first outlined by Barth (1969), it will add a useful case study to a discussion which has theoretical, humanistic, and practical significance. One has only to consider the displacement of millions of Southeast Asians in the last two decades, the homeless Palestinians, the fragile and embattled but influential Israeli state, the internal "problems" of ethnic minorities in Iran and China, the increasing Hispanic and Caribbean presence in the United States, the West Indians in Britain, the "majority minority" of Blacks in South Africa, and of Indians in Guatemala to realize that the lives and fortunes of Chamula colonists are not merely of provincial concern, but rather, constitute a local scenario of what is in fact a universal human problem.

THE CHAMULA TZOTZIL AND THE
GENESIS OF THE DIASPORA

Within the Tzotzil-Tzeltal group, the Tzotzil-speaking Chamulas are, numerically and symbolically speaking, the dominant Indian community in the Chiapas Central Highlands. Numbering over 150,000, they have by far the largest population of over thirty municipalities in the region which have significant (over five thousand) Indian populations. They occupy a large (364 sq. km), densely populated home municipality in the highlands called San Juan Chamula (approximately seventy-five thousand) and also live in over one hundred small- to medium-sized communities (two hundred to two thousand persons) which are scattered all over the state of Chiapas. Combined populations of these emigrant colonies, which were founded at various times and for various reasons over the last 150 years, number some seventy-five thousand, approximately equaling the Chamula population living in the parent municipality.

Because of their sheer numbers, wide geographic dispersal, and visibility as migrant day-laborers in commercial agricultural enterprises throughout the state, Chamulas have come to symbolize the Indian ethnic presence in the Central Chiapas Highlands. Although there are dozens of other groups (having distinctive dress, Tzotzil or Tzeltal dialect and customs) who also inhabit the area, common parlance in spoken Spanish of the region refers collectively to all Indians as "*Chamulitas.*" This usage is of course condescending and ignorant in that it assumes that "if you've seen one, you've seen them all." Nevertheless, this usage underlines the symbolic importance of the subjects of this study in the social and ethnic fabric of the state of Chiapas. Chamulas, to many "mestizos in the street," are the quintessential Indians of the state. Mestizos typically describe them as numerous, poor, troublesome, superstitious, childlike, hardworking, intransigent, and always available as day-laborers for modest wages. Also contributing to the mixed pejorative and feared image of Chamulas as a collective term for all Indians is the high visibility of the parent *municipio*, San Juan Chamula, as a successful conservative community.

Chamula is one of a handful of Indian municipalities in the region which are zealous about their ethnic separatism. They encourage and defend this separatist posture with regard to Mexican national culture. They permit no mestizo Mexican, not even a priest, to live or hold property in their municipal territory. They also possess a strong tradition of political and religious centralism which is in the hands of a small oligarchy composed of powerful families (Vogt 1973; Gossen 1974b: 5). This oligarchy cooperates with state and national officials on matters of state and federal jurisdiction, but insofar as local municipal affairs are concerned, it permits no factions to emerge which threaten the central authority structure. Some aspects of this strong centralized posture toward the outside world date at least from the mid-nineteenth century and have contributed to Chamula's focal role in two major "rebellions," one in 1868–70 , the other in 1909–11. In 1937, internal changes, authorized by state authorities, helped to consolidate the position of the oligarchy which presently controls Chamula's economic and political life (Wasserstrom 1977: 82). Fairly recently (1965), this group of *caciques* engineered the forced purge of Protestant converts in the community. They correctly saw in the Protestants a challenge to the traditional authority structure. Even more recently (1987), the parent community formally withdrew from the Roman Catholic Diocese of San Cristóbal to which it had belonged to affiliate with a renegade Eastern Orthodox bishop in Tuxtla Gutiérrez. The main issue in the schism was an old story: the Roman Catholics sought to make extended catechism a firm requirement for parents who wanted to have a child baptized. This requirement was regarded as both a nuisance and (correctly) as a ploy of the church to "modernize" and meddle in local beliefs and practices. The Eastern Orthodox bishop promised to respect their autonomy and, in so doing, gained seventy-five thousand token adherents overnight. Thus, it is fair to say that Chamulas are not only the major Indian demographic presence in the Central Highlands but also a bulwark of ethnic separatism which is willing to resort to violence and pragmatic artifice in order to sustain its ethnic, political and religious integrity.

Chamulas have been forced for many reasons to migrate permanently to form new communities over the last century and a half. Significant among these reasons are: (1) Chamula's relatively large, densely settled population which lives in the home municipality (seventy-five thousand); (2) the strong central political structure which does not permit factional splits in the home political and religious organization; and (3) the relative poverty of the community. Chamula was particularly hard-hit by the development of commercial coffee production and large-scale cattle ranching in the nineteenth century (Wasserstrom 1977; Favre 1971). By the mid-nineteenth century Chamula was already a major labor supplier for nearby San Cristóbal and for newly developing commercial agriculture in the lowlands. Population pressure, together with systematic quasi-legal acquisitions of desirable Chamula land by mestizo ranchers, created a significant exodus of population from the home municipality at this time. Many of these Chamulas were compelled to move with their families to become debt peons on Mexican-owned coffee plantations and cattle ranches. A major nativistic movement known as the "Cuzcat Rebellion," which developed in 1867–69 at the time of the Juárez Reform movement, led to another population exodus when losing principals in that conflict were expelled in 1870. These exiles joined other Chamulas to form a community known today as San Juan Bosque. A similar exile community was founded by losers in a civil-religious upheaval which took place in the home community in 1910–11. These exiles also joined Chamulas who had already emigrated to new lands in the highlands to establish Rincón Chamula.

Mexico's epic revolution of 1910–18 carried in its wake a set of agrarian reform laws which facilitated the recovery of most of the community's traditional lands which had been lost in the nineteenth century. These are actually four *ejidos* (units of Mexican agrarian reform land tenure and administration) which now comprise the home municipality and contiguous lands in adjoining municipalities. Still other Chamula squatters who occupied land in other adjoining municipalities have had their land rights recognized by agrarian reform officials in these communities. Dozens of other *ejidos* have been formed by Chamulas in the highlands and in the distant jungle lowlands. These *ejidos*, some of which date from the 1930s, are based on the legal formula of twenty heads of family per unit. Many other Chamulas have purchased private land in the Highlands and have moved as small groups of families to live there permanently. The most recent exodus has taken place since 1965 and has consisted of Protestant converts (some three thousand of them) who were forcibly expelled by the oligarchy which still controls the home community. These people, having lost their land, have generally emigrated to the outskirts of the old colonial mestizo town of San Cristóbal de las Casas, which shares a long boundary with San Juan Chamula. They constitute to this day the most depressed group of Chamula emigrants, living in several temporary encampments around San Cristóbal. A few of these Protestant Chamulas have become fairly prosperous middlemen, specializing in the orange and potato wholesale and retail trade. Other hundreds of Chamulas, many of them Protestant converts, have emigrated to other towns and cities, seeking steady jobs and higher wages which are generally available there. In sum, approximately as many Chamulas (seventy-five thousand) now live in these dispersed communities as remain at home.

The following typology derives from demographic survey data collected by me between 1977 and 1979 with the help of a Chamula assistant. Between 1965 and the present, I have had the opportunity to visit at least one community of each type and the descriptions below are accurate, albeit very general. The typology is basically historical; the categories are based on circumstances that figured in the founding of the colonies.

1. Nineteenth- and Early Twentieth-Century Highland Exile Communities.

These communities were founded by exiles who were expelled from the home township because of their involvement in religious and political conflicts, notably those of 1867–69 and 1910–11. They are among the older types and have evolved characteristic local styles, yet they preserve the Tzotzil language and truncated forms of the old social and religious organization.

2. Highland Squatter Communities Whose de facto Land Rights Have Now Been Recognized.

Many of these communities were founded illegally on unused lands of the great haciendas of the Porfiriato period (1870–1910). Postrevolutionary agrarian reform legislation has allowed many of these communities to have their land rights legally recognized.

3. New Highland Communities Founded on Privately Purchased Lands.

Most of these communities date only from the 1940s and later. Their purpose was largely to expand corn production and they are generally located in the Grijalva River Valley. Some members of these communities maintain homes and fields in both the home township and in the new communities.

4. Highland Agrarian Reform Communities.

These communities also date from the 1940s and later and were founded according to the provisions of Mexico's agrarian reform laws which were initially articulated in the Constitution of 1917, but not actually made operational until the regime of President Cárdenas in the 1930s. The unit of tenure was the *ejido*, generally consisting of twenty heads of family who arranged with agrarian reform authorities initial allotment of national lands, some of which were acquired by the breaking up of the prerevolutionary haciendas; other land had never been effectively exploited prior to allotment.

5. Lowland Agrarian Reform Communities.

These communities have been founded according to the same agrarian reform legislation as those in Type 4. However, they tend to be even more recent and are located in lowland jungle areas which were not accessible until very recently. Many are still accessible only by river and trail. However, they are most interesting from the point of view of this study, for they are located in ecological settings which are unlike the home township. This has led to radical changes in economic life. The lowland *ejidos* are also located in areas which have local Indian populations which do not speak either Tzotzil or Spanish. Thus the linguistic and social intercourse which results in these communities presents some unusual cases of adaptation and synthesis.

6. Remnant Hacienda-Dependent Communities Which Date From the Nineteenth and Early Twentieth Centuries.

Although major haciendas were broken up by the revolutionary agrarian reform laws, many remnants of these great ranches survive, largely in areas near the former "big house," that is, the grand house that was the home of the patrician criollo landowner. Though greatly reduced in territorial extent, some of these remnant haciendas retain Chamula tenant farmer colonies nearby to supply labor for the patron's economic pursuits. Although they are legally free to leave and receive wages for their labor, these Chamulas have continued the patron-client relationships which prevailed in Chiapas before the revolution. In a sense, these are social fossils which have much light to shed on the prerevolutionary social order.

7. Chamula Minority Enclaves in Other Highland Indian Townships.

These communities date from early in the twentieth century, perhaps earlier. Chamula residents own their small plots, either privately or as part of *ejidos*, but they are under the legal jurisdiction of other Tzotzil and Tzeltal majority civil and religious organizations.

8. New (post-1965) Communities Formed by Exiled Chamula Protestant Converts.

Since 1965, some three thousand Chamula Protestant converts have been forcibly expelled by Chamula municipal authorities from the home township. These people have generally fled to San Cristóbal de las Casas. At least a dozen Protestant exile colonies now form a ring around San Cristóbal. Although some have purchased small plots of land on the outskirts of the town, most live in temporary encampments and lead the lives of refugees, for they cannot go home even to work their ancestral lands for fear of life and limb. Some have become prosperous entrepreneurs; the majority live in extremely depressed circumstances and have yet to find permanent new homes. Chamula Protestant ideology is based on challenge of the central "Catholic" authority structure of the oligarchy which controls political and religious affairs of the home township. Therefore, these Chamulas appear to have the weakest link with the dispersed Chamula moral community.

9. Town and Urban Dwellers.

It is hard to speak of urban and town dwellers (with the exception of Type 8, above) as members of the tight Chamula communities. The reason is that individuals—usually groups no larger than single households—have emigrated to these centers for particular reasons. Many have emigrated to towns in search of good jobs; others are fugitives from the Chamula legal system; others have left home in the wake of family disputes and scandals.

CONTINUING UNITY IN DISPERSAL: SOCIAL AND ECONOMIC BONDS

All of the colonies derive at some point in the post-Independence period from the home community. Furthermore (with the exception of Type 9), they have been founded by groups large enough to sustain the use of the Tzotzil language in domestic and community life. This linguistic link is one of great power and helps to explain the tenacity of Chamula cultural styles and forms, particularly the retention of the Chamula domestic lifestyle, dress, and truncated forms of the old social and religious organization. Thus, the tendency has been to recreate microcosms of the old and familiar lifestyles.

In spite of the challenge of adaptation required by dozens of new social and ecological niches, new flora and fauna, different soils, crops and planting schedules, different neighbors, and new languages, the old order has usually persisted in the colonies. This, in turn, has encouraged direct social and economic transactions that link the periphery to the core. The most important of these—often pursued at great personal and financial cost—are the following: (1) occasional attendance at festivals and rituals in the regular annual cycle of the parent community; (2) maintenance of ancestor cults which require annual visits to the home community; (3) seeking of marriage partners and ritual kinsmen from the home township; (4) recourse to the traditional Chamula court system, located in the home township, for adjudication of matters which cannot be resolved by elders and civil authorities in the new communities; (5) visits to the home township on market days for purchase of traditional household, religious, and personal items, such as tortilla griddles, candle holders, blouses, and belts; (6) visits to the home township to seek services of traditional curers; (7) visits to the home township to seek loans; (8) participation in ritual positions (cargos) which require only temporary residence in the home ceremonial center for particular festivals or ritual sequences; and (9) visits to the parent community for the purpose of recruiting temporary laborers for service in the new communities.

THE MORAL INFRASTRUCTURE THAT BINDS THE DIASPORA

While the social and economic links of the colonies with the parent community are fairly visible as rational strategies for dealing with emigrant life— it's nice to deal with one's own—an even more powerful force, in my view, is the latent moral and ideological factor that figures in life in the colonies. These are, indeed, Maya colonies, not just rural proletarian colonies. They speak a Maya language and bear an ideology that is, if not directly linked to the Ancient Maya, at least demonstrably as unlike the mestizo world as Black South Africans are unlike the Afrikaner- and English-speaking South African world.

To understand the ideological world in which Chamula emigrants move, it is essential to note the world from which they derive. The Maya have been, since the pre-Columbian period, preoccupied with the prophetic power of their cyclical view of time (León-Portilla 1968; Villa Rojas 1968). The contemporary Chamulas in the home community share this point of view in their worldview and cosmology, and it is fairly well-documented (Gossen 1974a, 1979a). In the complex world-of-the-sun, in which they view themselves as those privileged to be at the center of the universe, Chamula is the measure of all things good and moral. Chamulas' historical vision is explicitly a cyclical one, in which the structure of events in the early epochs of their time framework repeats itself inexorably in major events of recent history and even in the present (Gossen 1978). In a way, the past behaves as a self-fulfilling prophecy, guiding people to make day-to-day decisions in specific ways which are consonant with the "deep structure" of their social order and cosmological vision. This type of decision making is not solely guided by economic rationalism; it is more fundamentally guided by a tendency to actualize what they believe to be the Sun/Christ's will with regard to keeping themselves in the center of the universe. The pattern of Chamula history suggests that this is so. For example, three modern revitalization movements or rebellions (as some historians prefer to call them) share many structural features. The highly visible movements of 1867–70 (the Cuzcat movement), 1910–11 (the Pajarito Movement), and the present one, 1965 to the present (the purge of Protestant converts), share important features: (1) desire to keep central Chamula control over Chamula affairs; (2) violent purging of nonbelievers; (3) explicit male/female roles in management of the new cults (women as initial spiritual impetus, "mothers of god," men as militant public defenders); (4) intolerance of pluralism or coexistence of rival cults. Others have observed some of these patterns in Chamula religious and political organization (Vogt 1973). Bricker has shown that Chamula "nativism" and native accounts of it share significant features with similar events and narratives from the larger Maya culture area (1981: 181).

It is my view that emigration of Chamulas into many new social and ecological niches is guided by a Maya ethical paradigm, which is at the same time a theory of knowledge, a theory of history, and a theory of ethnicity—one in which they are "chosen people," not emigrants whose identity merges easily and quickly with Mexican national culture. Chamula emigration behaves not only as an economic, demographic, and ethnographic phenomenon but also as a series of "historical encounters" with new neighbors and new ecological settings that must be made their own. These encounters must be carried out—concretely and conceptually—through application of existing cultural paradigms, and theories of knowledge and history. Chamula emigration may thus be considered as an extension of Chamula cyclical theory of history into space.

What does it mean to extend a theory of cyclical history into space, to turn metaphysics into emigration that produces a loose federation? To consider the act of packing up forever to go to a new land, with all of the perils and uncertainties, to be a "moral" act, must seem little more than rarified academic discourse. But one must keep in mind that Chamula emigrants are not *fleeing* from structure in order to surpass it, but rather, are moving to *reproduce* it. Why, even in the Protestant communities that so diligently claim to have left behind the tyrannical structure of centralist, pagan oligarchy, do they nevertheless reproduce communities that do not coexist with other Protestant Indian converts and exiles, but rather set up enclaves of their own?

At least part of the answer lies in the fact that Chamula time reckoning is not linear in the sense of Western time reckoning. This is implicit in the four-creation cycle in terms of which time present is but another episode in the Sun/Christ creator's continuing effort to sustain a viable human community. I. M. Lewis recently wrote in a general commentary on anthropology and history: "Since events are part of a never-ending stream and always pointing forwards, subsequent developments immediately suggest new interpretations of the past" (Lewis 1968: 10). This is only partially adequate as a description of traditional Chamula temporal perspective, for Chamula time, as Ancient Maya time, points backwards to events which have been and will be again (see Gossen 1977). That is the essence of a cyclical view of time: it is not a never-ending stream, but a series of structurally similar, repeated cycles. So real is this cyclical temporal perspective for traditional Chamulas that there is at least some reason to believe that the historical process of emigration, for participants, anticipates a reenactment or refounding of the old social order as much as it entails a promising future. Indeed, this historical vision of human life as reenactment of the conditions of moral order, rather than as a strategy for future-oriented individual pragmatism, may have something fundamental to do with the adaptive competence with which Chamulas have dealt with new circumstances.

SYMBOLIC HOLDING PATTERNS

The most interesting question to ask at this point is why Chamula Tzotzils, more than other dozens of Tzotzil and Tzeltal communities, produce emigrant colonies that survive as Indian communities, while others produce emigrant colonies that acculturate. The easy answers lie in demography; there are more Chamulas to start with. Is it simply the case that greater demographic mass produces more colonies that end up with preference for persistence over acculturation?

The obvious answer is "yes." In all of the cases known to me, sufficient numbers of emigrants (twenty to forty adult men and women) go to the colonies to produce a critical mass that makes it possible to reconstruct life—particularly domestic life—in the "provinces." This is the case from the earliest out-migration that I have been able to document (the 1869–70 exodus to

Bosque) to the contemporary cases (the Protestant exile communities of 1965–present and the lowland and highland ejido communities). In all cases, some based on politics (defeated rebel/exiles had to leave together) and others on conditions of land reform legislation (twenty heads of households had to petition for *ejido* lands as a collective unit), the people who emigrated not only left in numbers sufficient to create a viable unit (from forty to one hundred individuals, a number comparable to that of a typical hamlet in the home community), but also left together, as neighbors and relatives. Thus, in a larger society in which Indians constitute a non-national cultural entity, the terms were complementary. The we/they social order continued, because the Chamula Tzotziles, Ladinos, and other Tzotzil and Tzeltal groups were accustomed to circumscribed and separate ethnic relationships at home; they sustained these in new settings. Marriage partners and compadres were often imported from San Juan.

The only exceptions to this in the typology delineated above are the individual town and urban emigrants (Type 9, above). The most dramatic cases of conformity are the historic exile communities (Type 1), some of which are well over one hundred years old. They are identifiably Chamula in ethnic identity even today.

THE FEMALE DOMESTIC UNIT VS. THE MALE PUBLIC SECTOR

With this "adaptive advantage" of critical mass, how do the communities persist as small enclaves in new territory? The most fundamental continuity lies in the domestic unit, a sphere in which women, who tend to be monolingual Tzotzil-speakers, socialize new generations of Tzotzil speakers. They do this in one- and two-room homes that are veritable spatial replicas of the household layout at home in San Juan (i.e., females left/males right). Each generation of males moves out into the local social and economic milieu, learning new languages and new public activities, only to return to marry into a Chamula Tzotzil enclave community, wherein new generations of Tzotzil-speaking individuals and culture are reproduced. The female power in this process is extraordinary, for it is women, not men, who socialize children.

Thus, a historical dichotomy is reproduced in the Chamula colonies as it has been throughout Mexican history: the Indian female domestic sector versus the male public sector. Women stay at home. Men are obliged, by political and economic exigency, to deal with the cultural and linguistic demands of the public sector. This dual system is reproduced in language and custom. The result is a well-known Mesoamerican pattern in which the Indian, female, private world functions as a conservative counterpoint to the public sphere in which Indian males have often been forcibly drawn into the economic and political service of the mestizo-dominated national culture. Most Chamula diaspora communities reflect this pattern in the conduct of domestic and public life; and it is also reflected in the preservation of female traditional dress versus male "adaptive" dress.

THE CARNIVAL COMPULSION

With the demographic and female sustaining agents as key factors in the maintenance of the diaspora, it is nevertheless the case that Chamula men in many of the emigrant colonies move quickly, and with great effort and cost, to establish truncated forms of the old ritual cults. The cult of choice is overwhelmingly not any one of the various *Alférez* or *Mayordomo* cults of the saints, but rather the highly centrist and integrative cult of Carnival, the "Festival of Games," which is the cult to the Sun/Christ. This winter solstice festival is described in chapter 5. The chief symbolic motif of the festival is ethnic warfare and ritual destruction of the central authority system, which is then ritually reconstituted through a Firewalk on the fourth day of the festival. The prevailing choice of the Festival of Games as the symbolic replication of the old order suggests that Chamula political centrism and moral separatism—the bulwark of the home community's own self-image as depicted in its major annual fiesta—is in fact being reproduced in the diaspora. The only difference in the festival in the colonies is in scale (always smaller) and in content: The ethnic adversaries who are ritually represented and overcome so that the Sun/Christ may prevail are typically drawn from their new neighbors' own self-representations. Sometimes the key monkey characters (the Sun/Christ's mythological adversaries) are represented with no costume other than sunglasses and street clothes, i.e., they are Ladinos.

What is curious and instructive about the Carnival compulsion is that it is a *male-dominated public activity* in which women are ostensibly passive (i.e., they have no visible ritual roles). Yet it is the *passive power* of females that is the wellspring of the overt ethnic separatism and moral authority that Chamula Tzotzil males represent ritually in the festival.

THE POLITICS OF GENDER IN THE DIASPORA

While the ritual of Carnival, with its overt public announcement of ethnic separatism and virtue, is the most typical symbolic manifestation of Chamula ethnic identity in the colonies, it does not approach in importance the sustaining power of the female-dominated Tzozil-speaking household. It is here that the common denominator of the diaspora colonies is found; it prevails from old to new colonies, from traditional to Protestant, from exile colonies to colonies formed through purchase of private land. In all of these, the household is Indian in style, in distribution of domestic space between males (right of the main doorway) and females (left of the main doorway), in types of foods consumed, and in location of religious objects or shrines (to the right of the main doorway). It is to this place and space that males retreat from the public arena that they frequent in their economic and political lives, and it is, symbolically, not *theirs*; it is predominately *female* space with male spaces that are often empty. Men speak of their wives publicly as the "owner of my house" (*yajval hna*). Thus the deepest font of Tzotzil ethnic identity is female; and this is not inconsistent with what we know of Tzotzil mythology (the Virgin Mary/Moon was mother of, and logically prior to, the Sun/Christ); nor with what we know of the gender politics of the major Tzotzil and Tzeltal social movements, in which extraordinary women were the instigators of the Tzeltal Rebellion of 1708–13, the Cuzcat Rebellion of 1868–69, and the War of Santa Rosa of 1910–11.

In summary, these symbolic holding patterns of the Chamula diaspora are anchored in the social, economic, and reproductive functions of the female-dominated Tzotzil-speaking domestic unit. Where these functions are strong, the males tend to express them in the public arena and claim them in the name of the Sun/Christ, who is none other than the son of the female moon deity. Chamula demographic strength and population pressure have provided lots of opportunity for continuity and reproduction of these patterns of gender politics in the greater Chamula diaspora. By extension, I suggest that interethnic relations and acculturation of other Mexican emigrant communities may be best understood by beginning one's inquiry with the structure and meaning of domestic life and gender roles, for it is from these factors that the tone and quality of public life derive, not the other way around.

IS FEMALE TO MALE AS INDIAN IS TO MEXICO?

Within the social fabric of Mexico, the Chamula Tzotzil are a success story. Since European contact they have undoubtedly changed in significant ways, but they are nevertheless survivors. They have adapted as Tzotzil speakers to coexistence in the dual Ladino/Indian society and their numbers are increasing today. They are the local representatives of what Octavio Paz would recognize as *hijos de la chingada*, bastard children of Malinche, Cortés's mistress, the Indian traitor. Although they survive as ethnic Indians, they are, of course, from the perspective of modern Mexico, descendants of the vanquished. Mexico the nation is their master, if not their moral authority.

It is widely recognized in Mexico (Paz 1959) and Peru (Silverblatt 1987) that the conquest, symbolically, sexually, and historically was a male venture. Male soldiers not only ravished Indian America and took Indian women as concubines, but men, collectively, came to represent the conqueror; Indian

America became the vanquished, passive female. Most of the gender analogy is so well-recognized that it hardly bears repeating here.[1] However, this study of the Chamula diaspora adds another layer of meaning to this dialogue, that females are to male in this Indian society (dominated/dominating) as Indians collectively are to Mexican national society. The public role of women in Tzotzil society is passive and apparently without note, just as *el indio* is passive and vanquished in the Mexican national idea. Yet, clearly the female element is the key to both the distinctive identity of the surviving, prospering Chamula diaspora and to the idea of Mexico as a nation.

In closing, I hope to have added another nuance to the meaning of *subirle el indio a uno*. This metaphor means more than a capricious moment of stubbornness, violence, and retreat from the normative conventions of civilized behavior; it is the very essence of that behavior. "To lose one's cool" (to have the Indian in one's nature pop out suddenly) is not to go off the deep end, but to acknowledge the ambivalent origins of one's being, partaking of many emotions: anger and hostility at the betrayal of Malinche and the joy in redemption of the Virgin of Guadalupe, death and creation.

Eight

LIFE, DEATH, AND APOTHEOSIS OF A CHAMULA PROTESTANT LEADER: BIOGRAPHY AS SOCIAL HISTORY

This essay was first published in Spanish in 1989, and, later in the same year, in English. It was initially presented at a conference entitled "Biographies and Confessions of Indians in the Americas," held in Seville in 1987. Of all the essays in this volume, this one reflects the transition in my self-image as a scholar more than any other—so much so that I did not feel inclined to publish the same version in Spain and in the U.S. The Spanish version contained a structural analysis that sought to place the tragic protagonist of this piece in an ancient tradition of Maya heroes and historical reckoning, the template of which is laid out in chapter 6 of this volume. For the English version, I lacked the scholarly courage to mobilize these deep historical links, for I felt that "continuity arguments," binding the Maya past and present, were frought with so many sources of inferential error that presenting them as such would render me as "dated." So, I opted to edit the Spanish version to publish it in English as a much more present-oriented historical analysis (that is, focusing more on modern social history), thinking thereby to cast myself as a serious social historian rather than a romantic Mayanist.

In retrospect, my quandary as to which version to publish for which audience seems to have amounted to naught, for I have received more amused criticism from my colleagues for changing the versions than for the intrinsic merit of either version. Therefore, the essential argument of the original version is restored here as a post script. The reader may be the judge. I, in fact, regard both versions as honest accounts.

FORETHOUGHTS

Miguel Kaxlán, a Chamula Tzotzil, was born in 1912, on the eve of the Mexican Revolution, and died in 1982, at the age of seventy. His life and role as founder and leader of the post-1965 Protestant movement of San Juan Chamula surely do not count as great historical documents, perhaps not even in the context of Highland Chiapas. However, his life provides a glimpse, from a very local perspective, of the incredible transformation and abundant contradictions of Mexico in the twentieth century.

This essay charts new territory for me. It is an effort to place the biography of a remarkable person in a matrix of embedded contexts, from highly local cultural drama to Mexican national life. This biography developed over the twenty years of my association with the Harvard Chiapas Project as an almost clandestine undertaking, for any public association with Tzotzil Protestants would not have been politically appropriate for me in my dealings with the Chamula traditionalists with whom I had friendships and good working relationships. I have never heard anyone—Tzotzil Protestants, Chamula traditionalists, local Ladinos, INI (Instituto Nacional Indigenista) officials, or Protestant missionaries themselves—talk openly or eagerly about the subject of this essay to any but established or potential allies. When they do address the subject, the rhetoric is accusatory or defensive; it is not a subject for casual conversation. My association with the Chamula Protestant Movement has never been open or close, yet my interest has been nothing short of intense, for it was hard to hear hymns that I had known as a child in Kansas translated into Tzotzil and sung with the abandon of a full-blown revival without feeling some deep sense of déjà vu. How could this be happening in Chiapas?

While "objective" information on the subject of Protestant evangelical activity is hard to come by, there can be little doubt that this work of religious conversion has been one of the major agents of social change in the Chiapas highlands in the last few decades. One has only to observe, in the middle of the 1980s, the Indian Protestant entrepreneurs in the San Cristóbal market or the dozens of new Indian Protestant squatter settlements and refugee camps around the San Cristóbal Valley, or the relatively prosperous farming settlement of Betania on the Pan-American highway south of San Cristóbal, to realize that Protestant converts are major players in the modernization process and contemporary demographic picture of the region.

Data for this essay come from hearsay, opinion, oral history, and everyday conversation; that is, conventional fieldwork. They also come from Protestant publications (notably Steven 1976), as well as from an extensive biography of the protagonist of this essay that was commissioned by me and written in Tzotzil by his son Manuel Gómez Hernández. I first sought Manuel's help with his father's biography in 1977, after he sought work with me as a translator. One of the fruits of his association with the United States Presbyterian missionaries of San Cristóbal was a remarkable facility in written Tzotzil and with Spanish translation. He had, in fact, been employed by the mission for many years as a New Testament translator. I was less interested in his translation services than in what he could tell me about his remarkable and notorious father who, in 1977, was in the midst of a major political drama that I hardly understood. I was eager to find out more, for I was at the time engaged in a project on Chamula out-migration, and I found that Miguel Kaxlán was the topic of choice in many conversations with Chamula traditionalists. They regarded him as a harbinger of evil, being a bearer of the "new and dangerous words" that could easily, in their view, destroy the community of San Juan Chamula. How could one resist the desire to get to know him, or at least about him?

DEATH OF MIGUEL KAXLÁN

In the autumn of 1982, several weeks before the festivals of All Saints and All Souls (November 1 and 2), a group of Chamula men kidnapped their compatriot, Miguel Kaxlán, in broad daylight from the marketplace in San Cristóbal de las Casas, the old colonial town that today, as in the past, serves as a major trade center of the central Chiapas highlands. After capturing him, they bound his legs and arms and blindfolded him, telling him simply that they planned to take him to the town center of San Juan Chamula, his home *municipio*, in order to discuss with him the status of land and personal property that had recently been expropriated from his band of Protestant convert followers. On the surface the subject matter and purpose of the "trip" made sense. He was both the founder and leader of this movement, dating from 1964. His followers, indeed, had serious property claims against the public officials of Chamula who had, since 1965, systematically harassed the converts. At the time of the kidnapping in 1982, these officials and their predecessors had stripped the converts of their right to live in the community, thus effectively expropriating their land and property.

Once the kidnappers were well within Chamula, on a relatively isolated and very steep truck road that leads from the San Cristóbal Valley into the Chamula hamlet of Milpoleta, they murdered their victim and hacked him to pieces with their machetes. The dismembered corpse was found and taken for burial in San Cristóbal. At the present time, some six years later, no suspects have been arrested, nor even identified. The case is as though it never happened, as though it were a dream. Even if Miguel Kaxlán simply "disappeared," a view that is commonly held by all interested parties—Tzotzil Protestants and traditionalists and Ladinos—it is nevertheless the case that he lives as a symbol of the life and times of contemporary Mexico.

With Miguel Kaxlán's death, apparently carried out with knowledge of, if not at the behest of then-ruling municipal authorities, a bitter chapter in the recent social history of the Tzotzil area of Chiapas has come to a close. Although the initial charismatic moment has passed, the victory clearly belongs to Miguel Kaxlán and others like him. Protestantism is now a full contender for the hearts and minds of the Tzotzil and Tzeltal peoples of Highland Chiapas. There is now, more than ever before a broad range of choices for Indians who live under the political sovereignty of Mexico. Will they retain Indian identity in custom and language? Will they become mestizo laborers, farmers, merchants, and traders? Will they become Protestant

Mexicans? Will they become radicalized advocates of pan-national guerrilla movements? Will they become Vatican II modern Catholics? Will they continue into the late twentieth century as Indians who coexist with the Mexican State? Or will they become Christians or socialists for whom nationality is not the most important question?

In San Juan Chamula, as in other thousands of small communities in Latin America, the quest for modernity moves forward inexorably. Miguel Kaxlán, the Chamula, is not a great historical figure, even regionally; his murder was not even reported in the press of the state capital, Tuxtla Gutiérrez. Yet, even as "Mr. Nobody," his life and times are worth exploring, for his religious and political career allow one to glimpse possible answers to an important question: To what extent is a historical movement toward modernization and social change (e.g., Protestantism) to be understood as local, national, or global? Is Protestantism any of these? Or is it all of them? Or is it simply a convenient vehicle for the political and economic ambitions of individuals who can no longer live in their traditional communities? Or, is Protestantism but one more overlay in the complex mosaic of alien cultural forms that have been, over the centuries, "encapsulated" by the Indian communities of Chiapas to make these alien forms their own (see Vogt 1964).

THE LIFE OF MIGUEL KAXLÁN

Miguel Kaxlán was born in 1912 in the small hamlet of Ya'al Vakax in the *municipio* of San Juan Chamula. Then, as now, Chamula was a circumscribed, conservative, monolingual Tzotzil Indian community. Although the community's public life was radically transformed by colonial and Mexican national institutions, its domestic and economic life at the hamlet level was Maya in content and style, with most people making a living as subsistence farmers and artisans. Many Chamula men, then as now, also went as seasonal laborers to work on the distant coffee plantations and cattle ranches of the Pacific coastal lowlands. Chamula of that time was part of the great ethnic mosaic of Chiapas that continues into our time, a complex picture of hundreds of local Indian communities that live in strained coexistence with the dominant Mexican mestizo culture of the region.

Miguel Kaxlán was born in one of the poorest hamlets of a land-poor, densely settled community, made even more miserable by mestizo land encroachments that occurred in the nineteenth century. Eight days after Miguel Gómez Chakojchu was born, his mother died from complications of childbirth and influenza. Seven days after his mother's death, his father also died of influenza. Miguel, now an orphan, was grudgingly taken in by his paternal uncle. In this household he spent his early childhood. At the age of eight, hunger and domestic strife over his unwelcome presence drove him to seek a place as an intern in the community's first and, at that time, only school. This was located in the ceremonial and civic center of San Juan Chamula, at some half-day's walk from his uncle's home. At this school he studied Spanish and standard beginning primary subjects. He turned out to be an excellent student. In 1922, in recognition of his good performance, he was given the honor of raising the flag over the school on the occasion of the arrival of a distinguished Federal Education Ministry visitor to the school. This visitor was so taken by the child's promise and so moved by the orphan's tattered, torn Indian clothing that he gave him a set of new clothes from his own valise. These included a shirt, pants, and shoes and socks, all European style. Since the clothes were the only ones he had, he wore them all the time, and he was apparently the first Chamula ever to wear European clothing in the community. Hence, he was nicknamed Miguel Kaxlán. (*Kaxlán* is Tzotzil for *castellano*, referring to being of Hispanic or Ladino origin.) This nickname stuck and he was known from the age of ten by this name, which roughly translates as "Miguel the Ladino." The name would turn out to be both a curse and a self-fulfilling prophecy. He would never really go home again.

In 1925 he went off to another government school called Cerro Hueco, with was located in the lowland area of the state of Chiapas, near Tuxtla Gutiérrez, the capital. This school brought together students from dozens of Indian communities of the state, thus obliging all of them to speak Spanish as a lingua franca. In this multiethnic context he met and apparently had a fast love affair with a girl whose community of origin was ironic and prophetic. Her home was Rincón Chamula. This community is of historical interest in that it was settled in large part by political exiles from Chamula, who fled there following their defeat in a political and religious movement known as the "Pajarito Rebellion" that took place in San Juan Chamula in 1910–11. Rincón Chamula was thus ethnically Chamula, but physically and socially removed by relatively great distance from San Juan.

Miguel, at the age of fifteen, married the girl from Rincón and moved there to join the community of his own exiled countrymen. In these surroundings, Miguel, an orphan among exiles, became aware of the political circumstances in San Juan that had produced the Pajarito Rebellion and defeated the leaders of the movement. He became increasingly bitter when he realized that some of the forces—notably poverty and marginality—that had driven him to leave San Juan and to move toward the Ladino world had also driven out his wife's family as political and social exiles.

Miguel Kaxlán abandoned his first wife in 1929, at the age of seventeen, in order to continue his studies. He went to the state capital of Tuxtla Gutiérrez, specifically to the office of Public Education, in an effort to find a way to go to Mexico City to seek further education. Arrangements were made and he departed for Mexico. He went by train from the Pacific lowland town to Arriaga. This was his first experience on a train and it caused an extraordinary impression of fear and amazement. Upon arriving in Mexico City, he was astonished to find that there were more Spanish speakers than English speakers, for he understood, from his own teaching and background, that Mexico City was so strange as to be labeled the "Land of the English" (*slumal inklex*). While he was studying in Mexico City he had various amorous adventures. But, most significant to him was his study of the Mexican Revolutionary Constitution of 1917, a subject that captured his young imagination, for there was, stated there, the promise of social justice for all Mexicans, particularly the poor, the marginal, and the oppressed. At the same time that he learned these things, he was keenly aware that his being Indian in Mexico City, a fact that was apparent from his still-imperfect Spanish, led to ill treatment and rudeness from native Spanish speakers.

The coup de grâce came in the form of modern medicine. He became very ill and willingly submitted to receiving some injections as a cure, even though this mode of medical treatment was totally strange to him. By chance, the shots were not administered correctly, and he suffered a temporary paralysis in his arm. This was enough. In 1931 he left Mexico City and returned to San Juan Chamula, where his uncle felt obliged to take him in, although grudgingly. They allowed him to farm the land that had been his parents, but which had been passed, by custom, to his guardians upon his parents' death, as a way of compensating them for the burden of rearing their orphaned children.

Miguel married again, the wife in Rincón Chamula apparently forgotten. As a poor couple with no land for maize production, they became potters, an economic pursuit that required little more than house and patio and access to communal forest land as a source of charcoal. Between 1931 and 1940 they had six children, but things did not go well for them. Miguel apparently drank a great deal and frequently beat his wife. Furthermore, their children did not have adequate food or clothing. The younger ones apparently had no clothing at all. Miguel's disastrous domestic circumstances ruined his reputation and blocked his aspirations to become a political or religious official in the town center.

In 1940 he abandoned his second household and went to work on the coffee plantations of the Pacific lowlands. Here he spent seven years, never returning to San Juan during this period. The support of his family fell to his uncle's household. Between 1947 and 1950 he worked as a day laborer on the construction of a section of the Pan-American highway that was being constructed between Tuxtla Gutiérrez and the Guatemalan border. During this period Miguel embarked on a third long-term relationship with a Tzotzil woman, this time with a Zinacanteca. In 1951, with the Pan-American highway construction project completed and this source of income gone, his third living arrangement broke apart due to some of the same problems that had caused his other domestic misfortunes. These were poverty and alcohol.

Ruin was complete. He returned to San Juan broke, alcoholic, and totally disillusioned, for he had not, by any reckoning, achieved economic or social mobility, or even material goods, from his lifelong effort to master Spanish and the lifestyle of the Mexican mestizo world. Not only had he not prospered in the Ladino world, but he had nowhere to go but back home to *Ya?al Vakax* where, remarkably, his second wife and her family took him in. He had little choice but to revert, however grudgingly, to the traditional lifestyle. A few days after his uncelebrated homecoming he took a sweat bath in the household *temascal* and had an unexpected revelation. A vision came to him. He was sucked up into the vortex of a whirlwind and was bodily lifted out of the sweat bath and carried ten meters through the air and dropped on the ground. After this extraordinary event, he became desperately ill and dreamed continuously. During this period, an unspecified sacred being appeared to him and "called" him to a new career as a shaman. This vision was complex, but basically carried a single message: he was to return to the traditional life in Chamula and was commanded to become a shaman. The "man" in the vision spoke to him, using these words:

> **All that I have given to you,**
> **All that you have received,**
>
> **It is yours,**
> **I wish to leave it to you.**
>
> **From this moment you will serve me,**
> **You will help me to care,**
>
> **For my children,**
> **For my offspring.**
>
> **Receive my gift.**
> **Do not fail me.**
> **Take good care of it.**
>
> **For it will serve you in caring**
> **For my children,**
> **For my offspring.**

From 1951 to 1958 Miguel Kaxlán lived in San Juan, earning a very modest living as a curer. Once again, however, his old problems returned. He began again to drink heavily and to fight with his wife and in-laws. He lost most of his curing clients and his source of income. His life was again where it had been so often in the past, in complete ruin. The last blow in the destruction of Miguel's attempted life as a traditional Chamula came from an act that may or may not have happened as reported. Whatever really occurred, he was publicly accused in 1958 of stealing the clothing from a mother and her daughter when they were washing their hair at a water hole. The accusation said that he stole the clothing so as to disorient them so that he could rape the daughter. Then he was said to have left both mother and daughter naked in order to go off and sell their clothing. These events reached the village elders, and policemen were sent to arrest him. Public shame was heaped on him during the hearings, and he was sentenced to several days in jail and had to pay a fine of one thousand five hundred pesos. This sentence and payment of damages were perceived by the community as too light a punishment for the crime. Most of them felt that the women's family ought to have killed him. That he got off so "easily" was attributed to the mediation efforts of Erasto Urbina, then mayor of San Cristóbal de las Casas. This intervention itself is noteworthy, for Urbina was (and still is) regarded as a great hero by the local Indian community, for he was bilingual in Tzotzil and Spanish, being of mixed Tzotzil and Ladino heritage. Although he was a successful merchant and politician in the Ladino world, he constantly worked to improve the economic and social circumstances of Indians by guaranteeing their equal status before municipal and state law. In the context of his hardware business, he always found ways to offer short-term credit to Indians without requiring collateral or charging interest.

Erasto Urbina's help with Miguel's legal problems after the rape and the scandal left Miguel with an indelible impression of gratitude and awe. Urbina was a compelling role model as a man of Tzotzil background who had "made it" in the Ladino world. With his shamanistic career in ruins, and public shame that would not vanish, Miguel clearly had little alternative but to leave home once again. Perhaps he could follow the path of Erasto Urbina. From 1958 to 1965, Miguel literally lived at the edge of two worlds, Indian and Ladino, a pattern of social marginality that had characterized much of his life.

However, by now his choices were dwindling. He could never really go home again to Chamula. His children would no longer speak to him. His wife abandoned him. His in-laws would not have anything to do with him. His only choice at this point in his life was to work as a day-laborer in San Cristóbal and in the Pacific lowlands. His drinking problem grew worse. Fate had dragged him to a low ebb. Even his carefully cultivated Spanish language skills and willingness to "go Ladino" in custom and dress would not deliver to him his lifelong aspiration of becoming someone of note.

In 1964 his brother Domingo got a job as a gardener at the San Cristóbal home of the North American Presbyterian missionaries Kenneth and Elaine Jacobs. They had already spent some ten years in the missionary effort in the Indian communities of the Chiapas highlands, though their work had not yet penetrated San Juan Chamula. Their presence in Chiapas was with the full blessing of Mexican government agencies. This support reflected the honest commitment of the secular government to the complete freedom of religious belief and practice. The Protestant evangelical agenda also meshed with government goals of supporting modernization, literacy, and Western health programs for Indian communities. The Protestants did these things as part of the missionary enterprise, so it did not "cost" the government anything.

Domingo, Miguel's brother, converted to the Presbyterian sect and he, in turn, converted his brother. Miguel felt he had little to lose. His conversion provided for him both a place to live (in the missionary compound) and, best of all, a job as a New Testament translation assistant to the missionaries. For the first time ever, his Tzotzil-Spanish skills were worth something. He set to work translating selected books of the New Testament to the Chamula dialect of Tzotzil.

In time, both Miguel and his brother joined the missionary cause itself and began proselytizing among friends and relatives in Chamula. By 1965 there were 35 converts, among them (a bizarre symbol of reconciliation) the family of Miguel's son, Manuel Gómez Hernández, the author of the biography on which this essay is based. Manuel was among those who had suffered hunger and hardships in childhood due to his father's neglect. Between 1965 and 1969 the number of Chamula converts reached 120, a relatively small number, but enough to send waves of anxiety across the red hills and oak and pine thickets of San Juan. A clear and present menace to Chamula's jealously guarded ethnic conservatism and central authority system was loose.

Among the cherished articles of faith and practice of the new Presbyterian sect were concepts that truly threatened the traditional order. Among the most unthinkable and intolerable were the following: (1) refusal to pay municipal taxes to support the fiesta cycle, which in their view was a cult of paganism; (2) refusal to participate in any way in the public religious life of the community; and (3) refusal to consume alcoholic beverages, a major source of revenue for the civil-religious hierarchy.

The traditional oligarchy was also worried because a system of fairly workable relations had evolved over the years between the small group of politically prominent Chamula families and Mexico's (then) one and only official political party, the PRI (Partido Revolucionario Institucional). The Chamula oligarchy felt threatened for obvious reasons. First, the precedent for a tax rebellion was in place, even though the present numbers were few. Second, the Protestants refused to recognize the moral authority of the central town government in their own lives. Finally, the Protestants in no way respected the finely tuned understandings that provided for Chamula cooperation with state and federal political authorities in exchange for a hands-off policy regarding Chamula autonomy in religious and judicial matters that were essential for the maintenance of a traditional Chamula community with no apparent Mexican federal presence.

By 1967 the threat was perceived to be intolerable and the converts' homes were burned to the ground, with no subsequent investigations or formal charges brought against anyone. The municipal authorities looked the other way and the state authorities were unable to respond. The burned-out Protestants found themselves obliged to flee to San Cristóbal, where they took refuge in the Presbyterian missionary compound.

It happened that the fires that destroyed the Protestants' homes in Chamula killed several members of one family, including three girls. Two other girls escaped the blaze with severe burns and fled heroically to San Cristóbal in the middle of the night. These girls survived and became quasi martyrs for the Protestant cause. They became active missionaries themselves and traveled widely through the United States soliciting funds for the Chamula mission.

The confrontational episode that involved the burning of homes caused a great deal of negative publicity and the state government was forced to intervene on behalf of the Protestants, who did, after all, enjoy protection of land and property under Mexican law. There followed several years of peace and reconciliation, and the Protestants were allowed to return to cultivate their cornfields and pasture their sheep, although living permanently in the community was out of the question. In 1974 the peace collapsed. The Protestant numbers had increased significantly by that time and they were blamed for fomenting an embarrassing rebellion of several thousand people who sought to prevent the elected chief magistrate (*presidente municipal*) from taking office. Being a member of the oligarchy, he had been duly elected by the usual PRI-supported machinery. The rebels accused the oligarchy of financial and electoral fraud and sought, at gunpoint, to keep the elected official from taking office. The oligarchy responded to this challenge by jailing two hundred Protestants, who were reputed to be the leaders of the electoral rebellion. They were subsequently taken to San Cristóbal and forbidden ever to return to Chamula. The state officials looked the other way. This episode of violence broke the strained coexistence of the Protestant Chamulas with the traditionalists. Most important for his narrative, the key players in the persecution of the Protestants were the very people who, almost twenty years before, had been the ones who had jailed Miguel Kaxlán on the occasion of the rape and theft trial. The ingredients of vengeance and honor were unquestionably present, and Miguel Kaxlán sensed an opportunity to rectify past grievances.

After the events of 1974, Miguel Kaxlán moved quickly into the arena of religious politics, since Protestantism was proving to be a useful tool for vengeance against those who, for decades had succeeded, in his view, in excluding him from participation in Chamula traditional religious and political life. He proceeded to ally himself with the PAN (Partido de Acción Nacional) which, nationally, was associated with the economic and religious right wing of Mexican politics. In reality, it was but a vehicle of protest against the PRI establishment, and it was, in its way, useful to Miguel. He was able to mobilize large numbers of his compatriots for the cause of antiestablishment sentiments, for Miguel's antipathy for the ruling families was shared by many of his compatriots. With this political ploy, it was not difficult to turn religious conversion into a political statement. Indeed, many who could not have cared less about the tenets of the faith became Protestants precisely because of its antiestablishment political posture.

The cynical alliance of Miguel Kaxlán with PAN and Protestantism enraged both the oligarchy and the PRI. The reasons were clear. PRI responded by allying itself with the traditional oligarchy against the Protestants. No action was taken against the land claims. Why? Because the Protestants and PAN could easily end, with lightening speed, the comfortable cooperation that the state and federal governments had enjoyed for several decades with the Chamula oligarchy. This mattered more than a little bit because Chamula was, and is today, the largest and most influential Indian community in the state. It also has a long history as an epicenter of rebellion and violence in recent Chiapas history. What had Miguel Kaxlán wrought?

Miguel spent the years from 1976 to his death in 1982 trying to convince the state and federal authorities that the oligarchy of San Juan Chamula had acted against federal law, which guarantees freedom of religion and benefit of the usufruct of property. Miguel Kaxlán took these issues to the highest levels of grievance that were available to him, even to Mexico City, claiming that the authorities in San Juan Chamula acted against federal law by depriving citizens of freedom of religion and use of their land and property. This was a compelling, if not convincing, allegation, since over two thousand Chamula Protestants lived as exiles in the San Cristóbal Valley in 1976, unable to return to their homes. Neither the state nor federal authorities chose to respond to their grievances about alienated or estranged property.

As a consequence of the imbroglio that followed Miguel's attempts to get higher authorities involved in the Protestant grievances, he became a despised enemy, not only of the Chamula traditionalists but also of the local Mexican political officials and of the Presbyterian converts and missionaries themselves. The Chamula traditionalists became infuriated because he was attempting to destroy their authority in the community. The local and state PRI officials were stung by his public accusations that suggested that Mexican laws and constitutional guarantees were empty shells. The officials were also alarmed because Miguel Kaxlán had well over two thousand followers whom he might mobilize for a full-scale rebellion. This was to be avoided at all cost because Chamula had an impressive track record of trouble. In fact, the ringleaders of two violent Indian social movements, those of 1868–69 and 1910–11, were Chamulas. Both movements had been directed against the established Ladino political and religious authorities. Finally, the missionaries and the new Chamula Protestant converts were upset and embarrassed by the turn of events, for Miguel Kaxlán caused a factional split in the fledgling Chamula Presbyterian sect. One group, led by Miguel's son Manuel, was convinced that pacifism, spiritual purity, and an entirely new lifestyle were required for their survival. They should simply abandon their property claims in San Juan and build new lives elsewhere. The other faction, led by Miguel Kaxlán himself, consisted of converts who saw Protestantism as a useful medium for political protest and economic improvement within their own community.

Such was the inflammatory stage on which Miguel Kaxlán moved in the last years of his life. Thanks to Miguel and his son working with the missionaries, the two wings of the Protestant movement had in 1982 more than two thousand adherents. At this time nearly all had been exiled from San Juan. Most lived in slumlike temporary settlements around the San Cristóbal Valley, earning a miserable living as menial laborers and domestic servants in their new town. Many received support from the church. Still others took advantage to buy private tracts of land with favorable payment plans guaranteed by funds from the mission. Yet others became prosperous middlemen in the San Cristóbal market. For every winner, however, there were many losers, and the climate was very tense. When at last, in 1982, his own countrymen abducted and murdered Miguel Kaxlán, the whole community seemed to breathe a collective sigh of relief and joy. Indeed, to this day, the circumstances of the murder have not been investigated. No one has accused anyone. The Mexican politicians are silent, as are the Chamula traditionalists and the Protestants. It is as though all wish to forget him, as though he had never lived.

APOTHEOSIS OF MIGUEL KAXLÁN

I believe that Miguel Kaxlán lives in both the conscious identity and unconscious psyche of modern Chiapas, perhaps also in the soul of Mexico itself. His words, deeds, and death are both a small footnote to and the table of contents of Mexican life in the twentieth century.

Miguel Kaxlán was born, like Mexico itself, with an Indian soul. This means, in its Tzotzil variant, that his life and body were collective social entities that were predestined to develop in a certain manner since the moment of his conception (see Gossen 1975). His Indian identity and soul were not of his making, nor were they subject to his control. All that he was to be, as a Tzotzil, was given, or so it seemed. In spite of his birthright, he was from birth systematically cast out of the Tzotzil world. Both parents died within two weeks of his birth. His aunt and uncle did not want him around, for they could barely feed him. His own community rejected him and, in effect, sent him away. His nickname tells the tale. "Miguel the Ladino" was his identity from the age of ten, for the Mexican clothes that the government official gave him were his only clothes. Acculturation through changes in language and lifestyle seemed to be his only alternative for survival.

In spite of his obligatory plunge into the Ladino world, he tried, in very traditional ways, to go home again. Tzotzil women and Indian domestic life were the strategy of choice. He married or lived with at least three such women; indeed, they symbolized several variants of the Tzotzil world: an exile community, the home community, and a non-Chamula Tzotzil community, Zinacantán. He also tried to come home again through a career in traditional curing and through his abortive efforts to join the civil-religious hierarchy. He even tried in his last years to defend Indian rights generically; that is, to point out the contradictions between Mexican law and local practice when the matter of Indian property rights was at stake. In the last analysis, all efforts failed catastrophically. He was doomed to shed the Indian soul.

From birth, it would seem, the circumstances of the Western soul were imposed upon his Indian soul. He was compelled to become a pragmatist and opportunist, to exercise free will, albeit in a flawed and destructive manner. To become what he might through his own devices was thrust upon him. In his lifelong flight from the status of being a poor orphan, his newly discovered Western soul, identified with self determination, personal liberty, and free will, found expression though the only means that were available to him: education and acculturation.

In spite of his efforts to "re-dress" (in the sense of the Spanish *revestirse*) himself as a Westerner, his efforts to become modern, Mexican style, and to make his own destiny, did not work out. Indeed, these efforts utterly destroyed him. He could live neither with the contradictions of the Tzotzil world nor with those of modern Mexico.

Miguel Kaxlán tried all his life to be a member of the community into which he was born. This never worked out, nor did the alternative. With every turn, his every effort to move successfully in the Ladino world turned sour. Each time he sought refuge in a Tzotzil household, and each time he abandoned it. In every case, it was wives, lovers, even burn-scarred little girls (the Protestant martyrs), who gave him his chance to become a credible Tzotzil male, to become someone in the native context. Each time he played this card he failed, most catastrophically in the theft and rape case. The women outlasted him, in every case. They stayed; he went on to die.

Miguel Kaxlán's linguistic skill in Spanish and Tzotzil was noteworthy. He was in fact effectively bilingual from the age of twenty. He tried earnestly to use this skill to carve out a niche for himself in the Tzotzil world. He sought a job as a municipal scribe and later as a political official, yet he couldn't find a place in the Indian system, for the authorities did not believe that he was trustworthy since he had spent so many years wandering through the Ladino world. He even attempted to use his bilingualism and translation skills to create an Indian Protestant church, with its own Tzotzil texts, so that it would not become a de facto acculturation tool. This effort to act as an advocate for the Indian community failed as well, for he was swept away by his political agenda, also ironically, in defense of his people. He moved on to try to put his knowledge of Mexican law and of the 1917 constitution at the service of his people; all to no avail.

As he approached the end of his life, Miguel Kaxlán witnessed the chilling irony of the traditional Tzotzil community in open alliance with the federal and state political authorities in a concerted effort to circumvent constitutional guarantees having to do with freedom of religion and property rights. Miguel's own son abandoned him to found his own faction of their common adopted religion. In effect, his son seemed willing to write off the Protestant converts' legal rights to their land and property in order to get on with their lives, in spite of an overwhelming case for legal grievances under the Mexican Constitution of 1917, which Miguel knew well.

Toward the end, he came to believe that corruption, dishonesty, and compromise were failings not only of the traditional Tzotzil social order but also of the Mexican government, the Ladino social order, and of the Protestant movement itself. All the identities that he aspired to have—Indian, Ladino, Protestant, even Miguel Kaxlán—turned out, for him, to be impossible, for none was, in the last analysis, free of contradictions. In the end, I believe it is likely that he faced death with relief rather than with fear.

POSTSCRIPT

In chapter 6 I presented a structural template of Maya historical process that captures consistent patterns through which male and female protagonists interact with one another in mythical and historical time. I argued that the Maya proclivity for conceiving of time primarily as a cyclical phenomenon linked to daily and annual solar cycles—and secondarily as a linear process—led to surprising similarities between the structure of historical reckoning in the Ancient Maya world and the unfolding of events in modern history as contemporary Mayas interact with the Mexican State.

I am encouraged to reconsider the tragic tale of Miguel Kaxlán in this light through reflection on recent events relating to the Maya Zapatista Movement. Although the Zapatista Movement was (and is) a radical critique of traditional Mexican society and the role of Indians within it, it nevertheless reproduces some of the patterns that characterize the old template (see chapter 6). In particular, I refer to the apparent care with which the clandestine leadership of the EZLN coordinated some of the early events of the 1994 insurrection with key calendrical dates in the annual ritual calendar. Not only the January 1 launching date of the rebellion (with was also the inaugural date of NAFTA and of the annual civic office cycle), but also the dates of the kidnapping of former Chiapas Governor Absalón Castellanos by the Zapatistas (early January 1994) and of his subsequent release, unharmed (Ash Wednesday of 1994), coincide with dates that have heavy symbolic significance in the Maya communities.[1] Furthermore, gender and ethnic identity of key protagonists follow predictable patterns, by whose design I don't pretend to know. In particular, the first martyr of the armed movement on January 1 was a Canadian-born female Colonel, Janine Archembault, who died a few hours after the siege of Las Margaritas. A few months thereafter, there came a miraculous apparition of spectral light to a Tojolabal Indian woman, a Zapatista named Dominga Hernández. She then found an image of a "white Baby Jesus" propped up against a tree. She now maintains this shrine on behalf of the Zapatista faithful (Ross 1995: 7 and Furbee 1996). Widely publicized also was the trip last summer (1997) of EZLN Comandante Ramona, then dying of cancer, to attend an indigenous rights rally in Mexico City. Finally, public statements by the Zapatistas involve explicit demands for the economic and political equality of women, a cause that is also important to the Protestant movement.

Juxtaposed with these high-profile, primordial female symbolic associations is the mysterious male persona of the non-Indian Mexican Subcomandante Marcos, eloquent spokesman and chief military strategist of the EZLN. Like Miguel Kaxlán, Marcos has highly ambiguous ethnic loyalties and affiliations and uses them effectively to promote his cause.

It is also relevant to recall that both the Zapatista and Protestant movements responded to the same period of radical social change (1960s to the present), and both movements gained some of their initial and continuing momentum through the active participation of female symbolic paladins. In the case of Miguel Kaxlán 's tragic life history, women—including his several Indian wives and mistresses, the Indian mother and daughter who were the alleged victims of the rape and robbery, and the burn-scarred Indian sisters who became martyrs for the Protestant cause—played central roles in launching, confounding, and restarting his political and religious career. This key structural place of women protagonists in times of crisis has deep historical precedent. Miguel himself, like so many male heroes and antiheroes before him—including personalities as diverse as the white Sun/Christ himself, Pedro Díaz Cuzcat (1868–69 War of Santa Rosa), and Pajarito (1910-11 conflict)—and after him (perhaps Marcos himself), all had ambiguous identities and alliances that bound them, paradoxically, to both non-Indian and Indian communities in their respective quests for social change. Like them, he eventually moved out of the orbit of Indian culture, marginalizing or abandoning former female allies and co-religionists, to take his cause into violent conflict with the male-dominated social order of the Mexican State (and its Indian allies). Like some of them (e.g., Cuzcat and Pajarito), he lost his bid for power through violent death at the hand of his adversaries. All of this recalls vividly the storyline of the Maya historical process that is sketched in chapter 6.

Perhaps, therefore, Miguel Kaxlán is not dead; indeed, he may have been alive before he lived. So powerful is the hand of Maya cultural agency to condition individual lives and their action in history. (See chapters 9 and 10.)

Nine

>✐⌒

FROM OLMECS TO ZAPATISTAS:
A ONCE AND FUTURE HISTORY
OF MAYA SOULS

I first composed this essay in 1992, on the occasion of the Columbus Quincentenary, as a symposium paper at the University of Virgina. It was published in two English versions in 1994 and 1995. Its life history is given in the acknowledgments. As it was going to press in the American Anthropologist (1994) and in the symposium volume (1995), the Zapatista insurrection exploded in January 1994. What I had conceived as a commissioned piece on the role of animals in the collective and individual representations of identities of Native Americans quickly became larger than the spirit of the invited paper, for the Zapatista movement presented to the media an unusual configuration of personalities, among them the mysterious and eloquent Subcomandante Marcos and his directorate of then (and still) relatively unknown Indian Comandantes. These personalities were (and still are) relatively obscure, yet it seemed to me that Maya ideas about self, person, and society might illuminate why this opaque profile of the Zapatista leadership was a preferred mode of self-representation. I present here a brief postscript alluding to these issues (published in the 1995 version) that leads directly to the rationale for the essay that follows as chapter 10.

I am concerned here with the deep life history of an idea—the nature of the person in relation to society—that has been central to Maya thought for some three thousand years. To some extent, this theory of personhood informs the way Maya people act in history to this day.

HOW A TOYOTA WAGON IS LIKE A COYOTE

In the spring of 1985, Robert Laughlin of the Smithsonian Institution arranged a U.S. tour for the newly formed puppet theater troupe of Sna Jtz'ibahom, the Maya Writers' Cooperative of Chiapas, Mexico. My university was sponsoring one of the performances, and since one of the members of the troupe was a long-time friend and field assistant from San Juan Chamula, where I have done my principal fieldwork, our home in Albany was the logical place for the group to stay. My friend, Marián López Calixto, felt very much at home with us in Albany, just as he had for several years in

Chiapas when we were living there. Worldly and self-confident, he assured us that neither the United States nor our home in upstate New York surprised him very much.

He did, however, surprise me with some unsolicited ethnographic observations about me and my world. Over rum and soda one night, he casually provided a startling assessment of me based, oddly enough, on our car, a 1984 Toyota wagon. It was a strange, needle-nosed, long vehicle that looked rather like a space buggy from a 1950s-vintage science fiction movie. Furthermore, it was pure white. Amidst drinks and laughter, he asserted that our vehicle was a coyote and that our possession of it affirmed his long-standing belief that my animal-soul companion was a coyote, an aspect of my persona that he and I had never discussed in Chiapas. Furthermore, he stated that he had often dreamed that my animal soul was a coyote and that it really came as no surprise to him that we had such a vehicle. The link between motor vehicles and animals, by the way, is coded linguistically and perhaps cognitively; the noun classifier for animals (*kot*) applies to cars, trucks, and buses as well, for all of them are nonhumans that move about on four feet. On examining the wagon the next morning, Marián carefully pointed out first the feet (tires and wheel wells), then the nose (needle-nosed hood), mouth (bumper and small grill work), eyes (tapered front-door windows), ears (two rearview mirrors), and even the anus (the tail pipe).

This odd discussion was both funny and serious—also, by the way, strangely flattering to me—for all Tzotzils, indeed the vast majority of over 15 million Indians in Mexico and Central America today, have a private spiritual world of the self that is expressed through the concept of animal souls or other extrasomatic causal forces that influence their destiny. That my friend Marián chose to speak of the subject with me revealed a measure of trust and intimacy, for the nature and identity of one's soul is not a subject for casual conversation in Indian communities; even less is it an appropriate subject for discussion with strangers. Marian's assessment of me via the concept of my purported animal-soul companion was also interesting in another regard. In terms of the world of Tzotzil animal souls, ranked from jaguars for the rich and powerful to rabbits for the poor and humble, the coyote is vaguely in the middle. This is probably close to where I am in the social and economic hierarchy of my nation and my community. It could also be argued that my coyote-mobile had quite a bit to do with my daily rounds that were related to my given obligations, personal, social, and professional—my daily destiny.

The concept of animal souls and other coessences goes well beyond being a mere evaluative vocabulary. These ideas matter. They constitute a key node in Indian cosmologies and beliefs about health and general well-being. The individual soul is often revealed to one in dreams and interpreted by diviners, shamans, and other traditional health-care practitioners. Furthermore, Mesoamerican souls are fragile essences that link individuals to the forces of

Earth, society, the cosmos, and the divine. They provide this link because they originate or reside outside the bodies of their human counterparts, often in the bodies of animals. These alter ego coessences can become lost, afflicted, manipulated by witches, or frightened by sexual excitement or some unexpected event. If these forces are fatally injured, their human counterparts die. In other words, animal souls and their related individual coessences figure prominently in native theories of evil, well-being, fate, and destiny. As such, they are also centrally present in the language, beliefs, practices, and symbols used in traditional health maintenance and curing.

I believe that this set of beliefs and the language used for talking about them reside at the very core of what might be called a native metaphysics of personhood in Mesoamerica. However, the challenge of interpreting and understanding this belief system (if it is a "system") is nevertheless formidable. I began, therefore, with the Toyota-as-coyote-as-Gary Gossen anecdote, for it was really only on that occasion that I first experienced a spontaneous exchange on the theme—that is, a conversation that directly involved me as the subject rather than as the observer or interviewer. Through this experience, I was forced to realize that the concept of animal souls, which I have previously attempted to analyze as a coherent theory of selfhood, bears more resemblance to a fluid medium of discourse and practice for dealing with self, other, and human destiny than it does to any rigid system of belief (Gossen 1975). Indeed, I have found that several recent studies that comment on my own work in relation to this concept offer compelling evidence to the effect that the belief system is neither as consistent (from one native testimony to the next in the same community and from one Maya community to the next) nor as stable over time as I had once believed to be the case (see Rachun Linn 1989 and Watanabe 1989). All of this said, there is equally compelling evidence that the language of souls has fundamentally to do with Mesoamerican construction of self and social identity, destiny and power, as much now as has apparently been the case for two thousand years in Mexico and Central America.[1]

TONALISMO AND NAGUALISMO IN TIME AND SPACE

Among the many wonders and enigmas that the Europeans found in America, one of those that must have confounded them most was the unseen and, for them, unseeable world of the Amerindian human spirit. Although some form of individual and group affiliation with spirits of animals, plants, and other natural and supernatural beings has broad diffusion in virtually all corners of the Americas, these invisible forces have assumed regional characteristics that are highly distinctive. For example, the generic term *totemism*, now common in some cognate form in most Western languages, derives from the Algonquian (Chippewa) *ototeman* ("brother-sister kin"), a term that, in its original cultural context, referred to the lineal descent of members of a clan from its founding or sponsoring spirits, animal, plant, or other supernatural. The term has subsequently been used all over the New World, with varying degrees of accuracy, to describe similar kinds of collective ties between social groups and their associated charter spirits.

The characteristic form of this type of human-Other spiritual affiliation in Mesoamerica designates not group relationships with spirits but rather predestined and relatively immutable *individual* relationships with particular supernatural forces. In central Mexico these forces or coessences are called *tonalli*, while in the Maya area they are *chanuletik* (Tzotzil "animal souls"), or *ch'uleletik* (Tzotzil "souls"), or cognate terms deriving from the proto-Maya *way* ("sleep," "dream," or "witch[craft]") (Houston and Stuart 1989: 5). These forces are typically identified with animals but may also, in the same community, take the form of other coessences. Related to these concepts is the body of beliefs known as *nagualismo*, which generally refers to the transformation of humans into those animals or other spirits with which they have an individual relationship. The term *nagualismo* is associated particularly with the explanation of how shamans, sorcerers, and witches accomplish their goals for good and ill. Their means is temporary transformation into the animal(s) or spirit(s) with which they have special supernatural ties (Adams and Rubel 1967: 336).

The thread that unifies these various expressions of the concept focuses on the forces that influence the destiny of the self. These forces lie outside of the body and are thus not easy to change or manipulate. One must live within the general parameters of one's destiny. This destiny is linked to fragile essences that can become lost, frightened, or injured. These afflictions of the soul may cause sickness or misfortune, whereupon one can engage other supernatural forces (often the souls of shamans and witches who are available for hire) to intervene to restore equilibrium to one's charter destiny. The preferred route to spiritual health is propitiation and adherence to normative behavior—that is to say, health maintenance rather than remedial intervention, for the latter is uncertain and often expensive.

Reports and detailed description of these beliefs are omnipresent in the modern ethnographic literature of Mesoamerica. Furthermore, the expression of these beliefs varies greatly from community to community. In a recent comprehensive ethnographic study of this concept in Cancuc, a contemporary Tzeltal (Maya) community, Pedro Pitarch (1996) shows not only that these coessences are centrally important to the maintenance of political and religious authority but also that influential individuals may acquire more than one *lab* ("coessence") by means of inheritance; these may, in turn, be passed on to one's descendants. This conservative contemporary expression of the coessence concept invites comparison with the central role that coessences appear to have had in ancient Mesoamerican states.

These concepts have also been extensively described in sources that date from the contact period, such as Sahagún's *Florentine Codex* (1969), and the colonial period, such as Ruíz de Alarcón (1982) and Gage (1958). Non-anthropologists and Protestant missionaries in our time have also reported these "superstitions" with particular zeal and condescension, as does Hugh Steven in his missionary novel, *They Dared to be Different* (1976). Writing about the current efforts to convert the Chamula Tzotzil Maya to Protestantism, he accounts for his hero's early experience with paganism in these words:

> Mariano's heartbreak would stop, but not his fear and hate. As a child he dreaded his father, stood in awe of the healing power of the *ilol*, and felt sprays of ice-cold panic sweep up his back whenever someone talked about the *brujo* who could change himself into an animal with the power to kill. (1976: 51)

In the sections that follow, I will present evidence for the antiquity of the animal-soul concept in Mesoamerica and will than proceed to discuss its impressive power in our time as a source of internal social control and social therapy within Indian communities, and also, its strength as a tool of passive (perhaps now becoming active?) resistance to spiritual conquest of the region by Western culture. Whatever may have been the public role of these beliefs in the calendrical and dynastic rituals of pre-Columbian state religions, beliefs, and practices related to spiritual co-essences have survived and evolved in our time with a relatively low, often nonexistent, public profile. Today, they typically belong to the private sphere of spiritual life whose ritual expression seldom moves beyond the domestic unit and small outdoor shrines; they have no doubt been there for thousands of years. Because this intimate spiritual complex does not have a conspicuous, public cult of expression, it has been difficult to eradicate or change by force. Missionaries and others who have had an interest in planned social change in the area over the centuries have apparently been unable to deal with what they could not see, for *tonalismo* and related beliefs and practices have been, and remain today, largely invisible to outsiders. Indeed, there is compelling evidence that these beliefs are evolving in the modern era to serve as powerful ethnic markers as Indian communities negotiate relatively esoteric definitions of self and group that are not fully apparent, comprehensible, or significant to dominant groups that might seek, by persuasion, conversion, or violence to "nationalize" or otherwise "neutralize" Indian identity.[2]

ANIMAL SOULS AND COESSENCES IN EARLY MESOAMERICAN STATES

The iconography of ancient Mesoamerica is replete with representations of human-animal relationships: transformations, masks, anthropomorphic ani-

mals, zoomorphic deities linked with human dynastic leaders, ritual paraphernalia that suggest links of ritual practitioners with specific animals, calendar glyphs as stylized animals, and so forth. Indeed, the motif most fundamentally associated with the rise of the Olmec style, emblematic of one of
Mesoamerica's first great civilizations in the Preclassic period (2000 B. C. to
A. D. 250), is a were-jaguar creature that has hundreds of variant forms, all of
which appear to link human political and religious authority with the supernatural power of jaguars or other jungle cats. This iconography merges
human and jaguar facial features into a single countenance, making unmis-
takable the message that human, natural, and sacred power somehow come
together in this idea. Might this be an early expression of the coessence concept? (See Figure 21.)

Figure 21. Jade Effigy Axe (the "Kunz Axe") in the Olmec Style
Exact provenance and date unknown, though Central Tabasco, Mexico, circa fifth cen-
tury B. C., is plausible. Neg. No. 326909, photograph by Rota. Courtesy Department
Library Services, American Museum of Natural History.

During what is known as the Mesoamerican Classic period (A. D. 250 to A. D. 850), the iconographic power of human-animal association with theocratic statecraft reached new heights with the rise of the great cult of the plumed serpent, associated with the god Quetzalcóatl in the Mexican Central Valley and with Kukulcán in the Maya area. The plumed serpent, linked with divinely chartered human political authority and legitimacy, developed into what is perhaps the key sacred symbol in the art and architecture of many of the theocratic states that dominated Mesoamerica until the Spanish Conquest. Indeed, whole ancient cities were dedicated to Quetzalcóatl, and the legendary ruler of eighth-century Tula, Topiltzin Quetzalcóatl, was remembered in written and oral tradition of ancient Mesoamerica as the human embodiment of the plumed serpent deity whose name he bore. His cult inspired the rise of subsequent polities, such as the massive post-Classic urban center of Chichén Itzá. The staying power of this deity and the ideas he embodies are such that it can be credibly argued that shamanic power via coessences, together with associated claims to political legitimacy, may have provided a key ideological underpinning for statecraft in ancient Mesoamerica. Indeed, the link of shamanic belief and practice to divine coessences and political authority figures as one of the key arguments in a recent, major work on continuity and change in three thousands years of Maya civilization (Freidel et al. 1993). (See Figure 22.)

Until very recently it was impossible to offer other than speculative interpretations as to the nature of the link between animals, coessences, gods, humans, secular power, theory of self, and cosmically ordained destiny in the early Mesoamerican states. However, rapidly unfolding new discoveries in the decipherment of early Mesoamerican writing systems are providing testimonies written in native Mesoamericans' own hand that promise to illuminate the meaning of the iconography. With regard to the animal soul concept, a very early Mesoamerican text bearing on this subject was recently deciphered by John Justeson and Terrence Kaufman (1992, 1993). This brief glyphic text appears on the Tuxtla Statuette, which is in the style known as the epi-Olmec style and dates from A. D. 162 (see Figure 23). Justeson and Kaufman say that they statuette itself is probably a representation of a shaman who is calling up an animal-soul companion.

The figure on the statuette may depict this, or the shaman's impersonation of this companion, since it shows a human being in the guise of an animal, wearing a duckbill mask and a cape of bird wings and claws. In the great florescence of Maya Classic culture (A. D. 250 to A. D. 850), the hieroglyphic inscriptions routinely used a glyph that reads *way* (related to modern Maya words for "sleep" and "dream") to signify the link between humans and coessences, both animal and other. Houston and Stuart conclude their report on this subject as follows:

Figure 22. Lord Quetzalcóatl
Artist rendering of a reconstructed bas-relief facade from the seventh century A. D. Toltec Culture. Provenance: Cerro de la Malinche, Tula, Hidalgo, Mexico. From Díaz Infante (1963: 57). Reprinted with permission from the Universidad Veracruzana.

> In our judgement, the way decipherment fundamentally changes our understanding of Classic Maya iconography and belief. It indicates that many of the supernatural figures, once described as "gods," "underworld denizens," or "deities," are instead coessences of supernaturals or humans. More than ever, then, Classic Maya beliefs would seem to coincide with general patterns of Mesoamerican thought....Our final point concerns the certainty with which Maya lords identified their coessences. . . . For the Classic Maya, such self-knowledge may well have been an important marker of elite status. (Houston and Stuart 1989: 13)

Thus it is now possible to state with a fair degree of certainty that individual coessences and their link with human power and destiny are very ancient and very persistent ideas that date at least from the time of Christ.

TONALISMO IN THE AZTEC UNIVERSE (CA. 1550)

Some fifteen hundred years later these same ideas, no doubt somewhat transformed by new cultural and linguistic influences and by dozens of generations of theocratic states, were present in the Aztec empire. Bernardino de Sahagún's Nahuatl-speaking assistants recorded their soul beliefs in the middle of the sixteenth century as follows:

It was said
that in the thirteenth heaven
[in the uppermost of the heavens]
our destinies were determined.
When the child is conceived,
when he is placed in the womb,
his destiny (*tonalli*) comes to him there;
it is sent by the Lord of Duality.
(Sahagún 1969, Book VI, Chapter XXII)

In a recent commentary on this text, Miguel León-Portilla writes:

In several of the books where divine presences are depicted one finds also the hieroglyphs which denote the *tonalli*, the individual human destinies which, at given moments and places, are brought by the gods. The *tonalli*, destinies, will determine everything in each human life, from birth to death. The *tonalli* is essentially an individual's *i-macehual*, "that which is granted to one, that which one deserves." Thus, the *tonalli* bears, for all people on earth, the consubstantial origin and imprint of the divine source of life; it is this essence that determines what is going to happen in accordance with prearranged schemes. The unveiling of this predestined plan and propitiation of its divine source are vital to the human condition. (1993: 8)

Of this same belief system, Jorge Klor de Alva has recently commented on the fundamental difference between these premises about the Aztec self and the system which the Spanish missionaries sought to impose:

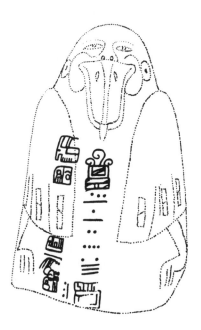

Figure 23. The Tuxtla Statuette (Holmes 1907: 692)
Iconography, writing, and long count date are in the epi-Olmec style. Provenance is San Andrés Tuxtla, Vera Cruz, Mexico. Date, as per inscription, is A. D. 162. The lower four glyphs in the column on the left side of the figure say: "The animal soul companion is powerful." (Justeson and Kaufman 1992, 1993: 1703)

There was no autonomous will at the core of the self since every human being was a microcosm reflecting the forces that made up the cosmos at large. Furthermore, there was no clear boundary between personal will and the supernatural and natural forces that governed the universe. Consequently, *acts* that were believed truly to harmonize the contrary influences of the gods (saints, spirits, "devils"), rather than right *intentions* per se, mapped out the terrain of the ethical individual. Therefore, behavior, performance and punctiliousness, rather than will, contemplation or motivation were the key concerns of the Nahua who strove to be moral.

Although the fragmented self was (and still is) believed to be composed of numerous physical and supernatural elements, three major entities, the *tonalli*, the *teyolia*, and the *ihiyotl*—all shared with animals, plants, and inanimate objects—seem to have constituted its core. (Klor de Alva 1993: 150)

There are many other native testimonies from the contact period that address the complex world of the Mesoamerican soul, although no source, to my knowledge, discusses the subject in such comprehensive detail. Another extremely rich primary source of data on this subject is the famous Quiché Maya epic history known as the Popol Vuh, which was apparently transcribed from a hieroglyphic text in the sixteenth century that subsequently disappeared (D. Tedlock 1985). This long account of the "dawn of life" and of the myriad events that lead to the modern era (early sixteenth century) contains literally hundreds of passages and motifs that can easily be interpreted within the matrix of the Maya variant of Mesoamerican *tonalismo* and *nagualismo*. (See, for example, Rosenbaum 1983.)

Thus, without belaboring the obvious, it can be stated without exaggeration that Spanish Christians, indoctrinated with the central theological doctrine of free will and choice (as these were given to humanity when God created us "in his own image"), encountered in Mesoamerica a fundamentally different construction of the human condition.

A SOUL WAR FROM THOMAS GAGE'S TRAVELS IN THE NEW WORLD (1648)

Although this essay will not consider the particulars of the collision in the course of the Spanish Conquest between two fundamentally different visions of self and destiny, a conflict that is still not resolved to this day, it nevertheless serves my present purposes to provide one extraordinary example of this spiritual encounter from deep in the Spanish colonial era. My goal is to illustrate that the labors of a full century of Christian missionization (1550–1650) did not manage to alter this belief system, much less eradicate it. The missionaries did, however, succeed in eradicating virtually all signs of it from public civil and religious practice. In private and domestic life, however, it survived, adapted, and evolved throughout the colonial period into our time.

The source I will use to illustrate this is no ordinary text. By the reckoning of some of us, it is one of the more colorful documents of colonial Mesoamerica, notable in large part because its English author, Thomas Gage, was a turncoat Franciscan priest who, midway through life became a Protestant, because it was expedient "so to do" during the Puritan Revolution in England, at which time he had to publish his travel journals in a new social and political climate. He thus brings both Roman Catholic and Protestant biases to his reporting.

Although Thomas Gage is a marvelous subject unto himself, full of ambiguous personal, religious, and ethnic loyalties, he was also a valuable chronicler of Mesoamerican Indian life in the colonial period for several reasons. First, he traveled widely to out-of-the-way places where colonial administration was in it grassroots mode; that is, where there was considerable slippage between Crown policy and local pragmatics. Second, he spoke not only Spanish but also several Indian languages; yet he did not have Spanish ethnicity or the colonial agenda to uphold or defend. Third, his observation of Indian religious and spiritual customs carried an unusual set of biases, reflecting both his newly Protestant and former Roman Catholic European self. These several unusual aspects of Gage's background may have provided a more objective lens for observing Indian life than one might expect from his Spanish contemporaries within the colonial establishment.

I reproduce the following testimony with little editorial comment, for Gage writes engagingly and obviously does not need my interpretive assistance. The passages below report an extraordinary episode from daily life among the Pokomchi Maya of Guatemala, among whom he lived, traveled, and provided pastoral care in the middle of the seventeenth century. Gage became involved with the following events through his ministry to a dying Indian named Juan Gómez and through gossip that emerged during preparations for his proper Christian burial. It turned out, to Gage's horror, that his death had not been "natural."

> There came unto me at least twenty of the chiefest of the town with the two majors, jurats [magistrates or sworn jurors] and all the officers of justice, who desired me to forbear that day the burying of Juan Gómez, for that they had resolved to call a crown officer to view his corpse and examine his death, lest they all should be troubled for him, and he be exhumed. I made as if I knew nothing, but enquired of them the reason. Then they related to me how there were witnesses in the town who saw a lion and a tiger fighting, and presently lost sight of the beasts, and saw Juan Gómez and Sebastián López much about the same time parting one from another, and that immediately Juan Gómez came home bruised to his bed, whence he never rose again, and that he declared upon his deathbed unto some of his friends that Sebastián López had killed him. For this reason they had López in safe custody. . . .

The crown officer was sent for and came that night and searched Gómez' body. I was present with him, and found it all bruised, scratched, and in many places bitten and sore wounded. Many evidences and suspicions were brought against López by the Indians of the town, whereupon he was carried away to Guatemala [City], and there again was tried by the same witnesses, and not much denying the fact himself, was there hanged. And though Gómez' grave was opened in the church, he was not buried in it, but in another made ready for him in a ditch. (Gage 1958: 275-77)

It is evident that Thomas Gage witnessed the tragic aftermath of what, in the view of the Indian community, had been a supernatural battle between the animal-soul companions of two powerful shamans. The lion and the tiger (perhaps an English reference to the puma and the jaguar, animals that are native to Guatemala) were the coessences of Gómez and López, and hence their battle in the forest involved both their bodies and those of their human counterparts. Gage's narrative leads us to believe that neither he nor the Crown officials fully understood what was going on, though all parties, whether Indian or Spanish and including Gage himself, ironically concurred in believing that López was guilty as charged.

ANIMAL SOULS IN CHAMULA (CA. 1980)[3]

One could go to San Juan Chamula today, or to any of thousands of small communities in Mexico or Guatemala, and listen to narratives of events remarkably similar to those reported by Gage in 1648. It is obvious from the tragic consequences that surrounded the Gómez-López encounter, that these beliefs systems could survive only in the private spiritual universe of closed Indian communities. It is also obvious to any ethnographer who works in contemporary Mesoamerican Indian communities (and who knows Indian languages) that *tonalismo* and *nagualismo* remain vitally alive in the late twenieth century.

San Juan Chamula is watched over and protected today by the sun deity, who is known as "Our Lord in Heaven." I have chosen to refer to this deity as the Sun/Christ, for his current "being" merges the concept of Christ, introduced by the Dominicans in the sixteenth century, with the pre-Columbian sun deity. (See chapters 1 to 3.) Central to the Sun/Christ's plan for managing and maintaining order in the universe was a scheme of delegation of certain powers to his mother (the Moon/Virgin Mary) and to several saints and other supernaturals. He gave to St. Jerome (known in Tzotzil as *jtotik bolom*, "Our Lord Jaguar") the responsibility for individual human destiny. The syncretic link of St. Jerome with wild animals is probably traceable to the traditional European legends wherein he was said to have made friends with animals while doing penance in the desert. Following this story, popular iconography of St. Jerome evolved the convention of representing the saint with a docile lion standing or lying at his feet. As St. Jerome has entered the Chamula Tzotzil pantheon, his senior aspect sits with the Sun/Christ on the third (highest) level of the sky. His junior aspect lives in a sacred mountain called Tzontevitz, which lies in Chamula territory and is the point of highest elevation in the township. In both aspects, St. Jerome carries out his mandate for overseeing human destiny through the medium of three types of spirits or souls that are associated with each and every human being.

The first of these spirits is called ʔora, meaning "time" or "predestined life span." (Perhaps it is analogous to the Nahuatl *tonalli*.) Irrevocable from conception onward, the ʔora for each person has the form of a multicolored candle that is placed by St. Jerome at the time of conception. Different lengths and thicknesses represent different life spans. The longer ones of course have potential for generating greater heat and burning longer than do the shorter candles; hence, the longer candles are associated with longer life spans. As long as the individual's candle burns in the sky, the associated person and his animal-soul companion live. When it goes out—either naturally, by burning up its fuel, or prematurely, through the invention of a witch (*jʔak'chamel*, or "thrower of sickness")—the person and his or her soul companion die. Because of its crucial importance to the predestined life span of the individual, the ʔora candle is nearly always symbolically present during curing ceremonies.

Related to the ʔora candle is a second type of individual spirit represented in the living human body by the *ch'ulel*, an invisible essence located at the tip of the tongue. It is the first spirit to become associated with the body as a fetus (symbolizing the lighting of the candle in the sky) and is the last to depart from the body several days after physical death (symbolizing the total extinction of the candle). It is this essence of the individual that goes to live eternally in the underworld and that returns to visit relatives each year at the Feast of the Dead (October 31– November 2) as long as they put out food for it. Since the *ch'ulel* has thirteen parts, any or all parts may become afflicted. This causes various degrees and kinds of human sickness, of a general class called *ch'ulelal*. A final significant fact about the *ch'ulel* is that it is also present, with all the same attributes, on the tip of the tongue of one's animal-soul companion.

This leads to the third type of individual spirit, the animal-soul companion itself, called *chanul*, deriving from *chon*, which means "animal." The *chanul* is assigned to the individual at birth by St. Jerome and the Sun/Christ. This animal shares every stroke of fortune that its human counterpart experiences. It is also of the same sex as its human associate. The *chanul* has two aspects, a "junior" (*itz'inal*) and "senior" (*bankilal*), each of which has thirteen parts. The junior aspect of the *chanul* lives in the sacred mountain named Tzontevitz (discussed above), where it is tended by the junior aspect of St. Jerome. The senior aspect of the *chanul* lives on the third layer of the sky, where it is tended by the senior aspect of St. Jerome. During the day, these soul animals roam about through the woods and fields of their territories much as ordinary animals do. However, at night, St. Jerome, in both his junior and senior aspects, herds them into corrals, the junior one on the sacred mountain and senior in the third level of the sky. Here they spend the night in relative safety from the perils of darkness, a time when most misfortunes, particularly those caused by witchcraft, occur. It is in order to guarantee this nighttime care that one must make occasional prayers of supplication to St. Jerome.

By far the most common cause of illness in Chamula is believed to be the loss of or injury inflicted on one or several of the twenty-six parts of the *chanul*. (thirteen for each aspect, junior and senior). Loss can occur during sexual intercourse, fright, excitement, anger, jealousy, or in the course of an accident. Thus human illnesses are typically caused by numerous afflictions of the *chanul* and—somewhat less frequently—the *ch'ulel*, associated with the candle of destiny in the sky. This makes a total of thirty-nine parts of the human spirit (twenty-six for the double *chanul* and thirteen for the *ch'ulel*) that can be afflicted singly plus a very large number of combinations that can be jointly afflicted or lost. It is the shaman's role to ascertain, by pulsing the wrist and by observing symptoms, what parts of the soul are afflicted. He or she must then prescribe the necessary candles, herbs, flowers, and foods and say the proper prayers at a formal curing ceremony, the purpose of which is to restore health and integrity to the soul configuration.[4]

All animal soul companions are wild animals with five digits. Furthermore, all are mammals or marsupials.[5] It is the sympathetic trait, the five digits of the hand or paw, that establishes the special tie between humankind and these animals. It is significant to note here that the Tzotzil word for "man" (*vinik*) is the same as the word for "twenty," indicating that the total of twenty digits is considered to be a striking aspect of human physiology and an important anatomical trait of soul companion animals as well.[6] Chamula animal souls are often ranked according to three levels, although there is considerable disagreement about which animals belong where in the ranking system. The third level is the most senior and thus includes those animals associated with rich and powerful individuals, while the second level is associated with moderately successful people, and the first, with the humble and poor. The only animal that all people agree to be a third-level *chanul* is the jaguar. The most powerful shamans and political and religious leaders, therefore, are logically thought to have jaguar soul companions. In the second level are generally ranked the coyote, weasel, and fox. The first and most junior level includes the rabbit, opossum, and skunk. There is general agreement about the jaguar's first-rank position and about the low rank of opossum, skunk, and rabbit. However, the second level is not consistently reported from individual to individual. (See Figure 24.)

Reflection and speculation (and disagreement) about this hierarchy of humanity in relation to the world of animal souls appear frequently in

Chamula narrative accounts about their world and its perils. An example of this type of testimony comes from Xun Méndez Tzotzek, a master story-teller. He gave me this account (here translated from the original Tzotzil) in 1969 as a part of a much longer narrative about the origin of the first of four cyclical creations. (See chapter 3 for full text.)

> You see, the people were occupied in increasing their numbers.
>> So it was when the first people emerged.
> Jaguars accompanied some of them;
>> Coyotes accompanied some;
>> Weasels accompanied others.
> But those whom the jaguars accompany,
>> These are the richest.
> Those whom the coyotes accompany,
>> These people are poorer.
> Those whom foxes accompany,
>> These are the poorest,
>> Just as poor as those of the weasel.
> Furthermore, those human counterparts of both the fox and the weasel,
>> They don't live very long.
> There was once a person those baby chicks had been eaten by some animal.
>> The owner of the chicks saw it happen.
>> So he shot the culprit with a shotgun.
> After the weasel died,
>> It was only three days until the owner of the chicks died.
>> He had shot his own animal soul and so died in no time himself. . . .
>> In this manner, whoever we are, we die just as our soul companions do.
> You see, long ago it was Our Father who thought about this.
>> Our Father long ago gave us dreams about our animal-soul companions.
> That is why it remains the same even today,
>> That not all of us have jaguars as animal souls.

The final line of this extract from Mr. Méndez Tzotzek's narrative dark-ly and cryptically observes, in the veiled language of this belief system, that human inequality and hierarchy are facts of life. His text both affirms and disagrees with some of my generalizations, stated above. However, the fact that a discussion of animal souls follows immediately after the account of the creation of viable human beings testifies to the saliency of souls in his reflec-tions about the human nature: our coessential consciousness, our strength, our frailty, our vulnerability, our inequality, and even our unwitting capaci-ty to destroy ourselves.

Death and misfortune, however, may also be caused by the malice of others, who use the languages and premises of animal-soul beliefs in the practice of "casting sickness." Although a normal person is said to have only one animal soul, a witch has one or several normal animal-soul companions plus an aberrant, anomalous creature that is outside the class of normal soul companions.[7] In some cases Chamulas note the number and type of a creature's digits as the traits that make it "different" from normal soul companion animals, as in the case of hooved animals and insects. It also appears that the anomalous classificatory position of domestic animals (neither wild nor human) gives them important intermediary power as witches' soul companions. Witches require the power of strong animal-soul companions from the "normal" class so as to be dominant over all other *chanuletik*, doing them ill if their clients so desire. They require anomalous animals for a different reason: anomalous animals give them a way to slip into places such as house compounds without being noticed. This enables them to do evils things surreptitiously, as when they take the form of a turkey or chicken, for potential victims would normally not expect a domestic animal or bird to hurt them.

All people, including witches, are said to learn the identities of their animal-soul companions through dreams. Typically, people have the same dream three times. Although an individual's animal-soul companion figures prominently in this dream, its meaning is not always clear. Often several animals appear in dreams, thus opening up the interpretive framework for uncertainty and multiple possible "readings" of the vagaries of one's destiny. In these cases, a shaman must be consulted. While shamans and witches can usually ascertain the meaning of their own and their clients' animal-soul dreams, ordinary people are often uncertain about the identities of their soul animals, even in adulthood. Even if they do know, they are reluctant to discuss the matter publicly.

In summary, then, the factors that determine individual fate and fortune are always to be understood and reflected on as phenomena that are *predestined* but also, secondarily, *subject to the agency and will of others*, both human and supernatural. These causal forces derive ultimately from the Sun/Christ, St. Jerome, the candle of one's life span, and the junior and senior aspects of the animal-soul companion. The healthy body carries this constellation of influences in equilibrium; it is the passive bearer of forces over which it really has no control. But this constellation can also be attacked and disoriented by others, both human and supernatural. The body, thus afflicted, suffers from a disequilibrium situation in the whole; a part is missing, injured, or destroyed. About the only ways people can affect their own destinies through preventive measures are by paying homage to the deities who are responsible for the soul animals, so as to encourage them to continue their vigilance and compassion for humankind, and by being conforming, sensible, and generous, so as not to attract the attention, anger, and jealousy of others. Once afflicted, the only traditional way to remedy one's condition is to hire a shaman to intervene on one's behalf by performing rituals whose primary goal is to restore equilibrium to the several individual spirits that influence

Figure 24. The Logic of the Concrete: Chamula Animal Souls

(Adapted from Gossen [1975: 435]) This table offers a structural examination of the logic of the coessence concept as presented in the data provided by several Tzotzils in 1969.

Wild soul companion animals (5 toes, like humans)		Domestic and other anomalous animals (Cloven hooves, claws, etc., unlike humans)
Carnivores	Herbivores and Omnivores	Herbivores and Omnivores
Stronger people, rich people, and cargo-holders	Weaker people, ordinary people	Witches have one of these plus a strong wild animal-soul companion
jaguar ocelot coyote fox weasel	rabbit skunk racoon opossum squirrel	cattle sheep pigs chickens turkeys wild birds insects
Early creation. Distant Habitat (lowlands, hot) Infrequently seen, nocturnal	Later creation. More frequently seen in highlands Nocturnal, diurnal, and crepuscular	Recent creation. Seen every day near house compounds Diurnal

the body's well-being. In practice, however, the shaman also addresses the matter of restoring harmony and equilibrium to one's social relations.

This is not an altogether comforting or secure worldview. People often express anxiety over whether or not they are complying with their pre-scribed destinies. Uncertainty with regard to this matter can easily affect key decisions in one's life and can limit a person's willingness to undertake such risky activities as building a new house or taking a new job. Might one be stretching one's "self"? Might one's neighbors and friends be thinking this? Although this belief system produces occasional private stress, its tendency to encourage social conformity and modesty may help us to understand why it continues to occupy an important niche in the life of Indian communi-ties and why individuals, perhaps including the clandestine Zapatista leaders, are reluctant to seek high profiles for themselves. Proof of the modern via-bility of this vision of self and destiny and the associated curing practices is that they coexist very successfully with Western medicine and other forms of planned social change, perhaps including the Zapatista movement. They constitute much more than a "system" of "folk medicine," since they give form to thought and reflection about the social reality that surrounds the individual.

Remedial rituals that are associated with this belief complex are called "see-ing" or "watching over" ceremonies. They do not seek to change the preor-dained path of the soul through the life cycle, but rather to defend it from, and guide it through, unforeseen attacks and perils. Curers seek neither to change nor to circumvent the inevitable, but rather to allow the niche that belongs to the patient to be fully realized, according to the will of the Sun/Christ and St. Jerome. Obviously, there is enormous latitude for interpretation here, a quality that renders this belief system both fluid and adaptable at the same time it pur-ports to address constant and unchanging truths. What remains constant, even within this realm of opaqueness and subjectivity, is a deep skepticism about individual autonomy and the very idea of the "self-made" individual who is guided only by pragmatic self-interest. In short, these ideas seem to deny the very pillars of Western liberalism.

Chamula beliefs in coessences coexist and compete successfully with Western medicine and political practice precisely because they address mat-ters of self and society that are beyond the individual body and person. In practice, this is a fluid language of social analysis and social integration. In contrast, Western medicine and politics are pragmatic, individual, and "demo-cratic" in that a given antibiotic or legal statute is supposed to accomplish the same ends for a rich person or a poor person. While not rejecting Western medicine or Western social practices, the Chamula system of coessences seeks in addition to encourage well-being by situating the individual in the cosmos and guiding him or her through the reality of social hierarchy and inequali-ty. Tzoztils today accept both systems, realizing full well that their own traditional system deals with issues and realities that are beyond the reach of Western medicine and conventional, individualistic political pragmatism.

THE FUTURE OF AN ANCIENT IDEA

As I move this discussion to a conclusion, I want to emphasize that I am dealing with a conceptual universe that is not only very ancient and very widespread in contemporary Mesoamerica but also, apparently, highly adaptive to our fast-changing times. It is clear that these beliefs once occupied a central place in the public religious and political life of precontact Mesoamerican societies. It is also clear, for reasons that I have attempted to demonstrate, that the political realities of colonial and modern periods have obliged the expression and practice of these beliefs to disappear from the public sector. They have survived in the private, domestic sector of people's lives, where they have remained for centuries—vital, important, but nevertheless discreetly veiled from public view.

In her well-known autobiographical commentary, *I, Rigoberta Menchú*, the 1992 Maya Indian Nobel Peace Prize laureate testifies to the importance of these ideas in the social fabric of modern Guatemala's Indian community:

> We Indians have always hidden our identity and kept our secrets to ourselves. This is why we are discriminated against. We often find if hard to talk about ourselves because we know we must hide so much in order to preserve our Indian culture and prevent it from being taken away from us. So I can tell you only very general things about the *nahual*. I can't tell you what my *nahual* is because that is one of our secrets. (Menchú 1984: 18-20)

In our time, there is evidence that the commitment of Indian communities to a self-definition of ethnicity and community maintenance, based in part on belief in coessences, is reemerging in the public arena as Indians in Guatemala and Mexico move to assert their own place in the ethnic mosaic that characterizes both modern nations. No one has stated this "emergent" quality of Mesoamerican soul beliefs more eloquently than John Watanabe, to whom I turn in closing:

> Having a soul means behaving in sensible ways, not just mechanically cleaving to established ways. Soul indeed demands mastery of cultural convention, but this precludes neither personal opportunism nor cultural innovation as long as one has the eloquence to persuade others of one's propriety. Although souls unequivocally situate individuals within a community, they constitute that community more as an inclusive, continually negotiated ground of social interaction than as an exclusive nexus of essential traits or institutions. I would suggest that greater appreciation of these "emergent" qualities of Maya souls might well clarify the tenacity of Maya ethnic identity in the face of rapid, . . . increasingly violent, social change. (Watanabe 1989: 273)

What, then, is the future of this idea? I know of few features of Mesoamerican life, ancient or modern, that demonstrate more tenacity than this unseen Mesoamerican essence. This tenacity has occurred not through obsessive maintenance of a precious gift from the past but through creative reinterpretation of a distinctively Mesoamerican vision of self, society, and ethnic identity. Perhaps, in the next century, as John Watanabe has suggested, the Mesoamerican Indian "soul" will evolve into something closer to the Afro-American use of "soul" as a generalizing metaphor for the spiritual essence of a historically oppressed people in a pluralistic society. When the dust settles in the wake of the Zapatista movement, I believe that its peculiar unfolding in early 1994—with a strikingly low profile for individual Indian leaders, sensitive reliance on collective judgments, and selective reliance on non-Indian allies—will make sense, Mesoamerican sense.

POSTSCRIPT (SUMMER 1994)

The Zapatista rebellion, which began on 1 January 1994 in the state of Chiapas, deep in the Mesoamerican heartland, speaks directly to the open-ended question that I have posed in the concluding section: What is the future of the idea of the Mesoamerican soul? Although the Maya Indians who constitute the majority of the small, poorly armed rebel army have yet to see any substantive results in terms of specific political and economic reforms that might improve their lot as impoverished peasant farmers, they have already achieved massive international publicity for their cause as an Indian underclass that has long been largely ignored by the Mexican state. Some observers have asserted that they have achieved that which the Mexico City Olympic riots in 1968 and the passage of NAFTA (the North American Free Trade Agreement) did not: that is, to force the democratization of Mexico's entire political process, which has, for sixty years, functioned as a de facto one-party system. While it is not my present purpose to support or refute these claims, I do want to highlight several aspects of the Zapatista movement that relate directly to the subject matter of this essay.

In spite of its revolutionary posture and its newsworthiness—qualities that might suggest easy access for both reporters and news consumers—the rebellion has an enigmatic, acephalous leadership apparatus that has not been easy for the press, the public, or even the politicians to understand. I refer to the relative invisibility of the Indian directorate, their apparent willingness to allow Subcomandante Marcos—a well-educated, sophisticated, light-eyed, and light-skinned non-Indian from Mexico City—to be their chief spokesperson. How does all of this make sense?

The present essay has attempted to interpret the extrasomatic, coessential, nonlocal nexus of causality and destiny in Mesoamerican thought. We have witnessed the studied privacy of discourse and practice involving the coessences and their identity, as Menchú notes in the quotation cited above. Moreover, we have seen that Mesoamerican Indians are reluctant to act publicly in ways that might be perceived by others as overtly self-serving, for fear that this might invite accusations of casting misfortune and sickness on others. As a corollary and counterpoint to this reluctance to engage in instrumental acts that suggest individual volition and exercise of power over others, such assertion of authority is permissible if it is mobilized in ways that are credible and legitimate in the eyes of the community and if authority so exercised can be viewed as beneficial to the community at large. In part, breach of this principle lies behind the intense hostility of the Zapatistas toward Indian elites, who, in collusion with the Mexican state, have overtly flouted the premises of this principle to facilitate their own gain at the expense of their own compatriots.

These traditional and evolving Mesoamerican ideas about self, Other, community, destiny, and political legitimacy, seem plausibly, even probably, to underlie the recent, dramatic events in Chiapas. Time will tell. However, I believe that the content of this essay contributes a foundation for understanding some part of the postcolonial order that is unfolding today.

ACKNOWLEDGMENTS

Parts of this article were presented at a conference entitled "American Identities 500 years after the Columbian Encounter," held at the University of Virginia, October 8-10, 1992. I am grateful to this institution, to Professor A. James Arnold, and to the Virginia Foundation for the Humanities for the opportunity to begin assembling a number of the ideas that are brought together in this essay. This version of the essay appeared in a symposium volume, *Monsters, Tricksters, and Sacred Cows: Stories of American Identities*, edited by A. James Arnold (1995), published by the University Press of Virginia. I am particularly grateful to my colleague John Justeson, who gave me permission to quote from his and Terrence Kaufman's unpublished 1992 paper. He also called my attention to the Houston and Stuart report (1989) listed in References Cited. I also thank my colleague Robert Carmack for calling my attention to the extraordinary passage from Thomas Gage is cited in the text. I also thank Duncan Earle, of Texas A & M University, and Jeff Tewlow, of the University of Texas, for sharing their ideas on the significance of the 1994 Zapatista rebellion, some of which contributed to my own thinking as recorded in the headnote to this essay.

Ten

> ~~~

MAYA ZAPATISTAS MOVE TO
AN OPEN FUTURE

This essay, first published in 1996, has a complex life history that is recorded in the acknowledgments. It is the product of many revisions—almost weekly at one point—that seemed to make it a story without end; which, of course, is what it was and is. This is the way life happens. I conceived of this piece in the spirit of journalism—fast reporting of unexpected current events with responsible background information. Neither politicians, nor the Mexican Army, nor journalists, nor scholars (including myself) had a clue that the events of January 1, 1994, were imminent. Yet I felt compelled to respond. What might I contribute to the interpretation of this unusual tale?

While San Juan Chamula was not then, nor is it today, involved in any public way with support of the Zapatista movement (indeed, the Chamula officials opposed it and publicly prayed to be spared from it),[1] _I was captivated by the magnitude and complexity of the story, for it seemed to embody the profound ambivalence of Maya people being both within and outside of modern Mexico. I was concerned with providing information about the deep cultural history of the region—something which most of the massive media coverage ignored. The story line, as reported by the media, consistently highlighted issues of land, poverty, and political inequality in a colonial backwater, all of which was and is true. However, from the details of its earliest moments to Subcomandante Marcos's eloquent public statements, the Zapatista movement has a postmodern cultural quality that confounds facile reporting, for it is both a rebellion against Mexican neoliberalism and a celebration of the Mexican national idea; an affirmation of ethnic autonomies and a manifesto of Mexican unity under the banner of cultural pluralism; all of this articulated in styles of public demeanor and discourse that are indirect and opaque just as they are highly accessible via communiqués and daily updates on the Zapatista website on the Internet._

As this essay first went to press in late spring 1996, it seemed that this complex Zapatista agenda had been understood and accepted by Mexican authorities, according to the peace accord that they signed with the Zapatistas in February 1996. This led me to conclude the published essay on an optimistic note, which I have deliberately retained here, even though I might have saved face by editing out the upbeat conclusion, for since then, things have fallen apart. The horrific Christmas massacre of December 22, 1997, in San Pedro Chenalhó (located immediately to the north of Chamula) demonstrated that my optimism was premature. Forty-five Tzotzil Mayas, said to be Zapatista supporters—including many women and children—were gunned down and hacked to pieces by a progovernment paramilitary group of fellow Maya Tzotzils. These events *cast some doubt on the wisdom of my earlier attempt (the body of this essay) to tell and interpret a very current and complex story as a "complete narrative" with an upbeat point of closure. Reality, apparently, is darker, more contingent, more open-ended, more ambiguous . . .*

I append to this essay as a postscript an editorial piece on the massacre that I published in my local newspaper (Albany Times Union) in January 1998. This postscript—an opening to another story—will, I hope, speak for itself as a conclusion to this book.

INTRODUCTION

This essay considers several layers of complexity that are manifest and implicit in the Maya Zapatista movement, known to most of the world only since the dramatic events of January 1, 1994, the date on which a Maya peasant army occupied, briefly, four major towns of the state of Chiapas, Mexico. This insurgent group is called the Ejército Zapatista de Liberación Nacional (EZLN, the Zapatisa Army of National Liberation). Through a postmodern mesh of profound social and economic asymmetries, armed confrontation, massive and carefully orchestrated media coverage, World Wide Web sites, e-mail, faxes, wooden guns, and poetically crafted communiqués, together with Subcomandante Marcos's extraordinary charisma as a non-Indian spokesperson and advocate for Indian petitions for social and economic justice, the three thousand poorly armed Maya peasants who constitute the EZLN have precipitated one of the most fascinating moments in twentieth-century Latin American history.

The Zapatista movement has served as a catalyst for the most grave political and economic crisis in Mexico since the 1920s, bringing to its knees the PRI-dominated, one-party political establishment that has ruled the country for much of the twentieth century; all of this amid the heady expectations that NAFTA and its associated neoliberal economic policies would transform Mexico into Latin America's first First-World nation. The last three years have produced nothing less than a referendum on the whole Mexican national idea: its own identity, the role of Indians in the country's past and present, and its place in the world community of nations. Amid all of this arises the mysterious persona of Subcomandante Marcos and also, through him, the metapersona of the Maya Zapatistas whom he represents. He seems to be articulating something fundamental about the whole Mexican national idea and its ever-ambivalent ties to its Indian past and present.

FROM POLITICAL ECONOMY TO CULTURAL AGENCY

Few events in recent Latin American history have so captivated the attention of the international media as the Zapatista rebellion. However, it has been almost universally interpreted as a peasant rebellion focused on agrarian issues and as a violent critique of Mexico's political system, which has systematically marginalized Indians and other underclass groups in the quest for economic growth. These economic and political appraisals are undoubtedly true, as we have seen in relentless media coverage and abundant written commentary, including many of the Zapatistas' own public statements.[2] A frequently voiced corollary in Mexican, European, and North American commentary focuses on the "obscurantist" theme: Interpretation of Zapatista causes in ethnic and cultural terms obscures the "real" issues. For example, a current essay by Michael Powelson, concludes as follows:

> Since the colonial period Chiapas has seen dozens of peasant revolts which were incited principally due to poverty and excessive exploitation. Despite this, from the colonial period to the present day, provincial, national and international elites, academics, and government bureaucrats have found that by focusing on the ethnicity of the rebels fundamental economic debates and problems can be avoided if not ignored altogether. On the other hand, the rebels themselves, whether in Tuxtla in 1693 or San Cristóbal in 1995, have shown little evidence that their movements are ethnically based, and both Ladinos and Indians have played key roles.
>
> The crisis that currently grips Mexico, and the reason for the rebellion in Chiapas, is rooted in that nation's decade-long effort to lift subsidies and tariffs to lower wages in order to increase profitability for both Mexican and transnational corporations. In the face of a major insurrection, the Mexican government is more than willing to engage in endless negotiations and debate concerning indigenous rights or community autonomy, since such discussions do not challenge the current trajectory of Mexico's increasingly market-oriented, and ruthless, economy. (Powelson 1996: 6)

However, while this prevailing opinion may be defensible and accurate with regard to proximate causes of the rebellion, it nevertheless proves to be somewhat myopic when it is examined in the light of the deep cultural history of the region and in cognizance of recent events in Chiapas and in the region as a whole, including both Mexico and Guatemala.

In December 1995, Chiapas and its Indian communities became, once again, foci of national political anxiety and military mobilization. However, this time the issue was not military challenge from the Zapatistas, but rather, cultural and symbolic warfare. The issue was the place name of Aguascalientes, the Central Mexican site of the abortive November 1914 meeting of several revolutionary leaders, including among others, Emiliano Zapata and Pancho Villa, national icons by anybody's reckoning. The intent of this meeting was to chart the future of the Mexican Revolution and of the emerging revolutionary Mexican state. The meeting failed, the leaders went their separate ways, and the bloody civil war persisted for several more years. The Maya Zapatistas resuscitated the name, memory, and intent of Aguascalientes, with more optimistic expectations, in July 1994. The new Aguascalientes forum, a celebrated, "revolutionary" political convention called the First National Democratic Congress, was held in the Lacandon jungle, in Zapatista-controlled territory, in a hastily improvised amphitheatre of posts and canopies. This was a deliberately provocative gesture: The Zapatistas invited candidates of the PRD (Partido Revolucionario Democrático, the principal left-of-center national political party), all of whom opposed the ruling PRI political establishment. They also invited a host of national and international media representatives to witness a political rally that advocated the defeat of the PRI and its so-called neoliberal policies in the ensuing state and national elections. Presumably everyone present, including the PRD representatives and candidates, supported the political agenda of their hosts, the Zapatistas.

The national elections were held on August 22, 1994. The PRI again prevailed, in both national and Chiapas gubernatorial contests, together with many local and regional allegations of electoral fraud that have not been resolved to this day.

The newly elected Mexican President, Ernesto Zedillo, inherited a catastrophic economic crisis that would require a bailout from the International Monetary Fund and the United States. At the behest of the United States and its banking interests, and as a condition for a multibillion-dollar bridge loan to cover its debt service, Mexico was obliged in the spring of 1995 to prove that the Zapatista threat to national stability was "under control." This brought a Mexican Army thrust into the Zapatista-controlled areas of the Mexican Southeast on February 9, 1995. Included in their operations were the total destruction and occupation of the site of the 1994 Aguascalientes convention. Crudely constructed Mexican army barracks now occupy the site, and it is sealed off with barbed wire fences from any intrusion by unauthorized personnel.

Aguascalientes, however, did not go away. The name, the place, the memory of the events held there in 1994, together with the Mexican Army's wanton destruction of the site, contributed to the formation of an even more potent, multilayered political symbol. Throughout 1995, the Zapatistas were engaged in cloning the Lacandon site in four new locations in Chiapas, all in regions either controlled by Zapatistas or with majority Zapatista support. The goal was to have them completed by January 1996 to commemorate the second anniversary of the 1994 insurrection.

The sites are Oventik (near San Andrés Larráinzar, in the Highlands), La Realidad, La Garrucha, and Morelia (the latter three located in the Lowlands). All of these ambitious public pavilions—mounted on a massive scale, complete with raised platform mounds crowned by posts covered with multicolored, plastic-laminated sheets—are called "New Aguascalientes." Deliberately constructed according to preindustrial Indian technology and reminiscent in form to the plazas of the ancient Maya ceremonial centers, these New Aguascalientes centers are potent political statements. During construction, leaders permitted no modern tools, no machines, no motorized vehicles, and no petroleum products supplied by PEMEX (Petróleos Mexicanos, the Mexican government monopoly that controls production, distribution, and sale of petroleum products). In this way they blocked any opportunity for quick PRI purchases of influence with fleets of Mercedes trucks and Japanese backhoes, a co-optation strategy for which the Government is well known. The four pavilions are located outside existing municipal centers in an apparent effort to separate them symbolically from the traditional colonial and modern seats of *cacique* rule. Zapatistas say that these New Aguascalientes Cultural Centers are "social" and "cultural" centers that will provide a forum in which they can meet the media and the public for the purpose of promoting their cultural policies (*Proceso* 1996). Whatever the Zapatistas' expressed intent, the Mexican government regarded these nonmilitary, cultural installations with alarm and in December 1995 sent the army to seal off all access to them via public roads. I do not know the details of the inauguration of the pavilions in January 1996, for neither national nor international media representatives were allowed access. We do know that Mexican Army military maneuvers in Oventik in late December 1995 resulted in bitter and hostile encounters between local Indian pro-Zapatista supporters and a formidable column of Mexican Army tanks and armed vehicles (Martínez 1995).

What matters in this discussion is relatively simple: The Zapatistas regard these New Aguascalientes centers as their permanent public forum, with other additional such centers planned for other locales in Mexico. The Mexican government regards them as a threat worthy of military harassment and obstruction of public access.

The plot has now become even more complex. The New Aguascalientes centers were indeed inaugurated in January 1996. However, coinciding with their inauguration, the Zapatistas sponsored another event, the Foro Nacional Indígena (National Indigenous Forum), in San Cristóbal de las Casas (January 3–8, 1996). The army and the government could not easily block access, for the town is the commercial center of the Chiapas highlands and also an important tourist destination. All Indian communities in Mexico, foreign and national observers, and Mexican Government representatives, were invited to this event. It is clear from the content of the agenda—ranging from cultural autonomy, to feminist issues, to equal access to the media, to bilingual/bicultural education, to agrarian reform, to democratic political reform at *municipio* level—that this was both a sophisticated and well-staged event that could not be ignored by Mexican government representatives.

Among the more moving documents circulated at the January Indigenous Forum was the "Preamble" to the "Resolutions of Roundtable One," on the subject of cultural autonomy. Brief excerpts follow here:

Autonomy

We are the people who were the original inhabitants of Mexico. We have exercised, and will continue to exercise, the right to determine who we are according to our own premises. We are bearers of our own culture and of our own agenda. . . .

In a profound sense, we consider ourselves to be Mexicans. This is so even though the founders of the Mexican state and all governments that have followed in their footsteps have ignored our existence. This is so even though many Mexican men and women regard us with condescension and ignorance, virtually denying our existence. Because of this, as we affirm once again on this occasion our existence as a people. We wish to make it known that our current struggle for acknowledgment of our separate identity does not seek to launch a fight with our fellow Mexicans, nor much less, to secede from a country that we consider as much our own as we do our separate identity as Indians. Through our act of demanding recognition of our Indian identity, we wish to contribute to the formation of a more fundamental unity of all Mexican men and women, a unity that recognizes the true diversity of the ethnic communities that make up modern Mexico. This is a fundamental condition for harmony among all Mexican men and women. Our quest for recovery and recognition of our own identity does not, in any way, constitute a challenge to national sovereignty.

We are not asking anybody to grant us autonomy. We have always had it and we have it today. No one can "give" us the capacity to be ourselves, to think and act in ways that are governed by our own way of looking at the world. However, we have not been free, either during the Spanish colonial regime or under the post-Independence Mexican state, to exercise freely our separate identity as a people. Throughout our long struggle of resistance, we have always been obliged to express our identity against a repressive backdrop of Mexican state representatives and Mexican state institutions.

Basta! We have had enough of this. We will no longer continue to accept being the objects of discrimination, being excluded from full participation in a homeland that belongs as much to us as to other Mexican men and women, a homeland that has been built with our hands, our labor, and our effort. We wish to enjoy the full freedom to continue being who we are. We wish to create conditions that will make this possible. We believe that Mexico itself will be truly free only when all of us are free. (Foro Nacional Indígena 1996; my translation)

A little more than a month after this meeting, the government made an announcement in San Andrés Larraínzar, a Tzotzil Maya town located only a few kilometers away from Oventik, one of the sites of the New Aguascalientes Centers. The government stated its intention to sign, in mid-February 1996, an agreement that would radically expand the rights of all Indians in Mexico. This cleared the way for a peace accord with the Zapatistas. The *New York Times* report of February 15, 1996, states:

The accord lays the foundation for "a new relation between the state and the indigenous peoples" throughout Mexico. Most of it will have to be carried out in practice by changes adopted in the state and national legislatures, including several constitutional reforms. The document recognizes for the first time the "autonomy" of Mexico's Indians, which translates into their right to adopt their own forms of government in their communities or towns according to their customs. It recognizes their right to "multicultural" education, including teaching in their own languages, and to "adequate" representation in local and national congresses. (Preston 1996: A12)

It can be defensibly argued that this breakthrough, which many of us never expected to see in our lifetimes, came in large part through the Zapatista-sponsored forum in San Cristóbal, even as the Zapatistas' own Aguascalientes cultural centers, their most ambitious expression of their nascent autonomy, were being systematically encircled and isolated from public access by the Mexican Army.

As one tries to assimilate and comprehend this melodrama of controversial cultural pavilions (the New Aguascalientes) and acceptable cultural pavilions (roundtables at the Indigenous Forum in San Cristóbal), it can hardly by argued that culture and ethnicity are moot issues in what the Zapatistas are trying to communicate to Mexico and to the world. Culture and ethnicity matter a great deal; they were the first items on the table, the subject of Roundtable One at the Forum.

While the prospect of this acknowledgment of "cultural autonomy" may be cause for celebration, it raises the question of just what constitutes the shared culture and identity of Mexico's many and diverse Indian communities. In the sections that follow, I will identify three themes in the events of the past two years that may guide us in thinking about both the Maya past and future. What constitutes the core of how Maya people have thought and acted in history over the past two thousand years? And, from these deep roots, even through them, how is change—such as that sought by the Zapatistas—being effected in the Maya universe today? And, finally, why is the Zapatista agenda so persuasive in all of Indian Mexico?

BREATH ON THE MIRROR: THE OPAQUENESS OF EVENTS

In an extraordinary recent book, *Breath on the Mirror* (1993), Dennis Tedlock discusses a central idea, perhaps *the* central idea, in Maya epistemology. It concerns the opaque nature of human access to reality. As recorded in the Popol Vuh, the founding epic of the Quiché people, both the downfall of our protohuman ancestors and the ascent of modern human beings involved the loss of vision. The gods were displeased with the fact that their newly created beings could see everything just as the gods could; their vision penetrated all parts of the cosmos, through the mountains and heavens. The gods were angered that humans were their equals; their knowledge reached too far (Tedlock 1993: 1-11). The Popol Vuh relates this critical moment in human history as follows:

> And when they changed the nature of their works, their designs, it was enough that their eyes be marred by the Heart of Sky. They were blinded as the face of a mirror is breathed upon. Their eyes were weakened. Now it was only when they looked nearby that things were clear.
>   And such was the loss of the means of understanding, with the means of knowing everything, by the four humans. The root was implanted. (Tedlock, trans. 1985: 166-67)

Such, then, is the human condition, that in the great scheme of things, people are never to have easy access to the true scheme of things. Virtually all human perception and related experiences rely on approximation of reality. The opaqueness of reality in the Maya world is not, as in Plato's parable of the shadows on the cave wall, merely a degraded or imperfect representation of an ideal form. Perceived reality in Maya thought derives from generative forces that are *not* fixed ideal forms; these causal forces are multiple, complex, constantly in flux, usually invisible, and interactive among themselves. Furthermore, these forces reside, for the most part, outside the body and individual consciousness.

The corollaries that flow from this basic principle in the ancient and modern Maya world are numerous. In the first place, nothing except that which is nearby is ever what it seems to be according to our sense perception. There is always something beyond and outside of the apparent reality that affects it. Such unseeable generative forces have expressed themselves in the everyday life of the Maya for two thousand years. In the ancient Maya world, the greatest of these outside forces was the tyranny of time. The divine mandate of solar, lunar, and Venus, and 260-day calendar cycles intimately affected the unfolding of each day for each individual and for the community in the ancient Maya world. This so-called chronovision was not a deification of time, but an acknowledgment that all things, human and natural, were programmed with shifting valences of cause and effect dictated by divine cycles located outside the body. Variants of these ancient beliefs persist today in the form of sacred solar cycles, individual coessences and ancestor cults; they figure centrally in the complexity of the extrasomatic configuration of causality. Humans have no choice but to adjust their behavior accordingly. There emerges here an almost unlimited opening for the interpretive skills and political control of shamans and secular leaders who claim to have a less opaque vision than ordinary people. It is probable, in my view, that such clairvoyant skills are attributed to, if not claimed by, the clandestine Indian leadership of EZLN.

What we have seen in the Lacandon jungle these past two years in Chiapas appears opaque to our own eyes, for it has undoubtedly been constructed and understood by the Maya as an effort to act in history in such a way that human uncertainty, the givenness of outside causal forces, and the effort to engage in instrumental behavior to effect change in a hostile environment, mesh together in a plausible, credible, and cautious pattern of counterbalances. The movement cannot have been conceived by a few and delivered as a plan of action to change history and destiny without being cast as something that was somehow destined to happen in the first place, yet for which no single Indian leader wished to assume responsibility as the *principal* leader, for all ethnic groups involved came from different communities of origin in which various readings of legitimate authority were operative. It would therefore have been inappropriate for any one individual to presume to conceive and direct an enterprise of such complexity and uncertainty. Perhaps this is the central reason why a relatively invisible pan-Maya directorate of men and women provides diffused Indian leadership, while conferring upon a non-Indian, Subcomandante Marcos, the role of spokesperson. This is also, undoubtedly, why the movement is tied emblematically to Emiliano Zapata and to the epic agenda of the Mexican Revolution itself. These icons link their own political aspirations with the relatively uncontested charter myth of modern Mexico. Given the Zapatistas' own Maya heritage of understanding history as a programmed, divinely ordained process, it is not unreasonable for them to attach their wagon to a well-known and powerful mythical star. The Myth of the Mexican Revolution is surely such a star.

The quasi-mystical link of their own agenda and destiny with that of Mexican "democracy" and other principles of the Mexican national idea is laid out eloquently in a communiqué dated February 26, 1994, from the Clandestine Indigenous Revolutionary Committee High Command of the Zapatista National Liberation Army. The following excerpt constitutes the first paragraphs of this document. We of course do not know from whose pen these words come; however, the poetic and opaque language bears the clear mark of contemporary Maya oratorical style, perhaps mingled with the romantic imagery of Spanish-speaking collaborators.

> When the EZLN was only a shadow, creeping through the mist and darkness of the jungle, when the words "justice," "liberty," and "democracy" were only that: words; barely a dream that the elders of our communities, true guardians of the words of our dead ancestors, had given us in the moment when day gives way to night, when hatred and fear began to grow in our hearts, when there was nothing but desperation; when the times repeated themselves, with no way out, with no door, no tomorrow, when all was injustice, as it was, the true men spoke, the faceless ones, the ones who go by night, the ones who are in the jungle, and they said:

"It is the purpose and will of good men and women to seek and find the best way to govern and be governed, what is good for the many is good for all. But let not the voices of the few be silenced, but let them remain in their place, waiting until the thoughts and hearts become one in what is the will of the many and opinion from within and no outside force can break them nor divert their steps to other paths.

"Our path was always that the will of the many be in the hearts of the men and women who command. The will of the majority was the path on which he who commands should walk. If he separates his step from the path of the will of the people, the heart who commands should be changed for another who obeys. Thus was born our strength in the jungle, he who leads obeys if he is true, and he who follows leads through the common heart of true men and women. Another word came from afar so that this government was named and this work gave the name 'democracy' to our way that was from before words traveled." [3]

THE EXTRASOMATIC LOCATION OF SELF AND DESTINY

Where does the individual stand in the opaqueness of the Maya universe that has just been described? The best short answer is "not alone," as the Zapatista communiqué, cited above, reiterates unequivocally. Since at least the time of Christ, the Maya world has evolved a variant of the broader Mesoamerican idea of the coessence, which, briefly stated, is a fundamental principle of personhood or self which asserts that each individual and his or her destiny are linked to one or a set of cospirits or coessences that reside outside the body. (See chapter 9.) These coessences are typically identified with animals in the Maya area but may also take the form of other spirit companions. They are often revealed to people in dreams and are therefore known in some parts of the Maya regions by terms related to the proto-Maya *way* (meaning "sleep" or "dream"). These spirits are given at birth and share with each individual the trajectory of his or her life, from birth to death. Since these forces lie outside the body, they are not easy to manipulate. One must therefore live within the general parameters of one's given destiny. Coessences typically have several parts, all of which are fragile and may become lost, frightened, or injured, singly or in various combinations. These afflictions of the soul may cause sickness or misfortune in the persona of the corresponding individual, whereupon the afflicted person engages other supernatural forces (often the souls of shamans and witches who are available for hire) to intervene to restore equilibrium to his or her charted destiny. Thus, these beliefs lie at the core of many traditional curing, divination, witchcraft, and sorcery practices that are found throughout the Maya region.

Epigraphers have recently made enormous strides in documenting this concept as it was expressed in the inscriptions and iconography of the late pre-Classic and Classic periods in the Maya and contiguous areas. Justeson and Kaufman have recently deciphered an epi-Olmec text that appears on the Tuxtla Statuette (state of Tabasco), dating to A. D. 162. The hieroglyphic text's discussion of the peculiar, masked figure specifically states that "the animal soul is powerful" (Justeson and Kaufman 1993: 1703). (See Figure 23, chapter 9.)

In the great florescence of the Maya Classic culture, the hieroglyphic inscriptions routinely used a glyph that reads *way* to signify the link between humans and coessences, both animal and other (Houston and Stuart 1989: 13). The sign representing this concept (Figure 25) is a dualistic image whose left side manifests the sign *a:ja:w*, for a human lord, and whose right side manifests the pelt of a jaguar, the quintessential companion of political leaders. (See chapter 5 on the use of the jaguar-skin belt in the "Dance of the Warriors" in the Festival of Games.) The imagery by which the ancient Maya represented the concept is itself the unification of the imagery of the coessences that comprise the *way*. The concept of the *way* appears to lie not only at the very center of Maya thinking about self, society, and destiny but also at the center of Maya theories of statecraft and political legitimacy via shamanic power. See, for example, the recent *Maya Cosmos: Three Thousand Years on the Shaman's Path* (1993), by David Freidel, Linda Schele, and Joy Parker. In this work, as the title suggests, the concept we are discussing is shown to have an impressive life history spanning almost three millennia.

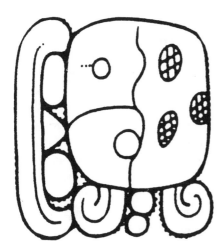

Figure 25. The Way Glyph
Detailed Drawing by Ian Graham of the *way* glyph as it appears in a text in the upper right corner on Lintel 15, Structure 21, at Yaxchilán. From Graham and Von Euw (1997: 39)

While it is true that the political and shamanic practice of these ideas occupied an important place in the public rituals of the ancient Maya, it is also true that the colonial and modern governments of Mexico and Guatemala, and the missionaries who have operated under their patronage, drove these practices and beliefs underground into the privacy of Indian homes and scattered outdoor shrines. It is primarily in this nonpublic location that they persist in hundreds of Maya Indian communities today. And yet they remain vitally important as an identity marker. In her recent autobiographical commentary, *I, Rigoberta Menchú*, the 1992 Nobel Peace Prize laureate of Guatemala, testifies to the studied privacy of these beliefs and practices among the Maya people of her country [1984: 18-2]. (See citation in chapter 9.)

Indeed, virtually all modern ethnographies of the Maya region agree not only on the importance of some form of these ideas to the maintenance of individual and community integration but also on the studied privacy that is appropriate for any discussion pertaining to these ideas.

Thousands of Maya Zapatistas undoubtedly bear such cognitive baggage in their languages, minds, hearts, and souls. These ideas cannot be irrelevant to an understanding of recent events. This raises the interesting question of why members of Zapatista guerrilla army are so often masked. Obviously, there is more than security and guerrilla theater going on here, for the masks are often worn in settings that do not involve interaction with outsiders. This will be discussed further below.

THE COMMUNITY AND THE OTHER

A third enigmatic theme that underwrites the Zapatista movement is expressed in elegantly constructed communiqués that seem to place their own goals within the framework of Mexico's own stated goals for itself. Zapatistas are, on the surface, simply demanding to be included in the Mexican national idea that states that Mexico embraces all of its people. This has been a centerpiece of Mexican revolutionary rhetoric for at least sixty years. How could a Maya indigenous insurrection movement be so charitably inclined toward the ideology and symbols of its stated adversaries? Indeed, the maximal hero of the Mexican Revolution, Emiliano Zapata, who is also the paladin of the Maya rebels, was, himself, a mestizo, not an Indian. Who are Subcomandante Marcos and the martyred Coronela Janina if not incarnations of the enemy? Where are the Maya gods, heroes, and leaders in this Maya insurrection?

I have attempted to comprehend a very similar pattern among the contemporary Tzotzils. The non-Indian Other appears to be a necessary precondition for collective identity within the Chamula pattern of historical memory and being in the present. (See chapters 1, 4, 5, and 9.)

A close examination of the Popol Vuh reveals that the ancient Quiché themselves linked their own political legitimacy to a powerful eastern city state known in legend as Tolán or Tulán, which, in terms of the ethnic identity of its inhabitants, was unlike the Quiché kingdom itself. In fact, it is represented as an imperial polity to which their own ancestors once paid tribute. There are at least a dozen surviving place-names in Mesoamerica that bear names related to Tulán or Tolán, and most of them lie outside the Maya area. The most famous of these is Tula Hidalgo, an early post-Classic site in the Central Valley of Mexico. This was the seat of the Toltec kingdom (non-Maya-speaking) and home of the legendary god-king Topilzin Quetzalcóatl, who was associated with arts, learning, peace, and prosperity. According to legends current at the time of contact and continuing into our time, he is said to have fled into the eastern sea A.D. 987 at the time of his defeat and the fall of Tula at the hand of the god of destruction and war. From the tenth century onward, Topilzin Quetzalcóatl was remembered in legend as a messiah who would one day return from the eastern sea to bring a new period of peace and prosperity to the entire region. In a recent, poignant testimony from one of the last surviving veterans of the Mexican Revolution (Lloyd 1994), an ancient man from a village in Morelos said that Zapata had not died in 1919, but had, like Quetzalcóatl, gone off to the East (to Arabia) and would return one day to help his people. Such commentary is reportedly heard these days in Chiapas in relation to the unusual powers of the fair-skinned Subcomandante Marcos.

It is highly likely that the Quiché narrators of the Popol Vuh were aware of this Central Mexican tradition and found it plausible to tie their own political aspirations and legitimacy to this foreign god-king and to the power of a distant polity that was not Maya at all. The plumed serpent, presumed to be Topilzin Quetzalcóatl's coessence, the source of his legendary power, is in fact often mentioned in the Popol Vuh.

My point is simple. Mayas have always constructed ethnicity, cosmology, historical reckoning, and political legitimacy by drawing freely from symbolic and ideological forms of other ethnic and political entities—particularly those perceived to be stronger than themselves—in order to situate and center themselves in the present. Therefore, what I have identified above as the apparently anomalous and peculiar link of the Zapatistas to foreign alliances and symbolic affiliations—including Marcos, white foreign martyrs, the paladin of Zapata and the Mexican revolutionary ideology that he embodies—is not at all strange to the Maya imagination. In fact, such alliances appear to have been a centrally important strategy for Maya cultural affirmation and political legitimacy since well before the contact period.

ZAPATA AND MARCOS IN THE WORLD OF THE SUN

I have sketched above three fundamentally Maya ideas about the nature of reality and of the place of individuals and groups within the cosmos. Briefly summarized, these are:

1. Reality is opaque; what can be experienced by human perception is seldom the whole picture of what is actually going on. Hence, trusted interpreters and leaders are indispensable.

2. The destiny of the individual self is always linked to extrasomatic forces that are beyond one's direct control. Therefore, the exercise of free will and acting only in one's own self-interest are probably doomed to failure.

3. Expressions of Maya collective identity, such as community membership and ethnic affirmation, depend heavily on concrete and symbolic acknowledgment, even inclusion of, other identities, in order to situate themselves in an ever-evolving present. The idea of a pure lineage of Maya identity is, I believe, foreign to the way Maya people have thought and acted in history.

What do all of these principles share? Quite simply, they encourage actors to account for and act sensibly in relation to their own moral community and "selves" by moving beyond themselves. Neither self, nor society, nor reality itself can be understood by focusing only on what is individual, local, tangible, and immediately accessible to the senses.

In a rather surreal manner, the several parts of this traditional template of Mesoamerican ideas about self and destiny have come together in the odd configuration of the Zapatistas' self-presentation to the world; with sublime confidence guided by forces beyond themselves, studied anonymity, acephalous organizational structure, and forthright alliance with foreign icons and non-Indian advisers and comrades-at-arms. Why should a blond, European, cosmopolitan Subcomandante Marcos preside with such frequency as the spokesperson for this extraordinary movement on behalf of Indian leaders, male and female, representing at least five of the major linguistic and ethnic groups in the state? Why is there no visible "Indian leader"? Subcomandante Marcos, I believe, is utterly plausible as a spokesperson for an Indian cause precisely because he is outside of, extrasomatic to, the Indian community. He is, after all a fair-skinned criollo who, by his own testimony, bailed out of the gilded upper-middle-class culture of Mexico City. He was identified by the Mexican government in March 1995 as a real person, Sebastián Guillén Vicente, who fit the social and demographic profile he himself had previously confessed.

Furthermore, one of the first and most widely publicized martyrs of the first days of the Zapatista revolt was Janine Pauline Archembault Biazot, a white ex-nun known as "La Coronela" (the Colonel). She was of French birth and Canadian residency and is said to have died heroically as she led the Indian troops in the siege of the town of Las Margaritas on January 1, 1994 (Mendivil 1994: 10).

Finally, on April 30, 1994, a Tojolabal Indian woman, a Zapatista named Dominga Hernández, found herself bathed in miraculous spectral light (*rayos lucentes*), whereupon she found an image of a *Niño* (a replica of a "white" Baby Jesus) propped up against an oak tree. The Child of Lomantán spoke and declared his solidarity with the poor, whereupon Dominga built him a modest shrine in her patio, where visitors and visionaries come now come to revere the Child as a patron of the Zapatista cause. The Bishop of San Cristóbal, Samuel Ruiz, has sent his priests to look for fresh signs of this miracle (Ross 1995: 7). The vitality of this new cult is currently such that both Zapatistas and pro-government Indian communities are laying claim to the Child's miraculous powers (Furbee 1996).

This "other world" of personal and collective destiny that is symbolized by Marcos, the Child of Lomantán, the martyred Colonel Janina, and perhaps also by the emblematic memory of Zapata himself—all of them white or mestizo—is but one of the several non-Indian places from which coessential power and causation in the Maya universe emanate. The individual and the community are not alone.

The masked, incognito mode of self-representation of the parties in these events appears to be linked to the Maya construction of self and society. The masking cannot be dismissed as guerrilla theater, nor merely understood as a military security measure. It is, rather, a logical strategy of caution and modesty in the arena of instrumentality (read "revolutionary change") whose goals are not yet achieved and whose benefits to the larger Indian community are not yet manifest. Thus, individual identities had best be masked, thus ritually "homogenized," lest the leaders be accused of self-aggrandizement and self-gain. If they were so perceived by others—without solid evidence for the overriding legitimacy of their exercise of power—they could easily become potential targets for malevolent supernatural action from within the community, as in the casting of sickness. They could also become specific targets for murder at the hands of Indian pro-government paramilitary organizations. (See postscript below). It is perhaps also for these reasons that the members of the Indian directorate of the Zapatista Movement have opted for a secret lateral organization of coequals rather than a public hierarchical chain of authority.[4]

If the unusual unfolding of the Zapatista movement can be partially understood within the matrix of ancient Mesoamerican ideas about self and society, I think these events have another quality that represents something relatively new, if not utterly revolutionary, in the modern era. I refer to the pan-Indian composition of the leadership and constituency of the Zapatistas.

Only on rare occasions in colonial and modern Chiapas history—notably, the Tzeltal Rebellion of 1712 and the War of Santa Rosa in 1867-70—have Indian political and religious movements in Chiapas crossed ethnic and linguistic lines in terms of their constituencies and military mobilization. When they have done so in such a manner as to become active and visible, these movements have been promptly crushed by the state. Indeed, the Spanish Crown created administrative policies, settlement patterns, and local civil and religious organizations that would, in effect, segregate Indians from Spanish and mestizo communities and also from one another. In functioning to encourage local identities, languages, customs, and loyalties, these policies served the Crown's purpose by discouraging pan-Indian opposition to state policy. In many respects, this configuration of ethnically and demographically isolated Indian townships that are indirectly controlled by the state through the *cacique* system has continued largely intact well into the late twentieth century. It is only now in the throes of disintegration. (See postscript below.) The New Aguascalientes centers express this in highly dramatic fashion in that they are totally removed physically from the old Indian municipal centers.

The quest for pan-Indian cultural affirmation has also been underwritten by a fundamental shift in the distribution of Indian populations in Chiapas. The demographic portrait of the lowland region that spawned the Zapatista movement matters a great deal in making sense of the pan-Indian solidarity that seems to be emerging in our time. The Zapatista homeland, in the Lacandon jungle lowlands of Chiapas, is actually a pioneer settlement area. Within the last few decades, tens of thousands of displaced individuals have emigrated there as refugees from poverty and political and religious persecution in their Indian townships of origin. The region is also home to thousands of Guatemalan Maya refugees who fled there to escape political violence in their own country. It therefore has no established social order that is dominated by any one Indian ethnic or linguistic group. This is also a region of great religious diversity, composed of thousands of newly converted Protestants and recently evangelized "progressive" Catholics who were, over the last two decades, the subjects of intense proselytizing by lay catechists and priests associated with liberation theology. No doubt there are also "traditional Mayas" who do not feel attracted to either Protestant or liberal Catholic teachings.

It is therefore not surprising that the composition of EZLN, although generally Maya, is actually fairly diverse in terms of ethnic, linguistic, and religious backgrounds that are represented. Tzotzil, Tzeltal, Zoque, Chol, and Tojolabal speakers, as well as Mexican mestizos and ethnically "white" Mexicans, are all united in pursuit of common political and social goals. What is Maya about the Zapatista movement must therefore be sought not in particular variants of Maya or other Indian cultural identity but rather in general principles of values and conduct that all might share, be they Tzotzils, Chols, or Zoques. This common ground is what I have tried to identify here.

While the immediate goals of the Maya Zapatistas appear to outside observers to be primarily of an economic and political nature, I believe that the pan-Indian nature of this enterprise has a powerful component of postcolonial ethnic affirmation that goes well beyond political action. Any serious observer of modern Guatemala, Chiapas, or Yucatán will be aware that well-organized pan-Maya cooperation now extends into many arenas of activity. Pan-Indian groups range from intellectual, educational, and religious organizations to craft guilds—for example, textile and ceramic cooperatives—catering to the tourist and export trade. There are also numerous writers' and artists' cooperatives whose members are working to create a corpus of literature in Maya languages, as well as graphic and performing arts that express the traditional and contemporary Maya themes. Guatemala is moving toward the creation of a parallel Indian education system, designed by the Mayas themselves (Centro de Estudios de la Cultura Maya), that recognizes—perhaps grudgingly on the part of the government—that literacy in Indian languages is in the national interest. Certainly, Mexico cannot be far behind. We have seen evidence of commitment to this end in the agreements on cultural autonomy of February 1996 in San Andrés Larraínzar.

The governments of Mexico and Guatemala now realize that the pan-Indian voice in these de facto multicultural nations is here to stay. Governments can no longer crush this voice with military action or buy it off with conciliatory "things" alone. They must enter into dialogue with it and add the contemporary Indian voice to the national idea. There is evidence, therefore, that Mesoamerica's "collective Indian soul" has emerged in the late twentieth century as an active and public voice in the modern nations of the region. And, most important, the Indian voice is commanding a broadly based respect in the national communities of both Mexico and Guatemala that has not been known for 450 years. The Zapatista movement is part of this quest for cultural acknowledgment and social and economic justice. We are privileged to witness, understand, and contribute to this optimistic turn in the modern history of Mesoamerica.

POSTSCRIPT (JANUARY 1998)

Timely and honest investigation of the tragic Christmas week 1997 massacre in San Pedro Chenalhó, Chiapas—in which forty-five Tzotzil Maya Indians, most of them women and children, were gunned down and hacked to pieces by Tzotzil Maya neighbors said to be allied with pro-government factions—may provide Mexican President Ernesto Zedillo an opportunity to avert full-scale civil war in Chiapas.

While the media have dutifully reported the tragedy and subsequent investigations and arrests, the magnitude of this story and its implications for the United States's Latin American policy have been missed. The massacre is symptomatic of a desperate and dying system of colonial political control whose end must be expedited if there is to be lasting peace in the area.

All of Chiapas has been convulsed and polarized by the events of January 1, 1994, when the rebel Zapatista Army of National Liberation, comprised largely of Maya Indians, occupied four towns and cities on the very day the North American Free Trade Agreement (NAFTA) went into effect.

Although dispersed by the Mexican army, the Zapatistas retain a powerful and growing body of supporters in Chiapas and throughout Mexico. Among these supporters were the victims of the massacre.

San Pedro Chenalhó, like dozens of other Chiapas townships, has a majority population of Maya linguistic and cultural descent. This township and its dependent hamlet, Acteal, site of the massacre, are remnants of a caste (*casta*) system created by Spain early in the colonial period to segregate Indians from mestizo and white communities into two "republics" or "kingdoms." Indians, having the duties of *casta*, had to be administered by the Spanish "missionary state" in ways that would effectively control them, convert them, and place them at the service of the Crown for purposes of tribute payment and forced labor.

The key controllers were local indigenous elites, known as *caciques*, who were placed by colonial authorities in positions of political and religious leadership in their own communities. They received numerous privileges—such as exemption from tribute payment and labor service, the right to settle local civil disputes according to local custom, and the right to preside over desirable tracts of communal land within their communities—in exchange for delivering political stability, loyalty, tribute payment, labor service, and day-to-day maintenance of religious offices to the missionary state.

Despite independence from Spain, nineteenth-century liberal reform legislation, and the epic Mexican Revolution (1910-17), *cacique* rule remains in many of Chiapas's predominantly Indian municipalities, including San Pedro Chenalhó. The mayor there, Jacinto Arias Cruz, local boss of the PRI (Institutional Revolutionary Party), has been arrested as the ringleader of the massacre. He is a classic *cacique*.

Throughout postrevolutionary Mexico, *caciques* have lived extremely well, while the majority of their compatriots have lived in abject poverty. *Caciques* have been the conduit for government largesse—such as hard-surfaced roads, clinics, schools and electrification, potable water, and agricultural extension projects. They have been in a position to take credit for all improvements in local infrastructure and social services from which they also, typically, reap a handsome profit. Logically enough, they use their power to orchestrate sometimes unanimous "votes" in favor of local and regional PRI candidates. In turn, the government has dutifully supported their local political interests and looked the other way when Indian bosses used draconian and violent means to stay in power.

This colonial political system is now under siege throughout Chiapas. Yet it will not die peacefully. Why? Because NAFTA and its related Mexican government policies (dubbed generally as "neoliberalism" by the Zapatistas) have removed most of the safety net of economic survival and hope for Chiapas's rural poor, just as these same policies stand to benefit the *caciques* with yet another bonanza of wealth and privilege. These policies include deregulation of the commodity market (which eliminates predictable prices for corn, the principal food staple; and coffee, a once-dependable source of seasonal labor and income for Indians); abandonment of agrarian reform, casting into limbo hundreds of pending petitions for new government-sponsored communal (*ejido*) land distribution; and the encouragement to privatize everything from current Indian *ejido* land holdings to financial institutions.

These policies were formally implemented by Mexico, in part, as U.S.–imposed conditions for getting NAFTA legislation approved by the U.S. Congress in 1993. The goal: a level playing field for making U. S. goods and services competitive in the Mexican market. The result: social chaos in rural Mexico.

The deteriorating social and economic conditions related to these policies in rural Chiapas have produced a number of responses and social transformations in the last few decades—all of which pose a threat to the centuries-old pattern of symbiotic collusion among Indian *caciques*, local white elites and the Mexican state.

These changes include large-scale conversion to Protestantism, massive population displacement, increasing social activism by the Roman Catholic Church, and, of course, the increasing appeal of the radical democratic reforms supported by the Maya Zapatista movement. Indian involvement in these expressions of discontent varies. In the northern fringe of the Tzotzil Maya-speaking area of Chiapas—where the massacre occurred—all of these dissenting elements are active and at variance with one another, as well as with the *cacique* establishment and their allies.

Therefore, the testimony of witnesses to the massacre, who say the victims were publicly nonaligned, but privately sympathetic to the Zapatistas, rings true. It also rings tragically true that Chiapas state officials failed to intervene when they were advised an attack was imminent. Finally, it is well known that the Mexican Army has been omnipresent in the area as a "precautionary measure" for the past few years. Thus it is clear that the means to suppress paramilitary, pro-government goon squads existed, but were not mobilized. As the crisis in Chiapas deepens, President Zedillo has urgent reason to revitalize and implement terms of the peace accord signed with the Zapatistas in 1996 and then abandoned. (It commits the federal government to constitutional changes guaranteeing democratic local political processes and various form of local autonomy.) Otherwise, the forty-plus Chiapas townships said to support democratically elected, clandestine local organizations sympathetic to the Zapatistas will perhaps find that they have nothing to lose by coming out of the closet to seize power from the PRI-allied local hierarchies.

This transition in power is not likely to be peaceful.

ACKNOWLEDGMENTS

This essay synthesizes several versions of a talk that I gave between February 1994 and March 1996, under the same or similar title, at conferences or as an invited lecture at UCLA, the Center for Latin American Research and Documentation (Amsterdam), the American Anthropological Association (Atlanta 1994), Colgate University, Carleton College, and the University of Texas. The essay has gone through many revisions, reflecting the fast-changing scenario and new documents that I attempt to interpret. I am grateful to my graduate students, Catherine Stanford, Nancy Forand, C. Matthew Samson and Bradley Tatar, of the University at Albany, and to Joshua M. Paulson, of Carleton College, for bringing new material to my attention. I also thank my colleagues, Robert M. Carmack, Duncan M. Earle, Jerome Levi, and Linda Schele, for their helpful critical comments and insights on various versions of this essay.

PERMISSIONS
ACKNOWLEDGMENTS

Chapter 1 was originally published under the same title, as is: 1993. *The Other in Chamula Tzotzil Cosmology and History: Reflections of a Kansan in Chiapas. Cultural Anthropology* 8 (4): 443–75. (This journal is published by the American Anthroplogical Association.)

A Spanish version, somewhat different from the English version, was published as: 1993. Ser indio en una matriz euroafricana: reflexiones personales sobre la identidad tzotzil chamula. In *De palabra y obra en el nuevo mundo*, vol. 3. *La formación del otro*, edited by Gary H. Gossen, J. J. Klor de Alva, M. Gutiérrez Estévez, and Miguel León-Portilla. Madrid: Siglo XXI de España, pp. 37–74.

Chapter 3 was originally published, virtually as is: 1993. On the Human Condition and the Moral Order: A Testimony from the Chamula Tzotzil of Chiapas, Mexico. In *South and Native American Native Spirituality: From the Cult of the Feathered Serpent to the Theology of Liberation*, edited by Gary H. Gossen and Miguel León-Portilla. *World Spirituality: An Encyclopedic History of the Religious Quest*, vol. 4. New York: Crossroad Press, pp. 414–35.

Chapter 5 was originally published, in part, under the same title in my edited volume (1986) and in a very different Spanish version (1992), also my coedited volume. The main corpus of the text for the present book has been considerably edited to vary radically from either published version. The former (partial) versions are: 1986. The Chamula Festival of Games: Native Macroanalysis and Social Commentary in a Maya Carnival. In *Symbol and Meaning Beyond the Closed Community: Essays in Mesoamerican Ideas*, edited by Gary H. Gossen. Albany, NY: Institute for Mesoamerican Studies, University at Albany, State University of New York, pp. 227–54. 1992. Las variaciones del mal en una fiesta tzotzil. In *De palabra y obra en el nuevo mundo: imágenes, interétnicas*, edited by Miguel León-Portilla, Manuel Gutiérrez Estévez, Gary H. Gossen, and J. Jorge Klor de Alva. Madrid: Siglo XXI de España, pp. 429–56.

Chapter 6 was published under exactly the same title as follows under joint authorship with Richard M. Leventhal: 1993. The Topography of Ancient Maya Religious Pluralism: A Dialogue with the Present. In *Lowland Maya Civilization in the Eighth Century A.D.*, edited by Jeremy A. Sabloff and John S. Henderson. Washington, D.C.: Dumbarton Oaks Research and Library Collection, pp. 185–217.

Chapter 7 was previously published in Spanish in two slightly different versions from the present, which appears in English for the first time. They are: 1983. Una diáspora maya moderna: desplazamiento y persistencia cultural de San Juan Chamula, Chiapas. *Mesoamérica* 5: 253–76. Antigua, Guatemala, and Woodstock, VT: Centro de Investigaciones Regionales de Mesoamérica (CIRMA). 1992. La diáspora de San Juan Chamula: los indios en el proyecto nacional mexicano. In *De palabra y obra en el nuevo mundo: encuentros intertnicos*, edited by M. Gutiérrez Estévez, Miguel León-Portilla, Gary H. Gossen, and J. J. Klor de Alva. Madrid: Siglo XXI de España, pp. 429–56.

Chapter 8 has been published in both Spanish and English versions, neither of which is entirely identical to the current text in this volume: 1988. Vida y muerte de Miguel Kasklán: héroe chamula. In *Biograf as y confesiones de los indios de América*, edited by M. Gutirrez Estvez. Special number of *Arbor* 131 (515–16): 125–44. Madrid: Consejo de Investigaciones Científicas. 1989. Life, Death and Apotheosis of a Tzotzil Protestant Leader: Biography as Social History. In *Enthnographic Encounters in Southern Mesoamerica: Essays in Honor of Evon Z. Vogt, Jr.*, edited by Victoria R. Bricker and Gary H. Gossen. Albany, NY: Institute for Mesoamerican Studies, University at Albany, State University of New York: pp. 217–29.

Chapter 9 has been previously published under the same title in American Anthropologist. Its content has been radically altered in the present volume to omit ethnographic redundancy. As originally published it was: 1994. From Olmecs to Zapatistas: A Once and Future Histor of Souls. *American Anthropologist* 96 (3): 553–70.

Chapter 10 has been previously published under a different title in American Anthropology. Its content has been altered in the present volume to omit redundancy. As originally published it was: 1996. Maya Zapatistas Move to the Ancient Future. *American Anthropology* 98(3): 528–38.

The postscript to chapter 10 was originally published as an editorial, and is reprinted with permission of the Times Union, Albany, NY.

NOTES

Chapter One

1. I offer the following as a modern English rendition of the passage from Robert Burns:

   > Would that some power might give us the small gift of seeing ourselves as others see us. It might thus serve to free us from many a blunder and foolish notion. We might even feel compelled to abandon pretentious ways of dressing and moving about. Perhaps it would even cause us to tone down the pretense of excessive piety.

2. These questions have been considered at length by others, including native Mesoamericans themselves, as recorded in colonial testimonies (Bricker 1981; Sahagún 1969; Farriss 1984; León-Portilla 1962; and Todorov 1984) and in ethnographies and narrative accounts of our time (Colby 1966; Gutiérrez, et al. 1988; Horcasitas 1972; Ingham 1986; Laughlin 1980; Sullivan 1989; Warren 1978; and Watanabe 1992). Thus, for many centuries, and continuing into our time, Mesoamerican Indians have considered the intellectual puzzle of what to make of powerful foreigners—gods, demons, amoral strangers, perhaps even friends.

3. This mood of modern ethnic self-affirmation is widespread in the Maya areas of Mexico, Guatemala, and Belize. In many cases, this expression involves pan-Mayan ethnic consciousness that goes well beyond local Indian communities. See Kay Warren's excellent synthetic piece on the subject (Warren 1992).

4. This and subsequent line drawings and related commentary were done by Marián López Calixto in 1978 and 1979. Mr. López Calixto produced these drawings as illustrations of narrative texts. He worked for me but in relative independence from me. His task was to find what in his judgment were salient items and themes in the transcribed narrative texts and to illustrate them. I hoped thereby to obtain an "independent" critical reading of information in the texts that might not have come to my attention at the time of original performance, transcription, and translation into Spanish.

5. See Sarah Blaffer's extensive comparative and historical analysis of the "black-man" and related demons in the oral traditions of Zinacantán, a Tzotzil community whose territory is contiguous to Chamula (Blaffer 1972).

6. Figure 4 is an illustration of a place called "The Place of the Calendar" (*yav kalintario*) in the Chamula cosmos. It is located at the point where the sun goes down into the western sea at sundown. The Sun/Christ is said to leave manufactured goods, particularly metal tools, books, metallic money, and calendars at this location.

The demons are said to be couriers who bring these goods through subterranean tunnels and deliver them to the earth lords, who then sell them to Ladino merchants, who in turn sell them at great profit to Indians.

7. Figure 5 is an illustration of a very popular motif in historical narratives. Indians who seek short-term gain (usually money) are said to make pacts with the demons or earth lords, exchanging their labor and/or loyalty for cash and other forms of well-being. These deals are usually catastrophic for Indians in the end, but some narratives yield a happy ending in which the Indian protagonist manages to foil the evil motives of the demon or earth lord. Several living rich men in Chamula are said to have gained their wealth in this manner.

8. See Pickands (1986) for a comparative study of this and apparently related heroic figures in ethnohistoric sources in the Maya area. See also Gossen (1974b: 319) for a more complete abstract of the story than that which is given in this chapter.

9. Although it is not the intent of this paper to speculate about possible pre-Columbian antecedents for the moral and evaluative valences of black and white, there can be little doubt that color symbolism and moral assignation and cardinal directional association were a relatively consistent and widespread feature of pre-contact Maya thought. Generally, red and white were associated with east and north and the waxing solar cycle (daily and annual) and with agricultural growth and sustenance; black and yellow, with the west and south and with the waning solar cycle (daily and annual), and with associated organic life cycles. In a related general pattern, the complementarity of light (day and sky) and dark (night and underworld) appears to have been a strong organizing principle in pre-Columbian thought and iconography. The individual values in both sets of color valences (white, red, black, and yellow; and light and dark) are clearly interdependent, complementary, and symbiotically linked. All parts of both sets are essential for the continuation of life. Thus, it is not unreasonable to suggest that the significance of the categories black, white, and Indian in current Tzotzil discourse is probably conditioned by long experience with similar ideas that date from the precontact period (Thompson 1934). (I am grateful to Michael Coe for his verification of this information and for his help in guiding me to the appropriate source.)

10. Nancy Farriss (1984) and Victoria Bricker (1981) have observed the strength of this type of logic as a survival strategy for Maya ethnicity and identity in the colonial and modern periods. Sahlins (1985) has also shown a similar logic to be operative in native Polynesian historical reckoning of their encounter with Europe.

11. Evon Z. Vogt, personal communication.

Chapter 2

1. Our Father of Nazareth derives from the Spanish Nuestro Señor de Nazaret, Jesus of Nazareth. His image, Christ with the cross on his shoulder, is in the Chamula church. However, as this deity has come into the Chamula pantheon, he is not the same as Jesus. He is a minor saint, vaguely related to Our Father in Heaven. He appears in the processions on Easter Sunday, but, again, as a vague relative of, not the same as, the Sun/Christ deity.

2. Through the Dominican missionization of Chamula, the Biblical Jews and Judases are linked conceptually with the pre-Columbian monkeys and demons as negative forces hostile to the social order created by and presided over by the Sun/Christ deity.

3. The halo of this passage refers to the rays of light and heat which shone around the young Sun/Christ's head. The forces of evil (Jews, monkeys, and demons) realized that this radiant heat and light would ultimately kill them; hence their interest in killing Our Father before he killed them.

4. There is some confusion about the relationship of San Salvador (Jesus the Savior) to Our Father in Heaven. It seems that they are two different aspects of the same deity. Our Father in Heaven travels in the third, outermost, layer of the heavens. Apparently, the radiance of his head—the light of the sun itself—which we perceive on the first, innermost layer of the heavens, is revered as San Salvador.

5. This passage means that the Jews were struck by a thunderstorm. The angels are familiars and companions of the earth lords and the terms are often used interchangeably. They live in caves high on the mountainsides and are seen visibly in the form of rainclouds and lightning and are heard in the form of thunder. They would have been able to intercept the Jews in the climb up to heaven through their celestial mobility, thus punishing them with a great storm.

6. This is said to be the origin of the custom of eating fish on Ash Wednesday (*melkulix ti? choy*, "fish-eating Wednesday"). However, Chamulas cannot afford dried, salted, or fresh fish, so the custom is ignored today.

7. The method described here is still part of ritual practice in the staging of the Crucifixion on Good Friday in the Chamula church. The image of Christ is literally nailed to the cross in almost exact repetition of the events recorded in this text, including the stake and the rope as aids in erecting the cross.

8. Seventh Friday is the Tzotzil way of saying Good Friday.

9. Each year on Good Friday, after Our Father is nailed to the cross, a straw-stuffed image of Judas, dressed as a Mexican mestizo, is burned. The charred remains are strung up by the rope and left to hang from the center of the main façade of the Chamula church until Easter Sunday.

10. The phrase "she saw the face of her son" means that, from her vantage point on earth, his face was all that she could see. To anyone on earth, this is all that is visible of the Sun/Christ's totality, which is a whole anthropomorphic body, according to Tzotzil belief.

11. This means not only that the sun and moon are conceived of as moving anthropomorphic deities but also that they follow similar circuits about the earth. The sun is believed to move in the third and highest level of the sky; the moon, in the second level. In both cases, the route is over the earth, into the underworld and up again from the eastern horizon. In both cases, it is the faces of the deities which we perceive as radiant reflection which penetrates through to the first level of the sky, which is the only layer of celestial phenomena that we can perceive from the surface of the earth.

12. Chamulas believe that all the dead go to live forever in the underworld. This follows, as the text explains, from the basic solar orientation of human life: We go to the underworld, for Our Lord Sun/Christ did that when he died. Unlike him, however, humans never return to earth as living beings. Their souls do return to

earth on the eve of the Festival of the Dead (November 1, All Saints' Day, and November 2, All Souls' Day). On this occasion, they go out around midnight to receive the food and drink offered to them by their relatives still living on earth. In practice, the only ancestors so honored are those who have left land and property to the living.

13. This cryptic line about "secret wisdom" is hard to understand. Most obviously, it is of interest that the initiative in creating the cosmic division of labor for presiding over night and day is attributed ultimately to the moon. It was she, not the sun, who made the first move (i.e., giving him birth) in establishing the cosmos. She also makes a second instrumental move in going to see him to make arrangements for day and night. Her secret wisdom may thus be read as latent female authority which lends a kind of egalitarian balance to a social order which on the surface appears to be dominated by male authority. Throughout the text, including the final verse, the narrative emphasizes joint responsibility for the maintenance of cosmic order between the moon and her son. Also suggested in the "secret wisdom" passage is the menstrual cycle which is associated by the Chamulas with the lunar cycle. "To menstruate" in Tzotzil is "to see the month." Thus, Chamula women share Our Holy Mother Moon's cyclical nature just as Chamula men share in the divine solar cycles through public ritual observance. Together, both men and women work to maintain the integrity of this cyclically patterned universe, with their different and complementary powers.

14. Marián, from the Spanish Mariano, is the older brother of Our Father Sun.

15. Xalik, from the Spanish Salvador, is a given name which means "Savior." In Tzotzil belief, this is one of the aspects of Our Father Sun.

16. The sweat house or bathhouse refers to the traditional dome-shaped sauna that is found throughout Indian Mesoamerica. It is typically made of stones or wattle and daub (mud stucco). The steam is produced by tossing hot water on very hot stones. The bathers beat themselves with branches of aromatic and medicinal herbs.

17. This and the following couplets refer to the sun's travels over (day) and under (night) the earth. The sides of heaven referred to are the eastern and western horizons, believed to be the edges (i.e., sides) of the earth.

18. Incense and other "essences" (for example, tobacco smoke, odor of aromatic plants, sky rocket explosions) are typically present in all Chamula ritual events. These ritual substances, together with ritual language and song, are "food" for Our Father Sun.

19. John the Baptist is the patron saint of San Juan Chamula, from whom the *municipio* takes its name. The image of San Juan (junior aspect) has the place of honor in the Chamula church, just above the main altar, facing west. His festival, June 24, is one of the largest and best attended of all Chamula fiestas. All Chamula saints have a junior (*itz'inal*) and a senior (*bankilal*) aspect. Furthermore, the *barrio* of Chamula which is considered the most senior in rank (*bankilal*) is San Juan. It is of interest that San Juan has close affinity with Our Father Sun, being one of his younger brothers. This special relationship to Our Father Sun is expressed not only in his favored position in the Chamula church but also in the fact that Barrio San Juan lies generally east and north of the ceremonial center, thus giving it a favorable directional orientation in relation to the other two *barrios*, which lie to the northwest (San Pedro) and to the west and south (San Sebastian). The highest point in

Chamula (and, indeed, in the Central Chiapas Highlands) is Tzontevitz ("Tree Moss Mountain," as it is translated in this text), which lies in the Barrio of San Juan. The senior aspect of San Juan lives in this mountain. Thus, the seniority of San Juan in the rank order of Chamula saints is only exceeded by Our Father Sun himself.

20. Xitalá is a place which everyone seems to know about, but to which no one of my acquaintance has been. I have been able to establish only that it is located in the *municipio* of Santa Catarina Pantelhó, which places it to the northeast of Chamula in an area which drops off quickly to the lowlands, known in Tzotzil as "Hot Country." The site of the old ceremonial center is said to have the remains of rock foundations and walls from an old church (or perhaps from a pre-Columbian structure).

21. Both these places lie within the present-day municipal boundaries of Chamula, thus placing them in the highlands in what is classified as "Cold Country." They are located due north of the present-day Chamula ceremonial center at a distance of about twenty kilometers. There are remains (mounds and foundations) of some buildings at Hol Ch'umtik, probably of pre-Columbian origin. *Ya?al Ichin* is still an inhabited hamlet of Chamula.

22. Please see the end of note 19 (above) for an explanation of the junior and senior aspects of all Chamula saints. In the case of San Juan, his senior aspect lives in Tzontevitz ("Tree Moss Mountain") along with St. Jerome, some other saints, and the soul companion animals of all people in the community. (See chapter 9 of this book for a full discussion of animal-soul companions.) The junior aspect of San Juan lives in the Chamula church, and it is he who is represented in the image of that name.

23. This must have been a great spectacle to behold, for the narrator explained that the helpers were none other than San Pedro and San Sebastián, the saints for whom the other two *barrios* of Chamula are named. With San Juan (the elder) in the lead, San Pedro next, then San Sebastián, and then the unnamed workers, they herded the great field of stones as though they were sheep.

24. The staff mentioned in this line refers to a common shepherd's staff, a typical accouterment in religious icons and images as well as in the everyday life of many Chamula rural households, both in the home *municipio* and in the diaspora communities. Sheep, with chickens, turkeys, dogs and cats, sometimes rabbits, are the most commonly kept domestic animals.

25. There are today dozens of places in Chamula that bear the names of Bejel Ton ("Round Stone") or Pajal Ton ("Fixed Stone"). Many of these places are names for wayward, uncooperative stones, still visible and conspicuous, which refused to be herded to San Juan's proposed church site in the ceremonial center. No ritual significance is attached to these places, although they serve as constant reminders of the past.

26. See note 23 (above) for a list of those gods who were involved in the stone-herding expedition. By this time, Our Holy Father Sun had joined in to help.

27. See note 19 (above). It is important to call attention to the genuine ambiguity regarding the residence of San Juan. Part of the ambiguity stems from the two aspects of the saint's being, junior and senior. All Chamulas seem to agree that the main image in the Chamula church is of the junior aspect of the saint. However, the junior aspect also "represents" (*sk'exol*, "as his substitute or shadow") the senior

aspect for purposes of prayer and cult practice. Thus, the senior aspect is not visible, but implicit. Although today the senior aspect of San Juan is believed to live in Tree Moss Mountain (Tzontevitz), he once apparently had a fully established house there. Whether this was a shrine or chapel no one seems to know. However, there is still a place-name near the top of Tzontevitz Mountain called San Juan's Window (*Sventana San Juan*). This "window" is a small cave opening. It has a cross shrine nearby which is often visited by curing parties. Indeed, it ranks as one of the holiest shrines in the community. I have visited this site in the company of Tzotzils, all of whom saw fit to say prayers asking forgiveness for having intruded on San Juan's domestic tranquility.

Chapter Three

1. This line and in fact this entire passage assume that the listener or reader knows that corn is Our Father's body and, therefore, sacred. The "place for his body" is the cornfield. While there is general agreement among all Chamula that corn came originally from Our Father's body, there is no general agreement about which part of his body it came from. The most common version is that corn came originally from the inner thigh, thereby explaining also that corn silk came from Our Father's pubic hair. Other explanations identify the biceps of Our Father's arm as the part of the body that provided the first corn, in which case the underarm hair is given as the origin of corn silk.
2. The reference to light here is a metaphor for Our Father Sun's light, heat, blessing, and good will. To follow any evil inclination is to invite destruction, which is, even in modern times, associated with the death of the Sun/Christ. Solar eclipses occasionally remind people of this threat, for these events are explained as demons who come from the edges of the earth to bite the sun to death. (See Figure 1 and related discussion in chapter 1.)
3. This whole passage refers to knowledge of sex.
4. In Chamula the custom of seeking godparents to help a couple baptize their child is typically the father's responsibility. For the mother to take the initiative in the search for *compadres* (Sp. for "coparents," the relationship between parents and godparents) invites the accusation that she is interested in her *compadre* for other than the accepted reasons of ritual solidarity, economic security, and friendship. As in Mexican national society, *compadrazgo* in Chamula establishes a lifelong, special relationship between the godchild and the godparents as well as between the parents and the godparents. Whereas it is common in Mexican society to seek *compadres* for several ritual events in one child's life (baptism, first communion, and marriage), the Chamulas give importance to the *compadrazgo* tie only for baptism. It is in Chamula a bond of special friendship and is usually accompanied by formal gestures of respect and consideration, not only upon establishment of the bond but also throughout the lives of the participants.
5. In addition to the general notion that sexual activity is evil, for it was first taught by the demon Pukuj, there is in Chamula general acceptance of the belief that women are accompanied by Our Father Sun from midnight to noon (the time of his rising aspect) and, potentially, by demons from noon to midnight (the time

of the falling aspect of the sun, when he moves from the zenith of the sky to the nadir of the underworld). Thus, women are believed to be virtuous from midnight to noon and vulnerable to sin and evil from noon to midnight. This is one of the reasons that Chamula men give for their preference that women carry water and wood—tasks which take them away from the home—in the morning. Women who wander about in the afternoon are believed to be more prone to commit adultery than those who remain at home in the afternoon. The explanation is a clear legacy from the First Creation, when the first woman learned about sex from the demon Pukuj, probably, some Chamulas say, in the afternoon.

6. "Successor" comes from the Tzotzil word *k'exol*, which is a ritual term that also means "substitute." It is typically used in change-of-office rituals, the new officeholder being called *k'exol,* or replacement for the past officeholder. In this passage, then, the Moon (Our Holy Mother) refers to the first woman as her "successor," the bearer of feminine tasks and responsibilities for humankind.

7. It is interesting to note at this point that contemporary Chamula outer garments are made of sheep's wool, which of course was introduced only after the Spanish conquest. The early First-Creation time dimension of this narrative is indicated by Our Holy Mother's teaching of weaving with cotton, which was native to the New World and which was no doubt used by the pre-Columbian Maya. Chamula women continue to be expert weavers, the loom being of the back-strap, portable type, but they now weave almost exclusively in wool, producing women's skirts, outer blouses, shawls, and head pieces and men's outer tunics. Women's inner blouses, some shawls, and men's shirts and pants are now made from machine-woven cotton or bought ready-made. It is important to mention, however, that several neighboring Indian communities continue to produce high-quality cotton textiles on back-strap looms. Thus, the technology that is reported in this text is still known and widely practiced in the Chiapas Highlands.

8. *Atole* is the standard Mexican word for a thick cornstarch gruel that is drunk sweetened as a beverage. This passage refers to unsweetened *atole*, which is used as a stiffening and adhesive agent for thread, both cotton and wool. Recently spun thread is soaked with atole to make it less fuzzy and easier to handle. It also keeps it from breaking easily.

9. The stiffened thread is attached to the pieces of the loom for the original, vertical threads (warp) of the cloth. These of course must be stronger and stiffer than the horizontal threads (weft).

10. There is a discrepancy here between the information in the text and actual modern practice, in which the threads are separated while still wet with *atole*.

11. This apparently means "no other duties besides weaving, cooking, carrying wood, carrying water, etc." The latter duties had already been assigned earlier in the narrative.

12. It is interesting to note that Our Father created the large and powerful animals first, perhaps thinking that the task of populating the earth required strong people; hence, the necessity of first creating the strong animal-soul companions and the weaker ones later.

13. This line is a fairly direct commentary on human inequality in the Chamula worldview. The fact that jaguars are not the soul companion animals of all peo-

ple explains why some are richer and others poorer; why some are more powerful and others weaker; and why some die as respected elders and others die
early in life without accomplishing much at all.

14. It is not clear here just what sequence of days is referred to. I believe, however, that
it refers to the four-day cycle that led to the victory of the Sun/Christ over the
forces of evil in the primordial creation story. (See chapter 1.) At the beginning of
this cycle, Our Father is killed by the monkeys, demons, and Jews, for they fear his
power to give heat and light to the world. He comes back to life, however, and on
the first day after his burial and resuscitation, goes to the western edge of the earth.
On the second day, he goes from the western edge of the earth down to the nadir
of the underworld. On the third day, he begins his upward swing toward the eastern horizon, where he finally emerges at dawn of the fourth day. By noon of the
fourth day, he reaches the zenith of the sky, thus giving the earth the full, uncontested benefit of Our Father's light and heat. He also at this time, according to some
versions, burns to death most of his enemies—the monkeys, the demons, and the
Jews—and frightens the few survivors into retreat outside the moral universe of the
sun. Henceforth, from this moment of "completion" of the four days of primordial
creation, the Sun's path marks the spatial limits of the universe and maintains the
elementary units of time: day and night and the annual solar cycle. Therefore, the
"third day" referred to in this narrative seems to signify the turning of the tide to
what might be called "cosmic optimism." The image of the "third day" suggests the
sun's position on the third day as Our Lord Sun/Christ moved upward from the
nadir of the underworld to the eastern horizon, from whence, on the fourth day,
he would finally establish the spatial and temporal categories of the universe. On
this, the fourth and final day of primordial creation, he completes the cycle by
emerging from the eastern sea in a ball of heat and light, causing the primordial
oceans of the earth to evaporate. Hence, returning again to the present text, the
third and fourth days of the sun's emergence cycle would have been the first time
when plants could have grown and survived on earth.

15. This passage refers to the emergence of typical features of the karst-type limestone topography of the Chiapas highlands. It is an area of heavy rainfall but
without many surface drainage features such as creeks and rivers. The area is very
mountainous, but for the most part internally drained, typical features being
subterranean streams, sinkholes, springs, deep water holes, seasonal swamps, and
ponds. The relatively heavy rainfall, combined with the limestone substructure,
has caused a pattern of weathered limestone surface features such as steep cliffs,
landslide formations, and thousands of basins, large and small, which have been
formed by collapse of the limestone substructure. There are, on the edges of
these collapsed basins, thousands of cave openings and rock shelters, large and
small, including some that lead to immense limestone caverns. The cracks in
rocks, referred to in the text as the "door to the demon's house," are often in fact
cave openings that lead to great cavern networks inside the earth. These "doors"
sometimes appear to be mere vertical cracks, but Chamulas note that they are
"meant" to deceive, being just large enough for a curious person to enter for the
purpose of exploration, sometimes, Chamulas say, never to return.

16. Earth lords (*yajval banamil*) and their external manifestations as clouds and lightning (Tz. *anjeletik*, from Sp. *ángel*, "angel") live in medium to large caves, often

those with prominent rock shelters. These caves are therefore intimately associated with rain, thunder, and lightning. The tie betwen caves and rain is probably explained, in part, by the internal drainage system of the Chiapas Highlands, as well as by the fact that rain-bearing clouds in this mountainous terrain appear to emerge from the mouths of caves.

Chapter Four

1. I choose "person" to translate *vinik* ("man," also "twenty"), for although it literally means "man" in contrast to "woman" (*antz*), it is clearly meant here to indicate the generic human condition, as in "humankind." Dennis Tedlock solved this problem another way in his recent book on the ancient and modern Quiché (see Tedlock 1993), by translating the Quiché cognate of this word as "vigesimal being," for the attribute of having twenty digits is a diagnostic feature of people in general, as well as being the word for "man" and "twenty."
2. For a full discussion of the Tzotzil concept of the soul, see chapter 9.
3. *Batz'i k'op*, "the true language," is the Tzotzil word for the Tzotzil language. The word *batz'i* also mens "true," "right," "genuine." Thus, a measure of linguistic chauvinism is built into the very name of the language.
4. This series of emotional phrases (verses 17-20) serves to emphasize that all did indeed speak a single language and were thus capable of communicating and working together.
5. The logic of this arrangement—Ladinos first, Indians second, in order of language acquisition—is consonant with the Chamula view that saints, who are the common ancestors of all people, are Ladinos. Like saints, Ladinos have greater power than Indians in most spheres of contemporary life. Furthermore, nearly all Chamula images of the saints, as well as of Our Father Sun and Our Mother Moon, have fair skin and non-Indian features. Paradoxically, it is nevertheless true that Chamulas believe themselves to be morally superior to Ladinos, and that it is Tzotzil, not Spanish, which is the "true language."
6. *Kaxlan* is the Tzotzil word which means Ladino, or bearer of the Spanish-speaking Mexican cultural tradition. It comes from *castellano*, which refers to Castilian or the standard Spanish language. Thus, ethnic and linguistic identity are explicitly tied together in Chamula thinking.
7. For several decades, it has been the goal of Mexican Indian primary education to teach Spanish to Indian children, thereby facilitating their participation in Mexican national culture. This policy is called *castellanización* and has generally used Indian language texts only for elementary teaching of the idea of sounds in relation to written symbols. After the first few years, Spanish is "ideally" the language of instruction. Teaching of literacy in Indian languages has never been a specific goal of Indian education in modern Mexico.
9. Father Miguel Hidalgo is also acknowledged by Mexican written history as being the father of Mexican Independence. He gave the famous "*Grito de Dolores*" ("Long live Our Lady of Guadalupe! Down with bad government! Death to the Spaniards!") on September 16, 1810, which launched the Mexican Independence Movement against Spain. This date is celebrated as Mexico's Independence Day. It

may be of some importance to Chamula historical reckoning (though it is not mentioned in this Chamula text) that Miguel Hidalgo was a parish priest who was close to poor village people. He felt a special affinity for mestizos and Indians and in many ways, both theological and intellectual, distanced himself from the Spanish criollo establishment. Among other attributes, he learned and used in his parish ministry a number of Indian languages. These aspects of his background, according to fact and legend as recorded in Mexican school textbooks and history books, contributed to his sensitivity to the problems of the poor and oppressed in colonial Mexico. Condemned to death as a subversive, he faced a firing squad on July 31, 1811.

Chapter Five

1. I have discussed elsewhere (Gossen 1972b, 1974b) the syncretic concept of the Sun/Christ. The Dominican Catholic missionization of the Chamulas in the sixteenth century achieved not a conversion, but still another overlay of theology and religious personages upon the sun and moon cults of the pre-Columbian Maya. They had, at the time of the Conquest, already incorporated many beliefs and concepts from the Toltec tradition of the central valley of Mexico into their cosmological and religious practice. Thus, the Sun/Christ and Moon/Virgin Mary relationship that emerged from sixteenth-century missionization simply added another "aspect" to the many faces of the sun and moon deities that already existed.

2. It should be noted that variants of this narrative differ on many details. One of the most common points of variation is whether the ascent of the Sun/Christ to the zenith of the sky occurs on the fourth primeval day (as I have paraphrased it) or on the third primeval day. In either case, the Sun/Christ commences his upward swing from the nadir of the Underworld at the beginning of the third day. The real difference, then, is whether the present order begins with the Sun/Christ deity first appearing on the eastern horizon, or with his rise to the zenith of his perceived orbit in the Middle of the heavens.

3. "Stinking Ladino woman" is from *xinulan* ("stinking woman"), which is modern colloquial Tzotzil for any Ladino woman. The stink is said to come from their bad breath, which is explained by their affinity for dogs, whose breath is also foul.

4. The reference to "open grasslands" (*jobeltik*) is linked to *jobel*, the Tzotzil word for San Cristóbal de las Casas, which is the adminstrative and commercial hub of the Chiapas highlands. This city has been, since the colonial period, identified with Spanish, Mexican, and Ladino ethnicity. Indeed, Indians were not legally permitted to spend the night there until the 1950s.

5. February 24 was the first day of the five-day Festival of Games in 1979. The date given in the text, of course, changes every year at this point to make it coincide with the Easter cycle in the Christian calendar. All dates given in this article are based on the 1979 calendar.

6. Bricker has noted that the Dance of the Warriors, as it is performed at the Chamula Festival of Games, has what appear to be clear links with pre-

Columbian Maya ritual practice in both Yucatan and Chiapas. The thematic link is calendrical and cosmological in Yucatan (it occurred during the five-day unlucky period at the end of the year) and military in Chiapas (the top-ranking military chief, *zba chilom*, was a kind of holy warrior identified with the cult of the jaguars (Bricker 1973: 112).

7. Venustiano Carranza and Alberto Pineda were revolutionary and counterrevolutionary figures, respectively, in the Mexican Revolution of 1910-18, as it was experienced in central Chiapas. Carranza went on to become president of Mexico. Pineda remained committed to the reactionary right wing of Chiapas politics until his death.

Chapter Six

1. The terms *center* and *periphery* refer, within this paper, to only the physical location associated with the layout of ancient and modern Maya settlements.

2. *El calendario del más antiguo Galván* is a broadside distributed in the central market of San Cristóbal de las Casas, Chiapas, Mexico.

3. Schele and Miller (1986) also mention the importance of the cyclical nature of time in terms of two types of dates: special records of the zero date and Lounsbury's contrived numbers. These numbers "record" the actions of the past, present, and future within a cyclical structure. These special records of zero dates and the contrived numbers emphasize the dominance of cyclical time in relation to linear time—the long count.

Chapter Seven

1. For a wake-up call, remember that the great moral arbiter of Spanish discourse on this issue in seventeenth-century Spain, Juan Ginés de Sepulvéda, declared— among his many "humanist" defenses of Indian subjugation to the will of Spain—that "these barbarians of the New World are as inferior to Spaniards as children are to adults, or as women are to men."

Chapter Eight

1. Thor Anderson, personal communication.

Chapter Nine

1. See, for example, Foster 1944; Saler 1964; Villa Rojas 1963; and Vogt 1965 and 1970.

2. See John Watanabe's excellent recent book (1992) on this subject.

3. The following discussion derives, in part, from a fuller consideration of this subject that is published elsewhere (Gossen 1975). I have, however, for reasons noted above, rethought and revised significant parts of my earlier interpretation.

4. See Vogt 1969 (pp. 416-76) for detail on curing ceremonies in neighboring Zinacantán and Gossen 1974 (pp. 209-16) for a shamanic prayer text that articulates in practice the beliefs described here.

5. I trust that it is obvious that this generalization refers only to a small sample of Chamula Tzotzils. The literature cited elsewhere in this essay reflects the enormous range of animate and inanimate coessences that exist in ancient and contemporary Mesoamerica.

6. It is relevant to recall that ancient Mesoamerican mathematics and calendrical reckoning were of a base-twenty type, suggesting that time itself was anthropomorphized.

7. In Pitarch 1996, a hyperbolic expression of this pattern in the Mesoamerican coessence concept is described wherein powerful individuals, both good and evil, may possess numerous soul coessences.

Chapter Ten

1. Jan Rus, personal communication, April 1994. See also Peres Tzu 1996.

2. What began with hundreds of news reports in 1994 has now exploded into a major corpus of analytical and interpretive literature. Major works include Collier 1994; Harvey et al. 1994; Ross 1994; and Subcomandante Marcos's collected letters and communiqués through August 1994 (1995). Collected essays on the subject appeared in *Cultural Survival Quarterly* 18(1) (1994) and *Akwe:kon: Journal of Indigenous Issues* (summer 1994).

3. English translation taken from Nigh 1994: 12, based on a Spanish document that appeared in *La Jornada*, February 27, 1994.

4. Another dimension of this buccal half-mask costuming of the Zapatistas may be a recapitulation of the concept of the coessence. Partly this is an expression of group identity, in that these half-masks are often worn to social events involving only the Zapatistas themselves. In these settings, masks may suppress individual identities, but they do not disguise them, for all participants are known to one another. Contextually, in suppressing individual identities, the wearing of the half-masks is expressing group identity—an identity that, like the way, is a relationship among a set of these individual identities, identities that are influenced by something beyond themselves. This representation in fact recapitulates, though it presumably does not continue, more ancient Mesoamerican symbolism of the coessence. The coessence concept among the modern Zoques of Chiapas and among their pre-Classic Zoquean forebears was designated by the word *jama*, which also meant "day." According to Justeson and Kaufman (1993: 1703), this concept is represented by the imagery of the Tuxtla Statuette—through the donning of a buccal half-mask. Furthermore, the diagnostic motif of an epi-Olmec glyph representing this word (*jama*) is a person wearing such a half-mask. The human identities in the glyphic and sculptural representations are still manifest; the half-mask imagery represents the coessence. The buccal half-mask imagery in the Zapatista case seems strikingly parallel in structure and content (Justeson, personal communication, March 1996).

REFERENCES

Adams, Richard. 1967. Nationalization. In *Social Anthropology*, vol. 6 of the *Handbook of Middle American Indians*, edited by Manning Nash, pp. 469–88. Austin, TX: University of Texas Press.

————.1970. *Crucifixion by Power: Essays on Guatemalan National Social Structure 1944–1966*. Austin, TX: University of Texas Press.

Adams, Richard N., and Arthur J. Rubel. 1967. Sickness and Social Relations. In *Social Anthropology*, vol 6. of *Handbook of Middle American Indians*, edited by Manning Nash, pp. 333–55. Austin, TX: University of Texas Press.

Aguirre Beltrán, Gonzalo. 1967. *Regiones de refugio: el desarrollo de la comunidad y el proceso dominical en Mestizo América*. Mexico City: Instituto Nacional Indigenista Interamericano.

————.1978. La antropología social. In *Las humanidades en México*, edited by Consejo de las Humanidades, pp. 545–644. Mexico City: Universidad Nacional Autónoma

Anderson, Arthur J. D., and Charles Dibble. 1951. Florentine Codex: General History of the Things of New Spain by Bernardino de Sahagún. *Book 2: The Ceremonies. Monographs of the School of American Research* 14 (3). Santa Fe, NM: School of American Research and the University of Utah Press.

Aveni, Anthony F. 1989. *Empires of Time: Calendars, Clocks, and Cultures*. New York, NY: Basic Books, Inc.

Bancroft, E., and R. Bancroft. 1980. *Rincón Chamula. Ethnographic Notes on an Established Chamula Colony in the Municipio of Solistahuacán*. Chiapas, México: unpublished field report.

Barth, Frederik, ed. 1969. *Ethnic Groups and Boundaries*. Boston, MA: Little, Brown and Co.

Baum, L. Frank. 1956 [1900]. *The Wizard of Oz*. Chicago, IL: Rand McNally & Co.

Berlin, Heinrich. 1968. Estudios Epigráficos II. *Antropología e Historia de Guatemala* 20 (1): 13–24.

————. 1979. How Metaphors are Used: A Reply to Donald Davidson. In *On Metaphors*, edited by Sheldon Sacks, pp. 181–93. Chicago, IL: University of Chicago Press.

Blaffer, Sarah C. 1972. *The Black-man of Zinacantan: A Central American Legend*. Austin, TX: University of Texas Press.

Bolles, David. 1978. *Post Conquest Mayan Literature*. Lee, NH: Private Publisher.

Bonfil, Batalla Guillermo. 1970. El campo de investigación de la antropología social en México: un ensayo sobre nuevas perspectivas. *Anales de Antropología* 7: 163–81.

Borhegyi, Stephen de. 1956. The Development of Folk and Complex Cultures in the Southern Maya Area. *American Antiquity* 21: 343–56.

Bouissac, Paul. 1976. *Circus and Culture: A Semiotic Approach.* Bloomington, IN: Indiana University Press.

Breslin, Patrick. 1992. Coping with Change, the Maya Discover the Play's the Thing. *Smithsonian* (August): 79–87.

Bricker, Victoria R. 1973. *Ritual Humor in Highland Chiapas.* Austin, TX: University of Texas Press.

———.1981. *The Indian Christ, the Indian King: The Historical Substrate of Maya Myth and Ritual.* Austin, TX: University of Texas Press.

———.1989. The Calendrical Meaning of Ritual among the Maya. In *Ethnographic Encounters in Southern Mesoamerica: Essays in Honor of Evon Zartman Vogt, Jr. Studies in Culture and Society*, vol. 3, edited by Victoria R. Bricker and Gary H. Gossen, pp. 231–49. Albany, NY: Institute for Mesoamerican Studies, University at Albany, State University of New York.

Bricker, Victoria R., and George A. Collier. 1970. Nicknames and Social Structure in Zinacantan. *American Anthropologist* 72 (2): 289–302.

Burns, Robert. 1970. *The Works of Robert Burns.* Philadelphia, PA: J. Crissy and J. Grigg.

Calnek, Edward E. 1962. *Highland Chiapas Before the Spanish Conquest.* Ph.D. Dissertation. Chicago, IL: University of Chicago.

Cámara-Barbachano, Fernando. 1964. El mestizaje en México: planteamiento sobre problemáticos socioculturales. *Revista de Indias* 24: 27–83.

Carlson, John B. 1980. On Classic Maya Monumental Recorded History. In *Third Palenque Round Table*, 1978, part 2, edited by Merle Greene Robertson, pp. 199–203. Austin, TX: University of Texas Press.

Carmack, Robert M. 1972. Ethnohistory: A Review of its Development, Definitions, Methods, and Aims. *Annual Review of Anthropology* 1: 227–46.

———.1996. Mesoamerica at Spanish Contact. In *The Legacy of Mesoamerica: History and Culture of a Native American Civilization*, edited by Robert M. Carmack, Janine Gasco, and Gary H. Gossen, pp. 80–121. Englewood Cliffs, NJ: Prentice-Hall.

Carter, William. 1969. *New Lands and Old Traditions: Kekchi Cultivators in the Guatemalan Lowlands.* Gainesville, FL: University of Florida Press.

Casagrande, Joseph, Stephen Thompson, and Philip N. Young. 1964. Colonization as a Research Frontier: The Ecuadorian Case. In *Process and Patterns in Culture: Essays in Honor of Julian H. Steward*, edited by R. A. Manners, pp. 281–325. Chicago, IL: University of Chicago Press.

Chambers, Erve, and Philip P. Young. 1979. Mesoamerican Community Studies: The Past Decade. *Annual Review of Anthropology* 8: 45–69.

Chase, Arlen F., and Diane Z. Chase. 1987. *Investigations at the Classic Maya City of Caracol, Belize: 1985–1987. Monograph 3.* San Francisco, CA: Pre-Columbian Art Research Institute.

Clifford, James. 1988. *The Predicament of Culture: Twentieth-Century Ethnography, Literature, and Art.* Cambridge, MA: Harvard University Press.

Clifford, James, and George E. Marcus, eds. 1986. *Writing Culture: The Poetics and Politics of Ethnography.* Berkeley: University of California Press.

Closs, Michael P. 1985. The Dynastic History of Naranjo: The Middle Period. In *Fifth Palenque Round Table, 1983.* Merle Greene Robertson, general ed., and

Virginia M. Fields, volume ed., pp. 65–77. San Francisco, CA: Pre-Columbian Art Institute.

Coe, Michael D. 1965. The Olmec Style and its Distribution. In *Archaeology of Southern Mesoamerica*, vol. 3, part 2 of *Handbook of Middle American Indians*, edited by Gordon R. Willey, pp. 739–75. Austin, TX: University of Texas Press.

Coggins, Clemency. 1979. A New Order and the Role of the Calendar: Some Characteristics of the Middle Classic Period at Tikal. In *Maya Archaeology and Ethnohistory*, edited by Norman Hammond and Gordon R. Willey, pp. 38–50. Austin, TX: University of Texas Press.

———.1980. The Shape of Time: Some Political Implications of a Four-Part Figure. *American Antiquity* 45 (4): 727–39.

Colby, Benjamin N. 1966. *Ethnic Relations in the Chiapas Highlands.* Santa Fe, NM: Museum of New Mexico Press.

Collier, George A. 1975. *Fields of the Tzotzil: The Ecological Bases of Tradition in Highland Chiapas.* Austin, TX: University of Texas Press.

Collier, George A., with Elizabeth Lowery Quaratiello. 1994. *Basta! Land and the Zapatista Rebellion in Chiapas.* Oakland, CA: Institute for Food and Development Policy.

Craig, Sienna and Macduff Everton. 1993. Maya Dreams: Pride and Resistance in the Highlands. *Summit* (Fall): 60–69.

Díaz Infante, Fernando. 1963. Quetzalcóatl: Ensayo psicoanalítico del mito nahua. *Cuadernos de la Facultad de Filosofía, Letras y Ciencias* 18. Xalapa, Mexico: Universidad Veracruzana.

Dolgin, Janet L., David S. Kemnitzer, and David M. Schneider, eds. 1977. *Symbolic Anthropology: A Reader in the Study of Symbols and Meanings.* New York, NY: Columbia University Press.

Douglas, Mary. 1966. *Purity and Danger: An Analysis of Concepts of Pollution and Taboo.* New York, NY: Praeger Publishers.

Drennan, Robert D., and Carlos A. Uribe, eds. 1987. *Chiefdoms in the Americas.* Lanham, MD: University Press of America.

Earle, Duncan. 1979. *Field Report from Nuevo San Juan Chamula, Municipio of Las Margaritas.* Chiapas, Mexico: unpublished manuscript.

Eber, Christine. 1995. *Women and Alcohol in a Highland Maya Town: Water of Hope, Water of Sorrow.* Austin, TX: University of Texas Press.

Edmonson, Munro S. 1982. *The Ancient Future of Itza: The Book of Chilam Balam of Tizimin.* Austin, TX: University of Texas Press.

Eliot, T. S. 1963. *Collected Poems, 1917–1962.* New York, NY: Harcourt, Brace and World.

Falla, Ricardo. 1978. *Quiché Rebelde.* Guatemala City: Editorial Universitaria de San Carlos.

Farriss, Nancy. 1984. *Maya Society under Colonial Rule: The Collective Enterprise of Survival.* Princeton, NJ: Princeton University Press.

Favre, Henri. 1971. *Changement et continuité chez les Mayas du Mexique: Contribution a l'étude de la situation coloniale en Amérique Latine.* Paris: Editions Anthropos.

Flannery, Kent. 1972. The Cultural Evolutions of Civilizations. *Annual Review of Ecology and Systematics* 3: 399–426.

———.1976. Formative Oaxaca and the Zapotec Cosmos. *American Scientist* 64 (4): 374–83.

————.1982. Review of *In the Land of the Olmec. American Anthropologist* 84: 442–47.

Flannery, Kent, and Joyce Marcus. 1976. Formative Oaxaca and the Zapotec Cosmos. *American Scientist* 64 (4): 374–83.

Foro Nacional Indígena. 1996. *Resolutivos de la Mesa 1. Autonomía.* Unpublished ms of a document circulated January 3–8 in San Cristóbal de las Casas, México.

Foster, George. 1944. Nagualism in Mexico and Central America. *Acta Americana* 2: 85–103.

————.1962. *Traditional Cultures and the Impact of Technological Changes.* New York, NY: Harper and Bros.

Freidel, David, Linda Schele, and Joy Parker. 1993. *Maya Cosmos: Three Thousand Years on the Shaman's Path.* New York, NY: William Morrow.

Friedlander, Judith. 1975. *Being Indian in Hueyapan: A Study in Forced Identity in Contemporary Mexico.* New York, NY: St. Martin's Press.

Furbee, N. Louanna. 1996. The Religion of Politics in Chiapas: Founding a Cult of Community Saints. Paper presented at the 95th Annual Meeting of the American Anthropological Association, San Francisco, November 23.

Gage, Thomas. 1958 [1648]. *Thomas Gage's Travels in the New World.* J. Eric S. Thompson, ed. Norman, OK: University of Oklahoma Press.

Geertz, Clifford. 1963a. *The Interpretation of Cultures.* New York: Basic Books.

————.1963b. Religion as a Cultural System. In *The Interpretation of Culture*, edited by Clifford Geertz, pp. 87–124. New York, NY: Basic Books.

————.1988. *Works and Lives: The Anthropologist as Author.* Stanford, CA: Stanford University Press.

González Casanova, Pablo. 1970. *Democracy in Mexico.* New York, NY: Oxford University Press.

Gossen, Gary H. 1971. Chamula Genres of Verbal Behavior. In *Toward New Perspectives in Folklore*, edited by A. Paredes and R. Bauman. Special edition of *Journal of American Folklore* 84 (311): 145–67. Reprinted (1979) in *Reader in Comparative Religion: An Anthropological Approach.* 4th ed., edited by William Lessa and Evon Z. Vogt, pp. 207–9. New York, NY: Harper and Row.

————.1972. Temporal and Spatial Equivalents in Chamula Ritual Symbolism. In *Reader in Comparative Religion: An Anthropological Approach*, 4th ed., edited by William Lessa and Evon Z. Vogt, pp. 116–28. New York, NY: Harper and Row.

————.1974a. A Chamula Calendar Board from Chiapas, Mexico. In *Mesoamerican Archaeology: New Approaches*, edited by Norman Hammond, pp. 217–53. London: Gerald Duckworth.

————.1974b. *Chamulas in the World of the Sun: Time and Space in a Maya Oral Tradition.* Cambridge, MA: Harvard University Press.

————.1974c. To Speak with a Heated Heart: Chamula Canons of Style and Good Performance. In *Explorations in the Ethnography of Speaking*, edited by Richard Bauman and Joel Sherzer, pp. 389–424. London: Cambridge University Press.

————.1975. Animal Souls and Human Destiny in Chamula. *Man* 10 (n.s.): 448–61.

————.1976. Language as Ritual Substance. In *Language and Religious Practice*, edited by William Samarin, pp. 40–60. Rowley, MA: Newbury House.

————.1977. Translating Cuzcat's War: Understanding Maya Oral History. *Journal of Latin American Lore* 3 (2): 249–78.

————.1978. The Popul Vuh Revisited: A Comparison with Modern Chamula

Narrative Tradition. *Estudios de Cultura Maya* 11: 267–83. Mexico City: Centro de Estudios Mayas, Universidad Autónoma de México.

———.1979a. Cuatro mundos del hombre: tiempo e historia entre los chamulas. *Estudios de Cultura Maya* 12: 179–90. Mexico City: Centro de Estudios Mayas, Universidad Nacional Autónoma de México.

———.1979b. One Hundred and Thirty Colonies of San Juan: A Modern Maya Diaspora. Paper presented at the symposium Continuity and Change in the Maya World. St. Paul, MN: Science Museum of St. Paul, May 19–21.

———.1980. *The Chamula Protestant Exile Settlements of San Cristóbal de las Casas, Chiapas, México.* Unpublished field report.

———. 1983. Una diáspora maya moderna: desplazamiento y persistencia cultural de San Juan Chamula, Chiapas. *Mesoamérica* 5: 253–76. Antigua, Guatemala and Woodstock, VT: Centro de Investigaciones Regionales de Mesoamérica (CIRMA).

———. 1985. Tzotzil Literature. In *American Indian Literatures. Supplement to the Handbook of Middle American Indians,* vol. 3, edited by Munro S. Edmonson and Victoria R. Bricker, pp. 64–106. Austin, TX: University of Texas Press.

———. 1986. The Chamula Festival of Games: Native Macroanalysis and Social Commentary in a Maya Carnival. In *Symbol and Meaning Beyond the Closed Community: Essays in Mesoamerican Ideas,* edited by Gary H. Gossen, pp. 227–54. Albany, NY: Institute for Mesoamerican Studies, University at Albany, State University of New York.

———. 1988.Vida y Muerte de Miguel Kashlán: héroe Chamula. In *Biografías y confesiones de los indios de América,* edited by Manuel Gutiérrez Estévez. *Arbor* 131 (515–16): 125–44. Madrid: Consejo de Investigaciones Científicas.

———. 1989a. El tiempo cíclico en San Juan Chamula: mistificación o mitología viva? *Mesoamérica* 18: 441–59. Special Number entitled *Matices de Historia: el caso de Chiapas.* Antigua, Guatemala, and Woodstock, VT: Centro de Investigaciones Regionales de Mesoamérica (CIRMA).

———. 1989b. Life, Death and Apotheosis of a Tzotzil Protestant Leader: Biography as Social History. In *Ethnographic Encounters in Southern Mesoamerica: Essays in Honor of Evon Zartman Vogt, Jr.,* edited by Victoria R. Bricker and Gary Gossen, pp. 217–29. Albany, NY: Institute for Mesoamerican Studies, University at Albany, State University of New York.

———. 1992. Las variaciones del mal en una fiesta tzotzil. In *De palabra y obra en el Nuevo Mundo: Imágines Interétnicas,* edited by Miguel León-Portilla, Manuel Gutiérrez Estévez, Gary H. Gossen, and J. Jorge Klor de Alva, pp. 195–236. Madrid and Mexico City: Siglo XXI.

———. 1993a. On the Human Condition and the Moral Order: A Testimony from the Chamula Tzotzil of Chiapas, Mexico. In *South and Mesoamerican Native Spirituality: From the Cult of the Feathered Serpent to the Theology of Liberation,* edited by Gary H. Gossen and Miguel León-Portilla, pp. 414–35. Vol. 4 of *World Spirituality: An Encyclopedic History of the Religious Quest.* New York, NY: Crossroads Press.

———. 1993b. The Other in Chamula Tzotzil Cosmology and History: Reflections of a Kansan in Chiapas. *Cultural Anthropology* 8 (4): 443–75.

———. 1994. From Olmecs to Zapatistas: A Once and Future History of Souls.

American Anthropologist 96 (3): 553–70.

———. 1996. The Religous Traditions of Mesoamerica. In *The Legacy of Mesoamerica: History and Culture of a Native American Civilization*, edited by Robert Carmack, Janine Gasco, and Gary H. Gossen, pp.290–320. Englewood Cliffs, NJ: Prentice-Hall.

———. n.d. *Four Creations of Man: A Maya Narrative Account of the Human Experience.* Unpublished manuscript.

Gossen, Gary H., and Victoria R. Bricker. 1989. Introduction. In *Ethnographic Encounters in Southern Mesoamerica: Essays in Honor of Evon Z. Vogt, Jr.*, edited by Victoria R. Bricker and Gary H. Gossen, pp. 1–6. Albany: Institute for Mesoamerican Studies, University at Albany, State University of New York.

Gossen, Gary H., J. Jorge Klor de Alva, Manuel Gutiérrez Estévez, and Miguel León-Portilla, eds. 1993. *De palabra y obra en el Nuevo Mundo: la formación del Otro.* Vol. 3 in the Quincentenary Series, *De Palabra y Obra en el Nuevo Mundo.* Madrid and Mexico City: Siglo XXI.

Graham, Ian, and Eric Von Euw. 1977. *Corpus of Maya Hieroglyphic Inscriptions*, vol. 3, part 1. Cambridge, MA: Peabody Museum of Archaeology and Ethnology, Harvard University.

Guiteras-Holmes, Calixta. 1961. *Perils of the Soul: The World View of a Tzotzil Indian.* Glencoe, IL: Free Press of Glencoe.

Gutiérrez Estévez, Manuel, Miguel León-Portilla, Gary H. Gossen, and J. Jorge Klor de Alva. 1988. Lógica social en la mitología maya-yucateca: la leyenda del enano de Uxmal. In *Mito y ritual en América, edited by Manuel.* Gutiérrez-Estévez, pp. 60–110. Madrid: Alhambra.

———. 1992. *De palabra y obra en el Nuevo Mundo: encuentros interétnicos*, vol. 2 of the Quincentenary Series, *De Palabra y Obra en el Nuevo Mundo.* Madrid and Mexico City: Siglo XXI.

Hammond, Norman. 1982. *Ancient Maya Civilization.* New Brunswick, NJ: Rutgers University Press.

Harvey, Neil, Luis Hernández Navarro, and Jeffrey W. Rubin. 1994. *Rebellion in Chiapas: Rural Reforms, Campesino Radicalism, and the Limits of Salinismo.* Revised edition. Transformation of Rural Mexico Series, 5. Ejido Reform Research Project. San Diego: Center for U.S.-Mexican Studies, University of California.

Haviland, William A. 1963. *Excavations of Small Structures in the Northeast Quadrant of Tikal, Guatemala.* Ph.D. dissertation, University of Pennsylvania, Philadelphia, PA.

Holland, William. 1963. *Medicina maya en los altos de Chiapas: un estudio del cambio sociocultural. Colección de Antropologia Social*, vol. 2. Mexico City: Instituto Nacional Indigenista.

Holmes, W. H. 1907. On a Nephrite Statuette from San Andrés Tuxtla, Vera Cruz, México. *American Anthropologist* 9 (4): 691–701.

Horcasitas, Fernando. 1972. *Life and Death in Milpa Alta: A Nahuatl Chronicle of Díaz and Zapata.* Norman, OK: University of Oklahoma Press.

Houston, Stephen and David Stuart. 1989. The *Way* Glyph: Evidence for Co-essences among the Classic Maya. *Research Reports on Ancient Maya Writing* 30. Washington, DC: Center for Maya Research.

Hunt, Eva. 1977. *The Transformation of the Hummingbird: Cultural Roots of a Maya Ritual Poem.* Ithaca, NY: Cornell University Press.

Ingham, John M. 1986. *Mary, Michael and Lucifer: Folk Catholicism in Central Mexico.*

Austin, TX: University of Texas Press.

Jameson, Frederic. 1981. *The Political Unconscious: Narrative as a Socially Symbolic Act.* London: Methuen.

Jones, Christopher, and Linton Satterthwaite. 1982. *The Monuments and Inscriptions of Tikal: The Carved Monuments.* Tikal Report No. 33, Part A, University Museum Monograph 44. Philadelphia: University Museum, University of Pennsylvania.

Justeson, John, and Terrence Kaufman. 1992. A Decipherment of Epi-Olmec Hieroglyphic Writing. Paper presented at the University of Texas Maya Hieroglyphic Workshop, March 17.

———. 1993. A Decipherment of Epi-Olmec Hieroglyphic Writing. *Science* 293: 1703–11.

Karasik, Carol. 1988. *The People of the Bat: Mayan Tales and Dreams from Zinacantán,* translated by Robert M. Laughlin. Washington, DC: Smithsonian Institution.

Kendall, Carl, John Hawkins, and Laurel Bossen, eds. 1983. *Heritage of Conquest Thirty Years Later.* Albuquerque, NM: University of New Mexico Press.

Kerouac, Jack. 1957. *On the Road.* New York, NY: Viking Press.

Klor De Alva, J. Jorge. 1993. Aztec Spirituality and Nahuatized Christianity. In *South and Meso-American Native Spirituality: From the Cult of the Feathered Serpent to the Theology of Liberation,* edited by Gary H. Gossen in collaboration with Miguel León-Portilla, pp. 139–64. Vol. 4 of *World Spirituality: An Encyclopedic History of the Religious Quest.* New York, NY: Crossroads Press.

Klor de Alva, J. Jorge, Gary H. Gossen, Miguel León-Portilla, and Manuel Gutiérrez Estévez, eds. 1995. *De palabra y obra en el Nuevo Mundo: tramas de identidad,* vol. 4 in the Quincentenary Series, *De Palabra y Obra en el Nuevo Mundo.* Madrid and Mexico City: Siglo XXI.

Knauft, Bruce M. 1996. *Genealogies for the Present in Cultural Anthropology.* New York and London: Routledge.

Köhler, Ulrich. 1975. *Cambio cultural dirigido en Los Altos de Chiapas: un estudio sobre la antropología aplicada.* Mexico City: Instituto Nacional Indigenista.

Laughlin, Robert M. 1969. The Tzotzil. In *Ethnology,* part 1. Vol. 7 of *Handbook of Middle American Indians, edited by Evon Z. Vogt,* pp. 152–94. Austin, TX: University of Texas Press.

———. 1975. *The Great Tzotzil Dictionary of San Lorenzo Zinacantán. Smithsonian Contributions to Anthropology* 19. Washington, DC: Smithsonian Institution Press.

———. 1977. *Of Cabbages and Kings: Tales from Zinacantán. Smithsonian Contributions to Anthropology* 23. Washington, DC: Smithsonian Institution Press.

———. 1980. In a Sense Abroad [Travel Journals of Tzotzils in the United States]. In *Of Shoes and Ships and Sealing Wax: Sundries from Zinacantan. Smithsonian Contributions to Anthropology* 25, pp. 2–139. Washington, DC: Smithsonian Institution Press.

———. 1994. The Mayan Renaissance: Sna Jtz'ibajom, the House of the Writer. *Cultural Survival Quarterly* 18 (4): 13–15.

———. 1995. From All for All: A Tzotzil-Tzeltal Tragicomedy. *American Anthropologist* 97 (3): 528–42.

Lawrence, D. H. 1923. *Studies in Classic American Literature.* New York, NY: Thomas Seltzer.

Leach, E. R. 1971. Two Essays Concerning the Symbolic Representation of Time.

In *Rethinking Anthropology*, London School of Economics, Monographs on Social Anthropology 22, pp.124–36. London: The Athlone Press, University of London.

León-Portilla, Miguel. 1962 [1959]. *The Broken Spears: The Aztec Account of the Conquest of Mexico.* Boston, MA: Beacon Press. [Originally published as *Visión de los Vencidos.* Mexico City: Universidad Nacional Autónoma de Mexico, 1959.]

———. 1968. *Tiempo y realidad en el pensamiento Maya.* Mexico City: Instituto de Investigaciones Históricos, Universidad Nacional Autónoma de México.

———. 1993. Those Made Worthy by Divine Sacrifice: The Faith of Ancient Mexico. In *South and Meso-American Native Spirituality: From the Cult of the Feathered Serpent to the Theology of Liberation*, edited by Gary H. Gossen in collaboration with Miguel León-Portilla, pp. 3–26. Vol. 4 of *World Spirituality: An Encyclopedic History of the Religious Quest.* New York, NY: Crossroads Press

León-Portilla, Miguel, Manuel Gutiérrez Estévez, Gary H. Gossen, and J. Jorge Klor de Alva, eds. 1992. *De palabra y obra en el Nuevo Mundo: imágenes interétnicas*, vol. 1 of the Quincentenary Series, *De Palabra y Obra en el Nuevo Mundo.* Madrid and Mexico City: Siglo XXI.

Lewis, I. M., ed. 1968. *History and Social Anthropology.* A.S.A. Monograph 7. London: Tavistock Publications.

Leventhal, Richard M. 1983. Household Groups and Classic Maya Religion. In *Prehistoric Settlement Patterns: Essays in Honor of Gordon R. Willey*, edited by Evon Z. Vogt and Richard M. Leventhal, pp. 55–76. Albuquerque, NM: University of New Mexico Press and the Peabody Museum, Harvard University.

———. 1979. *Settlement Patterns at Copan, Honduras.* Ph.D. dissertation, Harvard University, Cambridge, MA.

Lévi-Strauss, Claude. 1976. *Tristes Tropiques.* Harmondsworth: Penguin Books.

Linn, Priscilla Rachun. 1977. *The Religious Office Holders in Chamula: A Study of Gods, Rituals, and Sacrifice.* 2 vols. D. Phil. dissertation. Oxford University.

Lloyd, Susan. 1994. The Last Zapatista. In *These Times: The Alternative Newsmagazine* 18(4):10–11.

Lomnitz-Adler, Claudio. 1992. *Exits from the Labyrinth: Culture and Ideology in Mexican National Space.* Berkeley and Los Angeles, CA: University of California Press.

Lounsbury, Floyd G. 1980. Some Problems in the Interpretation of the Mythological Portion of the Hieroglyphic Text of the Temple of the Cross at Palenque. In *Third Palenque Round Table, 1978*, part 2, edited by Merle Greene Robertson, pp. 99–115. Austin, TX: University of Texas Press.

Madsen, William. 1967. Religious syncretism. In *Social Anthropology*, vol. 6 of *Handbook of Middle American Indians*, edited by Manning Nash, pp. 369–91. Austin, TX: University of Texas Press.

Marcus, George E., and Michael M. J. Fischer. 1986. *Anthropology as Cultural Critique: An Experimental Moment in the Human Sciences.* Chicago, IL: Chicago University Press.

Marcus, Joyce. 1976. *Emblem and State in the Classic Maya Lowlands.* Washington, DC: Dumbarton Oaks.

Martínez, Carlos. 1995. *Oventic Constructing Dignity: A United People, Chiapas, 1995.* Unedited video, viewed and cited with the permission of Tenoch Discs, Austin, TX.

Martínez Peláez, Severo. 1970. *La patria del criollo: un ensayo e interpretación de la real-*

idad colonial guatemalteca. Guatemala City: Editorial Universitaria.

McQuown, Norman, ed. 1959. *Report on the Man-in-Nature Project of the Department of Anthropology of the University of Chicago in the Tzotzil-Tzeltal Speaking Region of the State of Chiapas, Mexico*. 3 vols. (hectographed).

Menchú, Rigoberta. 1984. *I, Rigoberta Menchú: An Indian Woman in Guatemala*. Elisabeth Burgos-Debray, ed. London: Verso (New Left Books).

Mendivil, Leopoldo. 1994. ¡Murio Janine! La monja, cabeza de los "Zapatistas": Murió en combate. *¡Alarma!* 143 (February 8): 10–14. Mexico City.

Miami Herald. 1987. Mexican Tribe Splits with Catholic Church. July 20.

Miles, Suzanne W. 1952. An Analysis of Modern Middle American Calendars: A Study in Conservatism. In *Acculturation in the Americas, Selected Papers of the 29th International Congress of Americanists*, edited by Sol Tax, pp. 273–84. Chicago.

Modiano, Nancy. 1973. *Indian Education in the Chiapas Highlands*. New York, NY: Holt, Rinehart and Winston.

Molloy, John P., and William L. Rathje. 1974. Sexploitation among the Late Classic Maya. In *Mesoamerican Archaeology: New Approaches*, edited by Norman Hammond, pp. 431–44. Austin, TX: University of Texas Press.

Morris, Walter. 1987. *Living Maya*. New York, NY: Harry Abrams, Inc.

Moscoso Pastraña, Prudencio. 1972. *Jacinto Pérez "Pajarito" el último líder Chamula*. Tuxtla Gutiérrez, Chiapas, Mexico: Editorial del Gobierno del Estado de Chiapas.

Münch, Guido, et al. 1980. *El sur de México: datos sobre la problemática indígena*. Mexico City: Instituto de Investigaciones Antropológicas, Universidad Nacional Autónoma de México.

Nash, June. 1997. The Fiesta of the Word: The Zapatista Uprising and Radical Democracy in Mexico. *American Anthropologist* 99 (2):261–71.

Nigh, Ronald. 1994. Zapata Rose in 1994: The Indian Rebellion in Chiapas. *Cultural Survival Quarterly* 18(1):9–13.

Ochiai, Kazuyasu. 1985. *Cuando los santos vienen marchando: rituales intercomunitarios tzotziles*. Serie Monografías 3. San Cristóbal de las Casas: Centro de Estudios Indígenas, Universidad Autónoma de Chiapas.

Olivera, B. Mercedes, and Ana María Salazar. 1977. *Formas de trabajo y relaciones de producción en el café, el caso de Simojovel, Chiapas*. Mexico City: Instituto de Investigaciones Antropológicas, Universidad Nacional Autónoma de México. Unpublished manuscript.

Ortner, Sherry B. 1974. Is Female to Male as Nature is to Culture? In *Woman, Culture and Society*, edited by M. Z. Rosaldo and L. Lamphere, pp. 67–87. Stanford, CA: Stanford University Press.

Paz, Octavio. 1959. *Laberinto de la soledad*. Mexico City: Fondo de Cultura Económica.

Pear, Robert. 1982. Aliens who stay in clusters are seen to do better. *New York Times*, March 11, A24.

Pérez Castro, Ana Bella. 1980. Mitos y creencias en los movimientos mesiánicos y luchas campesinas en Chiapas. *Anales de Antropología* 17 (2): 185–95. Mexico City: Universidad Nacional Autónoma de México.

———. 1981. Duraznal: situación actual de una comunidad indígena. *Anales de Antropología* 18 (2): 173–86. Mexico City: Universidad Nacional Autónoma de

México.

Peres Tzu, Marián. 1996. The First Two Months of the Zapatistas: a Tzotzil Chronicle. In *Indigenous Revolts in Chiapas and the Andean Highlands*, edited by Kevin Gosner and Arij Ouweneel, translated by Jan Rus, pp. 121–30. Amsterdam: Center for Latin American Research and Documentation.

Pickands, Martin. 1986. The Hero Myth in Maya Folklore. In *Symbol and Meaning Beyond the Closed Community: Essays in Mesoamerican Ideas*, edited by Gary H. Gossen, pp. 101–23. Albany, NY: Institute for Mesoamerican Studies, University at Albany, State University of New York.

Pirsig, Robert M. 1974. *Zen and the Art of Motorcycle Maintenance: An Inquiry into Values*. New York, NY: Morrow.

Pitarch, Pedro. 1993. *Etnografía de las almas de Cancuc*. Ph.D. dissertation, University at Albany, State University of New York.

———. 1996. *Ch'ulel: una etnografía de los almas tzeltales*. Mexico City: Fondo de Cultura Económica.

Powelson, Michael. 1996. The Use and Abuse of Ethnicity in the Rebellions in Chiapas. *Blueprint for Social Justice* 49 (5): 1–7.

Pozas Arciniega, Ricardo. 1959. *Chamula: un pueblo indio de los Altos de Chiapas*. Mexico City: Memorias del Instituto Nacional Indigenista, vol. 8. (Reprinted in 1977, Colección de Clásicos de la Antropología Mexicana, no. 1 [2 vols.] Mexico City: Instituto Nacional Indigenista.)

———. 1962. *Juan Pérez Jolote: Biografía de un Tzotzil*. Mexico City: Fondo de Cultural Económica.

Preston, Julia. 1996. Mexico and Insurgent Group Reach Pact on Indian Rights. *New York Times*, February 15: A12.

Price, Richard. 1990. *Alabi's World*. Baltimore and London: The Johns Hopkins University Press.

Proceso. 1996. Conflictos postelectorales, encontronazos declarativos, presencia ominosa del ejército y asesinatos políticos, los ingredientes explosivos en Chiapas. *Proceso* 1000, January 1: 14–19.

Proskouriakoff, Tatiana. 1962. Civic and Religious Structures of Mayapan. In *Mayapan, Yucatan, Mexico. Carnegie Institution of Washington Publication 619*, pp. 87–163. Washington, DC.

Puleston, Dennis E. 1979. An Epistemological Pathology and the Collapse, or Why the Maya Kept the Short Count. In *Maya Archaeology and Ethnohistory*, edited by Norman Hammond and Gordon R. Willey, pp. 63–71. Austin, TX: University of Texas Press.

Rabinow, Paul. 1989. *Reflections on Fieldwork in Morocco*. Berkeley, CA: University of California Press.

Rachun Linn, Priscilla. 1977. *The Religious Office Holders in Chamula: A Study of Gods, Ritual and Sacrifice*. Ph.D. dissertation, Oxford University.

———. 1982. Chamula Carnival: the "Soul" of Celebration. In *Celebration: Studies in Festivity and Ritual*, edited by Victor Turner, pp. 190–200. Washington, DC: Smithsonian Institution.

———. 1989. Souls and Selves in Chamula: A Thought on Individuals, Fatalism and Denial. In *Ethnographic Encounters in Southern Mesoamerica: Essays in Honor of Evon Zartman Vogt, Jr.*, edited by Victoria R. Bricker and Gary H. Gossen, pp. 251–62.

Albany, NY: Institute for Mesoamerican Studies, University at Albany, State University of New York.

Redfield, Robert. 1941. *The Folk Culture of Yucatan*. Chicago, IL: University of Chicago Press.

———. 1960. *The Little Community*. Chicago, IL: University of Chicago Press.

Rosaldo, Renato. 1989. *Culture and Truth: The Remaking of Social Analysis*. Boston, MA: Beacon Press.

Rosenbaum, Brenda. 1983. El nagualismo y sus manifestaciones en el Popul Vuh. In *Nuevas Perspectivas sobre el Popol Vuh*, edited by Robert M. Carmack and Francisco Morales Santos, pp. 201–13. Guatemala City: Piedra Santa.

Rosenbaum, Brenda. 1993. *With Our Heads Bowed: The Dynamics of Gender in Maya Community*. Albany: Institute for Mesoamerican Studies, State University of New York.

Ross, John. 1994. *Rebellion at the Roots: Indian Uprising in Chiapas*. Monroe, ME: Common Courage Press.

———. 1995. The EZLN, A History: Miracles, Coyunturas, Communiqués. Introduction, *Shadows of Tender Fury: The Letters and Communiqués of Subcomandante Marcos and the Zapatista Army of National Liberation*. New York: Monthly Review Press.

Ruíz de Alarcón, Hernando. 1982. *Aztec Sorcerers in Seventeenth-Century Mexico: Treatise on Superstitions by Hernando Ruíz de Alarcón*, edited by Michael D. Coe and Gordon Whittaker. Monographic Series 7. Albany, NY: Institute for Mesoamerican Studies, The University at Albany, State University of New York.

Sahlins, Marshall. 1985. *Islands of History*. Chicago, IL: University of Chicago Press.

Sahagún, Bernardino de, compiler. 1969. *Florentine Codex: General History of the Things of New Spain*. 13 vols. Salt Lake City, UT: University of Utah Press.

———. 1980 [1564]. The Aztec-Spanish Dialogues of 1524, translated by J. Jorge Klor de Alva. *Ethnopoetics* 4: 52–193. [Originally published as *Colloquios*.]

Salazar Peralta, Ana María. 1977. *El papel del ejido en el proceso de integración de la población indígena en Chiapas*. Mexico City: Universidad Nacional Autónoma de México. Unpublished manuscript.

———. 1981a. *La participación estatal en la producción y comercialización del café en la región norte del estado de Chiapas*. Mexico City: Escuela Nacional de Antropología. Unpublished manuscript.

———. 1981b. La problemática cafetalera en la región de Simojovel, Chiapas. *Anales de Antropología* 18 (2): 187–98. Mexico City: Universidad Nacional Autónoma de México.

———. n.d. *Variabilidad cultural entre dos grupos mayas de Chiapas: tzotziles y choles*. Mexico City: Universidad Nacional Autónoma de México. Unpublished manuscript.

Saler, Benson. 1964. Nagual, Witch and Sorcerer in a Quiché Village. *Ethnology* 3: 305–28.

Sarup, Madan. 1993. *An Introductory Guide to Post-Structuralism and Postmodernism*. 2d ed. Athens, GA: University of Georgia Press.

Satterthwaite, Linton. 1965. Calendrics of the Maya Lowlands. In *Archaeology of Southern Mesoamerica*, part 2, vol. 3 of *Handbook of Middle American Indians*, edited by Gordon R. Willey, pp. 603–31. Austin, TX: University of Texas Press.

References

Schele, Linda. 1982. *Maya Glyphs: The Verbs*. Austin, TX: University of Texas Press.

—————. 1991. An Epigraphic History of the Western Maya Region. In *Classic Maya Political History: Hieroglyphic and Archaeological Evidence*, edited by Patrick Culbert, pp. 72–101. Cambridge: Cambridge University Press.

Schele, Linda, and David Freidel. 1990. *A Forest of Kings: The Untold Story of the Ancient Maya*. New York: William Morrow and Co.

Schele, Linda, and Mary Miller. 1986. *The Blood of Kings: Dynasty and Ritual in Maya Art*. New York and Fort Worth: George Braziller, Inc. and the Kimbell Art Museum.

Sharer, Robert J., and David C. Grove, eds. 1989. *Regional Perspectives on the Olmec*. Cambridge: School of American Research, Cambridge University Press.

Silverblatt, Irene. 1987. *Moon, Sun and Witches: Gender Ideologies and Class in Inca and Colonial Peru*. Princeton, NJ: Princeton University Press.

—————. 1988. Women in States. *Annual Review of Anthropology* 17: 427–60.

Siverts, Henning. 1969. Ethnic Stability and Boundary Dynamics in Southern Mexico. In *Ethnic Groups and Boundaries*, edited by F. Barth, pp. 101–16. Boston, MA: Little, Brown and Co.

Spicer, Edward. 1961a. Types of Contact and Processes of Change. In *Perspectives in American Indian Cultural Change*, edited by E. Spicer, pp. 7–93. Chicago, IL: University of Chicago Press.

—————. 1961b. Yaqui. In *Perspectives in American Indian Cultural Change*, edited by E. Spicer, pp. 517–44. Chicago, IL: University of Chicago Press.

—————. 1969. Political Incorporation and Cultural Change in New Spain: A Study in Spanish-Indian Relations. In *Attitudes of Colonial Powers Towards the American Indian*, edited by H. Peckham and C. Gibson, pp. 107–35. Salt Lake City, UT: University of Utah Press.

—————. 1972. Plural Society in the Southwest. In *Plural Society in the Southwest*, edited by E. Spicer and R. Thompson, pp. 21–76. New York: Interbook Inc.

Stavenhagen, Rodolfo. 1970. Social Aspects of Agrarian Structure in Mexico. In *Agrarian Problems and Peasant Movements in Latin America*, edited by R. Stavenhagen, pp. 225–70. Garden City, NY: Doubleday and Co.

Steven, Hugh. 1976. *They Dared to Be Different*. Irvine, CA: Harvest House Publishers.

Subcomandante Marcos. 1995. *Shadows of Tender Fury: The Letters and Communiqués of Subcomandante Marcos and the Zapatista Army of National Liberation*. Frank Bardacke and Leslie López, trans. New York: Monthly Review Press.

Sullivan, Paul. 1989. *Unfinished Conversations: Mayas and Foreigners Between Two Wars*. Berkeley, CA: University of California Press.

Tedlock, Barbara. 1982. *Time and the Highland Maya*. Albuquerque, NM: University of New Mexico Press.

—————. 1991. From Participant Observation to Observation of Participation: The Emergence of Narrative Ethnography. *Journal of Anthropological Research* 47 (1): 69–94.

—————. 1992. *The Beautiful and the Dangerous: Dialogues with the Zuni Indians*. New York, NY: Penguin Books.

Tedlock, Dennis. 1983. *The Spoken Word and the Work of Interpretation*. Philadelphia, PA: University of Pennsylvania Press.

—————. 1985. *Popol Vuh: The Definitive Edition of the Maya Book of Dawn of Life and the Glories of Gods and Kings*. New York, NY: Simon and Schuster.

―――. 1993. *Breath on the Mirror: Mythic Voices and Visions of the Living Maya*. San Francisco, CA: HarperCollins.

Thompson, J. Eric S. 1934. Skybearers, Colors and Direction in Maya and Mexican Religion. *Contributions* 10, Carnegie Institution Publication 436. Washington, DC: Carnegie Institution of Washington.

―――. 1966. *The Rise and Fall of Maya Civilization*, 2d ed. Norman, OK: University of Oklahoma Press.

―――. 1970. *Maya History and Religion*. Norman, OK: University of Oklahoma Press.

Tocqueville, Alexis de. 1946 [1835]. *Democracy in America*. London: Oxford University Press.

Todorov, Tzvetan. 1984. *The Conquest of America: The Question of the Other*. New York, NY: Harper and Row.

Tourtellot III, Gair. 1988. *Peripheral Survey and Excavation: Settlement and Community Patterns*. Memoirs of the Peabody Museum of Archaeology and Ethnology 16. Cambridge, MA: Harvard University Press.

Turner, Frederick Jackson. 1962 [1893]. *The Frontier in American History*. New York, NY: Holt, Rinehart and Winston.

Turner, Victor. 1967. *The Forest of Symbols*. Ithaca, NY: Cornell University Press.

―――. 1968. *The Drums of Affliction: A Study in the Religious Processes among the Ndembu of Zambia*. Oxford: Clarendon Press and the International African Institute.

Turner, Victor, and Edith Turner. 1982. Religious Celebrations. In *Celebration: Studies in Festivity and Ritual*, edited by Victor Turner, pp. 201–19. Washington, DC: Smithsonian Institution.

Villa Rojas, Alfonso. 1947. Kinship and Nahualism in a Tzeltal Community, Southeastern Mexico. *American Anthropologist* 49: 578–87.

―――. 1963. El naugalismo como recurso de control social entre los grupos mayances de Chiapas, México. *Estudios de Cultura Maya* 3: 243–60.

―――. 1968. Los conceptos de espacio y tiempo entre los grupos mayances contemporáneos. Appendix to León-Portilla, Miguel, *Tiempo y realidad en el pensamiento Maya*. Mexico City: Instituto de Investigaciones Históricas, Universidad Nacional Autónoma de México.

Vogt, Evon Z. 1964. The Genetic Model and Maya Cultural Development. In *Desarollo Cultural de los Mayas*, edited by Evon Z. Vogt and L. Alberto Ruz, pp. 9–48. Mexico City: Universidad Nacional Autonóma de México.

―――. 1965. Zinacanteco "Souls." *Man* 29: 33–35.

―――. 1969a. Chiapas Highlands. In *Ethnology*, part 1, vol. 7 of *Handbook of Middle American Indians*, edited by Evon Z. Vogt, pp. 133–51. Austin, TX: University of Texas Press.

―――. 1969b. *Zinacantán: A Maya Community in the Highlands of Chiapas*. Cambridge, MA: Harvard University Press.

―――. 1970. Human Souls and Animal Spirits in Zinacantán. In *Echanges et communications, mélanges offerts à la occasion de son 60ème anniversaire*, edited by Pierre Maranda and Jean Pouillon, pp. 1148–67. The Hague: Mouton.

―――. 1973. Gods and Politics in Zinacantán and Chamula. *Ethnology* 12: 99–133.

―――. 1976. *Tortillas for the Gods: A Symbolic Analysis of Zinacanteco Rituals*. Cambridge, MA: Harvard University Press.

―――. 1978. *Bibliography of the Harvard Chiapas Project: The First Twenty Years,*

1957–1977. Cambridge, MA: Peabody Museum of Archaeology and Ethnology, Harvard University.

———. 1994a. *Fieldwork among the Maya: Reflections on the Harvard Chiapas Project.* Albuquerque, NM: University of New Mexico Press.

———. 1994b. On the Application of the Phylogenetic Model to the Maya. In *North American Indian Anthropology: Essays on Society and Culture*, edited by Raymond J. DeMallie and Alfonso Ortiz, pp. 377–414. Norman, OK: University of Oklahoma Press.

Wallerstein, Immanuel. 1974. The Rise and Future Demise of the World Capitalist System: Concepts for a Comparative Analysis. *Comparative Studies in Society and History* 16: 387–415.

Warman, Arturo. 1980. *Ensayos sobre el campesinado en México.* Mexico City: Editorial Nueva Imagen.

Warren, Kay B. 1978. *The Symbolism of Subordination: Indian Identity in a Guatemalan Town.* Austin, TX: University of Texas Press.

———. 1992. Transforming Memories and Histories: The Meanings of Ethnic Resurgence for Mayan Indians. In *Americas: New Interpretive Essays*, edited by Al Stepan, pp. 189–210. New York and Oxford: Oxford University Press.

Wasserstrom, Robert. 1977. *White Fathers and Red Souls: Indian-Ladino Relations in Highland Chiapas, 1582–1973.* Ph.D. dissertation. Harvard University, Cambridge, MA.

———. 1980. Rural Labor and Income Distribution in Central Chiapas. Paper presented at the 1980 Meetings of the American Anthropological Association. Washington, DC.

———. 1983. *Class and Society in Central Chiapas.* Berkeley, CA: University of California Press.

Watanabe, John M. 1983. In the World of the Sun: A Cognitive Model of Mayan Cosmology. *Man* 18 (4): 710–28.

———. 1989. Elusive Essences: Souls and Social Identity in Two Highland Communities. In *Ethnographic Encounters in Southern Mesoamerica: Essays in Honor of Evon Z. Vogt, Jr.*, edited by Victoria R. Bricker and Gary H. Gossen, pp. 263–74. Albany, NY: Institute for Mesoamerican Studies, University at Albany, State University of New York.

———. 1992. *Maya Saints and Souls in a Changing World.* Austin, TX: University of Texas Press.

Willey, Gordon R., Richard M. Leventhal, Arthur A. Demarest, and William L. Fash, Jr. 1994. *Ceramics and Artifacts from Excavations in the Copan Residential Zone.* Papers of the Peabody Museum of Archaeology and Ethnology. Cambridge, MA: Harvard University.

Williams, Dan. 1987. 400-Year Church Ties Cut by Ancient Mexican Tribe. *Los Angeles Times*, July 5: 1, 12–13.

Winfield Capitaine, Fernando. 1988. La Estela de La Mojarra, Veracruz, México. *Research Reports on Ancient Maya Writing* 16. Washington, DC: Center for Maya Research.

Wolf, Eric. 1957. Closed Corporate Communities in Mesoamerica and Central Java. *Southwestern Journal of Anthropology* 13: 1–18.

INDEX

role in Festival of Games,
129; role in Maya past and
present, xxix, xxviii, 159,
162; role in Tzotzil Maya
rituals, 159; as shamans,
164, 183; Tzotzil, xxix; as
victims of exploitation,
xxix; in War of Santa Rosa,
24; in Zapatista movement,
xxix
women's issues, in
Protestant Movement, 223;
in Zapatista movement,
xxix, 223, 251
women's movements, 178
wood-gatherers, in Festival
of Games, 128–29, 136
Wood-gathering Expedi-
tion, in Festival of Games,
134
Wood-gathering Sunday, in
Festival of Games, 133
World System, of Meso-
america, xxii

Xalik, 44, 272(n15)
xenophobia, of Chamula
Tzotzils, 6

xenophobic nationalism, 29
Xibalban (Underworld
Lords), in Popul Vuh, 179
xinulan antz ("stinking
woman"), in Festival of
Games, 126
Xitalá, 48, 273(n20)
Xmucane, in Popul Vuh,
179

Ya?al Ichin, 273(n21)
Yaqui Indians, ethnic tenacity
of, 195
Yaxchilan, women associated
with bloodletting at, 181
yellow, as symbolic color,
270(n9)
Yucatán, *casta* social order
in, 191; Maya Indians in,
81, 192, 262

Zac-Kuk, Lady, as early
Palenque ruler, 180, 181
Zapata, Emiliano, 103, 249,
255; as mestizo, 258;
Quetzalcóatl and, 259
Zapatista Army of National
Liberation. *See* EZLN

Zapatista movement, xi, xiv,
xxi, xxii, xxvii, xxviii, 31,
54, 83, 222, 225, 242, 244;
effects of, xxiii, 247–66;
lack of support by San
Juan Chamula, 247; peace
accord of, 252–53, 265;
website for, 247, 248;
women's issues in, xxix,
223, 251
Zapatista rebellion, xi, xv,
77, 223, 225, 244, 245, 248
Zapatistas, xiv, 103, 223,
242, 249, 259; earth lord
petition involving, 185;
mask use by, 258, 261,
280(n4)
Zapotecs, as Juárez ancestors, 190
Zedillo, Ernesto, 250, 263,
265
Zinacantán, 214, 222,
269(n5), 280(n4)
zoomorphic deities, of
human-animal relation-
ships, 229
Zoque Indians, 262, 280(n4)

Index